Where to watch bi.

Somerset,
Gloucestershire,
& Wiltshire

THE *WHERE TO WATCH* BIRDS SERIES

Where to Watch Birds in Bedfordshire, Berkshire, Buckinghamshire, Hertfordshire and Oxfordshire
Brian Clews, Andrew Hervet and Paul Trodd

Where to Watch Birds in Cumbria, Lancashire and Cheshire
Jonathan Guest and Malcolm Hutcheson

Where to Watch Birds in Devon and Cornwall
David Norman and Vic Tucker

Where to Watch Birds in Dorset, Hampshire and the Isle of Wight
George Green and Martin Cade

Where to Watch Birds in East Anglia
Peter and Margaret Clarke

Where to Watch Birds in France
Ligue Française pour la Protection des Oiseaux

Where to Watch Birds in Ireland
Clive Hutchinson

Where to Watch Birds in Italy
Lega Italiana Protezione Uccelli

Where to Watch Birds in Kent, Surrey and Sussex
Don Taylor, Jeffrey Wheatley and Tony Prater

Where to Watch Birds in Scotland
Mike Madders and Julia Welstead

Where to Watch Birds in Somerset, Gloucestershire and Wiltshire
Ken Hall and John Govett

Where to Watch Birds in South America
Nigel Wheatley

Where to Watch Birds in Southern Spain
Ernest Garcia and Andrew Paterson

Where to Watch Birds in Wales
David Saunders

Where to Watch Birds in the West Midlands
Graham Harrison and Jack Sankey

Where to Watch Birds in Yorkshire and North Humberside
John Mather

Where to watch birds in

Somerset, Gloucestershire & Wiltshire

Ken Hall and John Govett

Illustrations by John Govett

Third edition

Christopher Helm

A & C Black · London

Third edition 2003
Second edition 1995
First edition 1988

Christopher Helm (Publishers) Ltd, a subsidiary of
A&C Black, 35 Bedford Row, London WC1R 4JH

© 2003, 1995, 1988 Ken Hall and John Govett
Line drawings by John Govett

0-7136-6614-5

A CIP catalogue record for this book
is available from the British Library

Printed and bound in Wales
by Creative Print and Design (Wales), Ebbw Vale

CONTENTS

ACKNOWLEDGEMENTS

We would like to record our thanks to the large number of people who have supplied us with information over many years and which has been drawn on heavily in writing this book. Perhaps our greatest debt is to all those who have submitted records to their local reports and publications but who cannot be mentioned individually here. The main reports covering the region are listed in one of the appendices along with the names and addresses of the organisations concerned. The three main county avifaunas are 'The Birds of Somerset' compiled by the Somerset Ornithological Society (Alan Sutton, 1988), 'Birds of Gloucestershire' by C.M. Swaine (Alan Sutton, 1982) and 'Wiltshire Birds' compiled by the Wiltshire Ornithological Society (Wiltshire Ornithological Society, 1991). A new edition of this last is currently nearing publication. In addition, breeding bird atlases have been published for Avon and for the North Cotswolds. 'The Birds of Exmoor and the Quantocks' by David K. Ballance and Brian Gibbs (Isabelline Books, 2003) and 'Sketches of Dean's Birds' by John Christian (Magpie Publishing, 1999) are two other books that cover limited parts of the region in more detail. All of these publications have provided a wealth of useful information.

Many local observers supplied extra details from their notebooks and commented on earlier drafts. In addition to all those who were listed in previous editions, we would like to thank the following who were particularly helpful in this third one and apologise to any that we have missed: John Austin, Simon Ayres, John Booth, John Brown, Linda Cady, Lorne Campbell, Paul Castle, Andy Davis, Stephen Edwards, Pete Foreman, Brian Gibbs, John Grearson, Gilbert Green, Tony Horner, Chris Klee, Geoffrey Lambert, Paul Marshall, Bruce Maxfield, Tim McGrath, Andy Middleton, Nigel Milbourne, Tony Parsons, Granville Pictor, Robin Prytherch, Chris Riley, Peter Rock, Chris Stone, Rob Turner and Gordon Youdale.

Finally special thanks are due to Nigel Redman and Mike Unwin (both of A.&C. Black) and to Lys Hall, all of whom showed great patience and understanding in waiting for the manuscript to be finished and normal life to resume.

INTRODUCTION

When we embarked on the first edition of this book, we had doubts as to whether it was really a good idea to make available detailed information that might bring additional pressures to bear on already beleaguered populations of birds. Now that we have reached the third edition, and can look back on the changes that have occurred over the past 15 or so years since then, it remains clear that whatever minuses there have been, and there certainly have been quite a few, disturbance from birdwatchers has played a very minor part in bringing them about. Habitat loss and degradation, agricultural intensification, urbanisation and climatic change have placed far greater stress on fragile bird populations than any number of rubber-necking birders peering at them. In fact, if it were not for the fact that many of the best places are already under some form of protection by conservation interests, or that pressure from the environmentally aware, including the majority of birdwatchers, had been brought to bear, the losses would be far greater than they have actually been. And on a more positive note, where species have increased in numbers and/or range, and there have been an encouraging number of these over the same period, the active interest of these same groups has ensured that significant populations have been established of several species that might otherwise have struggled to move beyond their initial toeholds. As we wrote then, there is no doubt that in today's crowded world those who wish to continue to enjoy birds and the natural world in general cannot pretend that threats will go away of their own accord, and although there are obvious risks involved, the more people who realise that a particular site is important, the better will be the chance that it can be defended. It is imperative that we are not apologetic about our concern that a wildlife-rich countryside is a fully justifiable land use and that constant pressure is brought to bear on those whose actions make it otherwise. The most straightforward way of doing this is to join one of the conservation bodies such as the RSPB, the WWT, county wildlife trusts, etc., but also be prepared to be vocal in support of a specific site that might be under threat.

So, what has happened over the past 15 years. Firstly, the county of 'Avon' has disappeared – not physically, of course, but in name at least, having been replaced by four unitary authorities. Although this has given us the chance to contract the title of the book, the term 'Avon' still occurs in several places as a useful shorthand, referring to the area around Bristol still used for recording purposes by local birders. The counties of Somerset, Gloucestershire and Wiltshire continue to be very much border country between the primarily lowland arable east and the upland pastureland of the west. This is true not only of the geology and the land usage, but also of the birdlife that distinguishes the region from other parts of Britain, many species reaching the edge of their range here, whether from the west or from the east. The heather-dominated hills and combes of Exmoor still hold many of their specialities, but Red Grouse have followed the Black into local extinction, and sadly Ring Ousels seem to be going the same way. Climatic change must be playing a part here, especially when one considers that Dartford Warblers have now become quite widespread in the same habitat as previously occupied by these 'northern' species. The nearby woods are still full of Pied Flycatchers, Redstarts and Wood Warblers, and all three species can be found in several other places in the western half of the region but they have become increasingly patchily distributed in the east, where they were never particularly common anyway. Birds more typical of rolling downland and farmland, such as Red-legged and Grey Partridges and Corn Buntings continue to be found in reasonable numbers in eastern Gloucestershire and Wiltshire, but have all declined in the more pastoral regions further west. In fact Corn Buntings, like the Cirl Buntings, no longer breed in Somerset at all, and Tree Sparrows, another bird associated with arable farmland, have continued to decline, with their range withdrawing eastwards. Nightingales remain patchily distributed, but although right on the edge of their range, there is no obviously geographical link to their fluctuating numbers, habitat factors no doubt being more important.

When it comes to overall distribution, on the plus side, and no doubt also associated with climate change as well as better protection, Little Egrets have appeared in ever increasing numbers, and have started breeding in several widely spaced localities. Cetti's Warblers, like the Dartford Warblers already mentioned, have likewise increased in numbers and range across the region, their calls being a typical sound throughout the year from many wetland habitats. Most of the bird of prey have benefited from protection and from the reduced use of pesticides in agriculture. Buzzards have continued to push east, and are now a typical sight throughout the whole area, previously having been relatively sparse much to the east of Bath. Peregrines have returned to nest on the cliffs of the Avon Gorge in Bristol, Salisbury Cathedral has been used as a roosting site, and in winter hunting birds can be expected over almost any wetland habitat. Sparrowhawks continue to maintain a healthy population, whilst Goshawk numbers have increased enough to allow viewpoints in the Forest of Dean to be set up where their spectacular spring displays can be seen. Red Kites have recently started breeding in Wiltshire, no doubt an offshoot of the introduced population of the Chilterns, and wandering birds are increasingly reported throughout the region. The army's control of large parts of Salisbury Plain continues to ensure the survival of several downland areas that would doubtless otherwise now be under the plough, attracting wintering birds such as Hen Harrier and Short-eared Owl as well as several specialised breeding birds. Protection by the RSPB has come to the aid of the Stone Curlews that breed on the downland in the same general area, although it is still not possible to publish exact details of their whereabouts. The introduced Mandarin is now well established in several parts of Gloucestershire, helping to reinforce Britain's position as a significant centre of the world population of this east Palearctic species, and so far it is felt to be a harmless addition to Britain's avifauna. Until recently the same was said about the North American Ruddy Duck, which winters in high numbers on the Bristol reservoirs, but which now stands accused of competing with the related White-headed Ducks native to Europe.

Two major physical features of the region certainly continue to deserve a mention. One is the River Severn, and especially its estuary. There is constant pressure to drain and build on the wetlands all along its shores, with the Cardiff Bay project across on the Welsh side being just one of many controversial schemes either in hand or planned. But so far the most intrusive of these (e.g. an airport, a tidal barrage) have not come to fruition, and its vast mudflats continue to host large numbers of wintering and passage waders, particularly the Dunlin which peak at over 50,000 on the estuary as a whole. The riverside grazing meadows near Slimbridge remain the winter home of one of the main flocks of White-fronted Geese in southern Britain, while large numbers of Shelduck remain in Bridgwater Bay for the annual moult which renders them temporarily flightless. At migration times, passerine movements can be impressive, with a good sprinkling of rarities to be found, although the overall numbers of birds involved seem to have declined.

The other area also under threat, but where there is much positive news to report, concerns the Somerset Levels. Drainage of this unique wetland area remains a continuing problem, but major work by the RSPB, the Somerset Wildlife Trust and other conservation bodies, together with an encouraging number of farmers, has improved the habitat for wetland birds quite spectacularly over huge areas. Not only have the water levels been raised in the damp fields of West Sedgemoor, to the benefit of both breeding waders and wintering wildfowl, but the worked-out peatland west of Glastonbury has been converted into a fascinating mosaic of reedbeds, meadows and swampy woodland which attracts a wide variety of birds throughout the year. The whole area is set to become one of the most important wetland habitats in the southwest.

So, despite many losses among what were once common woodland and farmland passerines, there are still plenty of birds to be found, and some rewarding places to find them in. Some continue to be crowded, but some still remain little watched. One or two sites have received attention by assiduous 'patch workers', who have turned up some amazing finds, so there is still plenty of potential out there. Certainly many woodland and inland areas, for instance, are visited only infrequently by bird-watchers. Even by the time of this third edition, we found some new places we did were not aware of before, and found others so changed as to be virtually new ones anyway. As ever, we would be delighted to receive further updating information and if readers of this book get as much pleasure exploring the region as we did during its writing, they will have much to look forward to.

The region

The region covered in this third edition is the same as in the previous two, although we have been able to shorten the title somewhat, following the abolition of the former county of 'Avon'. This has now been replaced by four unitary authorities: Bath & North-east Somerset, Bristol, North Somerset and South Gloucestershire. However, the word 'Avon' still appears quite frequently, not least because the name is still attached to both the Wildlife Trust and the Bird Report covering the area concerned, and its boundaries are still indicated on the Key to Sites map. The individual sites have been treated in what it is hoped is a logical geographical order, starting in the far west of Somerset and ending in the far southeast of Wiltshire. For this edition, even the more minor sites have been integrated into the main listing, using an abbreviated form of the standard format, so that as far as possible all the sites that are physically close together also appear near each other in the text.

Criteria for inclusion

The basic criterion for a site's inclusion is that it either holds a wide variety of species, is notable for certain more specialised birds, or is a good accessible representative of its habitat type. Within these general constraints we have tried to give details of as many places as space allows, spread as evenly as possible over the region. Although there is no doubt that most of the region's birds can be found in no more than half a dozen areas, we have worked on the assumption that people would like to see at least some of them without travelling long distances to do so, and hope that in this way the book will be useful to local birdwatchers as well as directing visitors from outside the area to the most productive places.

Measurements

Throughout the text we have given measurements in those units most readily understood by British readers. Distances are normally stated in miles, followed by the metric equivalent in kilometres. Altitudes are given in metres, as on all modern OS maps. For surface areas we have given the imperial measurement, followed by the metric one.

Habitat

This section gives a brief description of the main features of the area, concentrating in particular on those that may affect the birds. Also included are details of notable flora and fauna likely to be easily visible to non-specialists together with ownership or reserve status where appropriate.

Species

This section usually starts with a brief statement of the area's most significant group of birds, going on to give a sample of the main species of interest, and what they are likely to be doing at different seasons. The text is arranged in roughly chronological order starting with winter and resident species and then moving through the year to help follow the pattern of bird events at different seasons. Some attempt has been made to give the scale of numbers to be expected – whether single birds, small parties or flocks of hundreds of a particular species. Rare migrants and vagrants are by their nature unpredictable, but examples from the recent past have been given as a rough indication of what might be expected. The existence of a few rare and vulnerable breeding species has been ignored or their whereabouts treated vaguely and this seems reasonable general advice for anyone who comes across them. Common species are usually excluded unless they are of particular significance, e.g. prominent rookery, large numbers of roosting Starlings, etc. Specific dates are not usually included here as the 'Calendar' section gives full details on when each species usually occurs.

Timing

Includes such things as tides, time of day, weather conditions, periods of particular disturbance, etc. likely to affect what is seen, irrespective of the time of year.

Access

How to get there, starting from the nearest large town and main A-roads, but going on to give details of minor roads and paths, drawing attention to the most profitable parts of what may be quite an extensive area. For each of the main sites, use this section in conjunction with the outline maps, but for detailed exploration the 1:25,000 OS maps are invaluable, especially as they now cover the country in reasonably sized blocks; the numbers of the appropriate ones are given at the head of each section. At many reserves, detailed access maps are available, either on display panels or as leaflets and, where known, these have been indicated in the text. Wherever possible public rights of way have been recommended and details given of restrictions on access at the time of writing, but visitors are warned that on private land the owner's permission should always be sought before deviating from public paths, and nothing written here implies that access can be taken for granted. In many places the exact status concerning access is not clear, and in addition parking space may be extremely limited. Although in many cases a car is the only practicable means of access for most people, details of public transport are given where this provides a reasonable alternative. Facilities for the disabled are increasing all the time, and these have been indicated where known. Those leading parties of birdwatchers, and those with special needs, should contact reserve managers or the relevant controlling organisation in advance, even for those places where permits are not normally required. (For relevant addresses, see List of Organisations.) Many reserves and conservation organisations nowadays have associated Internet web sites and these are also useful sources of information. As web addresses seem to change frequently, only some of the more major ones are given here; search engines such as Google will generally locate up-to-date versions of these and other site-related addresses.

Calendar

A quick reference section, by seasons that correspond as far as possible to the main periods of avian activity. Within each section the most likely periods for each species or group of species is given; if no further qualifying comment is made, the bird concerned may be looked for with equal chance of success at any time during the season, or peaks may occur randomly throughout. The exact species mentioned are to a certain extent arbitrary – we have included those that seem to us most interesting or significant. In general, in richer habitats the commoner species are taken for granted unless there is good reason not to do so and this section should be used in conjunction with the species account, although in places some qualifying details are given.

Key to Maps

�	Sea/inland water
▢	Area of interest, eg. reserve
Ⓟ	Car parking
Ⓗ	Birdwatching hide
⒫ₕ	Public house
ⒼⒸ	Golf course
⊕	Church
■	Building
°° °°	Sewage farm
— · — ·	County boundary
– – – –	Footpath

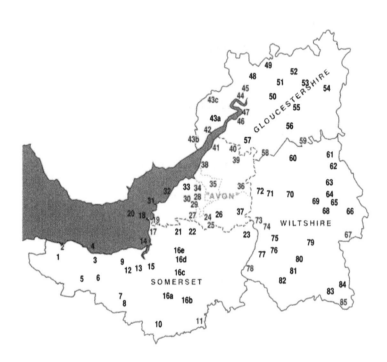

Habitat

The Exmoor National Park covers an area of c.265 square miles (686 km^2), but the heartland is the smaller, although still extensive, area of high moorland, wooded hillsides and river valleys from Dunkery Beacon to Pinkworthy in the north to Winsford Hill and Withypool Common in the south. Ploughing and reseeding with grass and heavy burning of heather, both in the interests of sheep farming, have reduced the extent of moorland dominated by deep heather to the northeastern part of the moor roughly from Dunkery through Wilmersham Common to Oareford. Similar habitat exists in the Withypool and Winsford areas but here burning has been more intensive, to the detriment of species such as Red Grouse. Dunkery Beacon reaches a height of 519 metres, commanding fine views in all directions, particularly of the Bristol Channel coast as far as Weston-super-Mare. The northwestern part of the moor from Alderman's Barrow to Pinkworthy is nearly as high, but is dominated by moorgrass, very waterlogged in places. The high ground is treeless, apart from a few clumps and lines of beeches, but the many streams draining in all directions shelter scattered rowans and hawthorns, these becoming more numerous lower down where they merge into the hedges of the farmland or the larger woods of the lower parts of some of the river valleys. North of Dunkery, particularly around Horner Water, there are fine sessile oakwoods, and the fringes of the moor hold several conifer-dominated Forestry Commission plantations. Bracken with some patches of gorse occurs widely in the river valleys and on the lower slopes of the moorland, providing valuable shelter for many breeding passerines. In some of the moorland valleys remains of farm buildings and drystone walls are used as breeding sites by Wheatears, and rocky outcrops occur near several of the streams. Unlike the situation on Dartmoor there is only one reservoir, the small, 24 acre (9.7 ha), Nutscale Reservoir.

Among mammals, red deer and Exmoor ponies are the most conspicuous, but there are plenty of badgers and foxes, but only small numbers of otters now remain. Adders can be found basking in sheltered places, whilst heath fritillaries are outstanding among a varied butterfly population. Although most of the area is in fact private land, there are plenty of waymarked footpaths and the whole area is popular with sightseers, walkers and horse-riders at all times of the year.

Species

Exmoor is renowned for its range of localised breeding birds; many of these leave in winter, to be replaced by a few specialised winter visitors. Hen Harriers winter regularly, one or two ranging widely over the high moorland, though they are most likely to be seen in the northwestern part. Short-eared Owls have occurred several times and are possibly overlooked, hidden in the bracken of the higher valleys before they start hunting in the afternoons and evenings. Buzzards and Kestrels are resident in good numbers and both Merlin and Peregrine hunt over the uplands in winter. Red Kites, usually singly, appear increasingly often in the winter or early spring, with birds from both the native Welsh population and from the reintroduction schemes elsewhere in the country being involved. Small birds can seem scarce on the open ground, even Meadow Pipits and Skylarks much reduced from their summer numbers, but a few Stonechats attempt to over-winter in the higher river valleys where they occur more commonly in the summer. There has been a scattering of Great Grey Shrike records in the autumn and winter, so it is always worth looking out for this elusive species, although it is certainly not a regular visitor. Ravens are wide-spread out of their breeding season which, like that of the resident Dippers down in the river valleys, starts early, the latter often being in full song before Christmas. With the trees bare, woodland birds can be easier to see, although total numbers of most species are lower at this time of year. Treecreepers, Nuthatches and the occasional Lesser Spotted Woodpecker join the roaming parties of tits, the Horner oak woods being one of the few places in Somerset where this ever elusive species still breeds.

One exciting new arrival on the moors has been the Dartford Warbler, whose numbers have risen well into double figures in the past few years, even more remarkable as historically they had never previously been recorded here as a breeding species. They are mostly resident, but easi-est to see once they start proclaiming their territories early in the year. Climate change is clearly playing a part in their increase, but there are losses as well gains with such species on the edge of their range. Sadly, Ring Ousels are becoming more and more difficult to find on Exmoor these days, but a handful of pairs can, for the moment at least, still be found in the heads of the river valleys on the north slopes of Exmoor. They are early arrivals, their loud fluting song often to be heard in late March. We can but hope that they will not follow Black and, more recently, Red Grouse into local extinction.

Most moorland birds prefer the relative shelter of the stream valleys, with Whinchat, Willow Warbler, Tree Pipit and Grasshopper Warbler occurring on bracken- and heather-covered slopes with scattered bushes. Curlew can be heard giving their evocative songs in flight over some of the more open combes, where a few pairs usually attempt to breed. Wheatears are more likely to be found on the grassland moors where drystone walls provide nesting sites.

Dartford Warbler

Exmoor is well known as a breeding area for Merlin, but they are not annual and are much prone to disturbance and predation from human and avian sources. If you should come across a suspected nesting pair, please move away from the site as quickly as possible in order not to draw unwelcome attention to it. Only one or two pairs occur, and this species is best looked for elsewhere. Hobbies also feed over the moor in spring and summer, and presumably breed in the general area. Passage migration as such is not outstanding, but flocks of up to 300 Golden Plover sometimes stop off on the high moors in both spring and autumn, and it's always worth checking for Dotterel on passage in late April/early May.

Lower down in the oak woodland, Pied Flycatchers, Wood Warblers and Redstarts are numerous, together with a good range of commoner woodland breeding species. A few pairs of Siskins and Redpolls breed in the coniferous areas, both species most easily located during their song flights. On warm summer evenings the distinctive churring of Nightjars can be heard along the woodland/heathland edges in several places. During late summer the woodland grows quiet as birds complete their breeding season and moult, but autumn can be quite rewarding with summer birds moving out into the heather, and Ring Ousels a little more widespread, small parties often attracted to the berries of the mountain ash trees.

Apart from the streams there is little surface water, so water birds are few at all times of the year, although a few Goosanders have recently moved into the area as a breeding species. Common Sandpipers occur on passage but have only rarely bred. Grey Herons occur singly at all times of the year, with small heronries near Withypool and Winsford. Nutscale Reservoir usually attracts only the occasional bathing gulls or Mallard, although Goosander and Canada Goose have been recorded.

Timing

At any time of year strong winds and rain make the moorland unpleasant and unrewarding for the watcher, and even the woodland birds will be subdued. Hunting harriers can be seen at any time of day, but Short-eared Owls are more active in the afternoons and evenings. For most breeding species morning visits are the most productive, and the more popular spots can become crowded with tourists on summer afternoons. Ring Ousels are often very elusive when not singing so visits early in the year are more reliable, or again later when they are feeding young. Nightjars are best listened for late on warm summer evenings.

Access

The most productive area, and certainly the one for a first visit to Exmoor, is around Horner and Dunkery Beacon. Approaching Porlock on the A39 from the east, turn sharp left along a lane signposted to Horner, c.½ mile (0.8 km) beyond the right-angled bend at Allerford and park in the village car park. One productive circuit is to walk upstream by Horner Water, looking out for Dippers and Grey Wagtails right from the start. After c.1 mile (0.8 km), fork left (signposted Cloutsham) and follow East Water upstream to where it crosses the road. Turning left up the road brings you to Webber's Post, where there is another car park. A wheelchair track here provides access for the disabled, and the bridleway next to it leads towards Horner, though you need to fork left off it along the Windsor Path to get back to the starting point. A minor road from Porlock to Wilmersham crosses the main Horner Water further west in the oak woodland, and provides another point of access. Pied Flycatchers and

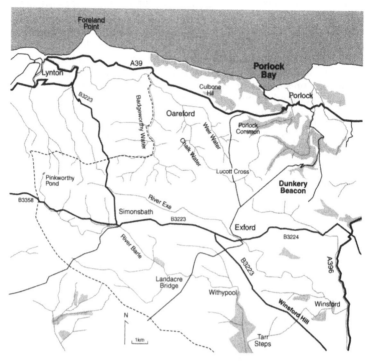

Redstarts are often easiest to see at the upper ends of the valleys, the latter in particular preferring the edges rather than the main woodland itself. Wood Warblers are rather more widespread throughout.

Webber's Post is reached by car by continuing up through Horner village and taking the first turning to the right at a minor crossroads. The road rises steeply through an area of beeches and conifers to reach a car park on the right where the road divides. This point provides an excellent site for scanning the woodland of the Horner valley, with soaring Buzzard and Sparrowhawk often to be seen. Taking the right fork (on foot is often best) brings access to the East Water stream as mentioned above, with Dipper, Pied Flycatcher and Redstart usually easily found. Directly east of Webber's Post, the lower slopes of Luccombe Hill hold breeding Grasshopper Warblers and Nightjars, both best listened for on summer evenings. During the day this is a good spot to search for Dartford Warblers, although they can be found almost anywhere there is thick heather and extensive low gorse. Redpolls and Siskins can be heard singing over the adjacent conifers, where both species breed, and it's worth checking here for Crossbills, especially after one of their periodic irruptions.

The left fork continues over the flank of Dunkery Beacon, with several pull-in places and a larger car park at Dunkery Gate over the brow of the hill all providing access to the heather moorland on either side of the road. The path past the cairn on the Beacon itself is not usually very productive although a Dotterel was seen there in 2001 and Golden Plover have occurred near the Robin How cairns just east of the road. Following the right fork at Webber's Post and crossing East Water (very narrow and winding like most of the roads where they cross the woodland streams) brings access to more heather-dominated moorland around Stoke Pero and Wilmersham Commons, where several obvious footpaths allow further exploration of the lower slopes of Dunkery on foot. There is a good chance of Ring Ousel in this area, plus Whinchats, Stonechats, Tree Pipits and Grasshopper Warblers in the sheltered valleys. The streams around Chetsford Water which is crossed by the road running north to Porlock Common are often productive. Nutscale Reservoir lies in this valley and can be viewed from its access track just off the minor road back to Porlock from Wilmersham Common.

For the western grass moorland, take the A39 west out of Porlock up the famous and extremely steep Porlock Hill, turning left in c.2 miles (3.2 km) along a road signposted to Exford and then right in 2½ miles (4 km) at Lucott Cross (alternatively approached from Chetsford Water). Park by a cattle grid across the road and walk west towards the ruins of Larkbarrow Farm. The open nature of the landscape gives a good chance of seeing any hunting birds of prey that may be present, especially in winter. Wheatears are attracted by the stone walls, and the beech trees around and beyond the farm hold breeding Redstarts. Various paths lead off across the surrounding moorland, although care should be taken in poor weather.

There are quite a few lesser-known areas worthy of exploration during a longer visit. Hawkcombe, which runs directly back from Porlock church, contains similar species to those of Horner Woods, including Pied Flycatcher, Redstart and Dipper, and Ley/Crawter Hills to the south have some nice gorse heathland with Stonechat, Yellowhammer, Dartford Warbler and Nightjar. The whole area is easily accessible from Porlock. Weir Water and Chalk Water near Oareford are attractive streams with Dipper and Whinchat in the valleys, and Wood Warblers and Redstarts in the nearby oak woodland. Park at Robber's Bridge car park and explore on foot. Redpolls, Siskins and Tree Pipits can be heard singing around the conifers on Culbone Hill, where the Worthy Toll Road from Porlock Weir emerges on the A39. The woods are private but there are footpaths through them. Pinkworthy Pond lies near the Devon border west of Simonsbath and is reached from the B3358 just before the county boundary. Park a short distance back from the bridge over the River Barle and follow this up to its source in the Pond itself beyond Pinkery Farm outdoor education centre. The surrounding grass moorland is extremely waterlogged but has attracted Golden Plover on migration. The Barle valley itself is an attractive stretch of farmland fringed with patches of heath and marsh and, although not outstanding for birds, a walk from Simonsbath past Cow Castle to the Landacre Bridge area should produce Dipper, Whinchat, Wheatear, Redstart and Buzzard, with the chance of dispersing Ring Ousels. Sand Martins and Kingfishers both sometimes breed in the Landacre Bridge area. Withypool Common immediately to the south is a tract of rather bare grass and heather moorland, though the area to the north of the bridge, where the footpath from Simonsbath emerges, has more in the way of ground cover. Winsford Hill has a larger area of heather moor with scattered hawthorns and scrub, attracting Tree Pipits and other open-ground breeding species, plus passing birds of prey in the winter. The oak-dominated woods upstream from Tarr Steps contain the usual woodland and river species including Pied Flycatcher and Dipper.

Calendar

All year: Grey Heron, Sparrowhawk, Buzzard, Merlin, Kingfisher, woodpeckers including Lesser Spotted; Meadow Pipit, Grey Wagtail, Dipper; Stonechat (scarce in winter), Nuthatch, Dartford Warbler, Raven, Siskin.

December–February: Hen Harrier, Peregrine, occasional Red Kite; Snipe, Woodcock, Short-eared Owl.

March–May: Hen Harrier and Short-eared Owl leave by early April. Golden Plover pass April; breeding Curlew arrive March. Stonechat and Ring Ousel return by late March; Chiffchaff and Wheatear early April; Cuckoo, Redstart, Whinchat, Pied Flycatcher late April. Most migrants in by early May, but Spotted Flycatcher may not arrive until mid–late May. Song at maximum May–June, when Siskin and Redpoll easiest to locate in display flights.

June–July: Breeding species include Curlew, Cuckoo, Nightjar; Sand Martin (localised), Tree Pipit, Redstart, Whinchat, Wheatear, Ring Ousel; Grasshopper Warbler (scarce), Dartford Warbler, Whitethroat and other common warblers, Wood Warbler, Pied Flycatcher. Song mostly fades in July, although Nightjar continues to August.

August–November: Majority of summer passerines leave by end of August; Redstart, Whinchat, Wheatear, Tree Pipit more widespread in low numbers in September. Parties of Ring Ousels in September. Winter raptors arrive from late October (wandering Peregrines throughout the year). Common Sandpipers pass August–September. Perhaps Great Grey Shrike late October–November or later into the winter.

2 PORLOCK MARSH & HURLSTONE POINT OS Outdoor Leisure 9

Habitat

Most of the north-facing coast of this part of the Bristol Channel from Minehead west into Devon is steep and rocky, so the break formed where the low-lying and fertile Porlock Vale reaches the coast provides a focal point for migrants moving along the coast and the vale itself channels those moving in a north/south direction. A shingle bar runs the whole width of the bay, but in 1996 this was breached, thereby altering the habitat completely. Whereas Porlock Marsh was previously a series of shallow mud-fringed lagoons backed by a small reedbed and scattered trees, the area is now effectively a tidal lagoon with patches of saltmarsh scattered in and around it. With rising sea levels, there are no plans to close the breach, but nevertheless it remains an important site for birds, although with a different mix of species.

Immediately to the east the rocky promontory of Hurlstone Point, with its old coastguard lookout, rises steeply to 109 metres by way of grass-grown scree and rocks. Further east are the mostly inaccessible cliffs on the north side of the Selworthy Beacon ridge, where there are some extensive stretches of gorse and heather. The attractive villages of Bossington and Allerford by the Horner Water river are sheltered by steep wooded slopes. More extensive woodland dominates the high ground rising towards Exmoor behind Porlock.

Species

Seawatching in winter has shown that Red-throated Divers are regular off-shore, numbers peaking around the turn of the year. The majority are only transient birds, though over 100 have been seen on occasion. Common Scoter also appear in the bay from time to time, but other seaduck are relatively rare. In general, Cormorants are the most usual diving bird, with Shags very seldom identified. Winter gales may bring hundreds of Kittiwakes offshore, and they also appear on spring passage. These days Porlock Marsh is much less attractive to dabbling ducks, though around 100 each of Teal and Mallard can usually be found in winter, whilst, among waders, Oystercatchers, Curlew and Lapwings are the most numerous species. The shingle and rough ground provide feeding opportunities for passerines, and the flocks of Linnets, Greenfinches and Chaffinches are always worth checking; for instance, a Little Bunting was found here in 2003. The occasional Snow Buntings stop off on the shore in autumn and winter and the resident Rock Pipits may be joined by a Water Pipit or two.

Early spring sees the first Wheatears on the grass behind the shingle, with Sand Martins and Swallows not far behind, skimming along the shore or over the marsh. A little later, the usual Pied Wagtails are joined by up to ten or so White Wagtails on their way to their Icelandic breeding grounds. Also Iceland bound are the Whimbrel which regularly stop briefly in early May. A pair or two of Redshank usually attempt to breed, but their success rate is very poor. However, the changed habitat is much to the liking of the Shelducks, over 100 occurring in winter, with a few young produced most years.

During the summer Hurlstone Point comes into its own as a vantage point for observing passing seabirds. These are rarely numerous but feeding parties of Manx Shearwaters are regular, and on occasion over 1000 birds have been seen in just a few hours' watching. Small numbers of Gannets also occur offshore in the summer, plus a few wandering Guillemots, Razorbills and the occasional Storm Petrel. A few Herring Gulls breed on the cliffs and prospecting Fulmars have become more frequent, the nearest colony being just to the west at Glenthorne on the Devon border. By this time the cliff-nesting Ravens have well-grown young which join the adults soaring overhead, and the resident Rock Pipits are joined by three or four breeding pairs of Wheatears, both species finding the rough scree ideal. Stonechats, Yellowhammers and Whitethroats occur nearby on the hill, recently joined by several pairs of Dartford Warblers in the gorse and heather. At dusk, the evocative sound of churring Nightjars can be sometimes be heard on North Hill. Peregrines doubtless breed on the cliffs along this stretch of coast, and like the numerous Buzzards can be seen throughout the year.

A feature of late summer has been the influx of Little Egrets, up to ten or so joining the more usual Grey Herons on the marsh, but unfortunately the trees where the latter used to nest are now all dead. The changed habitat seems to have reduced the numbers of waders on passage, but it still attracts the standard Curlews, Oystercatchers and Dunlin, whilst migrants like Ruff, Little Stint, Ringed Plover and Curlew Sandpiper occur in one and twos. Redstarts, Wheatears and Whinchats are regular passage birds, with perhaps a Black Redstart or Great Grey Shrike appearing late in the season. Autumn gales may make a seawatch off Hurlstone

Point worthwhile, as Storm Petrels, Manx Shearwaters or even one of the larger shearwaters have been seen in such conditions. Small numbers of skuas are seen most years, with Little Gulls and the occasional Sabine's if you are really lucky. Strong winds increase the chance of Guillemots and Razorbills being seen in the bay, although scanning the sea may produce sightings of birds offshore all year round.

Timing

For grounded migrants around the marsh early morning is best before there is too much disturbance. Because of the steeply sloping shingle, the state of the tide is generally not critical, and few waders feed on the seashore itself. The lack of cover makes watching in wet and windy conditions difficult on the marsh although seabirds may be brought in close to shore, particularly with northerly or northwesterly winds.

Access

Porlock is situated on the main A39 north coast road, often very busy at peak holiday times. From the town centre, Porlock Marsh (also called Sparkhayes Marsh) can be reached on foot via Sparkhayes Lane which leads directly into a waymarked footpath. This passes through arable farmland to reach the back of the marsh. If not flooded, you can cross directly to the shingle bank, whilst well-signed permissive paths run in either direction to Porlock Weir to the left or Bossington Beach to the right, skirting the developing saltmarsh.

Alternatively, drive along the B3225 to Porlock Weir where there is a car park (fee payable) just behind the beach. Walk a little way back along

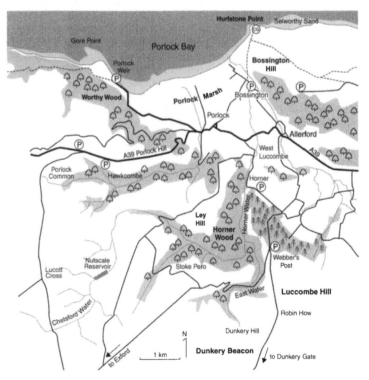

the road to where a flight of steps leads down onto the shingle, and then along the ridge to the breach. Do not neglect to scan the wooded ridge behind Porlock Weir for soaring Buzzards in spring and summer.

For Hurlstone Point and Bossington Beach, fork left at the east end of Porlock village along a narrow minor road signposted to Bossington, where there is a car park in the centre of the village. From here, the road leads on down to the beach where the Horner Water percolates through the shingle into the sea and the coastal footpath starts. For Hurlstone Head, cross the river by the footbridge by the car park, and turn left, following the stream (check for Dipper) and through some heathland to the point. For seabirds, scan from the shelter of the old lookout. Wheatears can be seen on the slopes directly below. A narrow and dangerous path leads a little way further east for views of the first of the cliffs. To proceed further would be foolhardy. A short way back from the point, another path runs up an open combe to Selworthy Beacon. Other footpaths lead on across the heathland further east, where Dartford Warblers occur, or down through the Allerford and Selworthy Woods to the starting point. Selworthy Beacon can be reached by road, but only rather tortuously from the centre of Minehead, following signs to North Hill. Greenaleigh Point, towards the eastern end of the ridge, is another seawatching lookout.

Calendar

All year: Cormorant, Grey Heron, Shelduck, Sparrowhawk, Buzzard, Kestrel, Peregrine, Pheasant, Oystercatcher, Herring Gull, Rock Pipit; Dipper (Bossington), Raven.

November–February: Red-throated Diver sporadically to April; occasional Shag, Eider, Common Scoter. Teal, Merlin. Water Rail, Curlew, Snipe. Kittiwake after gales. Kingfisher. Perhaps Firecrest, Chiffchaff, Snow Bunting (all rare).

March–May: Fulmar, Gannet. Winter duck leave during March. Redshank and occasionally Ringed Plover attempt to breed. Whimbrel pass late April–early May. Kittwake flocks on passage. Wheatear from late March; White Wagails in April. Chance of southern rarity from late April.

June–July: Fulmar, Gannet; Manx Shearwater feeding parties; occasional Storm Petrel, Guillemot or Razorbill. Maybe Sandwich or Little Tern. Breeding species include Nightjar and Dartford Warbler (Selworthy area), Whitethroat, Yellowhammer.

August–November: Seabirds during gales: Manx Shearwater, Gannet, perhaps Storm Petrel, even Sooty Shearwater or Sabine's Gull. Maybe seaduck offshore. Chance of Hobby (August–September). Passage waders in August–September include Ringed and Little Ringed Plover, Sanderling, Dunlin, Ruff, Grey Plover, Green and Common Sandpipers, Greenshank; Little Stint, Curlew Sandpiper, rarities more likely September–October. Maybe Grey Phalarope September–October. Common and Arctic Terns plus a few Arctic Skuas passing August–September. Pomarine and Great Skuas occur erratically. Trickle of passerines in August–early September including Redstart, Wheatear, Whinchat, hirundines. Visible migration of pipits, larks, finches in late September–October. Black Redstart, sometimes Snow Bunting October–November.

3 CROYDON HILL

Habitat

Croydon Hill is an extensive area of mostly coniferous plantations of varying ages lying to the south of the A396 Dunster to Timberscombe road. There are several large forestry clearings as well as an area of unplanted land dominated by heather to the eastern side on Black Hill and Rodhuish Common. To the north several small streams run into the River Avill valley where the woodland is more varied. A similar but less extensive area of coniferous plantation and heathland lies across the valley in the Grabbist Hill/Hoppcott/Wootton Commons complex. The whole area affords fine panoramic views of the Brendon Hills to the south and Minehead and the Bristol Channel coast to the north. Roe and fallow deer occur in the woodlands, emerging to feed in the open at dawn and dusk.

Species

In winter the plantations can appear fairly birdless, although Goldcrest, Coal Tit and Treecreeper are resident. Parties of Redpolls and Siskins feed among the tops of the conifers and in some years Crossbills can also be found, either quietly feeding on cones or giving their distinctive chipping calls as they fly from one area to another. On fine days the numerous resident Buzzards and Sparrowhawks start their soaring display flights or the latter can be glimpsed skimming over at tree-top height, and Ravens are often heard croaking overhead. In early spring Chaffinches, Robins and various tits reappear around the clearings, and on sunny days flocks of Siskins may be heard in communal sub-song. In recent years one or two pairs have remained to nest, giving observers the chance to witness full song and display flights. Redpolls breed in small numbers, and after 'irruption' years Crossbills have also raised young here. In late April and May other migrants appear, including a few pairs of Wood Warblers in the strips of beech that shelter the young conifers, with small numbers of Pied Flycatchers in the deciduous woodland around the river valleys. Stonechats and Whinchats breed on the open heathland, where both Tree

Nightjar

and Meadow Pipits can be heard singing. From late spring the main speciality of the area, the Nightjar, appears, most usually located by its distinctive churring song given at dusk from the edges of the larger clearings. Eventually one will be seen gliding low over the young conifers or heather, sometimes clapping its wings in display or giving its low *cuik* flight call. The reeling song of Grasshopper Warblers is also to be heard in the half-light, and there have been intriguing records of roding Woodcock in some years. Certainly the habitat looks ideal for this elusive species.

Later in the summer there is less song but, particularly in the morning and evening, birds are active feeding young. In August dispersing summer visitors may appear all around the clearings, including Redstarts and other birds which do not breed on the hill itself. Migration has been little watched, but there is the chance of the odd Ring Ousel dropping in on the higher open areas or a raptor circling over, before the wintering finches reappear again.

Timing
Mornings and evenings for small birds are best, particularly if the weather is calm. Nightjars do not normally start to call until the sun has set and calm warm conditions are essential for reasonable views. 9.30 pm is normally the earliest time, even later in midsummer. Soaring raptors such as Buzzard and Sparrowhawk prefer sunny conditions with at least a slight breeze to prompt them to undertake their display flights.

Access
From Dunster take the A396 southwest for c. ½ mile (0.8 km) and turn left along a minor road signposted to Luxborough. The road winds steeply uphill through mixed woodland with various footpaths leading off east and west. There is a picnic site at Nutcombe Bottom, on the left ½ mile (0.8 km) from the main road junction, where Pied Flycatchers can sometimes be heard singing in summer. There are waymarked trails here, south into the main woodland block, or east onto the open ground of Gallax Hill, where the Iron Age fort of Bat's Castle affords excellent views over the whole area. The road continues along the western edge of Croydon Hill, passing another parking area on the right c. ½ mile (0.8 km) beyond the first one. It is possible to park by the roadside in places but take care not to block any of the Forestry Commission/Crown Estate access roads which may be needed urgently in case of fire. Various tracks (some waymarked) lead southeastwards though the woodland and forestry clearings to open heathland around the triangulation point on Black Hill. The higher ground is normally the best for the heathland and conifer specialities, although Pied Flycatchers are more likely lower down in the deciduous woodland, such as in the Withycombe Scruffets valley, with Grey Wagtails and Dippers occurring near the streams. Stop and listen at the clearings for Nightjars, but do not forget to look up from time to time for raptors.

Another minor road runs west from the A396 along the south side of Grabbist Hill (park at the junction and walk up steep path for access to heathland on north slope). Other footpaths run up from near Wootton Courtney and from the north side of the hill. There is a similar mix of habitat here to that on Croydon Hill, and several pairs of Nightjars also breed in this area. The species is generally easiest to locate in large clearings up to five years after replanting; as this type of habitat is constantly changing with forestry operations the exact locations will vary considerably over quite a short period.

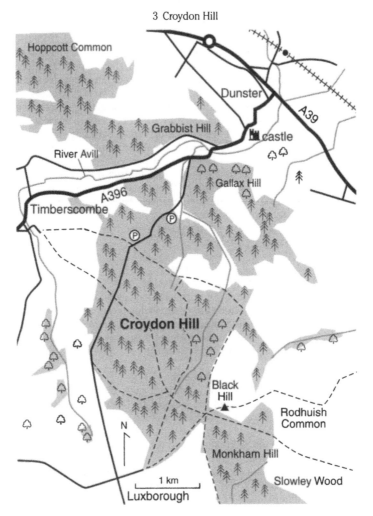

Calendar

All year: Sparrowhawk, Buzzard, Kestrel, Pheasant, Tawny Owl, Green and Great Spotted Woodpeckers; Kingfisher (River Avill), Meadow Pipit; Grey Wagtail, Dipper (River Avill), Stonechat, Coal Tit, Nuthatch, Treecreeper, Jay, Raven.

December–February: Woodcock, Siskin, Redpoll, Crossbill.

March–May: Siskin flocks in March, a few birds remaining to breed. Cuckoo, Tree Pipit, Whinchat, Blackcap, Pied Flycatcher arrive mid–late April; Garden Warbler, Whitethroat and Wood Warbler mainly early May; Nightjar from mid–late May. Redpoll.

June–July: Breeding species; song declining in July, but Nightjars remain vocal throughout. Maybe Crossbill irruption July.

August–November: Most migrants leave during August; dispersing Redstarts, Whinchat, maybe Ring Ousel occur September. Winter finches from mid-October.

Habitat

Stretching for c.4 miles (6.4 km) east of Minehead, the shore here has extensive expanses of sand and rocks exposed at low tide, contrasting with steep cliffs to the west and mudflats further east. The beach is backed at the western end by Minehead golf course, backed in turn by damp grazing meadows with deep ditches and a small reedbed. The railway to the south and the holiday camp to the west keep casual disturbance here low. The private holiday chalet development of Dunster Beach itself fronts a long narrow wetland strip called Dunster Hawn, with fairly open water at the eastern end, more overgrown with reeds and bushes to the west, and all surrounded by mature trees. The eastern rockier third of the beach to Blue Anchor is immediately backed by arable farmland. Minehead and Blue Anchor are both holiday resorts and the area is often crowded in July and August, although relatively undisturbed at other times of year.

Species

Around 200 Canada Geese (up to 600 on occasion!) can be found on the meadows of Minehead marshes at any time of year, and a few pairs breed. This flock regularly commutes between here and the Brendon Hills reservoirs of Clatworthy and Wimbleball, and is often accompanied by feral species which can include Barnacle Geese as well as other more obvious exotics. Truly wild geese are rare these days, apart from the Brent Geese which have become regular visitors to the beach and shoreline in recent winters, though only in single-figure numbers as yet. Up to 200 Wigeon are the most numerous winter duck, with a few Teal and Mallard also feeding here, their numbers swelled if and when flooding occurs. Among the waders, 150 or so wintering Curlew, Oystercatchers and Dunlin are the most numerous species, joined by flocks of several hundred Golden Plover in some years. Smaller numbers of Ringed Plover, Turnstone and Sanderling plus the odd Grey Plover and Knot add variety to the winter scene. The beach hosts a small winter gull roost, Herring, Black-headed and Common Gulls being the most numerous species, but joined on several occasions by Ring-billed and Mediterranean Gulls. Up to a dozen of the latter have been recorded in winter, though most reliably seen on autumn passage, and recently they have favoured the Blue Anchor end of the bay. Offshore, gales at this time may drive large numbers of Kittiwakes up-Channel. Peregrines patrol the coastline regularly in winter, with Merlin and Hen Harrier less frequent. The upper beach sometimes attracts wintering Snow Buntings, although, as everywhere on this coast, occurrences are patchy and in small numbers. Black Redstarts can also be found, although they are most likely in late autumn or on spring passage. The sheltered nature of the Dunster Hawn allows a small number of Chiffchaffs to attempt to overwinter, along with the now resident Cetti's Warblers, and they have been joined in several years by the odd Firecrest. Water Rails are regular, though normally detected only by their squealing calls, and Siskins and Redpolls feed on the alder seeds.

    Whether or not the first Chiffchaffs heard in March are wintering birds or migrants, there is little doubt about the Wheatears on the golf course or the Sand Martins over the beach. Migrating warblers can be numerous in the woodland, with Whinchats and Redstarts occurring in the more open areas. Pied Flycatchers have also occurred in several springs. The trilling calls of Whimbrel can be heard as birds move along the coastline, sometimes accompanied by one or two Bar-tailed Godwits, never a common species on this coast. White Wagtails in their smart grey and white plumage feed in small groups along the upper shore.

Breeding birds are not particularly notable, although a couple of pairs of Mute Swans nest on the Hawn, as do Coot and Moorhen. The strips of reeds hold a few pairs of Reed Warblers, and the recently arrived Cetti's Warblers have raised young on more than one occasion. Sandwich Terns may appear offshore during the summer, but terns are more regular in the autumn when Common and Arctic Terns also appear, up to a dozen or so to be seen resting on the sands at low tide. Their presence may attract an Arctic Skua to harry them for their catch. Wader numbers increase again, with up to 150 Ringed Plover sometimes recorded on passage. Small numbers of Sanderling also occur at the same time, though they can be found almost all year at this site. Freshwater species are not common, although Greenshanks can occur by the shore pools. Autumn passerines trickle through, but late autumn with visible movement of larks and finches is more reliable for numbers of birds, flocks of Linnets, Greenfinches and Goldfinches stopping to feed along the upper shore. Rarities such as Richard's Pipit and Yellow-browed Warbler have occurred at this time, the latter also having been seen exceptionally in late winter.

Sandwich Tern

Timing

For waders high-tide visits are best as the birds are nearer and also more active as the waters begin to fall. However, with a telescope, birds are still reasonably visible even several hours after high water, and it is possible to walk down the beach for closer views. At high tide some of the waders move up onto the grazing meadows to roost and feed, this area also providing a refuge for birds disturbed from the golf course, particularly in the afternoons. In the main holiday months the whole area can become very crowded, and early morning visits are much more productive.

Strong westerly winds in autumn may bring seabirds closer inshore. Calm days in winter are most likely to induce any wintering warblers to emerge from cover.

Access

Dunster Beach is signposted off the main A39 near Dunster. Drive through the village of Marsh Street, and turn right down a minor road that leads over an automatic level crossing to a car park (fee payable) by the beach. In winter you may have to park in the road if the car park is closed, which it often is at weekends and at night (take care not to get locked in!). A public right of way leads along the beach past the holiday chalet village to the golf course; at busy times a certain amount of tact is required of binocular-toting birdwatchers! Near the entrance to the holiday village, a stone causeway crosses the eastern end of the Hawn, where there is the largest section of open water, and leads to a nature trail running through the woodland at the back, recrossing the more overgrown end about halfway along or towards the far end. Other paths allow the western section to be explored, the whole area being attractive to migrants, especially since much of the golf course has recently been 'tidied up'. The marshes can be scanned from the footpath that runs back to Dunster station from the bridge over the small stream (the old River Avill) at the far western end of Dunster Hawn. There is a small rookery here, birds often flying down to feed on the beach with Carrion Crows and Jackdaws, and joining the gulls and waders bathing in the fresh water running across the beach. You can walk along the edge of the golf course as far as Minehead, checking the remaining patches of brambles for migrants, but take care not to interfere with the golfers. The most extensive areas of open beach are at this western end. The eastern half of the beach area is rockier and less disturbed, but usually attracts fewer birds. Access is via the bridge over the concrete channel of the diverted River Avill and then along the top of the beach to Blue Anchor (also accessible by road via Carhampton).

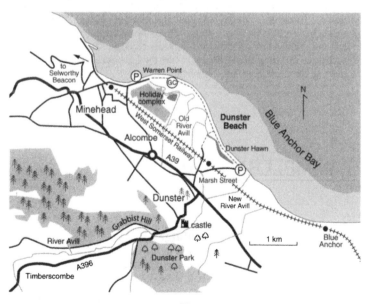

To approach from the west, drive to the eastern end of the Minehead seafront, where there is plenty of parking space beyond the Somerwest World entrance. A clearly marked footpath leads along the coast from the golf course entrance.

Calendar

All year: Cormorant, Mute Swan, Canada Goose, Kestrel, Moorhen, Coot, Rock Pipit, Cetti's Warbler, Rook.

December–February: Maybe diver or seaduck offshore. Shelduck, Wigeon, Teal, occasional Brent Goose, Gadwall, Shoveler, Tufted Duck. Peregrine, maybe Merlin. Water Rail. Oystercatcher, Ringed Plover, Grey Plover, Golden Plover, Dunlin, Curlew, Turnstone, Sanderling, Snipe. Gull roost may include rarities, e.g. Mediterranean, Ring-billed. Chance of Kittiwake in gales. Maybe Chiffchaff or Firecrest. Siskin, Redpoll; Snow Bunting (irregular).

March–May: Occasional Fulmar. Wintering waders move away in March; Ringed Plover, Oystercatcher and Whimbrel pass mid-April–mid-May, when usually also Common and Arctic Terns, maybe Arctic Skua. Sand Martin from mid-March; Wheatear, Chiffchaff, White Wagtail, sometimes Black Redstart, during April.

June–July: Small numbers of Fulmar and Manx Shearwater occur offshore. A few Oystercatchers, Ringed Plover, Sanderling, Curlew and Turnstones summer; other waders returning from mid-July.

August–November: Seabirds in gales may include Manx Shearwater, petrels, Gannet, Fulmar. Passing raptors might include Marsh Harrier (August), Short-eared Owl, Hen Harrier (October–November). Wader passage peaks August–September: Oystercatcher, Ringed Plover, Grey Plover, Turnstone, Dunlin, Sanderling; a few Whimbrel and Bar-tailed Godwit, occasional Greenshank. Terns from mid-August–mid-September include Common, Arctic, Sandwich, maybe Little. Migrants in August–September include Arctic Skua, Mediterranean Gull (rare), Whinchat, Wheatear; in October include Skylark, Chaffinch, Meadow Pipit. Snow Bunting, Black Redstart mostly October–November. Maybe wintering Firecrest from late October.

5 WIMBLEBALL LAKE   OS Outdoor Leisure 9

Habitat

This reservoir, which was first flooded in the late 1970s, covers an area of 374 acres (151 ha), and lies at c.200 metres above sealevel on the southern slopes of the Brendon Hills. It is mostly fairly steep-sided, forming long 'arms', and the northern part is surrounded by farmland. Woodland on the southeastern banks contains a high proportion of oaks, while the southern side is dominated by the steep slope of Haddon Hill, 355 metres high, where open heather and bracken heathland is backed by conifer plantations. The reservoir is dammed in the southwest corner, below which the River Haddeo runs through an attractive steep-sided and wooded valley to join the River Exe in c.3 miles (4.8 km). Again there are plenty of oaks, but with a good under-storey of hazel and rhododendron, plus alders in places by the river. The reservoir has been developed with recreation very much in mind, and is used extensively by sailors, anglers and windsurfers, as well as the general public. The South West Lakes Trust manage a small nature reserve at Hurscombe by the northernmost arm.

Species

As at many high-level, steep-sided reservoirs, overall numbers of winter wildfowl are rarely very high but always worth checking through. Currently the most numerous species are Coot, with up to 500 present in autumn and winter, and Mallard with around 200 maximum. Up to 100 Wigeon feed on the grassy banks, with similar numbers of Pochard and Tufted Duck out on the water. Surface-feeding ducks are relatively scarce, but Goldeneye are regular in single-figure numbers, Red-throated Diver, Smew and a few Scaup have been recorded, and gradually other species are being added to the site's list. Already both American Wigeon and several Ring-necked Ducks have appeared as vagrants. Among fish-eating species both Cormorants and Goosanders are increasing, over 80 of the latter having been counted at dawn and dusk when birds come to the lake to roost after having spent the day feeding on the surrounding rivers. Canada Geese are numerous, over 200 being not uncommon in winter, with a few pairs nesting. They are sometimes accompanied by the odd feral Barnacle Goose or other exotic. In the surrounding woodland, the alders attract wintering Siskins and the conifers hold occasional parties of Crossbills, whilst this is one of the few sites in Somerset where the increasingly localised Willow Tit is still seen. However, whether they still nest here is uncertain. Dippers breed on the surrounding streams, their rather Wren-like song being heard from very early on in the year.

Common Sandpiper

In spring Buzzards and Sparrowhawks start soaring above the surrounding woods, several pairs of both species being resident. Migrant hirundines and later Swifts gather to feed over the water, particularly in bad weather, and other passage birds may appear for a morning. The woods rapidly fill up with summer visitors, most notably 15 or so pairs of Pied Flycatchers plus Redstarts and Wood Warblers. Migrating Wheatears are regular on the open slopes of Haddon Hill, and from time to time remain to breed. Nightjars have also bred here in the past, although dependent on the stage of growth of the conifers which now cover part of this habitat. Tree Pipits, Stonechats and Redpolls are all to be found breeding on the heathland areas, while the woodland contains all three species of woodpecker. Siskins are also sometimes heard in summer but are difficult to pin down as far as nesting is concerned.

Autumn wader passage is generally thin, as normally very little mud is exposed. Common Sandpipers are the most numerous species, with a few Green Sandpipers and the occasional Greenshank. Moulting Canada Geese peak in July: throughout the year they are part of a flock which moves between here, Clatworthy and Minehead.

Timing

Generally not critical, although woodland passerines are always more active in the mornings. There is casual human disturbance around the reservoir margins at all times of the year, heaviest on summer weekend afternoons. The trout fishing season is from mid-April to late October, and in autumn and winter, Pheasant shooting causes a certain amount of noise and disruption in the adjacent farmland. For possible Nightjars, dusk on warm mid-summer evenings is the best time to try listening. As the majority of Goosander return to the lake to roost after feeding elsewhere, the highest counts are always made at dawn or dusk.

Access

The nearest main road is the B3190 north from Bampton to Williton, skirting to the southeast of the reservoir. At Haddon Hill this road turns sharp right at the entrance to a car park with fine views over the whole area. From here walk west to beyond the highest point over open heather-clad slopes from which, at the far end, the woods in the Haddeo valley can be scanned for soaring Buzzards. Redpolls sing regularly in summer over the car park itself, and the birch and scrub-covered slopes to the east hold Tree Pipits, Stonechats, Willow Warblers and Whitethroats. From the car park there is easy access to the reservoir banks directly below, and the oak woods along this southern shore hold Pied Flycatchers, Wood Warblers, Redstarts and Green and Great Spotted Woodpeckers. Goosanders seem to favour this part of the reservoir in winter. For the Haddeo valley, walk to the dam and continue on a signposted footpath through woodland on the near side of the river to a minor road from Brompton Regis to the hamlet of Hartford (vehicular access along this road is not advised as parking is virtually non-existent). Turn left to the end of this road, then follow the footpath, muddy in parts, that runs by the river all the way to Bury. Wood Warblers, Pied Flycatchers, Redstarts and other woodland birds can be found here, with Grey Wagtails and Dippers by the stream.

For access to the rest of the reservoir, continue towards Williton and turn left off the B3190 at Upton; if approaching from the Williton direction, turn right near two radio masts west of Raleigh's Cross Inn. In both

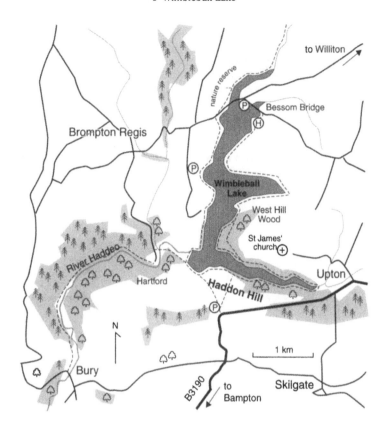

cases follow signposts towards Brompton Regis, eventually reaching a bridge and causeway across the northern arms of the reservoir. There is a small car park between the two arms, with toilets and a map of the site. This is probably the best point from which to scan for wildfowl, and the shallow water at the head of the arms is attractive to wildfowl and any waders present. At Bessom Bridge there is a nature trail along the west bank of the northernmost arm, through a damp bushy area where Willow Tits and a pair or two of Pied Flycatchers are sometimes found. On the western side of the lake is an information centre and café (closed in winter), accessed along a clearly marked turning from the road west of Bessom Bridge. There is ample parking here and the central part of the lake can be viewed from the bottom of the picnic site slope. A footpath runs round the whole shore, the only way to access the more distant extremities properly.

Calendar

All year: Little and Great Crested Grebes, Grey Heron, Sparrowhawk, Buzzard, Kestrel, Pheasant, Coot, Kingfisher, woodpeckers including occasional Lesser Spotted; Skylark, Grey Wagtail, Meadow Pipit, Dipper, Stonechat; Willow Tit (scarce), Nuthatch, Treecreeper, Raven.

December–February: Cormorant, Wigeon, Teal, Pochard, Tufted Duck, Goldeneye, Goosander, occasional Scaup, Smew or other rarer duck. Siskin, Redpoll, sometimes Crossbill.

March–May: Wildfowl mostly leave by end of March. Common Sandpiper, Swallow, House Martin passing late April–May. Wheatears pass April–May, sometimes remaining to breed. Cuckoo and summer passerines arrive from mid-April: Tree Pipit, Redstart, Pied Flycatcher; Whitethroat, Wood Warbler mostly early May. Redpolls singing May; maybe Siskin.

June–July: Breeding birds active, but less song in July. Nightjars, if present, churring throughout.

August–November: Wildfowl arrive during November, when strays most likely. Common Sandpiper, occasional Green Sandpiper, Greenshank and other waders August–September.

6 CLATWORTHY RESERVOIR

OS Outdoor Leisure 9

Habitat

Clatworthy, opened in 1961, is the older of the two Brendon Hills reservoirs, and is also smaller at 130 acres (52.6 ha). It is higher and more isolated than Wimbleball a few miles away to the west. Surrounded by rolling farmland, Clatworthy is a long narrow water with steep sides, so that apart from in drought years, little bare mud is exposed and emergent vegetation is restricted to the ends of the arms where streams flow in. Scattered woods with a high proportion of oak, plus beech and conifers, grow nearby, including some on the reservoir banks themselves. The area is visually attractive, and a small picnic site overlooking the reservoir is a focal point for visitors. Angling activities include both bank and boat fishing for trout.

Species

This is an underwatched area, partially because of its distance from the main centres of population, but also because it attracts only relatively small numbers of waterfowl at any time of year. In fact it is better considered as a woodland site with water attached! Feral Canada Geese are the dominant species, a flock of up to 200 birds moving between here, Wimbleball and Minehead, with a few pairs breeding nearby. Other wandering exotics attracted to this group include several feral Barnacle Geese. Other wildfowl are usually just in single figures, Cormorant, Little and Great Crested Grebes, Mallard and Coot the most frequent, with Wigeon, Teal, Tufted Duck, Pochard and Goosander occasionally appearing. Resident breeding species include Grey Wagtail, Sparrowhawk and Buzzard, joined in the summer by Wood Warblers, Tree Pipits and Redstarts and a nice range of passerines in the woodland nearby. Common Sandpipers and the odd Greenshank are the most likely waders to be seen on passage; other migrants no doubt pass through unrecorded, although Ospreys have been seen more than once, this

Canada Goose

spectacular visitor often preferring enclosed waters such as this to the more intensively watched lowland reservoirs.

Timing
Early morning in spring and summer is the best time for locating song-birds, while Buzzards are frequently on the wing in good weather throughout the first half of the year. Casual disturbance is likely to be highest on fine summer weekends, and during the fishing season from mid-March to mid-October.

Access
The main approach is to the southern side, either from the B3227 in Wiveliscombe or from the B3190 northeast of Upton. In both cases, follow signs to Huish Champflower, then Clatworthy, taking care on the narrow winding lanes. The picnic area lies about halfway along the southeastern side, close to the main dam, its access road marked by a large sign at the entrance. It has picnic tables, ample parking and toilets (including disabled facilities), but closes at 4.30 pm. The central part of the reservoir is overlooked from the car park, and a path leads down to and across the dam. The river valley below the dam is worth scanning for wagtails and soaring Buzzards. There is a waymarked nature trail around the wood on the far side of the dam, with Wood Warblers and Redstarts here in the summer. This is generally the best area but for a full exploration a permissive footpath continues on round the whole shore of the lake, passing through several copses, and allowing each of the inlet arms to be checked. If time is limited, walk back along the picnic site access road and take a gated path to the right, passing the fishermen's lodge to join the waterside footpath in the opposite direction round the shore. This first passes some bracken-covered slopes where Tree Pipits can be heard singing in the summer, and shortly allows the western end to be examined, this part being the shallowest, and thus attracting a wider range of species. There is a road down to this part of the lake from west of Raleigh's Cross, but it is in poor condition, and the gate at the end is often locked.

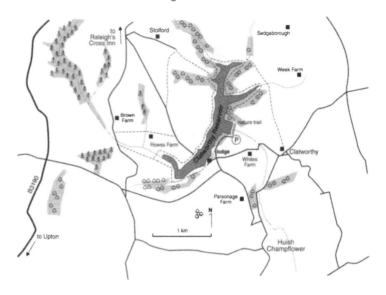

Calendar

All year: Great Crested Grebe, Canada Goose, Mallard, Sparrowhawk, Buzzard, Coot, Tawny Owl, Green and Great Spotted Woodpeckers, Grey Wagtail, Marsh Tit, Nuthatch, Treecreeper, Raven.

December–February: Little Grebe, Cormorant, Grey Heron, Pochard, Tufted Duck, Goosander, Stonechat, Siskin.

March–May: Common Sandpiper mid-April–May; chance of Osprey. Tree Pipit, Redstart, Willow Warbler, Chiffchaff arrive from mid–late April; Whitethroat, Garden Warbler, Blackcap, Wood Warbler a little later.

June–July: Breeding species active. Canada Geese may flock.

August–November: Little Grebe. Common Sandpipers pass during August–September with occasional Green Sandpiper, Greenshank. Summer passerines leave by early September.

7 LANGFORD HEATHFIELD   OS Explorer 140

Habitat

Although only covering 226 acres (91.5 ha), this SWT reserve is the largest area of lowland heath left in Somerset, having resisted many attempts to reclaim it for agriculture. Habitats are diverse within a small area, ranging from oak and ash woodland with a varied under-storey including crab apple, holly, elder, hazel and hawthorn, to more open wet heath with its specialised flora of meadow thistle, sneezewort, petty whin and saw-wort, among others. Sallow and birch scrub has encroached in several places and this, together with the bracken, has to be controlled in order to retain the variety of butterflies and flowers, the former including several fritillaries and the brown hairstreak.

Species
Spring and summer are the main times of interest here, and woodland birds the main group to be seen. Throughout the year Nuthatches, Marsh Tits, Tawny Owls and all three species of woodpecker can be found, the localised Lesser Spotted in particular finding the damp woodland with many rotting branches ideal for feeding and nesting. It is also one of the few sites where Willow Tits are still reported from time to time. Siskins and Redpolls swing among the birches during the winter months, and there have been chance sightings of Woodcock at this time – certainly the habitat looks ideal for this secretive bird. Buzzards circle low overhead, often causing alarm among the Jays and Carrion Crows, while the passage of a Sparrowhawk through the tree-tops produces a sudden silence from smaller birds. The nearby rookery is active from late winter, and Mistle Thrushes usually initiate the build-up in birdsong through the earlier part of the year to be swelled later by the arrival of the summer visitors. Cuckoo, Garden Warbler, Blackcap and Willow Warbler are all to be found in the woodland, while Lesser Whitethroat and Tree Pipit occur in the damp scrub and birch areas. Redstart, Wood Warbler, Grasshopper Warbler and Nightingale have all been noted here in the recent past, both on passage and as breeding species. A pair or two of Pied Flycatchers are a fairly recent addition to the bird population here, and it helps to be familiar with the song as they are well scattered in the woodland, and are not recorded annually. Once the main song period is over late summer and autumn are usually less productive with feeding birds hidden among the foliage, although there tends to be a flurry of activity among feeding passerines prior to migration. Barn Owls still breed in the area, and birds with young to feed might be seen during daylight hours.

Timing
Early morning is easily the most productive time for locating songbirds, and mid-afternoon is the quietest time for all species.

Access
The reserve lies c.3 miles (4.8 km) northwest of Wellington, and is reached by turning west off the B3187 to Milverton, and following signs to Langford Budville. From here, take the road signposted to Wiveliscombe; alternatively approach from the north from that town, signposted to Langford Budville. Either way, the road runs along the eastern edge of the common, with a layby at the southern end where cars should be parked. An SWT sign gives details of footpaths, which must be adhered to at all times to avoid damage to what is vulnerable habitat; the whole reserve can be adequately explored by following the paths, some of which are on raised boardwalks. The most extensive wet heath (sometimes very wet!) is in the southern part of the reserve. At the northern end a road signposted to Poleshill runs west through the more wooded part; again there is a layby on this road where cars can be parked, and another SWT sign giving details concerning access.

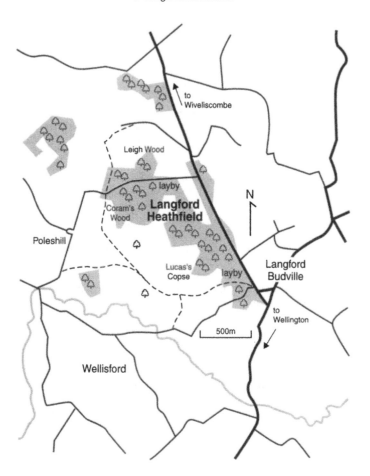

Calendar

All year: Sparrowhawk, Buzzard, Kestrel, Pheasant, Barn Owl, Tawny Owl, woodpeckers including Lesser Spotted; Marsh Tit, maybe Willow Tit; Long-tailed Tit, Nuthatch, Treecreeper, Jay, Rook; Raven (has bred).

December–February: Woodcock. Siskin, Redpoll. Rooks rebuilding nests from February.

March–May: Song from resident species builds up. Chiffchaff from late March; Cuckoo, Tree Pipit, Redstart, Pied Flycatcher from mid-April; Wood Warbler, Garden Warbler, maybe Grasshopper Warbler or Nightingale from late April. Spotted Flycatcher early–mid-May.

June–July: Breeding birds active throughout, song fading in July.

August–November: Summer visitors leave during August, stragglers through September. Woodcock may appear November.

Habitat

The top of the Blackdowns is a rolling plateau at around 250 metres, reaching a maximum of 315 metres at Staple Hill, with much of the area given over to dairy and livestock farming. The northern escarpment, overlooking the Vale of Taunton, is mostly clothed in woodland, part deciduous dominated by beech, but with extensive conifer plantations, some well matured. The only large area of open gorse and heather moorland now remaining is at Sampford Point, at the extreme northwestern end of the hills, although there are small patches scattered elsewhere. A multitude of streams rise in the Blackdowns, those flowing south into Devon cutting steep-sided valleys with patches of woodland and rough ground on their slopes. Standing water is restricted to a few small reservoirs and private lakes.

Species

Although not particularly outstanding, the Blackdowns provide the opportunity to see a variety of woodland and heathland birds otherwise local in this part of the county. In winter the woods and fields are likely to be fairly quiet, although Woodcock are regular, if under-recorded, visitors to the copses and plantations. Little Grebe, Mallard and a few Tufted Ducks are the most likely waterfowl to be seen on the few areas of open water, although the odd Goosander has been recorded. More interesting resident species include Dipper on some of the streams, and the localised Willow Tit may still survive in the conifer plantations, while Buzzard and Sparrowhawk are widespread. After an invasion year,

Curlew

Crossbills may stay throughout the winter in any of the larger plantations. In summer, the beech woodlands attract Wood Warblers, another declining species, in addition to the commoner Willow Warblers, Chiffchaffs and Blackcaps. Several pairs of Redstarts breed, especially where lines of old beech trees, a distinctive feature of the Blackdown landscape, provide nesting sites. Nightingales are widely if patchily distributed wherever the right cover conditions occur. The open heathland around Sampford Point attracts species such as Meadow Pipit, Whitethroat, Whinchat and Stonechat, all in rather variable numbers. This is another site where Dartford Warblers have been seen recently, and hopefully they will increase as elsewhere in Somerset. One or two pairs of Curlew can sometimes be heard giving their plaintive and evocative songs, though whether they ever breed successfully is rather uncertain. Conifer plantations have encouraged Redpolls to spread into the area, their twangy rattling flight calls and song drawing attention to their presence, but the Turtle Doves that used to occur here have not been seen for several years – they have become a very rare bird in the southwest. Wherever clearings have been opened up in the conifers, as well as on the remaining heathland, there is a good chance of locating Tree Pipits, and the same habitat holds a few pairs of Nightjars, which have recently returned as a breeding species to the Blackdowns.

Timing

Spring and early summer mornings without too much wind provide the best conditions for seeing most of the breeding species, both in woodland and more open habitats. Nightjars need to be listened for after sunset, but otherwise factors are few.

Access

Suitable habitat for birdwatching in the area is very fragmented and in many parts access to private land is strictly forbidden. In addition, parking space is often restricted, and a detailed map showing the footpaths is essential. A road runs along the ridge of the hills, linking the main sites of interest. At its western end, it sweeps round north towards Wellington, but a minor road leads straight on for another ¼ mile (0.4 km) to the start of a private road (but public footpath) leading west to Sampford Point and Black Down Common (the later actually in Devon). Another minor road (Green Lane) approaches the common from the north, with slightly more space to park where the footpath starts. There is plenty of gorse and bracken on the flat-topped ridge, overlooking a sweep of damp grassland on the west-facing slope. This is the best area for heathland and open-country birds, and provides a good viewpoint for soaring birds of prey. Returning along the ridge road, there are NT car parks in the woodland near the Wellington Monument, where the SWT has a reserve. Further east, near the Fish and Game pub, access is possible to Forestry Commission land at Buckland Wood, and to the adjoining SWT woodland reserve at Quants. The small reservoirs at Luxhay and Leigh are only visible with difficulty from the road. Commoner warblers, including a few Wood Warblers, breed in the area while Redstarts occur around Culmhead where there are fine beeches by the road but very restricted access.

The Holman Clavel Inn marks a useful centre point for the eastern half of the hills. To the south, just beyond Otterford, there is a small SWT/WW reserve (park in car park at northern entrance) where two lakes joined by a fast-flowing stream attract a few duck and Little Grebes, while the

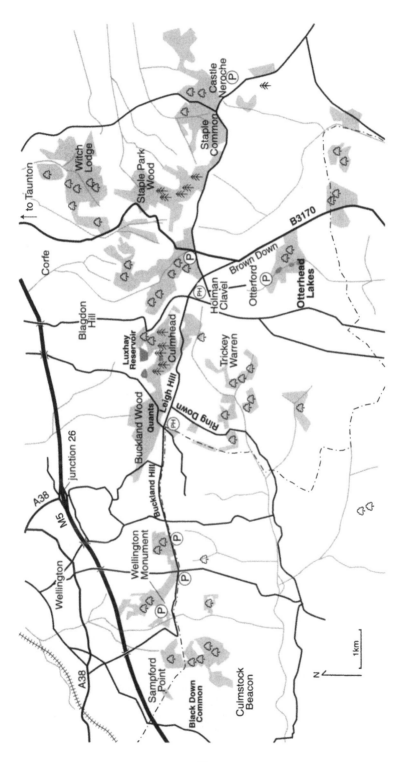

willows and alders by the stream hold wintering Redpolls and Siskins. Dippers and Kingfishers are also sometimes reported. The footpath round the nature trail is clearly marked. Immediately east of Holman Clavel, there is a small parking area by the road from which footpaths lead east through the plantations around Staple Hill, Staple Park Wood and Mount Fancy Farm, which are more varied than most, and where Tree Pipits and Crossbills have occurred. Any of the clearings here are worth checking for Nightjars. East again, there is another parking area for the Castle Neroche forest trail, with Wood Warblers and Redstarts in the mixed beech and coniferous woodland and the chance of a few Nightingales around Curland Common. Due north, beyond Staple Fitzpaine, several lanes to the east lead to Thurlbear Wood, where the SWT has a reserve. As ever, parking is tricky, but various footpaths run through the wood, one of the most reliable spots in the area to hear Nightingales in the spring.

Calendar

All year: Sparrowhawk, Buzzard, Pheasant, Green and Great Spotted Woodpeckers, Meadow Pipit, Grey Wagtail; Dipper (scarce), Stonechat; Dartford Warbler and Willow Tit (both scarce), Yellowhammer.

December–February: Little Grebe (has bred at Otterhead), Mallard, Tufted Duck; maybe Goosander (Otterhead), Woodcock, maybe Crossbill.

March–May: Breeding Curlew return March. Lesser Black-backed Gull passage through Taunton Vale. Cuckoo, Tree Pipit, Nightingale, Redstart arrive mid–late April; Whitethroat, Wood Warbler early May.

June–July: Breeding birds include Nightjar, common woodland passerines, Redpoll. Curlew leave end July, when Crossbills may arrive.

August–November: Most summer passerines leave by end August. Return passage of Lesser Black-backed Gulls October–December.

9 THE QUANTOCK HILLS   OS Explorer 140

Habitat

The Quantock Hills, 12 miles (19.2 km) long and averaging just over 3 miles (4.8 km) in width, although not as extensive as Exmoor, encompass a wide range of habitats within an area of c.38 square miles (98 km²). The hills rise steeply from both Taunton Vale to the south and from the coastal strip bordering the Bristol Channel to the north, reaching a maximum height of 384 metres at Will's Neck, although the main ridge is of much the same height for most of its length. The predominantly thin soils overlying sandstone give rise to open country dominated by heather, western gorse, whortleberry and bracken over much of the higher ground. On either side deep combes have been cut by fast-flowing streams, bush-clad and open on the southern escarpment but with some fine oak woodland on the northern slopes. At the eastern end of the hills there are extensive Forestry Commission conifer plantations, with smaller patches at the western end of the range. Elsewhere there are lines of mature beeches, particularly at Alfoxton and Crowcombe Parks. The whole area is very popular with ramblers and horseriders, but the fact that only one road crosses the central part of the hills means that disturbance is less heavy than might be expected. Red deer are the outstanding mammals to be seen, but badgers and foxes are common, and adders and slow-worms can frequently be found sunning themselves in quieter parts of the moorland.

Species

The Quantocks are primarily a place for seeing a wide variety of breeding woodland and heathland birds in a relatively small area, and in winter can be fairly quiet. Parties of tits, Nuthatches and Treecreepers move through the woodland, and the few Dippers remain on the streams throughout the year. Meadow Pipits and Skylarks on the ridge may attract an occasional Merlin or Hen Harrier, but these birds range widely and are thus not often reported. Ravens can be seen overhead, sometimes in small groups, throughout the year, and several pairs breed. Early spring is a good time to learn the songs of the resident woodland birds as they start to re-establish their territories. Mistle Thrushes, early and loud songsters, are rapidly followed by plenty of Robins, Song Thrushes, Marsh Tits, etc. All three woodpeckers breed in the deciduous woods, this being one of the more reliable areas for Lesser Spotted, although always difficult to pin down. Fewer species are found in the coniferous areas, Goldcrests and Coal Tits being the most numerous birds, although Long-eared Owls have occasionally nested, and the possibility that overwintering Crossbills may do so cannot be discounted.

With the arrival of the summer migrants, the oak woods become a hive of activity. Wood Warblers are numerous throughout, and Pied Flycatchers can be found in loose colonies in several places, these attractive birds currently enjoying a population boom. Redstarts are also characteristic of this habitat. The woodland edge and bushier parts of the hills hold plenty of Tree Pipits, Whitethroats and Yellowhammers, while higher

Pied Flycatcher

up there are Whinchats and smaller numbers of Stonechats. As on Exmoor and the Mendips, Dartford Warblers have recently become established here, and can be looked for throughout the year anywhere where there is extensive gorse and heather, particularly at the western end of the hills. In the coniferous areas Redpolls can be heard in May giving their metallic calls and song in flight and a few pairs of Siskins have bred recently: both species are more commonly seen in autumn and winter. A few Tree Pipits and Redstarts also occur around the forestry clearings. The open tops themselves hold fewest species, although Meadow Pipits are common. Buzzards and Sparrowhawks are widespread, and luckier sightings may be had of a Hobby, often just passage birds, hawking for insects over the heather. Late in the spring another speciality of the Quantocks arrives: the Nightjar, to be heard churring in several places at dawn and dusk.

In late summer woodland birds become hard to see, but in early autumn there is a resurgence of activity as the migrants move out onto the heathland to feed prior to migrating. Wheatears occur in small numbers on spring and autumn passage and it is always worth checking for Ring Ousels at the same time.

Timing
Spring and summer mornings are when woodland birds are the most vocal and active. Avoid wet and windy days on the higher ground as birds are very difficult to locate in these exposed areas under such conditions. For Nightjars warm summer evenings are essential – note, however, that it may be almost dark before birds begin to sing. On certain days pony-trekking events take place and the hills may be very crowded, and the whole area is very popular with walkers and cyclists.

Access
The main Bridgwater to Minehead road (A39) skirts the northern side of the hills, cutting across the western end at West Quantoxhead. The A358 Taunton to Watchet road runs parallel to the hills on the southern side and affords fine views of the escarpment. For the best oak woods, turn off the A39 in Holford where the youth hostel is signposted (the other two minor lanes nearby are very narrow) and then take the second right towards Hodder's Combe/Alfoxton as far as Holford Green where there is a small car park on the left. The mature gardens around the Green itself hold plenty of common woodland birds, easily visible. The nearby woodland of Holford Glen, around the lower end of the valley, holds woodpeckers and there are Dippers by the stream. For this area, walk back along the road over the stream and follow its right bank by road and then footpath to where a picturesque wooden bridge overlooks the valley.

Back towards the hills, there are paths by the rivers up Holford Combe and Hodder's Combe, or more directly onto the heathland between the two towards Black Hill. Walking up Hodder's Combe following any of the streams will bring you to the ridge path from where you can return over heathland habitat via Black Hill to the south or Longstone Hill and Alfoxton Park to the north. The Holford Combe streams bring you out nearer the Crowcombe/Nether Stowey Road from where access is also possible to the open ground of Dowsborough and Woodlands Hill, over which more paths lead back to Holford. Both combes hold similar birds. Look for Pied Flycatchers, usually several pairs together, in the middle and upper reaches of the valleys. Redstarts are mostly at the woodland

edges or near clearings. Tree Pipits occur around the edges of the woodland and onto the bushier open areas. These latter attract Whinchats,
which also particularly like the steep bracken-covered slopes either side
of the ridge. The ridge path itself is one of the poorest parts for birds,
although the Stonechats seem to prefer these highest areas, and Dartford
Warblers forage in the heather and gorse.

For the western end of the hills, take the Bicknoller road from the A39
at the Windmill Inn at West Quantoxhead, and at the crossroads in Staple
turn left up a steep and narrow no-through-road leading to a public car
park at Staple Plain/Beacon Hill. Several clearly marked paths lead up
onto the top, but the main areas of interest here are the conifer plantations on the northwest slopes with Nightjars audible from the car park.
The exact location of the birds will depend on where recent clearings
happen to be at the time. There are attractive steep combes in this area
above Weacombe and Bicknoller with Whinchats and Tree Pipits numerous, while the woodland edges hold a few Wood Warblers and Redstarts.

The main coniferous plantations at the eastern end are accessible
from a variety of points and are interlaced with well-marked forest paths.
From Nether Stowey, follow minor roads to Adscombe and on to the
rough tracks of the Forestry Commission's 'Great Wood' car parks and picnic sites at the bottom of Ram's and Quantock Combes. Alternatively
access is possible from the Crowcombe/Nether Stowey road at
Crowcombe Park Gate and the Dead Woman Ditch car park. From the
Taunton road c.2 miles (3.2 km) south of Nether Stowey a lane runs the

length of Cockercombe to end after 2 miles (3.2 km) on the ridge at Triscombe Stone where there is a car park. There are more tracks into the conifers in this scenically attractive valley, and to the southeast the bushy heathland of the adjoining Aisholt Common and Wills Neck is another area where Nightjars can be heard. Further southeast again, the woods and heathland around Cothelstone and Broomfield Hills are also worth exploring. The SWT has its headquarters at nearby Fyne Court (NT), with an easy-access nature trail suitable for disabled visitors.

Just to the east again lies the small, 32 acre (13 ha), Hawkridge Reservoir. This is easily viewable from the roadside, and is worth a quick look in passing, although disturbed by trout fishermen from March to October. Pochard and Tufted Ducks occur in small numbers in winter, the latter sometimes attempting to breed. Great Crested and Little Grebes are also regular and also sometimes breed. Most other ducks are rare, although Goldeneye, Goosander and more than one Ring-necked Duck have been seen. The surrounding woodland is attractive, with Nuthatches and woodpeckers to be heard from the bridge at the upper end, a footpath from here leading to the nearby SWT reserve of Aisholt Wood. The reservoir can also be reached from Bridgwater via Durleigh and Spaxton (see Durleigh Reservoir entry).

Calendar

All year: Little Grebe, Tufted Duck (Hawkridge Reservoir); Sparrowhawk, Buzzard, Tawny Owl, Stock Dove. Woodpeckers include Lesser Spotted. Skylark, Meadow Pipit, Grey Wagtail; Dipper (scarce), Stonechat, Dartford Warbler, Nuthatch, Treecreeper, Raven, Yellowhammer.

December–February: Great Crested Grebe, Pochard, occasional Goosander or Goldeneye (Hawkridge Reservoir). Wandering raptors include Merlin, Hen Harrier, maybe Red Kite. Woodcock. Stonechats increase at end of February. Siskin, Redpoll, Crossbill.

March–May: Little and Great Crested Grebes and Tufted Duck may breed at Hawkridge Reservoir. Wheatear and occasional Ring Ousel pass mid-March–April. Summer breeders arriving: Cuckoo, Tree Pipit, Redstart, Pied Flycatcher mid–late April; Whinchat, Grasshopper Warbler, Wood Warbler end April–early May. Siskins flock in March, a few remaining to breed. Redpolls singing in May. Nightjars arrive end May. Maybe migrating Hobby in May, or sporadically through to September.

June–July: Breeding species, including most common woodland and heathland species. Nightjar active throughout. Wood Warbler, Pied Flycatcher elusive from mid-June. Maybe Crossbill irruption July.

August–November: Most summer passerines leave in August, but dispersing/passage Tree Pipit, Whinchat, Wheatear, Redstart to mid-September. Stonechats disperse. Maybe passage Ring Ousel in September. Siskin and Redpoll numbers increase from September.

Habitat and Species

This small reservoir just northeast of Chard comprises 60 acres (24 ha) of open water surrounded by a thin belt of mixed woodland, which is currently been replanted with native trees and shrubs. It holds a few pairs of breeding Little and Great Crested Grebes, with up to 50 of the latter here in winter. Several hundred Mallard also winter here, with smaller numbers of Cormorants, Teal, Shoveler, Tufted Duck, Pochard and the odd Goldeneye. Over the years it has amassed a creditable list of rarer winter visitors, including Smew, Goosander, Ruddy Duck, Scaup, Long-tailed Duck, Ring-necked Duck and Slavonian Grebe, while Little Gull, Black Tern, Osprey and Garganey are among more interesting passage migrants. Little Egrets, up to six, have become regular late summer visitors, one or two usually staying through to the spring. The woodland fringe holds a good range of common breeding passerines such as Nuthatch, Treecreeper, Goldcrest, Chiffchaff and Blackcap. Green and Great Spotted Woodpeckers also nest here, and Lesser Spotted Woodpeckers are sometimes seen in the damp woodland, particularly in winter. Siskins and Redpolls come to the alders and birches in winter, whilst in summer a few Reed Warblers breed in the lakeside reeds. Buzzard, Grey Wagtail and Kingfisher can be seen throughout the year, all three breeding not far away.

Access

Previously difficult to watch, the reservoir is now a nature reserve owned by South Somerset District Council, and is well signposted from the town centre. Leave Crewkerne on the A30 towards Yeovil, and at the edge of the town turn left into Oaklands Avenue to reach a small car park at the end of the road. Information boards give full details of access, and there is a hide among the trees at the southern end of the reservoir from which the whole water surface can be scanned. Note that some of the woodland paths are closed from March to June inclusive to avoid disturbance to breeding birds.

11 SUTTON BINGHAM RESERVOIR   OS Explorer 117 and 129

Habitat

A few miles south of Yeovil, Sutton Bingham Reservoir is rather remote from other popular birdwatching sites and is relatively underwatched. The 142 acre (57.5 ha) reservoir, which dates from the mid-1950s, is dammed at the northern end, its two main tributary rivers making it 'hammer-shaped'. The banks are mostly gently sloping grazing land, appreciable areas of bare mud only being exposed when the water levels are well below normal. There is an extensive area of semi-submerged willows at the end of the main southern section of the reservoir with some flower-rich meadows nearby. Conifer plantations lie c.½ mile (0.8 km) to the west, and there are several scattered copses in the vicinity. There is an active sailing club and anglers use the reservoir during the trout-fishing season.

Species

The numbers of wildfowl wintering have continued to decline here, for reasons which are elusive. Twenty years ago, Sutton Bingham held significant numbers of the full range of species, but currently the diving ducks in particular are at a very low ebb. To start with the species doing well, inevitably Canada Goose and Cormorant feature prominently. Several pairs of the former raise young here each year, and over 300 birds are present at peak times in late summer and winter. Cormorant numbers are currently around the 50 mark in winter, and both species can be seen throughout the year. Great Crested Grebes have also increased considerably, with 10–20 pairs breeding, and numbers sometimes rising to over 100 in late summer when the birds form moulting flocks. The most numerous ducks are Wigeon, Mallard and Teal, with up to 200 or so of each still to found here on autumn passage or during the winter. Tufted Duck and Pochard numbers rarely break the 50 mark these days, and visits by Goldeneye and Goosander have become increasingly erratic. An American Wigeon spent several weeks here in 2000, and past rarities have included Ring-necked Duck and Green-winged Teal.

Particularly in the winter, the reservoir is used as a staging post for gulls on their way to their south coast roosts. Picking out the rarities depends of the enthusiasm of locals for this form of birdwatching, but Mediterranean Gulls are still reported on occasion, and more recently there have been a few sightings of Yellow-legged Gulls, typically from late summer onward.

The expanse of water is inevitably attractive to spring migrants, with hirundines passing through in some numbers. Water levels are usually high at this time so waders are normally limited to Common Sandpipers which join the resident Grey Wagtails on the concrete embankments. The

Grey Wagtail

48

local Buzzards and Sparrowhawks are at their most visible, soaring and displaying over the nearby woods and hillsides, and Ravens have also started to nest nearby. Hobbies can be seen overhead from time to time throughout the summer. Breeding birds in the damper fringes of the reservoir include several pairs of Reed Buntings, and it is good to be able to report the arrival of Cetti's Warblers. Ospreys have always occurred here on spring and autumn passage, but an exciting feature of recent years has been the habit of single birds to stay for long periods, often for several months at a time. Whether this will lead to anything more significant, only time will tell.

As summer turns to autumn a trickle of passerine migrants such as Yellow Wagtail, Tree Pipit, Whinchat, Sedge Warbler, Willow Warbler and Chiffchaff move through the waterside fields and vegetation. If the water levels are low, small numbers of Common and Green Sandpipers stop to feed along the reservoir margins, sometimes accompanied by other waders such as Little Ringed Plover, Redshank, Ruff or Little Stint. As ever, anything could turn up and the site has an impressive list of rarities to its credit, a Pectoral Sandpiper in September 2001 being one of the more recent of a long list of American waders seen here. Common, Arctic and Black Terns occur with rather more regularity than in the spring and autumn gales may bring a storm-driven Grey Phalarope or Kittiwake.

Timing

Not particularly critical for most waterfowl, although strong winds may drive birds into obscure corners for shelter. If the reservoir should freeze, then most wildfowl will leave, although freezing conditions further north and east will bring increased numbers of birds. Calmer conditions are best for observing resting gulls as they are difficult to pick out on choppy water. Terns on passage seem to appear most often under calm, rather cloudy conditions, when they are able to feed well on insects just over the water surface. For waders, low water levels are essential, the lower the better to expose the maximum areas of mud, although in extreme drought conditions the mud can dry out and become less attractive. Sailing takes place throughout the year, with maximum activity on weekend afternoons. Waterfowl normally just move to less disturbed parts of the lake. Model-boat sailing on the western arm can cause some disturbance in this area. Trout-fishing takes place from mid-March to mid-October.

Access

From Yeovil, take the A37 Dorchester road, and turn right after c.1½ miles (2.4 km) at the point where there is an obelisk by the main road. In about another 1¼ miles (2 km) the road passes under a railway bridge and emerges onto the causeway across the western arm. Park on the roadside here to scan the arm and the whole northern part of the reservoir. Check the causeway itself for any waders or wagtails, and look carefully along the far edges of the arm for waterbirds hidden in emergent vegetation. Just to the south of the causeway there is a small picnic site, open in the summer months, where it is possible to park if exploring further on foot. For the rest of the reservoir, drive or walk south along the road, stopping at each gate or gap in the hedge to scan the water. It is possible to view almost the whole water area from the roads; further access is forbidden except to the small hide (which has access for the disabled) near a layby towards the southern end. If the water levels are low, this

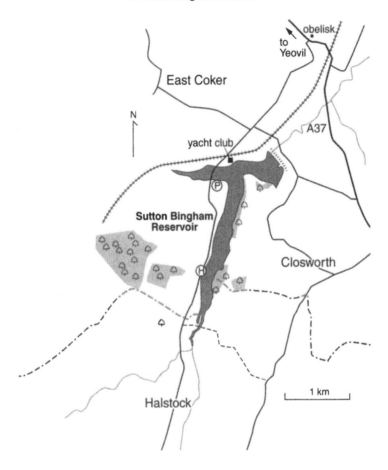

southern part has the best muddy areas, and the edges of the normally submerged willows at the far end are worth examining for Water Rails at the appropriate season. The road gains in height at the far end and at the top of the rise a footpath to the left just beyond a cottage leads to a bridge over the river where the willows and alders can be viewed more closely. Do not forget to scan the nearby hillsides, particularly those to the west and southeast, for soaring raptors.

Returning to the northern end and passing under the railway bridge, take the first turning on the right and under the railway again to the out-flow below the dam where Grey Wagtails are likely, and wintering Siskins and Redpolls possible in the nearby alders. At the road junction a little further on, a private road to the fishing lodge by the dam allows the northeastern part of the reservoir to be scanned, though further access is for anglers only.

Calendar
All year. Great Crested Grebe, Cormorant, Grey Heron, Canada Goose, Sparrowhawk, Buzzard, Coot, Grey Wagtail, Raven, Reed Bunting.

December–February: Wigeon, Teal, Pochard, Tufted Duck, sometimes Shoveler, Goldeneye, Goosander and Ruddy Duck; chance of rarity, e.g. Ring-necked Duck, Green-winged Teal. Peregrine sometimes seen. Snipe, Jack Snipe. Maybe Mediterranean or Ring-billed Gulls among commoner species.

March–May: Winter wildfowl depart during March. Possible Garganey. Buzzards soaring; chance of Osprey April–May on passage. Common Sandpiper mid-April–mid-May. Rarer gull possible through March. Occasional Common, Arctic or Black Tern late April–May. Sand Martin from mid-March, other hirundines April.

June–July: Little and Great Crested Grebes sometimes breed as do small numbers of Mallard and Tufted Ducks. Canada Geese peak July. Osprey have summered. Hobby through to September. A few Sedge and Reed Warblers breed, along with other commoner warblers, perhaps Cetti's Warbler also.

August–November: Chance of Black-necked Grebe or Garganey on passage. Winter wildfowl start arriving from September, most from November, when rarities most likely; some may stay into winter. Chance of Osprey August–September. Light wader passage July–September: Ringed and Little Ringed Plover, Green and Common Sandpipers, Greenshank, maybe Wood Sandpiper; Little Stint and Curlew Sandpiper and rarities more likely in September. Snipe numbers build up. Black, Common and Arctic Terns plus Little Gull (August–October). Sightings of Kingfisher most frequent. Trickle of commoner passerine migrants in August.

12 ASHFORD RESERVOIR   OS Explorer 140

Habitat and Species

A small reservoir a few miles west of Bridgwater, notable as one of the few regular breeding sites for Sand Martin in Somerset. Otherwise it holds a few Pochard and Tufted Ducks in winter, the latter having bred. It attracts the occasional Green Sandpiper on passage, and Little Grebes also sometimes breed.

Access

The reservoir lies just off the A39 west of Cannington and can be viewed from the footpath along its southern side. A minor road to Charlynch passes below the dam to where the footpath emerges next to the overflow culvert. The Sand Martins nest in holes in the wall at this end of the reservoir.

13 DURLEIGH RESERVOIR

Habitat

Durleigh is a small 78 acre (31.6 ha) reservoir just southwest of Bridgwater, mostly surrounded by farmland but lying less than 6 miles (9.6 km) from Bridgwater Bay and the River Parrett and thus visible to birds using the river as a guide-line. Apart from the dam at the eastern end, the banks are entirely natural. At the western end, where the Durleigh Brook enters, there is a small reedbed surrounded by a damp thicket of willows and other trees. The banks along the rest of the shore are relatively bare of vegetation, but only a small drop in the water level produces a strip of bare mud around almost the whole margin. Formerly a trout lake, the reservoir is now used for coarse fishing throughout the year, and there is an active sailing club.

Species

As at several sites, numbers of wintering wildfowl are currently much reduced here. It may be that as the habitat on the nearby Levels has improved, the reservoirs no longer provide the same attraction, and a series of mild winters has also meant that its former status as an ice-free refuge rarely applies these days. Certainly in early 1997, when there was a period of cold weather, over 150 Bewick's Swans roosted here, briefly re-establishing what was formerly a regular habit. At the same time over 200 Wigeon and Teal arrived for a time, whereas recently few individuals of either species stay for very long. Other dabbling ducks, even the former speciality, Pintail, are scarce, and diving ducks are restricted to small numbers of Tufted Duck and Pochard. Cormorants continue to increase, and often roost here overnight, most departing to feed on the levels during the day. Possibly because the reservoir is not watched so regularly these days, rarities are mostly just that, but more unusual wildfowl in the past have included include Ferruginous Duck and Green-winged Teal as vagrants, and there are winter records of Scaup, Long-tailed Duck and Red-breasted Merganser. Cold weather may bring a rare grebe or diver, but these rarely stay long.

Through most of the year, Canada Geese are the most conspicuous species, a pair or two usually raising a few young, and post-breeding flocks sometimes rise to over 400 birds in autumn. Several pairs of Great Crested Grebes usually try to breed, albeit often foiled by falling water levels, and up to 40 can occur later in the year, there always being a few about. High water levels in the spring means that passage at this time is normally unremarkable. Common and Black Terns in ones and twos may stop off briefly, joining the hirundines catching insects low over the water surface.

The shallowness of the water means that a muddy margin quickly appears when the water level drops in autumn, attracting small numbers of passage waders most years. Greenshank, Common and Green Sandpipers, Spotted Redshank, Ruff and Little Ringed Plover are the most likely, but Curlew Sandpiper and Little Stint sometimes turn up later on. Strong westerlies may bring a storm-driven Grey Phalarope from the nearby coast, or the chance of an American vagrant, and as at any migration spot, anything could turn up at this time of year. Little Egrets, numerous on the nearby coast, are also sometimes seen here in autumn, and it is worth remembering that rarities seen at Steart have often moved here for short periods, so the reservoir is often worth checking if one 'goes missing' from the coast (and vice versa, of course).

Timing
Low water levels are essential for waders. Disturbance from anglers, active throughout the year, can be a problem, so weekday visits are slightly more productive, although the birds can usually find an undisturbed corner unless fishing activity is particularly intense. The sailing club is also active the whole year round. Calm, rather overcast conditions seem to produce most terns. Cold weather may attract higher numbers of wildfowl, which often linger here even when most of the water is frozen.

Access
From the A38/A39 junction in Bridgwater turn left at the traffic lights c. ½ mile (0.8 km) west, signposted to Durleigh and Spaxton (see map with Bridgwater Brickpits entry). Turn left again c. 1½ miles (2.4 km) (the road straight ahead leads to Hawkridge Reservoir; see the Quantock Hills entry) to the dam, where there is a small car park opposite the church. The WW ranger has his office at the top of the slope, next to the sailing club. Although there is no formal public access, birdwatchers are usually allowed to walk along the southern side of the reservoir as far as the hide (currently rather dilapidated) at the western end. Being a conservation area, the upper end of the reservoir is the least disturbed by fishermen and birds often seek shelter along the marshy fringe. If the water level has dropped, waders can be seen anywhere along the far shore and around the top end, although various emergent creeks and islands can conceal smaller species for some time. If the entrance gates are locked, continue past the dam and then bear right on the road that overlooks the southern side of the reservoir. Just before the point where the road drops down to cross one of the tributary streams there is a gateway on the right from where the western end of the reservoir can be scanned, though a telescope is helpful. With care, most of the water surface can be viewed from here, or from various points back along the roadside.

Calendar
All year: Little Grebe, Great Crested Grebe, Cormorant, Grey Heron, Canada Goose, Coot, Grey Wagtail, Reed Bunting.

December–February: Possibility of diver or rare grebe. Cormorant; Teal, Mallard, Pochard, Tufted Duck in small numbers; sometimes Bewick's Swan, Wigeon, Gadwall, Pintail in cold weather. Water Rail.

March–May: Shelduck. Most wildfowl move out in March. Sometimes Little Gull, Black Tern (April–May). Sand Martin from mid-March, other hirundines mid-April.

June–July: Little and Great Crested Grebe may breed. Mute Swans peak July–August. Reed Warbler. Return wader passage starts late July. Little Egret most likely in late summer and early autumn.

August–November. Canada Geese peak August. Wader passage August–September: Greenshank, Green Sandpiper, Spotted Redshank, Ruff; Ringed and Little Ringed Plover, Black-tailed Godwit peak August, Curlew Sandpiper, Little Stint peak September. Few waders after mid-October. Common, Arctic and Black Terns (August–October). Storm-driven vagrants possible September–October.

14 STEART & BRIDGWATER BAY   OS Explorer 140

Habitat

The Bridgwater Bay NNR runs from Lilstock in the west to Stert Island in the east, including that part of the River Parrett immediately upstream, with Steart itself attracting the most birdwatchers. The coastline here is low-lying with vast mudflats exposed at low tide and can be very bleak when a northerly wind is blowing in across the bay. A shingle ridge runs along most of the shore from Stolford to Stert Point, and Stert Island in the mouth of the Parrett is mostly bare shingle and sand. To the west the landscape is dominated by the Hinkley Point nuclear power stations, fronted by extensive flat rocks at low tide, amongst which emerges the channel of a warm-water outflow. Most of the north-facing coast is backed by damp grazing land with hawthorn hedges and several fresh or brackish small pools. There are some extensive areas of saltmarsh along the shore and the west bank of the Parrett immediately upstream, and a *phragmites*-dominated reedbed has developed west of Stert Point. Several scrapes and pools have been excavated on the saltings in front of the hides that overlook the river mouth. Habitation in the immediate area is restricted to the collection of farms at Steart and Stolford.

On the east shore, the River Brue emerges opposite Stert Island and forms a natural barrier to the southward spread of Burnham-on-Sea. Between here and the point where the Huntspill River (a broad canalised drainage channel closed by a sluice) emerges, the steep muddy banks of the Parrett have been strengthened by concrete but in general the shore on either side of the Parrett and the Brue consists of steep mud and a fringe of saltmarsh, backed by grass-covered banks that protect the meadows immediately inland. Most of the area of 6200 acres (2510 ha) is a NNR under the management of EN. In addition to the bird population there is an interesting maritime flora, including the flowers of yellow horned poppy along the shingle beach.

Species

The waders which throng the area in winter make Bridgwater Bay by far the most important site for both numbers and variety of species on the eastern shore of the Severn Estuary. The Dunlin population is of international significance, with well over 10,000 regularly present in the bay in midwinter, and the sight of these birds turning and twisting in flight, particularly prior to roosting, can be very spectacular. Winter counts of both Knot and Curlew can also be impressive, both exceeding the 1000 mark on many occasions. Several hundred Grey Plover and Redshank are usually present on the open shore, with smaller numbers of Oystercatchers and Turnstones, the latter mostly on the rockier coast west of Stolford. Two winter specialities of recent years are Spotted Redshank and Avocet, both of which are now regular at the mouth of the Parrett in small numbers, up to 20 or so on occasion. They can, however, be very difficult to locate, and are most easily seen at high tide on or around Stert Island. They seem to survive the cold spells reasonably well, such conditions often bringing hundreds of Golden Plover and thousands of Lapwings to the coast, although both species are annual here in winter whatever the weather. They tend to prefer the fields inland for feeding, but also occur on the open shore.

This wealth of potential prey inevitably attracts raptors, including Peregrine and Merlin chasing the wader flocks at high tide, and Hen Harrier and Short-eared Owl quartering the saltmarsh and reeds. All four species are regular, with two or three individuals of each often present. Kestrels are resident, while Sparrowhawks often hunt along the upper shoreline and nearby fields.

Wildfowl numbers have steadily reduced in recent years, though several hundred Wigeon, Teal and Mallard are usually present, their numbers swelled if there is a cold snap. The Stolford to Hinkley Point shoreline regularly attracts up to 50 Pintail, which is usually a freshwater bird elsewhere in region. Nowadays it is generally only cold weather elsewhere that will bring any grey geese to the fields, but single-figure groups of dark-bellied Brent Geese have become almost annual visitors to the shore, in line with their build-up nationally. Other wildfowl occur irregularly in ones and twos, again most frequently after cold weather. Goldeneye and Tufted Duck are the most likely to be seen, but Great Crested Grebe, Red-breasted Merganser, Scaup and Common Scoter sometimes appear.

As late winter merges into early spring, the wader population changes daily as wintering birds are replaced with passage birds, many on their way to Iceland and Greenland. Over 200 Ringed Plovers may be present for a brief period in spring, whereas it may be hard to find even a dozen in winter. Grey Plover, Redshank and Turnstone numbers increase for a

Pintail

time and Bar-tailed Godwits pass through, normally only in double-figure numbers, although easterly winds have exceptionally produced thousands. Sanderling are most likely at this time, although they prefer the sandier flats of Berrow to the Parrett mud. Sadly, the Whimbrel roost on Stert Island is currently a shadow of its former self, as the birds that mostly feed on the Somerset Levels during the day seem to roost inland as well, now that the number of refuge areas there has increased.

The damp fields close to the estuary prove attractive to migrant wagtails, both White and Yellow Wagtails being regular in small numbers. Swallows, House Martins and Sand Martins coast north steadily as they follow the line of the Parrett and then the Severn. Chats such as Whinchat and Wheatear stop for a day or so, and Black Redstarts sometimes occur. As at any time of year, westerly winds may bring seabirds to the shelter of the Parrett for a time, Common, Arctic and Sandwich Terns (rarely more than ten of each) attracting the attention of a few Arctic Skuas. Kittiwakes are also seen under such conditions in the spring, but other seabirds are rare at this time of year. Marsh Harriers are probably annual and vagrants or rare migrants from the south may appear; for instance Spoonbills have occurred several times and could possibly become more regular as their European population increases.

During the summer, two or three pairs of Ringed Plovers and Oystercatchers usually attempt to breed on the shore or on the slightly more secure Stert Island. Herring and Lesser Black-backed Gulls no longer breed on the island although both nest on the Hinkley Point power station roof. Rock Pipits are resident in the Hinkley Point area, and one or two pairs of Yellow Wagtails breed in the meadows either side of the Parrett. The copses a little way inland contain ten to twenty pairs of Nightingales, mostly easily located on the Hinkley Point nature trail, and the fields hold a small population of Grey Partridges, not an easy species to find in the southwest. In late summer up to 2500 flightless Shelduck keep to the low water area at this, their major British moulting site. Several hundred are present along the shore at most times of the year, with lowest numbers in midwinter. These days it is a rare visit to Steart that does not produce a Little Egret, with over 50 sometimes to be seen during their late-summer influx. Significant numbers remain all year, feeding on the upper shore or around the various pools on the saltmarshes.

The return passage of waders starts early. Ringed Plover and Redshanks may reach 400 and Curlew over 1000 at this time. Icelandic Black-tailed Godwits are much reduced these days, with counts rarely exceeding 100, and the wintering flock that used to occur seems to have moved away. Later in the autumn small numbers of Greenshanks, Common Sandpipers, Little Stints and Curlew Sandpipers are regular, and vagrants have included several American species. A Spotted Sandpiper which overwintered on the River Brue attracted much interest, as did a Semipalmated Sandpiper at Burnham in September 2000. Small parties of Yellow Wagtails are not uncommon in early autumn, their chirruping calls being a characteristic August sound. Reed and Sedge Warblers occur in good numbers in the reedbeds, and under suitable conditions, Aquatic Warblers have proved themselves regular visitors, although normally only seen when picked out of a mist-net. Under any conditions migrant terns, usually Common or Arctic, appear offshore, but strong westerly gales can bring a wide range of seabirds, which take shelter in the mouth of the Parrett after having been blown against the lee shore at Burnham. Manx Shearwaters,

Storm and Leach's Petrels, Great, Arctic and occasional Pomarine Skuas have all been seen fighting their way out to sea again. A Wilson's Petrel in October 1999 was the reward for many hours spent staring at the sea for the lucky observers. Careful watching has also produced the occasional Mediterranean, Sabine's and Glaucous Gull although Steart is not noted as a gull-watching site, the large winter gull roost, mostly Common and Black-headed Gulls, on Stert Island being difficult to view. However, the warm-water outfall at Hinkley Point has attracted both Forster's Tern and Bonaparte's Gull in winter, so is always worth checking.

Finch flocks are generally small and rarely outlast the autumn. Lapland and Snow Buntings are regular in ones and twos and Black Redstarts are another late autumn species that occurs annually. Richard's Pipits have become virtually annual in Somerset, and this is as good a spot for them as any.

Timing

High-tide visits are more essential here than at most other estuarine sites, as at low tide the mudflats are mostly 2 miles (3.2 km) wide, and the wader flocks rapidly follow the receding waters over them. The hour before high water and the two hours afterwards are generally considered the most productive, as waders are concentrated into their roosts in the *spartina* and grassland at the river mouths. Before high water birds are visible as they wheel and turn before gathering to rest in tight groups, and as the waters fall again they spread out over the nearest stretches of exposed mud to feed. With flocks most concentrated at this time, birds of prey are also more likely to be seen as they try to pick off the unwary straggler. Rising waters are the most likely to bring an unusual duck, grebe or diver into the Parrett mouth, and seabirds also will approach nearer to the coast over water rather than mud. If the tide is low, Stolford and the Hinkley Point area may be more productive as the shore slopes more steeply here. Strong winds from the west or northwest may bring seabirds well up the Channel, either to seek shelter in the Parrett Estuary itself during the gale, or beating their way along the north-facing shore as the winds abate. Under such conditions, watching for passerines is almost impossible. Calm, overcast conditions in spring and autumn may cause falls of migrants. Such conditions during light southeasterlies in late August are the most likely to produce Aquatic Warblers in the reedbeds. Short-eared Owls tend to be most active in the afternoons and evening, and an evening high tide may prompt a Peregrine or Merlin to make another kill before nightfall. Water-skiers in the Parrett Estuary can cause disturbance, as can people landing on Stert Island, both more likely at weekends.

Access

There is good birdwatching to be had from both east and west shores of the Parrett, although the Steart side is usually more productive.

West Side: For Steart, turn off the A39 into the village of Cannington, and then north along the minor road towards Hinkley Point and Combwich (see Bridgwater Brickpits entry for access to flooded pit at Combwich). About ½ mile (0.8 km) past the road to Combwich, turn right towards Otterhampton and Steart, then right again after c.1 mile (1.6 km) along a no-through-road to Steart itself. The road reaches the coast at Wall Common, where there is an expanse of rough grassland behind the shingle beach. If you have missed high tide, it may be best to park here and walk west along the seawall scanning the mud for waders. Small numbers roost on the shingle in this area, and others move west from the point as the tide falls. Reasonable views can be had for up to 2½ hours after high water as the flats are narrower here. In addition, the shingle along this stretch shelters several areas of brackish water and wet grassland which is more attractive to Little Stints, Ruff and 'freshwater' waders than the open shore. Buntings, finches, pipits and larks also favour this type of habitat in autumn and winter. Similar terrain continues intermittently all the way to Catsford Common, where remains of old drainage systems provide patches of open fresh water. Check the bushes along the seawall and the fields just inland for migrants. East of Wall Common the saltmarsh stretches well down the shore in a broad strip to Stert Point, and is backed for most of its length by reeds, attractive to passerines, hunting Short-eared Owls and Hen Harriers.

If you have arrived just before high tide, continue past Wall Common for 1 mile (1.6 km) to the EN visitors' car park on the left-hand side of the road. A waymarked track leads directly down to the shingle beach and then right towards the point. Alternatively you can walk on along the road to where a gate bars further progress by car. At the far end of the shingle bank there is an open area and a small hide looking out north over Stert Flats. Waders gather here on moderate tides. The rebuilt tower hide gives panoramic views over the mouth of the river and, with a telescope, provides an excellent vantage point for watching the waders gathering at high tide or picking out a Peregrine on the grassland. For closer views, there are three more hides overlooking the point itself and the adjacent pools; they are reached via a stile and path straight on past the tower hide. The largest numbers of waders congregate in the saltmarsh just up-river on the west bank of the Parrett and are sometimes forced onto the grass immediately in front of these two hides. On the highest tides they move to Stert Island, although this is generally more favoured by gulls, terns, Cormorants and Oystercatchers. Little Egrets, as well as waders, often come to the pools to feed.

For the western end of the shore, follow signs towards Hinkley Point from Combwich, and then roads signposted to Stolford where there is limited parking behind the shingle. Either walk east for Catsford Common, or follow the seawall west towards the nuclear power stations. There are several cattle-grazed fields just inland, and the shore itself is a mixture of mud and rocks. The footpath leads all the way along the concrete seawall on the outer edge of the perimeter fence of the power stations and on towards Watchet. Turnstones, Oystercatchers and Rock Pipits find the flat rocks and pools here attractive, and the warm water outfall at the eastern end (not the gantry a little to the west) is a focal point for gulls and terns (including the odd Little Gull in winter). Purple Sandpipers are rare on the Severn, but one or two winter on the stretch west from here, Helwell Bay at Watchet being the most regular site in recent years. The power stations can also be reached by continuing to the end of the road from Combwich. There is a car park and visitor centre here, usually open from 10 am to 4 pm every day, apart from winter Saturdays (1 October to 31 March) when it is closed. However, with the heightened security of recent years, access may be restricted at short notice. A waymarked nature trail with disabled access traverses woodland and scrubland habitat where several pairs of Nightingales are the main attraction, although there is a varied selection of other birds (e.g. Lesser Whitethroat), plus an interesting flora, to be seen.

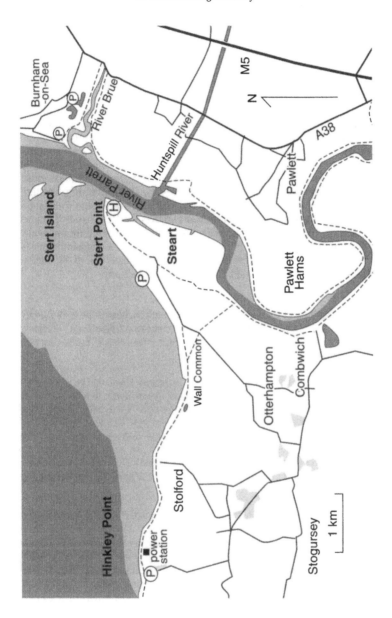

East Side: There is a small high-tide roost at the mouth of the Brue, and this can be observed from the very southern end of Burnham-on-Sea promenade, where there is ample parking. At low water a few gulls may gather on the beach just to the north where there is a fresh-water outflow but on the whole most waders move off to feed on the west side of the river. It is possible to walk along the north bank of the Brue from here, and into Apex leisure park on the left. Although well-used by the public, there are wildflower meadows, some newly planted woodland and a large reed-fringed pool here which holds Cetti's Warblers throughout the year, as well as Great Crested Grebes, Coots and the occasional Scaup, tern or other rarer visitor. A Little Bittern in April 1997 was a big attraction, for instance, so it's always worth a look. The other side of the river is reached via Highbridge: just north of where the A38 crosses the Brue, Clyce Road leads west to a sluice barrier where the tidal water ends. Cars can be parked in the road here, though with due consideration for the locals. A footpath crosses the sluice and on along the grassy seawall on the southern side to the river mouth. The grassland and pools at the end are worth checking for small birds and waders and are favoured by hunting Short-eared Owls. From here to the Huntspill River the area is rather sterile and overgrazed, but provides a good vantage point for scanning the river and (through a telescope) the Steart shore. Although most waders move over to the far side as the tide falls, wintering Spotted Redshank seem to prefer the Brue/Huntspill side for feeding (although roosting at Steart). It is possible to walk up-river on the eastern bank of the Parrett: few waders seem to use this stretch because of the relatively steep banks, but Wigeon, Curlew, Golden Plover and the occasional hunting harrier may be seen in the extensive sheep-grazed fields of Pawlett Hams, and a few Yellow Wagtails sometimes breed here.

Calendar

All year: Little Egret, Cormorant. Grey Heron (breeds at West Huntspill church and Lower Hill Farm, Otterhampton). Shelduck, Kestrel, Oystercatcher, Red-legged and Grey Partridges; Rock Pipit (breeds Hinkley; September–February elsewhere).

December–February: Occasional Great Northern Diver or Great Crested Grebe on the river. Brent Geese. Wigeon, Teal, Pintail, a few Shoveler. Sometimes diving duck, e.g. Scaup, Goldeneye, Common Scoter. Hen Harrier, Sparrowhawk, Merlin, Peregrine; Avocet, Golden Plover, Grey Plover, Knot; Snipe, Jack Snipe; Black-tailed and Bar-tailed Godwits (scarce), Curlew, Redshank, Turnstone, a few Spotted Redshank; one or two Purple Sandpipers (Hinkley Point and west). Occasional Glaucous, Little or other rare gull. Kittiwake and auks after gales. Short-eared Owl. Water Pipit (scarce). Winter thrushes.

March–May: Wintering wildfowl and raptors mostly leave during March, Short-eared Owl to early April. Chance of Marsh Harrier late April–May. Wader passage includes Ringed Plover, Grey Plover, Sanderling, Turnstone (all peak May), Whimbrel late April–early May, a few Greenshanks mid-April–May. Common and Arctic Terns, sometimes Arctic Skua, late April–May. Wheatear from mid-March; Whinchat, Yellow and White Wagtails in April. Swallows moving late April–May. Nightingale arrives late April.

June–July: Peak numbers of moulting Shelduck. Occasional Peregrine. Oystercatcher and Ringed Plover usually breed. Breeding passerines include Yellow Wagtail, Nightingale, Lesser Whitethroat, Reed and Sedge Warblers. Wader passage starts July, including Whimbrel, Dunlin.

August–November: Seabirds in gales (September–October) may include Fulmar, Manx Shearwater, Storm and Leach's Petrels, Gannet, skuas; also Grey Phalarope. Wildfowl mostly arrive from November; occasional Red-breasted Merganser October–November. Peregrine from August, Merlin,

Hen Harrier, Short-eared Owl from late October. Wintering waders build up steadily throughout, others pass through: Black-tailed Godwit, Whimbrel peak August, Ringed Plover, Redshank peak August–September, Bar-tailed Godwit, Little Stint, Curlew Sandpiper peak September, Turnstone in October. Vagrant waders sometimes in August, but most September–October, especially Americans. Kingfisher (from September), Yellow Wagtail (August), Aquatic Warbler (late August); chance of Black Redstart, Snow and Lapland Buntings October–November, sometimes rarity such as Richard's Pipit at same time.

15 BRIDGWATER BRICKPITS   OS Explorer 140

Habitat
Either side of the River Parrett, both upstream and downstream of Bridgwater, are a series of worked out pits in various states of dereliction but providing a useful addition to the wetland habitat of the area. Mostly the pits are deep and steep-sided, but reedmace and *phragmites* grow extensively in some while others are surrounded by dense patches of hawthorn, brambles and willows. All are under threat of major change, either from increased use by angling and boating interests, or from infilling for tipping and housing development. The M5 motorway strides through the largest area, helping to further fragment the habitat.

Species
This was the site from which Cetti's Warbler started its colonisation of Somerset, and although they are now much more widespread, this remains an important site for this species. At least a dozen singing males can usually be heard throughout the year, although this resident species is always in danger of decimation by cold winters. The Kingfisher,

Cetti's Warbler

another bird affected by cold weather, is also resident. Reed, Sedge and occasionally Grasshopper Warblers all occur in summer in and around the pits, the first being the most numerous, and attracting parasitic Cuckoos. Among more occasional summer visitors, Nightingales are sometimes noted at Chilton Trinity, attracted to the remaining areas of dense bushes. Waterfowl are rarely numerous, a few dozen Tufted Duck or Pochard on any one pit being the most frequent, but the proximity to the River Parrett and Bridgwater Bay means that a wide range of irregular autumn/winter visitors can be expected, diving species such as Goldeneye, Goosander and Slavonian Grebes being the most likely. Two or three pairs of Great Crested and Little Grebes, Mute Swans and Canada Geese breed, though with variable success because of human disturbance. Water Rails are regular here in winter, and may have bred, and wintering Bittern and Bearded Tits have both been recorded on several occasions. Gulls on their way to coastal roosts drop in for an evening bathe and preen, but like most passing birds, have not been studied carefully so it may be that rarities are being overlooked. Savi's Warbler, Spotted Crake and Garganey have all been recorded as passage birds in the past.

Timing

Early morning and dusk are the best times for observing reedbed birds: the warblers and any Nightingales are most vocal then, and Bittern and Water Rails are also active as they move to new nocturnal feeding areas. In addition, gulls stop over from mid to late afternoon in winter to bathe. Strong winds make small birds virtually impossible to locate in this kind of habitat, and if the pits freeze over most species move out. On the other hand strong winds and cold weather elsewhere may force seabirds, including wildfowl, onto these more sheltered waters. Casual disturbance can be chronic, so weekday visits are often more productive. Noise from the M5 can be very intrusive at all times at the southern pits.

Access

The most productive pits are at Huntworth, Dunwear, Chilton Trinity and Combwich; others are either filled in, strictly private or of very restricted access. For the first group, take the minor road from M5 junction 24 through Huntworth to the canalside car park by the Boat and Anchor Inn (the road leads on round to join the A38 between junction 24 and Bridgwater itself). A track over the railway level crossing (taking due care and attention) leads to the reserve of Screech Owl pit on the far side on the right, scannable from the raised crossing approach. A little further on a bridge leads over a ditch to paths providing access through the reeds to the water's edge. The area is used by anglers and is often wet and muddy, so care needs to be taken here. A track to the left leads on to more ponds and reeds on the far side of the motorway. This area is owned by Summerhayes Fisheries but, although angling is the primary concern, it is managed sympathetically for wildlife and access is often allowed to birdwatchers as long as they report to the security hut first.

For Dunwear, take the A372 from the centre of Bridgwater – note that there are no road bridges, apart from the motorway, over the Parrett between Bridgwater and Burrowbridge 5 miles (8 km) southeast – and turn right immediately before the motorway into Dunwear Lane. In ½ mile (0.8 km) there is a small car park on the right with access to the edges of two pits with quite extensive open water, and a strip of bushes and emergent vegetation all around. Access is relatively straightforward

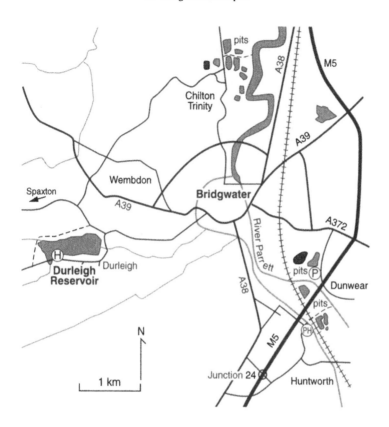

here, but the proximity of the town means that these pits are the most popular with the public. For Chilton Trinity, turn west off the A38 at its northern junction with the A39, passing the supermarket, docks and sports centre, and then follow road signs north to the village. A no-through-road to Hallick's Farm passes the main pits on the right, and although they are private, they are viewable from the road. Hopfield Fish Farm/Trinity Waters occupies part of the area, and their access track marks the start of a public footpath to the river bank in one place.

There is an outlying pit at Combwich, less reliable for Cetti's Warbler, but being close to the mouth of the River Parrett, more likely to attract wildfowl. Turn into the centre of the village from the Hinkley Point road (see Steart entry), and where the road turns sharp left, a private road (access on foot only) to the right ends just beyond a row of modern houses. Footpaths from here lead to the right to the flooded pit, or to the left over a stile to the River Parrett. It is possible walk all the way round the pit, although the path can be very muddy in places.

Calendar

All year: Little Grebe, Great Crested Grebe, Mute Swan, Canada Goose, Mallard, Kestrel, Kingfisher, Cetti's Warbler, Bullfinch, Reed Bunting.

December–February: Occasional rare grebe or diving duck, e.g. Slavonian Grebe, Goldeneye. Sometimes Cormorant. Grey Heron, maybe Bittern.

Teal, Pochard, Tufted Duck, Water Rail, Snipe, Jack Snipe, Herring and Black-headed Gulls. Chance of Bearded Tit. Chiffchaffs sometimes over-winter.

March–May: Little and Great Crested Grebes usually breed. Maybe Marsh Harrier (late April–May). Water Rail may breed. Summer migrants arriving: hirundines on passage April–May, Cuckoo and Nightingale from mid-April, Grasshopper, Sedge and Reed Warblers from late April, Whitethroat and Lesser Whitethroat early May.

June–July: Breeding species gradually fall silent, though Cetti's Warblers sing all year.

August–November: Grey Heron. Occasional Common and Green Sandpipers August–September. Sometimes hirundine (August–September) and Starling roosts in reeds.

16 THE SOMERSET LEVELS

OS Explorer 128, 129, 140 and 141

Habitat

The Somerset Levels comprise a vast area of low-lying former marshland bounded by Bridgwater Bay in the west, and a horseshoe of higher ground running from the limestone of the Mendips in the north round via the Dorset Downs, the Blackdown Hills and the Brendons to the Quantocks in the southwest. Much of this land lies below the 10 metre contour, and has to be continuously drained to stop it from flooding, while the sea defences have gradually been built up to stop inundation with salt water.

At present, the majority of the land is given over to grazing, and there are always fears that over-zealous efforts on the part of the drainage authorities may lead to ploughing as has happened in the East Anglian Fens. However, increasing numbers of landowners and farmers are taking advantage of grants available for environmentally beneficial farming practices, raising water levels in the summer and leaving winter flood-water on the fields for longer periods. In addition, several of the more important parts are under the control of nature conservation organisations and consequently the future for wildlife looks a lot more rosy than it did a few years ago. In addition to the fringe of hills, there are several low ridges that divide the region into fairly distinct parts, in particular the Polden Hills from Bridgwater to Street which separate those areas to the north drained by the Rivers Brue and Axe from those to the south drained by the Parrett and the King's Sedgemoor Drain. These strips of higher ground hold scattered farms and villages, with orchards, copses and a few larger areas of woodland providing a contrast to the relatively treeless levels themselves, where hedgerows have to provide the majority of cover. The main exception to this is the heaths around Shapwick, just north of the Poldens, where blocks of birch and alder woodland grow on a rich bed of peat. Peat extraction is a major industry in this region, and a large part of the former woodland has been destroyed; however, once peat extraction has finished, the ground tends to flood, allowing recolonisation by reedmace, *phragmites* and other wetland vegetation. Several larger pools of open water have been formed, and more are likely in the future. Large parts of this area ('the Avalon Marshes') is now managed by nature conservation bodies, with the RSPB creating a major reedbed reserve at Ham Wall. The network of drainage ditches and rhynes attract an interesting invertebrate fauna, with a wide range of dragonflies to be found. Roe deer occur in the woodland, brown hares and the introduced mink are widespread and there are otters in small numbers. Both the woodland and especially the meadowland flora, is a rich and often spectacular one in many places.

Species

As a breeding site the Levels are particularly important for waders, holding the southwest's largest lowland concentration of Lapwing, Snipe, Redshank and Curlew. A few pairs of the rare Black-tailed Godwit have attempted to breed in one area, but despite protection measures by the RSPB they are rarely successful in raising any young. Buzzards are numerous, Barn Owls thinly but widely scattered and Hobbies may be seen anywhere all summer. Grey Herons are a common sight, and there are several large heronries. The peat heaths hold a specialised breeding population that includes Grasshopper Warbler and Nightingale, while Yellow Wagtails and a few Whinchats can be found more widely. Redstarts used to nest in the pollarded willows that lined the ditches but are now virtual extinct here. Winter brings large numbers of wildfowl, particularly if there is extensive flooding. Bewick's Swans are regular, with Pintail, Wigeon, Teal and other surface-feeding ducks occurring in nationally significant numbers. Flooded fields also attract waders, particularly Dunlin, Ruff and Snipe while Golden Plover and Lapwing flocks occur more widely. Among predators, Peregrines have become regular recently, with Merlin, Hen Harrier and Short-eared Owl in small numbers. Among passage species, the most notable is Whimbrel, large numbers of Icelandic birds feeding in the rich grassland on their way north in spring.

There are many rewarding sites on the Levels, the major ones being listed below.

16a WEST SEDGEMOOR & CURRY MOOR
OS Explorer 128

Habitat

West Sedgemoor contains the most extensive area of 'unimproved' grazing left on the Levels, with rough sedgy fields often remaining wet well into the spring. The valley floor has few trees or bushes, especially in its central part, although there are two or three small areas of withy beds. One main rhyne runs down the centre, fed by subsidiary cross ditches. The southern side is enclosed by a steep escarpment mostly clothed in deciduous woodland, while to the north there is a lower open ridge where several villages are surrounded by arable and grazing farmland. To the north again lie Curry and Hay Moors, where rich grass meadows lie either side of the sluggish River Tone. The RSPB owns or leases a substantial part of West Sedgemoor, and consequently habitat management is more sympathetic to wildlife than in the past, with much higher water levels in both summer and winter.

Species

With the water levels normally being held at a higher level than in the recent past, the numbers of wildfowl here in the winter can be spectacular. In some years West Sedgemoor has been the most important single wintering site in the UK for Teal and the fourth for Wigeon, with well over 10,000 of each species being present. Shoveler and Pintail numbers can also be high, with over 1000 of each counted in some recent winters. Up to 100 or so Bewick's Swans regularly spend the winter on the Levels, although they tend to move around from one site to another in different years. West Sedgemoor and nearby Curry Moor continue to attract some of these birds most years. Mallard and up to 100 Mute Swans are the other two most numerous wildfowl here, although if flooding is deep as sometimes occurs on Curry Moor, a few hundred Tufted Ducks and Pochard will stay until the waters recede. At other times, small numbers of these two species plus a few Goldeneye can be found on the rivers and wider ditches. The raised water table of recent years has also produced higher average numbers of waders in winter, and the area has become of international significance for Lapwing; for instance nearly 45,000 were counted in January 1999, 10% of the UK winter population. Golden Plover, formerly mostly a passage bird, now regularly winter in flocks of as many as 3000 birds, and there can be over 1000 Snipe hidden in the marshes in some years. A few hundred Dunlin and small numbers of Ruff add to the variety. All in all it is very gratifying to see such positive results after all the conservation effort put in over the years.

The abundance of prey attracts Peregrines on an annual basis, birds often sitting for long periods on the ground in the middle of the open fields. One or two Hen Harriers and up to seven Short-eared Owls wander widely, while Merlins can be seen dashing after small birds or

Wigeon

perched quietly on posts. Great Grey Shrikes have been seen several times, but are probably only transient birds.

Early spring sees the Buzzards soaring over the wooded ridges nearby, and at any time of year this is a noticeable species anywhere on these moors. Grey Herons nest early, and Swell Wood contains the largest heronry in the region, around 120 pairs jostling among the bare tree-tops. As the winter birds move away, breeding waders move in, with noisy Lapwings hurling themselves through the air in ecstatic display flights while the strange bleating sound of drumming Snipe and the shrill calls of Redshank add to the general noise level. Curlew also breed here, and with a few Black-tailed Godwit at least summering, West Sedgemoor is the most important lowland breeding site for waders in the West Country. Yellow Wagtails, Whinchats, Sedge Warblers, Reed Buntings and Skylarks add life to the fields, while woodland species include a few pairs of Nightingales.

In late summer, the vegetation grows extremely lush and most birds fall quiet although Quail can sometimes be heard calling, this being a reasonably reliable site for this elusive species. Post-breeding flocks of Lapwings gather on the mown hayfields but the other breeding waders move away. Hobbies range widely over the moors throughout the summer, with feeding groups of up to a dozen appearing in the spring and again in the late summer. Autumn is a relatively quiet time, until increasing thrush numbers mark the start of another winter.

Timing

For winter wildfowl and waders, the more water on the fields the better, though if flooding is too deep birds often move away temporarily. Conversely if the fields are dry then few if any of these species will be present. During the summer a dry spring will reduce the habitat available for breeding waders, and their numbers may also be low if the previous winter has been severe. Cold weather further north will usually bring influxes of ducks, Golden Plover, Lapwings and thrushes, although they may move away again if standing water freezes. Strong winds make watching difficult, but slightly breezy days through the spring are best for bringing out the soaring Buzzards. The heronry is active through the spring and is best viewed before there are too many leaves on the trees.

Access

From Langport, take the A378 west through Curry Rivel, and c.2 miles (3.2 km) west of there, take a minor road to the right, marked with an RSPB sign. There is a small gravelled car park almost immediately on the left, in the corner of Swell Wood. A short walk leads to a hide from which excellent views of nesting herons can be obtained, and of woodland birds at the feeders throughout the year. Also starting from the car park there is a clearly marked circular woodland trail (with disabled access) which allows further exploration without disturbing the herons. Permits are not required although groups should contact the RSPB in advance.

For West Sedgemoor itself, walk down the road from the car park to the Moorland Hide at the foot of the hill, partially obscured by farm buildings. Parking is not allowed here (except for the disabled), and the short walk down the steep slope affords panoramic views of this part of the moor. A pool has been created in front of the hide, but the whole of the expanse of the moor and the escarpment should be scanned carefully. For further exploration it is possible to walk along the (often muddy)

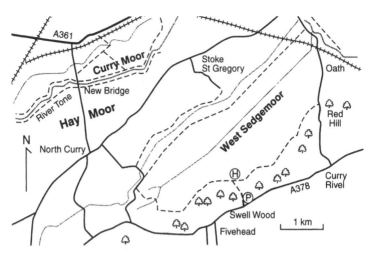

drove that fringes the southern edge of the moor; walking east will eventually bring you to Dewland's Farm, near Oath, where a road runs back south up Red Hill (a good 'scanning point') to the A378 at Curry Rivel. Continuing north, good general views of the east end of the moor can be obtained from the railway bridge at Oath, and a little further on, past the Black Smock pub, another drove along the northern side of the moor starts. These droves are not public rights of way, but access is usually allowed. Do not, however, use the droves that run out into the moor (none cross over the central drain anyway) unless specific authority has been granted by the RSPB or the farmers. Everything can be seen from the edges without disturbing the birds themselves.

Curry and Hay Moors can be scanned for wildfowl from the minor road that runs from North Curry to West Lyng on the A361 west of Burrowbridge. Public footpaths run in either direction along both banks of the River Tone which reaches its tidal limit at the bridge. There is often deep water on the moors in winter as they are used for temporary flood-relief. Taking the north bank allows a circular walk as in c.1 mile (1.6 km) in either direction there are droves which run back parallel to the river through the fields, crossing the road a short distance north of the bridge. The withy beds often seem to hold concentrations of passerines and a variety of other species in the winter.

Calendar

All year: Grey Heron, Mute Swan, Sparrowhawk, Buzzard, Kestrel, Lapwing, Snipe, Stock Dove, Little Owl; Barn Owl (irregular), Tawny Owl, woodpeckers including Lesser Spotted; Skylark, Meadow Pipit, Nuthatch, Treecreeper, Rook, Reed Bunting.

December–February: Grey Herons start nesting February. Bewick's Swan, Wigeon, Teal, Mallard, Pintail, Shoveler; sometimes Pochard, Tufted Duck, Goldeneye. Hen Harrier (irregular), Merlin, Peregrine. Water Rail (has bred). Golden Plover, Dunlin, Ruff, Snipe, Jack Snipe, occasional Green Sandpiper. Short-eared Owl. Stonechat, Redwing, Fieldfare.

March–May: Short-eared Owl to early April; maybe Marsh Harrier late April–May; Hobby from late April, seen irregularly to September. Golden

Plover, Whimbrel pass April–early May. Breeding waders active from March: Lapwing, Redshank, Snipe, Curlew, maybe Black-tailed Godwit. Resident woodland birds active throughout; Cuckoo, Yellow Wagtail, Nightingale from mid-April; Sedge Warbler, Whinchat late April.

June–July: Breeding species active through June, then quieter period starts. Grey Herons desert heronry late June. Waders disperse early July, but Lapwings flock. Quail calling.

August–November: Quiet period until winter birds return from mid-November.

16b WET MOOR & WITCOMBE BOTTOM
OS Explorer 129

Habitat
These grassland moors close to the River Yeo have traditionally remained waterlogged for long periods in winter, and therefore attractive to wildfowl. Wet Moor is very open, with only a few trees scattered about the ditch-lined meadows, while Witcombe Bottom just to the east has rather more in the way of hedges, and also contains some wider and deeper drainage channels and some water-filled clay pits. Although both areas can be extensively flooded in winter, water is often quickly pumped off in the spring, leaving the fields free to produce a lush but ornithologically rather dull hay crop in the summer, with few rushy areas remaining. However, at least some farmers are maintaining higher summer water levels, with a consequent improvement in the breeding wader population, and hopefully this trend will continue.

Species
The Wet Moor meadows are one of several sites where Bewick's Swans feed on the levels, although in recent years they have tended to be much more fickle. If flooding occurs, they will be accompanied by significant numbers of Wigeon and Teal, into the thousands at times, with smaller numbers of other wildfowl, rarely over 100 of any one species, but sometimes including diving ducks such as Pochard and Tufted Duck, while rarities such as Ring-necked Duck have been seen. Lapwings, again into the thousands, are the most numerous wader, but up to 300 Dunlin and Golden Plover with sometimes as many as 20 Ruff also occur. Snipe numbers can be high if conditions are right while a few Jack Snipe and the odd Green Sandpiper also winter. In spring, parties of Whimbrel feed during the day on the fields, their trilling calls often being the first indication of their presence. As long as it is not too dry, a few pairs of Redshank, Snipe and Lapwing breed, with Yellow Wagtails, Reed Buntings, Meadow Pipits and a scattering of Whinchats and Sedge Warblers regular in the same habitat.

Timing

At all times of the year, the more water the better is the general rule. In many years breeding waders are active early in the season but leave if the fields dry out and become unsuitable as nesting habitat.

Access

The starting point for exploration is the road bridge over the River Yeo in Long Load. There is limited parking here, and you may have to find somewhere in the village and walk back. Public footpaths run either way along the raised banks; the southern side is generally the most productive. Wet Moor is the area to the west of the road and can also be viewed by taking the first turning right in Long Load south of the river (Church Lane) towards Muchelney; a couple of droves run north from this road back towards the river. They are the best means of access in summer, as the river bank paths are often overgrown at this time. A little further south in Long Load a turning to the east leads through Milton to the southern side of Witcombe Bottom. The road turns sharply right at a crossroads junction with two farm tracks. It is possible to park here and walk north along one track to the river where a footbridge allows access to King's Moor on the far side, this sometimes also flooding in winter, but in general the area to the west of Long Load is more productive. For something slightly out of the ordinary, a short distance beyond the turning to Milton the next turning right leads to the Town Tree Nature Gardens, where there is a car park and a waymarked trail. This is a private venture, for which a fee is charged, but is an interesting (and, for some, inspiring) example of what can be done in the way of habitat creation by an enthusiastic private individual.

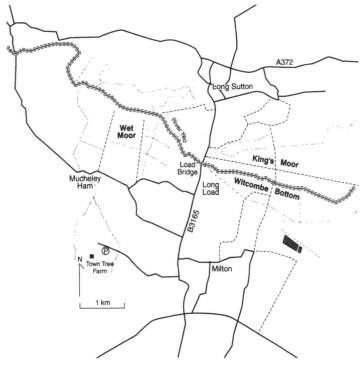

Calendar

All year: Grey Heron, Mute Swan, Buzzard, Kestrel, Lapwing, Meadow Pipit, Reed Bunting.

December–February: Bewick's Swan, Wigeon, Teal, Mallard, sometimes Pintail, Shoveler, Pochard, Tufted Duck. Occasional Short-eared Owl, Peregrine or other predator. Lapwing, Golden Plover, Dunlin, Ruff, Snipe, Jack Snipe, sometimes Green Sandpiper. Black-headed Gulls. Redwing, Fieldfare.

March–May: Breeding Lapwing, Snipe and Redshank displaying. Whimbrel late April–early May. Maybe other passage wader, e.g. Ruff, Black-tailed Godwit March–April. Yellow Wagtail from mid-April.

June–July: Breeding waders, Yellow Wagtail, Sedge Warbler, sometimes Whinchat. Lapwings flock from late June. Maybe Quail calling.

August–November: Quiet until winter birds arrive from November. Golden Plover possible from October.

16c CENTRAL LEVELS, INCLUDING KING'S SEDGE MOOR & GREAT BREACH WOOD

OS Explorer 140 and 141

Habitat

King's Sedge Moor, and Somerton Moor immediately to its east, are both relatively well drained, and rarely flood in the winter. Parts, especially in the northwest, have been ploughed for arable farming, but the majority of the low ground is given over to grazing meadows, damp and rough in places and mostly fairly open near the central drainage channels although there are some hawthorn hedges with willows along the southern fringes. Southlake Moor and North Moor lie to the south, the former having been regularly flooded in winter in recent years. The land rises relatively gently to the north and west, but the moors are enclosed further east by steep wooded slopes around High Ham and again where the eastern tail of the Polden ridge curves south near Compton Dundon. There is a small amount of grassy downland in a couple of spots here, with extensive mixed oak and ash woodland and patches of dense scrub at Great Breach and Copley Woods. Great Breach Wood is a SWT reserve, and is outstanding for butterflies, with over 50 species including marsh and other fritillaries, Duke of Burgundy, purple hairstreak and white admiral, and Collard Hill, on the Poldens, is the site, owned by the NT, where the large blue has been successfully reintroduced.

Species

This area of the Levels is not so well-watched as some others, but has a scattering of breeding waders, while the woodland provides a contrasting bird population to that of the open ground. In winter, Lapwing flocks are often several thousand strong, and can include up to 500 Golden Plover. Fieldfares and Redwings also occur in good numbers, feeding in the arable fields as well as in the meadows. The presence of prey species attracts regular wintering Peregrines, with Merlin, Short-eared Owl and Hen Harrier recorded more erratically. Buzzards are resident in all the nearby woods, and are often to be seen perched on any vantage point they can find out on the moors. If flooding occurs, for instance as at Southlake Moor, wildfowl attracted include Bewick's and Mute Swans, Pintail and Shoveler, with several hundred Snipe and Dunlin and rather fewer Redshank and Ruff the most frequent waders. In some years, Bewick's Swans also occur on King's Sedge Moor, feeding on the remains of arable crops. In addition a few Wigeon, Teal and occasional diving duck or Cormorant may be seen on the main drains.

In spring, those parts of the moors that remain damp attract a few breeding waders, Lapwing being the most numerous, with a few Curlew and sometimes Redshank and Snipe. Feeding parties of Whimbrel occur in spring. Meadow Pipits and Skylarks breed in some numbers, with a scattering of Whinchats and Yellow Wagtails. Inevitably, the Corn Buntings on the old airfield at Westonzoyland have now departed, as from the rest of Somerset. Woodland species include Nightingale and sometimes Tree Pipit, though the latter is dependent on the presence of clearings among the trees, and has not been recorded recently. Several Marsh Harriers have been seen on spring and autumn passage, and other rarer visitors have included Quail and Corncrake, the former sometimes nesting.

Whimbrel

Timing

Early morning visits are best for seeing breeding waders, as they are far more active then, and numbers are likely to be higher after a wet winter and spring. Southlake Moor is only productive when flooded, and the other moors are best in wet conditions. Early morning or late evenings produce the best chance of hearing Nightingales in the woodland, and birdsong generally is greater in the morning.

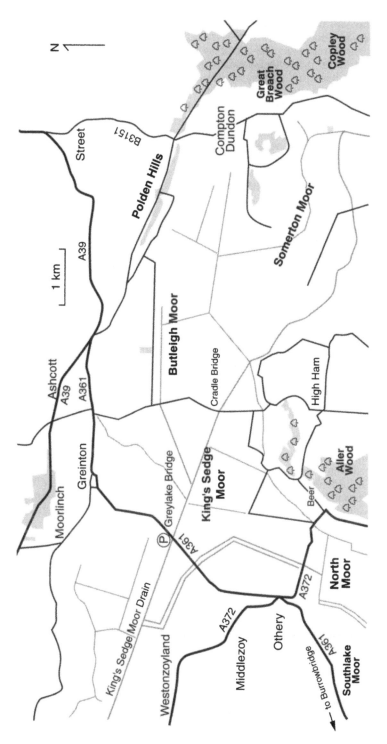

Access

The A361 north of Othery crosses the main King's Sedge Moor drain at Greylake Bridge, where there is a car park by the sluice gate across the channel, from which the best area of moor can be overlooked. The area to the west, including the arable fields on the north side which sometimes attract finches, buntings, thrushes and swans, can be viewed by walking along the north bank of the drainage channel. For the fields east of the road take the southern bank as far as the next road at Cradle Bridge. In summer these banks are often very overgrown, and the droves then provide better access. Few are actually public rights of way, and although this is generally not a problem any notices indicating private access (usually over shooting and fishing rights) should be respected. The RSPB has recently purchased land in this part of the Levels, and so both the variety of birdlife and the access will no doubt improve further. To the north of Greylake Bridge, turning left just before Greinton into Moorlinch brings access to droves running south again into an area of damp fields. To the south, the A372 from Othery runs east across the top end of North Moor which can be viewed from the roadbridge across the main drain. Buzzards can often be seen over the wooded ridge to the east. At Beer Door a minor road to the left skirts the southern edge of the moors, crosses the main drain at Cradle Bridge and eventually provides access to Butleigh and Somerton Moors. This eastern area is less productive, although seemingly more favoured by birds like Stonechat and Whinchat. For Southlake Moor, take the A361 south from Othery to the conspicuous mound of Burrow Mump, with its ruined church. There is a car park at its foot and the hill provides an excellent lookout point over the main flooded area, often holding good numbers of Bewick's Swans.

For Great Breach Wood, take the B3151 south from Street and turn left towards Kingweston at the crossroads at the ridge of the Polden Hills. The road runs through woodland, most of which is private, and just before it emerges into open farmland again, there is a locked and gated track off to the right. There is very limited parking by the road, but if the warden is present you may be allowed to park inside the gate. Following the track brings you to signs indicating the SWT reserve, where there are various paths into the woodland. Clearings among the oaks have been opened up for the benefit of butterflies and flowers, but have also attracted a few Tree Pipits in the past. Nightingales are most likely to be heard on the lower western slopes where there is the most hawthorn and blackthorn scrub.

Calendar

All year: Grey Heron, Mute Swan, Mallard, Sparrowhawk, Buzzard, Kestrel, Lapwing, Stock Dove, Barn Owl (scarce), Kingfisher, Green and Great Spotted Woodpeckers; Skylark, Meadow Pipit, Stonechat.

December–February: Bewick's Swan, Wigeon, Teal, Pintail, Shoveler, Pochard, Tufted Duck. Merlin, Peregrine; Hen Harrier and Short-eared Owl irregular. Lapwing, Golden Plover, Dunlin, maybe Ruff, Green Sandpiper. Redwing, Fieldfare.

March–May: Occasional Marsh Harrier (May). Golden Plover leave March. Breeding waders displaying: Lapwing, Curlew, maybe Snipe, Redshank. Whimbrel late April–early May. Yellow Wagtail arrive on moors from mid-April, Whinchat late April. In woodland, Nightingale, Tree Pipit and common warblers from mid–late April.

June–July: Breeding species active. Quail sometimes breed on moors. Lapwings flock from late June.

August–November: Summer visitors mostly leave during August. Finch flocks August–October in arable areas. Maybe Marsh Harrier August–September. Golden Plover from October.

16d HAM WALL & THE
AVALON MARSHES OS Explorer 140 and 141

Habitat

This unique part of the Levels lies between the Polden ridge and the River Brue to the west of Glastonbury and Street, and contains the remnants of the raised bogs that once stretched to within a few miles of the coast. Shapwick Heath NNR contains the most extensive examples of the vegetation types which range successively from poor fen through bog myrtle pastures to birch and alder carr. Adjoining areas contain flower-rich hay meadows and rough damp grazing. The dominant land-use, however, until recently has been commercial peat digging for horticultural purposes, this having destroyed the original vegetation over a wide area, giving parts of the heathland the look of an open-cast mining region. The industry is now in its final stages, and large areas have already been handed over to conservation bodies. The SWT has long been associated with the area, and has now been joined by the RSPB which is developing a large reedbed-based reserve at Ham Wall. There is an interesting butterfly and dragonfly population, and plants such as royal fern, marsh orchid and sundew occur in undisturbed habitat. Otters occur in reasonable numbers, although outnumbered by the introduced American mink, and roe deer also seem to find the habitat ideal. The former peat moors are increasingly known under the general heading of the 'Avalon Marshes', this also including Westhay Moor immediately to the north (see next section).

Species

Localised breeding species remain a major attraction here, although developments at Ham Wall and on the Catcott Lows reserve have vastly increased the range of species in the area at other seasons. Redpolls and Siskins can be found swinging among the alders and birches most winters, whilst flocks of tits, Goldcrests and Treecreepers move through the carr woodland, occasionally joined by an elusive Lesser Spotted Woodpecker. There are no recent breeding records for this last species, and similarly there have been no recent sightings of Willow Tit, which used to nest, despite the fact that the habitat still seems idea. However, on the plus side, the explosive calls of Cetti's Warblers can be heard throughout the year, well over 100 singing males having been counted during a recent survey, though actually seeing one is never easy. Another bird which also usually remains well hidden is the Water Rail, several wintering among the reedmace-filled ditches and pools, and probably breeding most years. Gratifyingly, considering the amount of conservation effort put in, one or two Bitterns usually winter in the Ham Wall reedbeds, and the hope is that they will in due course stay to breed. The more open farmland attracts large flocks of winter thrushes, and Barn Owls have remained regular although much reduced elsewhere. Among the birds of prey, Buzzards and Sparrowhawks are both common, and in most winters are joined by one or two Hen Harriers, usually 'ring-tails'. Like the Peregrines that also occur at this time, these birds are very wide-ranging, their hunting territories seeming extending as far as the coast, so a certain amount of luck is required to see one. An attraction for predators (and also birdwatchers) is the spectacular winter Starling roost in the reeds at Ham Wall or Shapwick, sometimes topping a million birds.

The retention of shallow floodwater at Catcott Lows has substantially raised winter counts of wildfowl, Wigeon, Teal and Mallard having occurred in their hundreds, with smaller numbers of Pintail, Shoveler and Bewick's Swans joining them when conditions are particularly favourable. In addition, many of the worked-out peat-diggings are now extensively flooded, attracting Gadwall, Tufted Ducks, Ruddy Ducks, Coots and Great Crested Grebes throughout the year, all five species raising young in varying numbers. Wintering Goosander and Goldeneye are also seen far more often than in the past. Garganey are virtually annual spring visitors, and probably breed, as do the occasional pair or two of Teal and Shoveler, though proof for any of these species is always difficult. Mute Swans are conspicuous residents, and a non-breeding flock of up to 40 birds remains throughout the year along the main drainage channels. A few feral Greylag Geese now appear to be firmly established on this part of the Levels, up to 100 sometimes occurring.

Whimbrel have always been regular spring migrants here, but other waders are already finding the flooded fields at Catcott an ideal stopover on their way north. Over 600 Whimbrel and 150 Ruffs on one May morning was probably exceptional, but both species are regular visitors,

Garganey

and other waders passing through at this time of year include Ringed and Little Ringed Plovers, Little and Temminck's Stints, Curlew Sandpiper and both godwits. The coming of summer brings a wider variety of breeding birds. Among commoner species, Garden Warblers, Whitethroats, Tree Pipits and Reed Buntings find plenty of habitat in the scrub-grown peat diggings and carr, with a few Grasshopper Warblers and a small population of Nightingales. The numbers of Sedge and Reed Warblers are steadily increasing as the reedbeds expand. Lapwing breed in the open meadows, sometimes joined by Redshank, and it is hoped that the breeding wader population will increase in future, as both Snipe and Curlew have bred in the past. Sand Martins used to nest among the peat stacks but are now only seen on passage. At any time during the summer there is a good chance of seeing a Hobby skimming over the trees and ditches in search of dragonflies and small birds, and hovering Kestrels are a typical sight all through the year. Marsh Harriers are a recent welcome arrival to these northern Levels, hunting birds ranging widely throughout the summer, with odd birds to be seen all year. In late summer, there is the now-normal influx of Little Egrets, this now being a characteristic bird of the area throughout the year, with a few pairs already breeding on the Levels. Nearly 50 have been seen gathering to roost at Shapwick in autumn, though during the day they can be remarkably elusive.

As the fields have traditionally tended to be dry in autumn, the return passage is seldom as good as in the spring, but there are signs that this is changing along with the habitat. Certainly, Green Sandpipers have always occurred from later summer onwards, and recently migrants like Spoonbill, Osprey and various waders have been seen during the autumn, ahead of the return of the winter birds.

Timing

Early morning and evening visits are usually the most productive, and are essential for several species, especially for Nightingales and Grasshopper Warblers. Late afternoon and evening also gives the best chance of seeing hunting Barn Owls, and Hobbies also are often active around dusk, although calm warm midsummer days will see them hunting dragonflies at midday. In the winter and spring, the fields at Catcott Lows need to be well flooded for wildfowl and waders to occur in any numbers.

Access

The main starting point for Shapwick Heath is the road between the villages of Westhay on the B3151 and Shapwick just off the A39. It is possible to park by the road just south of the large South Drain but do not block any of the gateways or entrances to peat storage areas. A broad track runs in both directions along the south side of the channel. To the west it reaches a point where the east end of Catcott Lows can be viewed; to the east (accessible by wheelchairs) it runs all the way to the Ham Wall entrance, providing good views over Shapwick Heath to the south. A footbridge over the drain here leads to a hide overlooking Meare Heath to the north, and the path to the south leads to another viewing screen. A short distance south from the bridge on the Shapwick/Westhay road, you will see EN signs indicating points of entry to their reserve both to the left and right, waymarked trails taking you though a representative sample of the main carr woodland and bog myrtle meadows. A little further on along the road is a public footpath running west near Canada Farm. Where this path turns sharp left, a path to the right leads to another

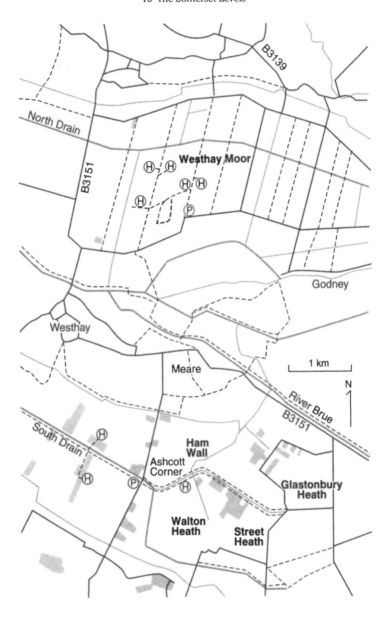

hide overlooking open water and reeds. As peat digging ceases, new wetland habitats are being created throughout this section, and there are
plans to construct hides and screens, overlooking other selected areas.
In general access is allowed along some of the droves, though there are
few actual public rights of way; with the changing situation, any instruc-
tions in force at the time should be followed, particularly concerning
disturbance to breeding species and the vegetation.

A couple of miles (3.2 km) to the east, the road between Meare and
Ashcott crosses the South Drain and the entrance to Ham Wall RSPB

reserve. There is a small car park by the bridge, where the track from the Shapwick end finishes. The track continues east, still on the south side of the channel (access by car for the disabled only), crossing an old bridge to reach a viewing platform on the left and a series of boardwalks on the right. The former looks north across the South Drain to the pools and reedbeds of Ham Wall. Access to the reserve itself is by arrangement with the RSPB, but the platform affords excellent views over the whole area. The boardwalks lead to several screens overlooking similar habitat on Walton Heath to the south. One can continue east by the main channel to reach a minor road off the B3151, from which Walton, Street and Glastonbury Heaths can be viewed. Peat extraction continues here but in due course should extend the wetland habitat even further.

To reach Catcott Heath, take a minor road west from the southern edge of Westhay village, signposted to Burtle. Turn left in 2 miles (3.2 km) at the Burtle Inn, then straight ahead for 1 mile (1.6 km) towards Catcott village. At the second of two right-angled bends, turn left along an unsurfaced track to a small car park and the Lady's Drove hide. This overlooks the damp meadows of the SWT reserve of Catcott Lows, usually the most productive area for birds. Alternatively, walk east from the double bend along a muddy drove to Catcott Heath itself. The first track left off this drove brings you to Jane's Drove hide which also overlooks the main area liable to flooding. More open meadowland with a few patches of alder, birch and other woodland can be found to the west on Edington Heath and Chilton Moor. Again, minor roads and various droves allow the fields to be scanned; those who wish details of further access should contact the SWT who manage reserves here and elsewhere on the Levels.

Calendar

All year. Little and Great Crested Grebes, Little Egret, Grey Heron, Mute Swan; Greylag Goose (feral), Gadwall, Mallard, Tufted Duck, Ruddy Duck. Marsh Harrier (erratic in winter), Sparrowhawk, Buzzard, Kestrel, Water Rail, Barn Owl, Cetti's Warbler, Reed Bunting.

December–February. Wigeon, Teal, Shoveler, sometimes Bewick's Swan, Pintail, Goldeneye, Goosander and other wildfowl. Hen Harrier (erratic), Merlin, Peregrine. Snipe, occasional Green Sandpiper; Water Pipit (scarce); Siskin, Redpoll.

March–May. Garganey, Teal and Shoveler sometimes breed. Marsh Harrier (from mid-April). Hobby irregularly from May to September. Water Rail and Lapwing breed, maybe Redshank, Snipe or Curlew. Ruff, Whimbrel and other passage waders (April–May). Passage of hirundines from April. Summer visitors arriving: Cuckoo, Tree Pipit, Yellow Wagtail, Nightingale, Blackcap from mid-April; Whinchat, Whitethroat, Grasshopper, Reed, Sedge and Garden Warblers late April.

June–July. Breeding residents and summer visitors. Influx of Little Egrets in July.

August–November. Occasional Green Sandpiper August–September. Other migrants occur if the fields remain wet.

16e TEALHAM, TADHAM & WESTHAY MOORS
OS Explorer 141

Habitat
Of the ornithologically important areas on the Levels, these are nowadays the most northerly, lying in the lower River Brue basin between the peat moors/heaths to the south and the Wedmore ridge to the north. Tealham and much of Tadham Moor contain extensive open and frequently wet meadows, many of the fields being rough and tussocky, and the rhynes usually full of water. Further east on Tadham Moor there are well developed hedgerows with mature oaks, ashes and pines, and even a small wood. East again, Westhay Moor provides something of a contrast, as peat extraction has created several large pools in addition to there being rough meadows and alder/birch carr. The worked-out diggings have been converted into another extensive SWT/EN reserve, in habitat terms an extension of the 'Avalon Marshes' to the south (see previous section). The moors to the northwest and to the east are drier, but have enough hedgerow cover to provide habitat for a good population of commoner species.

Species
The variety of habitats and the generally high water table give this area a rich and varied bird population at most times of the year. If the winter is reasonably mild and wet, waterlogged fields on Tealham and Tadham Moors attract large numbers of Lapwings, sometimes accompanied by smaller numbers of Golden Plover and Dunlin. Up to 300 Snipe plus a few Jack Snipe can also be found scattered throughout the area. Stonechats in twos and threes appear for the winter and noisy flocks of Starlings, Fieldfares and Redwings add to the vitality of the scene. A disturbance among any of these species often draws attention to a hunting Merlin, Peregrine or Sparrowhawk, the first two being regular winter visitors while the latter is resident, along with the widespread Buzzards and Kestrels. Other predators include Short-eared Owl in some winters, and like the resident Barn Owls, one can often be seen hunting in daylight. Deep flooding rarely lasts for long periods, because of the improved drainage, but while it does will attract some hundreds of Mallard, Teal and Wigeon, with smaller numbers of other surface-feeding ducks. A non-breeding flock of Mute Swans, up to 100 birds, remains all year, with scattered pairs nesting, and in winter they are sometimes joined by a few Bewick's Swans, exceptionally the odd Whooper.

Small numbers of Pochard, Tufted Ducks, Goldeneye, Great Crested and Little Grebes now occur regularly on the deeper flooded peat workings on Westhay Moor, particularly in cold weather. These pits are of local importance for Goosander, up to 30 gathering here to feed and bathe, and other diving species such as Smew drop in from time to time. Careful planning of reedbeds in the reserve area has paid off, most notably with the appearance of wintering Bitterns on a virtually annual basis. Single Green Sandpipers lurk in the sheltered ditches, mostly unseen until disturbed by chance.

There is a brief lull once the winter birds leave, but soon noisy Redshank and Lapwings take up residence in the damper meadows,

Sedge Warbler

where Snipe can sometimes be heard drumming, and the resident Grey Herons are back repairing their nests. Tealham Moor is noted for its Yellow Wagtail population, these attractive birds always at their best early in the year, and sometimes a pair or two of Whinchats nest in the rougher patches at the field edges. Reed Buntings, Skylarks and Meadow Pipits all breed commonly on the open moors, with Green and Great Spotted Woodpeckers, Little Owl and Lesser Whitethroat among a good range of farmland species. Notable among passage birds are the parties of Whimbrel in spring, sometimes accompanied by a few Ruff.

At Westhay Moor, both Great Crested and Little Grebes nest in the overgrown peat workings, and Mute Swan, Coot and Moorhen are well established. Sedge and Reed Warblers are relatively abundant, joining the resident Cetti's Warblers in the summer. The strange reeling sound of Grasshopper Warbler can sometimes be heard coming from places where the undergrowth is denser. Marsh Harriers are seen with increasing regularity through the spring and summer, ranging widely over the whole of the Avalon marshes, though breeding records are sporadic. Hobbies are often seen for a few days in spring, and wide-ranging feeding birds may be seen at any time from late April to September. A Red-footed Falcon accompanied them one spring, and other southern vagrants have included Purple Heron on more than one occasion. In fact as these northern Levels have become better watched, an impressive number of vagrants have been found, particularly in spring, including Night Heron, Spoonbill, White-winged Black Tern and Penduline Tit. One former vagrant that can now be seen at Westhay throughout the year is of course the Little Egret. It would be nice to think that some of the others might become equally common in future!

Most breeding waders move away as the vegetation becomes lusher in midsummer, but Lapwings gather into post-breeding flocks in the mown fields. Rougher areas produce thistles in abundance, attracting Goldfinches and Linnets in some numbers, with migrant Whinchats joining them at intervals. Dry early autumn conditions mean few feeding opportunities for waders, but Snipe and Green Sandpipers may be flushed from the ditches and peat workings.

Timing

The open nature of the terrain means that strong winds, especially from the west, make watching difficult at any time of year. Early morning is best for breeding waders in display flights, while late afternoon or evening in winter may produce a hunting Barn or Short-eared Owl, the former also sometimes hunting in daylight in summer if there are young to be fed. Heavy flooding will produce the most ducks, but the fields only have to be waterlogged to keep wintering waders happy. Freezing conditions will immediately drive off Lapwings and Golden Plover, but Dunlin and Ruff often feed on icy fields for several days, moving off only if a thaw is too much delayed. As elsewhere on the Levels, fog can persist all day over the moors, even if the marginally higher ground nearby is bathed in sunshine.

Access

The B3151 from Wedmore to Westhay runs north–south across the area with Tealham/Tadham Moors to the west and Westhay Moor to the east. Once down off the higher ground around Wedmore take the first through road west: this narrow but straight road leads across Tadham Moor to Tealham, the two merging into each other imperceptibly. Tadham has more in the way of trees, the first wood on the right holding the main heronry. Walkable droves lead off left and right, those to the north being the most productive and linking with others parallel to the road. A road to the right marks the beginning of Tealham Moor, which generally holds the most waders, winter and summer. Continuing on the road ahead eventually brings you a right turn just after the bridge over the major North Drain. Using your car as a hide anywhere along the whole route will often give excellent views of waders and wildfowl, although pull-in spots are limited. Access on foot along the droves is generally allowed, although only some are actually rights of way. It is totally unnecessary to enter any of the fields, which are strictly private.

Returning to the B3151 and turning left or right will bring you to minor roads running east along the north and south sides respectively of Westhay Moor, with another road linking the two at its eastern edge. Four droves, all of which are public footpaths, run north–south across the moor, making satisfactory rectangular routes for exploration. There is a car park at the southern end of the third one east (where the road bends sharply), with information boards showing the main access routes and hides of the reserve. The largest area of open water, favoured by Goosander and other diving ducks, is in the northwestern western half of the reserve, viewable from a screen just off the drove. Other hides and screens overlook the pools and reedbeds in various places, providing the best opportunity of seeing Bittern, Water Rail and other birds of the dense vegetation.

Other moors lying further east are drier, but Lapwing and Curlew sometimes breed on them.

Calendar

All year. Little and Great Crested Grebes, Little Egret, Grey Heron, Mute Swan, Gadwall, Mallard, Sparrowhawk, Buzzard, Kestrel, Lapwing, Barn Owl, Little Owl, Green and Great Spotted Woodpeckers, Skylark, Meadow Pipit; Cetti's Warbler (Westhay Moor), Treecreeper, Reed Bunting.

December–February. Bittern (scarce), Bewick's Swan, Gadwall, Teal, Wigeon, Pochard, Tufted Duck, a few Goldeneye, Goosander and other diving duck. Merlin, Peregrine, Water Rail, Lapwing, Golden Plover, Dunlin,

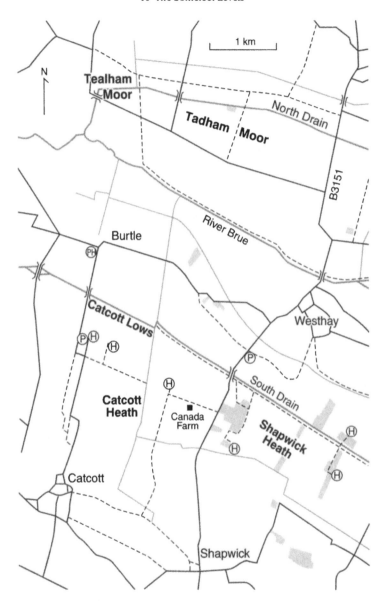

Snipe, Jack Snipe, Green Sandpiper, maybe Ruff, Little Stint. Black-headed and Common Gulls. Short-eared Owl (scarce), Stonechat, Redwing, Fieldfare, Siskin, Redpoll.

March–May: Golden Plover leave March; breeding waders active: Lapwing, Redshank, sometimes Snipe or Curlew. Short-eared Owl to early April; maybe Garganey from mid-March or Marsh Harrier from late April. Yellow Wagtail, Whinchat from mid–late April.

June–July: Breeding species include occasional Teal, Garganey and Water Rail. Feeding Hobby occasional May–September.

August–November. Green Sandpiper August–September. Finch flocks August–September include Linnet, Goldfinch. Whinchat on passage September. Golden Plover from early October, other waders November.

17 BERROW

OS Explorer 153

Habitat

There are sand dunes along most of the coast south from Brean Down to Burnham-on-Sea, but they are mainly productive for birds near Berrow, where they enclose a brackish marsh, now almost entirely overgrown with reeds. The dunes have been extensively stabilised with marram grass and sea-buckthorn, the latter providing ample cover for small birds and there are a couple of small ponds. A golf course lies immediately east of the marsh, and extends north and south, comprising open grass with scattered clumps of bushes, and a few trees along the edge. The shore near the dunes is sandy, giving way at low tide to vast areas of mud-flats around the Parrett Estuary. Although in places the marsh and reeds have continued to spread, there are ongoing problems with drainage which potentially could damage the site, and in recent years the bushes, which provide valuable habitat for breeding and wintering passerines, have been cut back across much of the golf course. Nevertheless it remains an important site, with an interesting dune and wetland flora which include species such as evening primrose and marsh orchid.

Species

In winter, Berrow marsh is noted as one of the more reliable sites in the area for Jack Snipe, along with the more numerous Common Snipe, though both have become increasingly difficult to see as the reedbed has expanded, and the amount of open wet marsh has reduced. Also skulking in the reeds are several pairs of Water Rails, present throughout the year but hard to see and most often located by their squealing calls. Cold weather, particularly later in the winter, will sometimes bring large numbers of Fieldfares, Redwings, and other thrushes to feed on the bright orange berries of the sea-buckthorn which they tend to ignore while other food is available. The same habitat also holds a significant win-tering population of Blackcaps, maybe approaching 100 birds in this extensive area. Winter predators include Merlin and Peregrine, while Sparrowhawk and Kestrel are always around. Short-eared Owls are erratic winter visitors, but if present, might be seen over the dunes and beach during the daytime. There are few recent records of Hen Harriers, although they are always a possibility, and the reedbed was a roost site in the past. In general the wader population is an offshoot of that of the Parrett Estuary just to the south, and any of the species mentioned there might be seen. Oystercatchers, Dunlin and Curlew are the most regular, but Knot and Bar-tailed Godwits sometimes appear in numbers on the shore, although they can be difficult to view apart from during a short period at high tide. However, the upper sandy part of the beach is favoured by another of Berrow's specialities, the Sanderling, which is present in small numbers throughout the winter, with over 100 sometimes present on spring and autumn passage. Ringed Plovers have a similar pattern of occurrence, with up to 500 between here and the Brue Estuary in August on occasion.

There is a trickle of spring migrants, with Wheatears and Stonechats appearing around the golf courses; up to four of the latter overwinter but have not bred in recent years. Arctic Skuas can sometimes be seen offshore, accompanying the passage Common and Arctic Terns. Other terns are much more irregular in occurrence. Migrant Marsh Harriers in spring sometimes pass along this coast, but rarely if ever stop, unfortunately. Among breeding birds, the main speciality of the reedbeds is the Bearded Tit, but one which might disappear unless the drainage regime can be stabilised. Up to five pairs breed most years, with up to 30 remaining throughout the year. Recently they have been joined by a few Cetti's Warblers, which likewise remain throughout the winter. Both species are of course also extremely vulnerable to cold weather. Summer visitors to the reeds include both Sedge and Reed Warblers. Out on the mudflats, Shelduck numbers build up during the summer, as adults bring their young to the safety of the shore from inland breeding sites. Numbers are swelled to a July peak by the arrival of moulting birds in Bridgwater Bay. August and September bring an increase in numbers and variety of waders, Little Stints and Curlew Sandpipers being more visible than most species as they prefer the upper shore to the open flats, although parties of over 400 Oystercatchers are easy enough to pick out. This is also a good time to check the gulls on the beach for Mediterranean and Yellow-legged Gulls which are both increasing visitors to the general area, and both of which have been seen here at this time. In late autumn Berrow shares in the diurnal passage of finches, pipits and other small birds that is a feature of the

Bearded Tit

Severn Estuary, the direction of movement here being mainly southerly. Redpolls, Siskins and Brambling occur in small numbers, and sometimes a Lapland Bunting may be picked out by its rattling call or plaintive whistle. Snow Buntings also occur here, sometimes stopping for a few days to feed along the lengthy upper tideline before moving on again.

Timing

Not particularly critical for reedbed birds, although high winds make location of small birds almost impossible. Diurnal migration in the autumn is most visible for the first two or three hours after dawn, with southerly winds and overcast skies most likely to produce the best passage. High tide is essential for most wader species; note however that the flats are uncovered extremely rapidly, and wader-watchers are probably better advised to try further south on this coast for extended views. The beach is fairly heavily used by walkers and horse-riders at all times of day but particularly in the afternoons. Strong westerly or southwesterly winds at any time of year may bring seabirds up against the coast, particularly in autumn. Birds are mostly visible while the gales are in progress as they soon move away offshore as the winds abate. Cold weather in the winter brings big movements of Lapwings and Golden Plover going southwest and also peak numbers of thrushes to the sea-buckthorn.

Access

Berrow is reached by the B3139/40 from the south and the B3140 from the east (see also map with next site). At their junction in Berrow village, there is a small car park from where a footpath runs past the pub opposite out to the golf course. Cross directly ahead (the right-of-way is clearly marked) taking care not to obstruct play or be hit by flying golfballs. The reedbed lies in front and can be crossed at this point by a walkway which gives access to the beach. The main areas of interest lie to the north. For shorebirds walk up the tideline in front of the dunes, scanning the shore but also keeping an eye on the debris along the high-water mark for small birds. Gulls and waders sometimes gather to bathe at the point where the main freshwater outflow from the reedbed runs across the beach. The dunes can be crossed at the far end of the marsh, not far from the church, and access southwards is possible along the edges of the golf course, but do not trespass onto the fairways or greens themselves. The reedbed can be viewed along the whole of its eastern border from the golf course, while the dunes provide viewpoints in a few places on the western edge. A second main access route is via the church at the north end of Berrow village, but you may have to park a little way away as the car park by the church is for worshippers and golf club members only. The bushes by the church and nearby gardens are worth checking for migrants and wintering passerines at the appropriate seasons.

Calendar

All year: Cormorant, Shelduck, Sparrowhawk, Kestrel, Oystercatcher, Herring Gull. Cetti's Warbler, Bearded Tit, Linnet.

December–February: Occasional diver or grebe; possible Bittern or goose. Wigeon, Teal, occasional Shoveler or diving duck. Hen Harrier (rare). Merlin, Peregrine, Water Rail, Dunlin, Curlew, Common and Jack Snipe; Short-eared Owl (irregular). Stonechat, Redwing, Fieldfare; wintering finches in small numbers. Wintering Blackcaps, maybe Firecrest.

March–May: Possible Common Scoter offshore (April–May). Chance of Marsh Harrier (late April–May). Water Rail and Jack Snipe leave by end March. Spring wader passage, especially Ringed Plover and Sanderling (May), Whimbrel (late April–early May); also Oystercatcher, Knot, Bar-tailed Godwit. Common and Arctic Tern pass late April–May, sometimes Great or Arctic Skuas. Other terns irregular May–July. Trickle of passerine migrants mid-April–May e.g. Tree Pipit, Yellow Wagtail, Whinchat, Lesser Whitethroat.

June–July: Manx Shearwater, Gannet irregular offshore. Peak numbers of Shelduck. Maybe Common Scoter. Wader passage from late July, small numbers summering, especially Oystercatcher, Curlew. Breeding Cetti's, Reed and Sedge Warblers, Whitethroat, Lesser Whitethroat, Bearded Tit.

August–November: Chance of storm-driven seabird (including auks, petrels). Water Rail and Jack Snipe from mid-October. Wader passage includes Ringed Plover, Sanderling (peaking in August); Knot, Oystercatcher in September. Small numbers of Little Ringed Plover (rare), Little Stint, Bar-tailed Godwit, Whimbrel, Turnstone mostly September; Greenshank or other 'freshwater' wader rare. Winter Dunlin, Curlew build up from October. Short-eared Owl from mid-October. Visible migrants include Grey Wagtail and hirundines (September), Chaffinch, Linnet and Meadow Pipit (October); Lapland or Snow Buntings possible October–November. Sometimes influx of Bearded Tits or Cetti's Warblers in November.

18 BREAN DOWN   OS Explorer 153

Habitat

Occupying a dominating position on the eastern shores of the Severn Estuary just south of Weston-super-Mare, Brean Down is an isolated peninsular of carboniferous limestone, c.1½ miles (2.4 km) long and reaching a height of 97 metres. The ridge and western end are covered by close-cropped grassland, but the slopes to north and south have extensive areas of hawthorn, bramble and bracken which provide shelter for migrants and breeding birds. Cliffs are restricted to the southern side, apart from the small quarries at either end. There are fine views all round over the mudflats of Weston Bay and Berrow Flats to north and south, and out towards Steep Holm and Flat Holm offshore. The Axe Estuary (see next site for more details) emerges on the north side from the flat grassland of Bleadon Level, past a small area of shingle and rocks just to the east of the Down. The whole area is owned by the NT and is heavily used by the general public at times. The grassland is noted for its limestone flora, in particular as one of the few sites for white rock rose, abundant on the southern slopes. The area is grazed in part by cattle and goats.

Species

Brean Down is mainly noted as a migration watch-point for passerines and seabirds. The Down itself is relatively quiet in winter although the resident Kestrels are joined by regular Peregrines, and the less frequent Merlin. Turnstones feed in small numbers on the rocks, but the wider range of waders using the Axe Estuary can be seen from the eastern end of the Down at high tide when they gather on the shingle and nearby grassland to roost. There is also a small gull roost in the same area. Sea-duck are uncommon in the Severn Estuary but a few Eider, almost invariably immature birds, occasionally appear offshore in winter. More usual, although mainly in hard-weather conditions, are Goldeneye and Goosander, plus the odd Red-breasted Merganser. Mallard, Teal and a few other dabbling duck occur regularly throughout the winter, plus Brent Geese in ones and twos, again at the Axe Estuary.

In early spring seabirds appear off the Down in larger numbers. Kittiwakes, up to 50 at a time, are regular from March to May, although gales may bring storm-driven birds during the winter. Common Gulls also move through at this time. Arctic Skuas, probably on their way overland via the Severn Estuary, occur in small numbers, joined very occasionally by Pomarines. Single Great Skuas are more regular throughout the summer, tending to peak slightly in August. More frequent watching from the point has shown there to be a marked up-river passage of Common and/or Arctic Terns in the spring, although very few occur in the autumn. Black Terns and a few Little Gulls are also regular spring migrants. There are no breeding seabirds although Fulmars are sometimes seen just off the point and large numbers of Herring and Lesser Black-backed Gulls move to and from their breeding colonies on Steep Holm throughout the year. A few Razorbills and Guillemots are seen offshore in spring but rarely stay long. Common Scoters fly past on their way north but few other ducks are seen moving through at this time.

The prominent position of the Down makes it attractive to spring passerine migrants, and among the earliest are the regular Ring Ousels, mostly just singles these days. Wheatears, Sand Martins and Chiffchaffs are followed by Tree Pipits and Yellow Wagtails, the latter two species mostly identified by their distinctive calls as they pass overhead, while a variety of other birds can be found in the cover of the brambles and bushes, up to a dozen singing Grasshopper Warblers at a time being among the more notable species. Sparrowhawks pass through in small numbers and there is always the chance of the occasional Red Kite and Marsh Harrier.

Breeding birds include several pairs of Stonechats plus both Rock and Meadow Pipits. The dubious origin of the occasional Red-legged Partridges seen here was underlined by the identification of at least one as a Chukar! Shelducks no longer breed but can be seen in moderate numbers on the nearby shores, particularly in the late summer. Mid-summer parties of up to 300 Manx Shearwaters, probably non-breeding sub-adults, occur offshore, particularly in unsettled windy weather, and up to 100 Gannets have occurred at this time of year. Cormorants moving to and from Steep Holm where they breed and roost are often seen.

As summer turns to early autumn, Willow Warblers, Whitethroats and other common migrants feed among the bushes, moving on again during the night on their next stage south. Later in the autumn the picture is dominated by diurnal migrants, when Chaffinches, Starlings, Meadow

Pipits and Skylarks can be seen passing overhead, generally to the south just after dawn. Accompanying them are smaller numbers of a whole variety of less common birds, including Bramblings, Siskins, Redpolls and Goldfinches, plus the odd Lapland and Snow Buntings. Rarities such as Richard's Pipit and Yellow-browed Warbler have also been seen in the autumn. Two recent additions to the Somerset list both came from here: a Pallas's Warbler in November 2000 was followed by a Sardinian Warbler in October 2001. Just to show what easily gets missed, searchers for the latter flushed a Corncrake, which then disappeared, never to be seen again! Winter thrushes also pass through and there is a return passage of Ring Ousels. Careful searching of the Goldcrest parties has turned up Firecrests on several occasions, and they are probably annual. Merlins, Peregrines and Sparrowhawks are all regular migrants, while Buzzards can occasionally be seen drifting south, and there have been reports of Hobby and Osprey. One or two Black Redstarts often stay through the winter, though frequenting the more sheltered rocky corners and generally being rather elusive. Another elusive species worth searching for, now that their Somerset breeding population is building up, is Dartford Warbler, which has a habit of dispersing to coastal locations for the winter, and which has been seen here more than once. Autumn gales can bring numbers of storm-driven seabirds, including Storm and Leach's Petrel, Grey Phalarope and Sabine's Gull, although large numbers are unusual this far up the Channel.

Timing

For waders at the Axe Estuary high-tide visits are essential, as birds quickly disperse to feed over a wide area. Brean Down is heavily used by the public in the summer holiday season so early morning visits are recommended at these times; in addition any migrants using the Down are most likely to be seen early on as they may disperse or fall quiet later in the day. Light southerlies with mist or rain around dawn are most likely to produce numbers of spring migrants. Visible migration in the autumn occurs for the first two to three hours after dawn, falling away to a trickle later. A reasonably strong headwind (between south and west) usually produces the most birds, as do overcast conditions. In bright sunny weather the birds are usually passing too high overhead to be identified. For storm-driven seabirds, southwesterly gales pushing the birds up the Channel bring the highest numbers, although the best watching may be just after the gales abate and the birds move back down-river again. In strong winds, small birds are almost impossible to see on the Down owing to the exposed conditions.

Access

Brean Down lies at the end of the coast road north from Berrow and Brean, the latter also being reachable via various rather tortuous lanes from the A370 between Weston-super-Mare and Brent Knoll. During the summer there are buses to here from Burnham-on-Sea and Weston. Park at the end just behind the seawall, unless the Tropical Bird Gardens and café at the foot of the Down are to be visited, in which case their car park can be used. Incidentally this collection is well worth a visit if only to identify the strange variety of calls which have been known to confuse the unwary birder. Access to the Down is unrestricted on foot, the approach being either to the left of the tearooms and on up a steep flight of steps or on along the road and via a more gentle slope a little to the

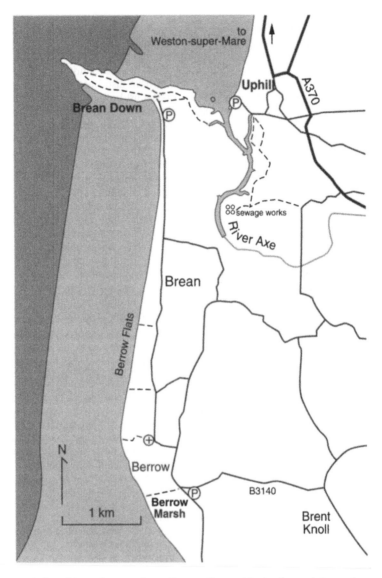

east. An old road runs along the northern side to the point, passing through the most extensive areas of cover. Another path runs along the main ridge and is probably the best route to take for early morning sightings of such species as Wheatears or Ring Ousels, before too many visitors are about. For seawatching, shelter can be gained from the old military emplacements at the western end, currently being restored, which also can be attractive to Black Redstarts. Note that seabirds are often well offshore, appearing to be nearer to Steep Holm than to Brean, although they also pass quite close.

Do not neglect the eastern end of the Down which gets less disturbance and has plenty of cover for migrants. The Pallas's Warbler in 2000, for instance, was seen in the trees on the slope by Brean Down Farm. This end of the Down also provides an excellent vantage point for scanning the birds gathered at the Axe Estuary, although a telescope is essential. For closer views follow the path along the foot of the Down past Brean Down Farm to the riverside seawall. The path continues by the River Axe but the foot-ferry to Uphill on the Weston-super-Mare side no longer operates.

Calendar

All year: Cormorant, Shelduck, Kestrel, Peregrine; Red-legged Partridge (scarce), Herring and Lesser Black-backed Gulls, Stock Dove, Little Owl, Stonechat.

December–February: Occasional diver or grebe to April. Maybe passing Brent Goose, Bewick's Swan. Mallard, Teal, sometimes Wigeon at Axe Estuary. Diving duck irregular (Eider, Red-breasted Merganser, Scaup). Oystercatcher, Redshank, Dunlin, Curlew, Turnstone at Axe Estuary. Kittiwake; Black Redstart, sometimes Dartford Warbler.

March–May: Fulmar and Manx Shearwater from late March. Shelduck. Chance of Common Scoter passing February–May. Maybe migrant raptor, e.g. Marsh Harrier (late April–May), Hen Harrier, Red Kite. Regular migrants include Common Gull (March–April); Common and Arctic Terns, Arctic Skua (April–May); Whimbrel (late April–May); Black Tern, maybe Pomarine Skua (late May–early June). Passerines include Ring Ousel, Wheatear mid-March–April, then Tree Pipit, Yellow Wagtail, common *Phylloscopus* and *Sylvia* warblers, Redstart, Whinchat, mid-April–mid-May; Grasshopper Warbler late April.

June–July: Fulmar; peak period for Manx Shearwater and Gannet; chance of Storm Petrel. Great Skua irregular April–September. Breeding Stonechat, Rock Pipit.

August–November: Chance of Storm or Leach's Petrel (September–October); Manx Shearwater, Fulmar rare after mid-September. Peregrine, Sparrowhawk, Merlin on passage (September–October). Wintering waders at Axe Estuary arrive from September. Light passage of common chats and warblers August–September; hirundine movements sometimes marked at same time. Visible migration late September–early November of common finches, pipits, Starling. Scarcer species, e.g. Lapland Bunting, Woodlark, Ring Ousel, mostly October. Firecrest (scarce); Black Redstart may winter from late October.

19 THE AXE ESTUARY   OS Explorer 153

Habitat
The River Axe winds its way through the flat grassland of Bleadon Level before emerging into the southern end of Weston Bay, cutting Brean

Down off from access from the north. Although it has always been an important site for waders, its interest has increased recently with the construction of a sewage treatment works nearby, and the designation of parts of the area as nature reserves. The limestone grassland at Uphill, the last section of the Mendip Hills before the coast, has an interesting flora including several orchid species, and is also important for butterflies. Areas of scrub and non-intensive farmland add to the interest of the surroundings. The seawall has been breached deliberately in places, as part of a 'managed retreat' scheme to expand the saltmarsh habitat, including several pools and small reedbeds. There is a small area of shingle and rocks just to the east of Brean Down, used by waders as a high-tide roost site.

Species

The Axe Estuary is primarily a site for watching wildfowl, waders and gulls from the autumn to spring, but with the habitat changes and increased protection is worth visiting throughout the year. The most numerous wintering waders are Dunlin, with over 1000 usually present, although they can be widely spread across Weston Bay at low tide. A few Redshank are present all year, with over 300 wintering. Around 100 each of Curlew and Oystercatcher make up the bulk of the rest, plus usually around 30 Ringed Plovers favouring the beach. Grey Plover and Knot rarely seem to appear here, much preferring the Steart mudflats. For several years there was a wintering flock of Black-tailed Godwits here, but this species seems to move from one site to another on the Severn Estuary every few years, so there are either over 100, or next to none. The grassland either side of the River Axe provides feeding grounds for over 1000 Lapwings, sometimes accompanied by a few Golden Plover. Both species move to the shore in cold weather or if disturbed.

The pools in and around the sewage works hold upwards of 50 Pochard, Tufted Ducks and Shoveler, and provide a refuge for the rather larger numbers of Wigeon, Teal and Mallard that tend to feed a bit more widely. Up to 500 Shelduck winter, mostly feeding out on the mudflats. It's always worth scanning the skies if the waders and wildfowl rise en masse, as the most usual reason will be a Peregrine somewhere overhead. Short-eared Owls have become rather more scarce along the Severn in recent years, but this is one of the better sites for them, with up to three hunting over the reeds and saltmarsh some winters. The same habitat conceals a few Snipe, Jack Snipe and Water Rails, never easy to see, of course. The rough ground attracts flocks of Linnets and Greenfinches, and one winter a few Twite were found, a species which seems to have deserted the Severn in recent years. Other scarce visitors at this time of year include the odd Water Pipit, maybe a few Brent Geese out on the mud, or diving ducks such as Scaup, Goldeneye or Goosander, especially after severe weather. A small gull roost contains mostly Black-headed and Herring Gulls but Mediterranean Gulls are increasingly reported, possibly feeding during the day on the Mendip Hills with Common Gulls.

Come the spring, and there is a trickle of migrant waders, including a few Whimbrel and Sanderling. Little Ringed Plover are regular at the sewage farm, and have bred here on more than one occasion. Little Grebes have also started to nest here, after a build-up in wintering numbers. Both Oystercatchers and Lapwings also attempt to breed, but the success rate is minimal because of disturbance and predation. The old quarries around Uphill provide crevices for Little Owl and Kestrel, while the nearby farmland still holds a few Grey Partridges. As at any coastal spot, anything might turn up on migration: Marsh Harrier, Avocet and even Spoonbill have been seen here in late spring and early summer. During the late summer, there is an influx of Little Egrets to the area, not yet into double figures but not far off, and nowadays birds can be seen here almost all year.

Early autumn sees a build-up of waders at the Axe Estuary, where small numbers of 'freshwater' species such as Greenshank, Common Sandpiper and Ruff are regular. A little later, in good years, a few Little Stints and Curlew Sandpipers appear for a time, and rarer visitors have included Wood Sandpiper and Grey Phalarope, the latter following gale-force winds. The odd Black Tern will stop to feed over the pools for a time, but the outstanding rarity to date was the American form of this species which turned up in October 2000, the first record for Britain. The differences from the European form are subtle, so it was fortunate that it stayed for several days, even more so if it is 'upgraded' to full species level at some time in the future. Other birds which have stopped to feed on the pools in autumn include Black-necked Grebe and Garganey, and no doubt the list will grow – the Axe Estuary has always been a focal point for migrants. Willow Warblers, Whitethroats and other common migrants feed among the bushes before the late autumn build-up of finches and pipits begins. Black Redstarts have appeared here in autumn and have wintered in the Weston area several times.

Timing

For waders at the Axe Estuary high-tide visits are the most productive, as birds quickly disperse to feed over a wide area. The paths through the nature reserves are popular with the public, especially dog-walkers, but tend to be quieter early in the day. Strong winds in the autumn may bring birds like Grey Phalarope to the shelter provided by Brean Down. Cold weather in winter may bring Goosander and other wildfowl to the coast.

Access

From Weston-super-Mare, follow signs south to Uphill village, and then towards the beach (see also map with previous site). One can park at the entrance to the boatyard on the left, or in Uphill Way a short way back from here. Alternatively drive on to the beach, or park in the road just before the sands, and scan the river mouth and Weston Bay from here. The main access is along public footpaths through the boatyard and past the quarries below Uphill church. Some of the paths are surfaced and suitable for wheelchairs. Check the cliffs for Little Owl and Kestrel, and the pool on the right for waterbirds. Part of this area is the Uphill Local Nature Reserve, with the Walborough reserve of the AWT immediately adjacent. The path continues through several bushy areas and past open grassland (explore this for flowers and butterflies), with good general views from the lower slopes of the hill. It then drops down to the farmland, with saltmarsh on the right. A hide overlooking the first wetland area is obvious, and there are several boards explaining the interest of the area and the main points of access along the route. Continuing along the main track, you pass more reed-fringed pools on the right, and open farmland to the left before emerging on the access road for Weston Sewage Treatment Works. (There is restricted access to this point by car for limited periods, for the disabled only, along this access road, which is reached via the A370 south of Weston. A notice near Way Acre Drove Nursery gives the details.) Turn right here, passing another hide overlooking the pools, to reach the sewage works. The site itself is private, but the first pools can be scanned from the public right of way that passes to the left of the entrance.

The mouth of the Axe can, of course, also be scanned from the eastern end of Brean Down (see previous site for details).

Calendar

All year: Cormorant; Little Egret (fewest in spring), Shelduck, Kestrel, Peregrine; Grey Partridge (scarce), Coot. Herring and Lesser Black-backed Gulls, Little Owl.

December–February: Brent Goose (erratic). Teal, Mallard, Wigeon, Shoveler, Pochard, Tufted Duck. Other diving duck irregular (Scaup, Goldeneye, Goosander). Oystercatcher, Redshank, Dunlin, Curlew, Snipe, Jack Snipe; Golden Plover sometimes in fields with Lapwings. Chance of Mediterranean Gull. Water Rail. Short-eared Owl. Water Pipit (scarce). Stonechat, maybe Black Redstart.

March–May: Maybe migrant raptor, e.g. Marsh Harrier (late April–May). Regular scarce migrants include Sanderling (May) and Whimbrel (late April–May). Wheatear mid-March–April.

June–July: Little Grebe sometimes breeds. Small numbers of Oystercatchers, Curlew and Redshanks summer. Little Ringed Plover, Yellow Wagtail may breed. Common passerines, e.g. Whitethroat breeding.

August–November: Little Egret numbers peak. Maybe Garganey or Pintail. Wintering waders arrive from September; trickle of passage birds (most September) including Ringed Plover, Ruff, Bar-tailed Godwit, Greenshank, Common and Green Sandpipers, a few Knot, Little Stint, Curlew Sandpiper. Maybe Wood Sandpiper or Grey Phalarope. Short-eared Owl on passage from October. Maybe passage Hobby (August–September) or Merlin (October–November).

20 STEEP HOLM & THE BRISTOL CHANNEL   OS Explorer 153

Habitat

The island of Steep Holm lies midway between the Welsh and English coasts, c.3½ miles (5.6 km) from Brean Down, the nearest point of land. Like the Mendip Hills, of which it is a continuation, it consists of Carboniferous limestone, and is surrounded by steep cliffs. The plateau top, 50 acres (20 ha) in area, is covered in a characteristic undergrowth of elder, privet and, in summer, mini-forests of alexanders up to 1½ metres high. Other plants include hemlock, henbane and wall pellitory, plus the famous, but rare, wild peony and wild leek. There are no trees apart from a few sycamores on part of the eastern slopes. Several of the more specialised herbal plants may have been introduced by thirteenth-century monks who used to occupy the island. More recent occupants have been the military who have left conspicuous and rather ugly fortifications over much of the island. It is now owned by the Kenneth Allsop Memorial Trust and managed as a nature reserve and ringing station.

Species

Breeding birds and passage migrants provide the main interest here, although very little watching has been carried out in winter when the island is virtually inaccessible. At this time large Starling roosts have sometimes formed and gulls also spend the night on the island. However, in early spring the gulls start to re-establish their territories, nesting widely on the plateau top. Herring Gulls are gradually rebuilding their numbers, having crashed to around 200 pairs in the early 1990s (there were 6000 plus in the 1970s). There are currently around 1000 pairs, having overtaken Lesser Black-backed Gulls at around 500 pairs. About 30 pairs of Great Black-backed Gull also breed, their numbers also increasing slowly. Another notable resident is the Cormorant with around 70 pairs nesting on the northern cliffs, birds regularly flighting back and fore to the mainland to feed. This is another species currently on the increase here. After several rather erratic attempts at breeding after a long absence during the 'pesticide era', Peregrines have nested successfully each year since 1999, and it is to be hoped that they are firmly re-established. Unfortunately, although still seen regularly, Ravens have once again ceased to nest here, probably due to the extinction of the local rabbit population and subsequent lack of food.

Among smaller birds, up to 30 pairs of Dunnocks have been the subject of long-running studies, and there are a few pairs of Rock Pipits, Blackbirds, Robins and Wrens which find enough sustenance to breed successfully. Shelduck and Mallard breed erratically, and Oystercatchers, the only wader recorded at all regularly, sometimes attempt to nest.

Spring passage is not spectacular, though the same mix of species as at nearby Brean Down can be expected, but in autumn large numbers of birds use the island as a staging post. Whinchats, Redstarts, Wheatears and all the common *Phylloscopus* and *Sylvia* warblers are regular, good numbers sometimes being grounded in misty conditions. Swallows, House Martins and a few Sand Martins pass in small groups, and Tree Pipits and Yellow Wagtails in ones and twos can be located by their calls as they fly over. A little later these are replaced by parties of Meadow Pipits, plus a few Skylarks, Grey and Pied Wagtails. October mornings see finch flocks passing the island, the predominant direct being from northwest to southeast from the Welsh coast to the Somerset side. Chaffinches, Greenfinches, Linnets and Goldfinches predominate, with smaller numbers of Redpolls, Siskins, Yellowhammers and Reed Buntings. Inevitably among the more regular species, rarer ones turn up from time to time, raptors such as Sparrowhawk and Kestrel being annual, while birds like Wryneck and Richard's Pipit are more in the way of vagrants. Large numbers of Goldcrests with sometimes a few Coal Tits are a notable feature of late autumn passage, and with these have appeared several Firecrests, which once was once something of a Steep Holm speciality, but is increasingly recorded elsewhere on passage.

As far as seabirds are concerned, little watching has been carried out from the island itself but rather more has been noted from boats plying between Weston-super-Mare, Ilfracombe and Lundy, particularly in summer and early autumn, although naturally more birds are seen the further out one goes. Fulmars and Manx Shearwaters are the most usual species but Gannets also occur regularly in the upper Bristol Channel, with Storm Petrel, Great Skua and Common Scoter rather more occasional. Kittiwakes, Guillemots and Razorbills tend to be seen most often in the spring. In gale conditions any of these birds could well be seen nearer the island.

Timing

Not critical for breeding birds, although strong winds may make access to (and from!) the island impossible. Grounded migrants are usually seen in highest numbers on misty mornings after a night that started clear with light winds. Clear still mornings in October produce the best conditions for large numbers of diurnal migrants, with a southerly or easterly headwind tending to bring flocks lower.

Access

Most visitors arrive by boat from Weston-super-Mare (Knightstone Harbour). There are usually between two and five sailings per month from April to October. Departure time varies between 8.45 and 11.00 am, and day-trippers are usually brought off between 6.15 and 8.30 pm. However, all intending visitors must contact the Kenneth Allsop Trust in advance for full up-to-date details as changes to boat times (and cancellations) are frequent. Be prepared to bring waterproof clothing and footwear on all visits, particularly in case bad weather should spring up during the day. There is no landing jetty, and the terrain on the island is fairly rough.

Pleasure boat trips to Lundy and around the upper Channel are arranged on a regular basis throughout the summer, and provide a chance of looking for any seabirds in the area. Full details of sailings are available from Waverley Excursions Ltd, Gwalia Buildings, Barry Docks CF6 6XB (http://www.waverleyexcursions.co.uk), and timetables are displayed in the main coastal resorts.

Calendar

All year: Cormorant, Peregrine, Pheasant. Herring, Lesser Black-backed and Great Black-backed Gulls, Rock Pipit, Wren, Dunnock, Robin, Blackbird, Song Thrush, Magpie, Raven.

December–February: Sometimes roosting gulls and Starlings (latter less frequent since the Peregrines returned).

March–May: Maybe Fulmar, Kittiwake, Guillemot, Razorbill offshore (especially May). Breeding gulls very active. Migrants (especially April) include Tree Pipit, common *Phylloscopus* and *Sylvia* warblers, Redstart, Whinchat.

June–July: Best time for Fulmar, Manx Shearwater offshore. Shelduck and Oystercatcher sometimes breed.

August–November: Maybe Gannet offshore in August. Kestrel, Merlin, Sparrowhawk (especially September–October). Gulls start deserting the island in August. Tree Pipit, Yellow Wagtail, Willow Warbler, Blackcap, Garden Warbler, Whitethroat, Lesser Whitethroat mostly August–early September; hirundines, Whinchat, Redstart, Chiffchaff to early October; Goldcrest, Coal Tit late August–October, plus chance of Firecrest September–October. Skylark, Meadow Pipit, common finches and buntings peak October.

21 CHEDDAR RESERVOIR OS Explorer 141

Habitat

Lying at the foot of the Mendip Hills, Cheddar Reservoir is an almost circular concrete-banked bowl of water, raised above the surrounding levels, and fed mainly by water pumped up from the River Axe to the south. The steep escarpment of the hills provides a barrier to birds moving north and a leading line for those moving east–west, while to the south and west the mostly flat damp grazing land stretches clear to the Bristol Channel. There is next to no marginal vegetation, but if the water levels do drop, a muddy shoreline and low gravelly islands become exposed. The steep grass-covered banks overlook some old clay pits to the south where there is a small group of willow and reed-fringed pools. The nearby levels are mainly well-drained but some fields to the southeast have coarser grass and occasionally flood in winter. The lake is stocked with coarse fish, particularly pike, and there is an active sailing club.

Species

Diving ducks find Cheddar Reservoir particularly attractive and of the local reservoirs, it is the one where divers, sea-duck and the rarer grebes are most likely to appear. The most numerous species in winter is the Coot, over 2000 birds being regularly present, with Pochard numbers in midwinter reaching the 400 mark in mixed flocks with up to 100 Tufted Ducks. Two other diving duck are also well represented with up to 50 each of Goldeneye and Goosander to be seen here. Both species, however, often disperse during the day to feed on rhynes and small pools scattered over the levels to the south, returning to the reservoir at dusk to roost. Among dabbling ducks, Mallard and Teal are the most regular, but midwinter numbers are rarely far into three figures although large numbers can occur in the autumn, particularly if the water level is low. Gadwall, Wigeon and Shoveler prefer the same conditions but small numbers of all three will stay on even when the waters rise. However, it is the rarer diving birds that tempt most watchers. Of the divers, Great Northern is the most regular, virtually annual in recent years and often staying for long periods. There have been a few multiple occurrences, four birds one year, sometimes giving their evocative calls, normally not heard in winter. Black-throated are much less frequent, but again have stayed for several weeks at a time. Red-throated occur mostly after severe storms and normally succumb unless they have the strength to move off

John Govett

Slavonian Grebe

to sea again. Long-tailed Ducks are almost annual, usually the duller immatures and they too can be long-stayers, and Scaup turn up rather unpredicably most winters. Common Scoter can appear at almost any time of year, but are transient birds not normally staying very long. Of the rarer grebes Black-necked on spring or autumn passage are the most frequently recorded, whereas visits by Slavonian in winter have recently become more erratic. Red-necked are rare and normally only appear after cold weather and easterly winds, but are by no means unknown. Ruddy Ducks, although numerous at Chew and Blagdon on the other side of Mendip, require those waters to be frozen before being driven to Cheddar in any numbers. Similarly Smew tend only to turn up here if the weather is cold. Rarities have included Blue-winged Teal and Ring-necked Duck. Bewick's Swans drop in from time to time as they move from one feeding area to another, and small numbers have been known to roost here if feeding on the nearby levels during the day.

There is a small winter gull roost, dominated by Black-headeds, 3000 being the usual maximum, accompanied by smaller numbers of Common, Herring and Lesser Black-backed Gulls. Some birds stay, while others drop in for a preen and a bathe before moving on towards the coast. The increased interest in this group has lead to the discovery of Mediterranean and Yellow-legged Gulls on several occasions, plus Ring-billed and Iceland Gulls as true rarities. A Franklin's Gull in March 2000 had been seen earlier in the winter in Dorset and was subsequently seen near Bristol, providing a rare opportunity to track the movements of a bird presumably on spring migration, even if it was on the wrong side of the Atlantic!

With the coming of spring, most water birds move away, and the concrete banks are normally only attractive to up to 40 or so Common Sandpipers among passage waders, species such as Ringed and Little Ringed Plover, Sanderling and Dunlin rarely stopping for more than a morning. Terns are more regular, particularly Common and the increasingly identified Arctic, with some Blacks later. Little Gulls can also be expected, occasionally several together, while spring gales sometimes drive passage Kittiwakes this far inland. Hirundines and Swifts gather in large numbers on both spring and autumn migration, and the wagtails feeding around the reservoir margins include Iceland-bound Whites in parties of up to 20.

After a quiet summer, the quality of the autumn wader passage depends heavily on the water level, but in recent years, even with the mud exposed, numbers have been much lower than in the past, a feature shared with other reservoirs in the region. Dunlin, Ringed and Little Ringed Plover, Greenshank and Common Sandpiper are the most frequently noted, with Little Stint, Curlew Sandpiper and Ruff more likely if the water level does fall. The strategic position of the reservoir makes it particularly susceptible as a landfall for birds from the west, and past American rarities have included Pectoral, Buff-breasted and White-rumped Sandpipers.

Low water levels attract larger numbers of dabbling ducks than normal and the Teal are worth scanning carefully for small numbers of Garganey under such conditions. A bizarre and continuing speciality of Cheddar is the Red-crested Pochard, with odd birds still turning up in the autumn, though not quite as frequently as in the past; whether they are wild or feral remains a mystery. Irrespective of the water level, Black, Common and Arctic Terns can be seen dipping low after insects, with Little Gulls once again also regular. Rarer visitors such as White-winged Black Terns sometimes appear at this time also. Westerly gales have produced storm-driven Grey Phalaropes on many occasions with a good chance of Storm or Leach's Petrel, Kittiwakes, a Gannet or other seabird under the same conditions, although these normally move off again fairly quickly. A growth of weeds on uncovered banks may attract flocks of Linnets and other finches and buntings. Rock Pipits stop briefly on passage, while single Water Pipits often remain around the reservoir margins all winter.

Timing

The major factor here is disturbance from sailing activities, as both boats and windsurfers use the whole area, prompting the majority of the ducks to leave the reservoir and head temporarily for Blagdon Lake, though they are usually back again by the next morning. Large numbers of boats are normally active on weekend afternoons, sailing mostly getting under way in late morning, so visits should be timed accordingly, and a certain amount of weekday sailing also takes place. It is unusual for all the water birds to leave, so the 'thinning out' by the boats sometimes makes spotting the rarer visitor slightly easier, though use of this policy has obvious risks! The lower the water level, the more waders are likely to be present; in addition, once mud starts becoming exposed, sailing activities are very much curtailed. Anglers, although present all year, are mostly stationary and cause little disturbance to the birds. Those looking for storm-driven seabirds should arrive as soon as possible after (or even during) the gale as most species move off as soon as the winds abate. Phalaropes and waders usually stay a little longer.

Access

Cheddar Reservoir has two main entrances, starting from the adjoining villages of Cheddar and Axbridge respectively. For the northern, Axbridge, entrance, take the eastern approach to that village from the A371 by-pass road, and within 200 metres take a gated road (also a public footpath) to the left, signposted to the Corinthian yacht club. At the far end there is a small car park just to the right of the entrance gate. Public access is

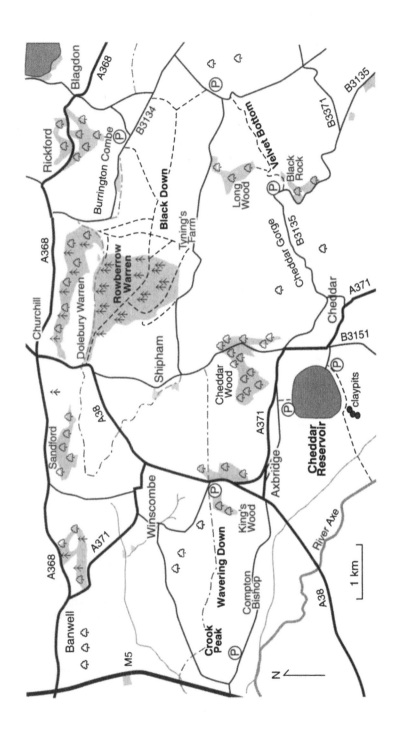

permitted to the reservoir perimeter track, subject to restrictions indicated on information boards at the entrance. Climb over the stile (access by car is for sailors only) and walk in either direction round the perimeter track from which the whole water surface is visible. The eastern half is normally the most favoured by waterfowl, and it is here that mud is normally most exposed under low water conditions, so a clockwise route is usually favoured. Passing the sailing clubhouse and boatpark brings you to a pumping tower, and the second access road and car park. This is reached from the A371 west of Cheddar by taking the B3151 signposted to Wedmore and, almost immediately, beyond the bridge over the now dismantled railway line, turning right along Sharpham Road, taking the middle of a three-way fork in 300 metres to the car park. It is worth walking round the whole perimeter as, especially in windy conditions, birds can be easy to miss near the concrete margins if the reservoir is merely scanned through a telescope.

Cheddar claypits are privately owned and there is no unauthorised access, although the public footpath that starts along the left-hand of the forks at the 'Cheddar' entrance passes quite close. Generally only twos and threes of the commoner ducks are found here, but warblers are attracted during migration times, and small numbers of Sedge and Reed Warblers breed. The levels nearby are well-drained and rather barren, but Stoke Moor, to the east of a minor road from Draycott to Wedmore, is a bit rougher than most and sometimes attracts wintering plovers and thrushes in some numbers.

Calendar

All year: Great Crested Grebe, Cormorant, Coot, Green Woodpecker, Grey Wagtail.

December–February: Maybe diver or rare grebe. Wigeon, Gadwall, Teal, Shoveler, Pochard, Tufted Duck, Goldeneye, maybe Scaup, Long-tailed Duck or other 'sea-duck'. Other diving and dabbling ducks in small numbers plus occasional rarity. Gull roost may include Mediterranean, Ring-billed or Yellow-legged Gull. Occasional Peregrine. Water Pipit. Winter thrushes nearby.

March–May: Wildfowl mostly leave during March. Common Sandpiper mid-April–mid-May; occasional Ringed and Little Ringed Plover, Sanderling or other wader April–May. Common, Arctic and Black Terns late April–May; Little Gull, maybe Kittiwake April. Hirundines and Swifts in large numbers from late April. White Wagtail, Wheatear in April–early May.

June–July: Small numbers of Coot, Great Crested Grebe. Breeding Sedge and Reed Warblers (clay pits). Start of wader passage mid-July. Common Scoter sometimes appear in July.

August–November: Maybe Black-necked Grebe. Seabirds after gales, especially petrels, Kittiwake, Grey Phalarope. Garganey and Red-crested Pochard (August–September), maybe rarer duck, e.g. Ring-necked into winter. Winter wildfowl start to return, mostly from mid-October. Possible Osprey (August–September). Wader and tern passage August–October including Ringed and Little Ringed Plover, Greenshank, Green Sandpiper, maybe Wood Sandpiper, peaking in August; Curlew Sandpiper, Little Stint and American rarities more frequent in September. Most waders leave by mid-October when water level usually high. Little Gull and Black, Common and Arctic Terns peak September. Rock Pipit in October, Water Pipit from late October.

22 THE MENDIP HILLS   OS Explorer 141 and 153

Habitat

Running roughly east–west along the border between Somerset and what was Avon, south of Bristol, the Mendip Hills are flat-topped and plateau-like in form, mainly of Carboniferous limestone, and reach a maximum height of 325 metres at Black Down. Towards their western end they are steep-sided both north and south, although at the east they widen and become less distinct from the lower ground either side. The main areas of ornithological interest lie west of the Bristol to Shepton Mallet road (A37). The broad open hillsides of Crook Peak and Wavering Down are typical of the limestone grassland found mainly along the top of the southern slopes. Limestone cliffs outcrop in various quarries, some of which, particularly the one at Batts Combe, are still very much active while the spectacular natural cliffs around Cheddar have an interesting flora, including the rare Cheddar pink. The upper ends of the gorges contain dry valleys ('bottoms') with mixed scrub and grassland. Deciduous woodland is most extensive on the steep northern and southern slopes: interesting examples occur at Cheddar Wood and Stoke Woods while on the plateau itself there are large Forestry Commission conifer plantations, notably at Stock Hill and Rowberrow. Damp heather-dominated heathland is restricted to a small number of patches where old red sandstone outcrops, as at Black Down. Pools formed after eighteenth-century lead mines were abandoned occur at Charterhouse and Priddy but standing water is otherwise rare, and many streams disappear underground via swallets, to emerge again at the foot of the hills, as at, for example, the cave system at Wookey Hole. The limestone grassland holds a rich flora which in turn attracts a wide range of butterflies, for instance, marbled white and chalkhill blue. Adders are common in the same habitat, and both roe deer and badgers are widespread.

Species

During the winter birds are very patchily distributed on Mendip, as many even so-called 'resident' species move off the plateau and out of the woodlands to lower ground. Conspicuous in the grassland areas are flocks of up to 2000 Common Gulls: other species are rarer, but flocks are worth scanning for the odd Mediterranean Gull which has been seen on several occasions. Carrion Crows and Magpies are widespread and Ravens are now a frequent sight, with several pairs breeding in the area. Siskins and Redpolls occur in the conifer plantations, as do Crossbills on an irregular basis, and it is possible that the latter have bred when one of

Stonechat

their periodic invasions has boosted the population. A former speciality of the conifers was the Willow Tit, but there have been no sightings at all in recent years. Short-eared Owls, invariably singly, are seen from time to time quartering the heathy areas, where, despite the exposed position, Stonechats attempt to stay resident. Water Rails, Snipe and a few elusive Jack Snipe are attracted to the marshy pools of the old lead-mining areas.

Spring tends to come relatively late to Mendip, with winter thrushes lingering to overlap with the occasional migrant Ring Ousel in the early spring. With so many species declining it is good to be able to report a welcome recent arrival in the form of the Dartford Warbler. A small population has built up in places where heather and gorse are dominant, perhaps as many as 20 pairs, although it is a difficult species to census accurately. They seem to be mostly resident, though easiest to see in early spring when establishing breeding territories. The bracken-covered slopes of the upper Cheddar Gorge system hold a currently healthy population of Redstarts although this species has declined drastically on the nearby Somerset Levels. Pied Flycatchers are regular spring migrants through the woodland, and one or two pairs have bred recently. So far, however, they have not become firmly established, despite the provision of good numbers of nestboxes in selected woods. Tree Pipits, Whitethroats, Willow Warblers and other summer birds soon follow, being particularly attracted to the bushier middle slopes. The damper heathery areas around Black Down hold several pairs of Stonechats, Meadow Pipits are common, Whinchats breed irregularly in the bracken, and a few pairs of Grasshopper Warblers can be heard giving their reeling songs, especially on warm mornings or evenings. Curiously, one or two Reed Buntings are resident in the same habitat. More typically they occur around Priddy Pools, where the reeds attract a small population of Reed and Sedge Warblers, and there are more Stonechats and Tree Pipits. Water Rails have been heard here in the summer and may well breed. Little Grebes certainly have been proved to raise young on several occasions. Displaying Curlew in the spring have raised hopes that they too may nest in less disturbed areas up on the high ground, and breeding has been proved at least once.

Sparrowhawks are well distributed, and Buzzards a frequent sight. Both species can easily be seen in spring displaying over their breeding sites in the scattered woods along the escarpments, but they are also widespread on the plateau. Feeding Hobbies are attracted by the dragonflies of the pools, and later by the hirundines of the same habitat. The limestone cliffs, both natural and man-made, support large numbers of Jackdaws, with Kestrels, Stock Doves and, more recently, Peregrines, favouring the same habitat. Winter storms have wreaked havoc with some of the conifer plantations, opening up some huge clearings. Their appearance has prompted the welcome return of a few pairs of Nightjars after several years' absence. The conifer plantations also shelter a pair or two of Long-eared Owls, not a common species in the southwest. The arable farmland is generally of less interest at most times but during the summer a few Quail can be heard in the cereal fields around Priddy Hill Farm in good years. Sadly, the Corn Buntings of the plateau and the Cirl Buntings of the lower slopes are now a thing of the past.

In late summer large numbers of tits, warblers and Chaffinches move in mixed parties around the bushier areas of the middle slopes but migration of small birds is mainly marked by a gradual diminution in numbers before the quieter winter picture returns.

Timing

For most of the woodland and heathland breeding species, morning visits are best, as birds tend to be more active and vocal then. However, in some of the deeper valleys and gorges actual dawn choruses can be a little disappointing as the sunrise can be artificially late. Tourist pressure in the Cheddar Gorge and Burrington areas is heavy on fine summer afternoons. For Grasshopper Warblers evening visits usually find the birds most vocal, and Nightjars are also active at dusk. In the winter timing is less important as far as most species are concerned although any Short-eared Owls present are more likely to be seen after mid-day. Migrant species (e.g. Wheatear, Whinchat, Ring Ousel) are best looked for in the mornings before they are disturbed by walkers. The weather on the plateau will often be considerably worse than that on the nearby lower ground and in wet or windy conditions the exposed nature of much of the habitat makes viewing extremely difficult.

Access

The A371/A368 Weston-super-Mare to Bath road runs along foot of the northern escarpment while minor roads from Weston through Bleadon and Loxton to Axbridge then the A371 to Wells provides the main access route from the south (see also map with previous site). Taking the Mendips from west to east, the main areas of birdwatching interest are as follows.

Crook Peak and Wavering Down form one of the largest areas of limestone grassland, and the tops attract migrant Wheatears at both seasons. From time to time they use the stone walls as nesting sites. The bushes and bracken on the upper slopes are worth checking for Ring Ousels in spring, although their occurrences have been rather erratic of late. Stonechats breed on the southern slopes, and there are several pairs of Dartford Warblers in this area. Access at the western end is by footpaths up from Rackley (where there is a small roadside car park) or Compton Bishop village. The woods at the foot of the slope here hold a few pairs of Nightingales. At the eastern end there is an area for parking in Winscombe Hill, just off the A38. A footpath from here leads up through King's Wood and then over the highest ground, eventually bringing you to Crook Peak, with fine views north and south. A detour to the south through more of King's Wood and up over Cross Plain covers a wider range of habitats.

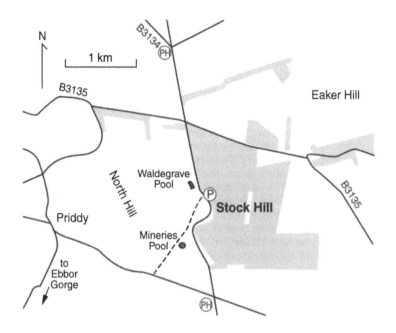

Cheddar Wood (SWT) and the nearby quarries are of restricted access but can be scanned from the Shipham road. The Cheddar Gorge cliffs are most peacefully viewed from the footpath along the top of the southern side, though roadside laybys in gorge itself can be used by those who do not mind the traffic.

For woodland and scrubland species the best area is formed by the Long Wood/Velvet Bottom/Charterhouse series of reserves in the upper reaches of Cheddar Gorge, mainly managed by the SWT. There is limited parking by the road towards the upper end of Cheddar Gorge, then public access on foot (nature trails indicated on board near the road). Alternatively continue to the B3371/B3135 junction, fork left and then left again at the King Down Farm crossroads. In c.1 mile (1.6 km) the road dips to cross Velvet Bottom with footpaths east to Blackmoor pools (small car park here just east of Charterhouse church) or west towards Cheddar Gorge and Long Wood. Tree Pipit, Redstart, Yellowhammer and Whitethroat all occur in this area.

The highest point around Black Down is reached by various paths up from Burrington Combe (B3134). Park at the bottom near the garden centre, opposite which a road, then path, runs up the west side of the combe past Mendip Lodge Wood where Wood Warblers have been heard in summer. Alternatively park near the top of the combe and walk up onto the north slopes where Tree Pipit, Grasshopper Warbler, Reed Bunting and sometimes Whinchat can be found. The extensive heather on the tops is another area for Dartford Warbler, plus several pairs of Whitethroats and Meadow Pipits. Redpolls, Siskins and Crossbills can be looked for in the Rowberrow plantations to the west, and Nightjars have been heard on the fringes of them.

The old Bristol road from Wells northwards passes the Stock Hill plantations east of Priddy, where there is a car park and picnic site, closed at night, just off the road north of the Hunter's Lodge Inn. The grassland to the west holds Stonechat and Tree Pipit, while Little Grebe and Reed Warbler breed at the pools with Jack Snipe and Water Rails wintering. The conifers attract Crossbills, Redpolls and Siskins in winter, and Buzzards and Sparrowhawks throughout the year. At dusk on summer evenings, this is the best place to listen for churring Nightjars, several pairs breeding in the extensive clearings, and at the same time you may see a hunting Long-eared or Barn Owl over the adjacent grassland, as these nocturnal birds emerge rather earlier when they have young to feed. Access in this area is fairly general along the paths.

Other areas are less productive, but worth mentioning in passing. Buzzards can be seen over Bleadon Hill, near Weston-super-Mare, from the Bleadon to Loxton road on the southern side, but in general this section is too well cultivated to attract a wide variety of species. The arable fields and rough ground between Charterhouse and Priddy hold open-country species and sometimes a few pairs of Quail, but the firing range means that observations have to be made mainly from the roadsides. Ebbor Gorge, between Priddy and Wells, holds the commoner woodland species in dramatic surroundings, with well-marked trails starting from the car park by the minor road from Priddy to Wookey. Dippers can sometimes be seen immediately downstream from where the River Axe emerges from Wookey Hole. East of the A39, Emborough Pool can produce a few winter duck and sometimes a pair of Great Crested Grebes will breed, while the farmland to the west holds a few Golden Plover in winter. East again, there are a series of small woods where the commoner species can be found but access is less straightforward here, partially because of quarrying activities in the area.

Calendar

All year: Sparrowhawk, Buzzard, Kestrel, Peregrine, Stock Dove. Long-eared Owl (scarce), Barn Owl, Tawny Owl, Skylark, Meadow Pipit, Grey Wagtail; Dipper (Wookey Hole). Stonechat, Dartford Warbler, Nuthatch, Jackdaw, Raven, Reed Bunting.

December–February: Maybe Hen Harrier or Short-eared Owl (to April). Golden Plover (scarce), Woodcock. Common Gull flocks may hold Mediterranean Gull. Fieldfare, Redwing. Crossbill some years; Siskin, Redpoll.

March–May: Little Grebe sometimes breed. Hobby irregular May–September. Water Rail has bred. Occasional Curlew displaying. Migrant Common Gulls peak March. Redwing and Fieldfare to late April. Arrival of summer breeders: Cuckoo, Tree Pipit, Redstart, Chiffchaff from mid-April; Nightingale, Whinchat, Grasshopper Warbler late April; Nightjar, Whitethroat, Wood Warbler early May. Passage Wheatear from mid-March (rare breeder), Ring Ousel March–April, Pied Flycatcher April–May. Yellowhammers return to high ground April.

June–July: Breeding species include Quail (irregular) and Nightjar. Maybe Crossbill irruption.

August–November: Most summer visitors gone by end August; passage Whinchat, Wheatear, Chiffchaff, maybe Hobby to end September. Winter thrushes from late October. Finch flocks near farms and under beeches.

23 ORCHARDLEIGH PARK & LAKE

OS Explorer 142

Habitat and species

This private park lies just north of Frome, and its ornamental lake fringed by deciduous woodland provides the main ornithological interest. Black-necked Grebes bred here in 1932, and nowadays both Little and Great Crested do so regularly. In winter, parties of Tufted Duck (which have bred) and Pochard are a regular feature, while Gadwall, Shoveler, Teal, Wigeon, Garganey, Goosander and, more recently, Ruddy Ducks, have been recorded in small numbers. Grey Wagtails and Kingfishers are frequent visitors, while the mature trees of the surrounding parkland hold Nuthatches, woodpeckers and other woodland species, and Buzzards nest in the neighbourhood.

Access

A minor road from Oldford, on the B3090 north of Frome, leads to Lullington, and public footpaths from this lane or from the village lead through the grounds of Orchardleigh Park. The lake (at ST 780510) can be surveyed from the dam at the eastern end as well as from the path along its southern shore.

24 CHEW VALLEY LAKE

OS Explorer 141 and 154 or 155

Habitat

Completed in 1956, Chew Valley Lake covers an area of 1200 acres (486 ha), and is roughly 2½ miles (4 km) long by 1½ miles (2.4 km) wide. Apart from the dam at the northern end and a couple of road causeways, the rest of the 8 mile (12.8 km) perimeter is naturally vegetated: open or rough grass in many places, with *phragmites* steadily encroaching from the large reedbeds at the southern end. There are several plantations dotted around the shore, the conifers dating from the reservoir's flooding gradually being thinned and replaced with native species, whilst the small island in the northeast part of the lake is well covered with mature deciduous trees. Two bays on the western side and Herriott's Pool cut off by the road causeway at the southern end provide more sheltered conditions. The surrounding countryside is rolling mixed farmland and the shallowness of the lake together with the fertile soil has provided a rich food source, sometimes too rich in hot years when eutrophic conditions can lead to 'algal bloom'.

Being only c.8 miles (12.8 km) south of Bristol, the lake comes under pressure as a source of recreation. There is an outstanding brown and rainbow trout fishery, and a thriving sailing club, as well as two public picnic sites and a nature trail. The south end is maintained as a nature reserve, and is the centre of activities of the Chew Valley Ringing Station. There are at present six birdwatching hides strategically placed around the shore.

Species

This is by far the area's most important reservoir for birds and holds nationally significant numbers of some wildfowl; interest is by no means restricted to ducks as a wide range of other species (current total c.270) use the lake at all times of the year. On a winter's visit, however, it is the large numbers of wildfowl which catch the eye first, although peak numbers of several species in fact occur in late summer and autumn. Among the surface-feeders, Mallard and Teal each at around 800 are the most numerous (the figures given are recent winter averages – twice as many may be present on peak occasions). Up to 600 Shoveler occur in the autumn, with smaller numbers through the winter, and Gadwall generally average around 200. Wigeon numbers have steadily declined here in recent years, probably owing to habitat changes and increased disturbance, with only occasional counts over 100. Pintail numbers rarely exceed 20, but they do occur annually, particularly in the early part of the winter. Of diving species, Pochard and Tufted Ducks are the most numerous, at around 500 each, although numbers of the latter are higher in spring and during the autumn moult. Pre-migration spring gatherings of Goldeneye can be impressive, sometimes topping 200, with around 70 or so occurring during the rest of the winter. Among the sawbills, Goosander have declined recently, with rarely more than 20 present whereas there were over 100 in the early 1990s. A decline in the numbers of coarse fish in the lake is thought to be the main cause. Smew, however, continue to be annual visitors, though usually in single figures, with 'red-heads' predominant. Red-breasted Mergansers turn up in ones and twos most years. A speciality of Chew is the introduced, and these days controversial, Ruddy Duck from North America, with currently several hundred spending the winter here, these birds mostly breeding in the North Midlands. Another introduced species doing well is the Canada Goose with recent counts exceeding 800. Feral Greylag and Barnacle Geese associate with them, numbers of all these geese peaking during the late summer moult. Other wild geese are nowadays much rarer, Brent Geese probably being the most likely 'vagrants'. Far more likely to be seen is one of the wide range of exotic escapes which have included Swan Goose,

Ruddy Duck

Australian Wood Duck, Black Swan and Chilöe Wigeon: the large expanse of water and the presence of other birds seem to attract them. Over the years other fugitives have ranged from the huge Pink-backed Pelican to the minute Red Avadavat. Truly wild visitors, however, also occur regularly, including Long-tailed Duck in winter and Common Scoter on passage, as well as vagrants such as Green-winged Teal and Ring-necked Duck, both of which have occurred several times. The formerly regular autumn appearances of Bewick's Swans have become increasingly infrequent and brief, possibly due to poor feeding conditions here.

The other group dominating the scene in winter is the gulls, roosting numbers of which have increased spectacularly in recent years: the most recent midwinter census showed 36,000 Black-headeds, 18,500 Commons, 3200 Lesser Black-backed and 700 Herring Gulls making up the bulk of the roost. Spice for patient watchers is provided by the rarities among the commoner species. Mediterranean Gulls are regular with up to four or five seen on some days, the white-winged adults being easier to identify than the more Common Gull-like first-years. Yellow-legged Gulls have also been proved to be regular visitors, with up to 30 in late summer and smaller numbers throughout the winter. Ring-billed Gulls in ones and twos are seen in most years and one individual spent several whole winters at the lake. Iceland and Glaucous Gulls are both extremely rare visitors to Chew, usually only appearing in 'invasion' years.

Numbers of wintering Cormorants can reach over 250 with smaller numbers throughout the year. Perhaps because of a series of milder winters, sightings of divers have become more sporadic recently; in some years a Great Northern will stay all winter, unlike the rarer Red- and Black-throated which usually succumb or move on. Slavonian Grebes are no longer annual, usually appearing in winter, but Black-necked have increased, especially on passage, and have bred once. Red-necked usually only appear if driven west by cold weather on the Continent but then may stay until spring, sometimes attaining breeding plumage. Around 100 Great Crested Grebes, although sometimes far less, winter at the lake, but most Little Grebes move to smaller waters at this time. Bitterns are almost annual if elusive visitors to the reedbeds, this habitat also providing shelter for up to a dozen wintering Chiffchaffs, several Water Rails and the occasional party of Bearded Tits. The explosive song of Cetti's Warblers can be heard throughout the year, a series of mild winters having allowed their numbers to build up significantly. The concept of 'pairs' is not really appropriate to this polygamous species, but a dozen males have been heard, and over 20 young have been trapped in some years.

Before the winter birds have moved away, Great Crested Grebes start their head-shaking displays all around the lake and the reeds resound to the trilling duets of Little Grebes. Up to 80 pairs of the former and 20 pairs of the latter breed, although numbers and success rates fluctuate wildly with the water levels. Goldeneye and Tufted Duck numbers peak in early spring as birds congregate prior to moving north. The first summer visitors are normally the Sand Martins, with Garganey also appearing early: rarely a pair will stay to breed. Soon Chiffchaffs, Willow Warblers and Swallows are everywhere, finding rich feeding around the lake margins, with Sedge and Reed Warblers arriving a little later; the breeding population of the latter is in excess of 600 pairs. In most years a Marsh Harrier is seen for a day or two over the reeds, but spring visits by Ospreys are generally fleeting. Overshooting vagrants such as Purple Heron and Great Reed Warbler have occurred at this time. Water levels are generally high, so wader passage is usually limited, although Common Sandpipers and Sanderlings find food even on the concrete causeways and Ruff sometimes also appear briefly. Common, Arctic and Black Terns pass through regularly, hawking for insects over the middle of the lake, sometimes accompanied by one or two Little Gulls.

Among ducks, Mallard (around 30 pairs) and Tufted Ducks (up to 25 pairs), are the most numerous breeding species, with small numbers of Gadwall, Pochard and Ruddy Duck also producing young most years. Coots (up to 100 pairs), Mute Swans (up to 10 pairs) and one or two pairs of Shelduck are the other main breeding waterfowl. Grey Herons are a typical sight at all times of the year, and over 40 pairs now nest on Denny Island. Buzzards are frequently to be seen soaring over the nearby hillsides, while among smaller birds the thriving Reed Warbler colony attracts several parasitic Cuckoos. In midsummer, moult gatherings of several species occur: Canada Geese, including local breeders, reach over 800, Mute Swans up to 100, while Great Crested Grebes peak at around 500 a little later. For several years up to four Ruddy Shelducks have appeared in late summer, though their origin is a source of dispute. Also at this time the now expected influx of Little Egrets occurs, nine being the current maximum, with numbers declining through the winter and into the spring. They are very mobile and, considering their size and plumage, can sometimes be difficult to locate. They must be high on the list of potential breeding species for the lake.

The late summer and autumn water level is a critical factor in determining the size and quality of the wader passage, and in recent years the water company's policy has been to keep the lake relatively full. Hence, although the range of species is still quite wide, numbers are generally a mere fraction of what they were a decade or so ago, and few species, apart from Lapwing, get into double figures these days. A thin band of shoreline does not worry the Common and Green Sandpipers, so these can be reliably encountered throughout the autumn. Given more exposed mud, species occurring annually include Dunlin, Ringed and Little Ringed Plovers, Greenshank, Ruff and Black-tailed Godwit, followed by Little Stints and Curlew Sandpipers later in the season. More erratic migrants include Wood Sandpiper, Spotted Redshank and more 'coastal' species such as Curlew, Knot, Sanderling and Oystercatcher. The lake has a long list of vagrant waders, with Pectoral Sandpiper and Temminck's Stint among those seen more recently.

Autumn passage is by no means restricted to the waders. Parties of 40 or more Common and Arctic Terns can be expected most years and numbers of Black Terns sometimes reach as high as 200; Sandwich and Little Terns occur sporadically, but both the formerly regular White-winged Black Terns and Little Gulls have become rarer of late. A migrating Arctic Skua may drop in momentarily, but other seabirds mostly occur only when storm-driven. Garganey gather in the shallows, with up to ten eclipse birds often present among the Teal to provide a neat identification challenge. Late summer is also a good time to look out for migrant parties of Common Scoter out in the middle of the lake. There are usually a few Hobbies over the lake through the autumn, especially if they have bred nearby, and the assemblies of hirundines roosting in the reeds may attract both this species and the resident Sparrowhawks to make an evening kill. At this time of year an Osprey may be tempted to stay for several days, finding easy pickings on its way south and low water levels and warm weather have attracted Spoonbills on a few occasions.

Autumn gales bring a few seabirds, most likely a Kittiwake or Grey Phalarope, but not so regularly as at Cheddar Reservoir, nearer the sea and on the other side of the Mendips. Late autumn usually produces a few surprises, however, with local rarities such as Eider, Avocet and Lapland Bunting all having occurred in November. Red-breasted Mergansers are most frequently seen at this period, with one or two wintering in recent years. One or two Rock Pipits may appear briefly, but are soon replaced for the winter by up to six of their Alpine relative, the Water Pipit.

Timing

Low water levels in autumn, the lower the better, are essential for a good variety of waders, and also produce better feeding conditions for sur-face-feeding ducks, including Garganey. (The only exception is that in extreme drought years the mud may dry out or become matted with veg-etation and thus be less attractive to waders.) However, after a dry sum-mer, feeding conditions for waterfowl are often excellent as rising levels flood encroaching lakeside vegetation, producing large concentrations of both diving and surface feeders. Windy conditions tend to concen-trate water birds into sheltered bays, and may bring storm-driven seabirds in autumn or winter. The major source of disturbance is from trout fishing, which is at a fairly high level throughout the day from mid-March to late November (the exact dates vary from year to year) although most intense at the beginning and end of the season. Bank fish-ermen are excluded from the nature reserve at the southern end, but those using boats can go right up to Herriott's Bridge as long as they do not land. Sailing is mainly from mid-morning to late afternoon on week-ends throughout the year, causing birds to move out of the sailing area to other parts of the lake. Feeding terns and gulls are not normally affected. The former are usually more active from midday onwards, presumably linked to insect activity: rarities are more likely in calm and overcast con-ditions, especially in a southerly or easterly airflow. Freezing conditions may bring an influx of wildfowl from further north or east, although birds disperse if the lake itself freezes over. Roosting gulls gradually build up from mid-afternoon, and rarities have been seen quite early on, with the advantage of better light. Calm conditions with light overcast giving a flat light are ideal; rough water makes settled birds difficult to pick out; with easterly winds the birds tend to stay far out in the centre of the lake. Evening visits give the best chance of encountering a wintering Bittern or raptors hunting the roosts.

Access

From the north, Chew Valley Lake is most easily approached along the B3130 which links the A38 and A39 via Chew Magna. The B3114 from there via Chew Stoke runs down the west side of the lake and joins with the A368 in West Harptree. Turning left here brings access to Herriott's Bridge, a causeway between the main lake and Herriott's Pool where silt from the inflowing River Chew has a chance to settle. Continuing north-east through Bishop Sutton, turning left at the Red Lion pub, and keeping left on minor roads eventually bring access to the northeast corner of the lake: continuing over the dam returns you to Chew Stoke. There are reg-ular bus services from Bristol to the main villages. Permits, available on a per day or season basis, are available from BW, and must be purchased by those wishing to use the hides.

Herriott's Bridge is a good starting point, and you may find out 'what's about' from other watchers here. There is ample parking by the road, although crowded on summer weekends. The pool attracts many ducks, particularly diving species, and is somewhat of a refuge. Ruddy Ducks are usually present, though they often move into the fringing reeds. A series of lagoons has been created at the back, with several islands in the pool itself. These attract, but also hide, ducks, waders and terns, so a certain amount of patience may be needed. Take care to scan the whole area: waders may feed along the causeway, and Bitterns lurk in the edges of the reeds. The hillsides to the southeast are favoured by soaring Buzzards; some are very pale and prone to misidentification, although rarer species do sometimes appear along the ridge. Occasionally the water level is dropped for a time giving a better chance of seeing a feeding Water Rail in the open, and waders and surface-feeding ducks including Garganey are attracted by such conditions. One of the main gull roost flightlines is along the river valley and directly over the bridge. Birds overhead can be difficult to identify, but a proportion stop to preen and bathe in the pool before moving on the main lake. A Ring-billed Gull wintered here from 1986 to 1992, feeding on bread along with the other gulls and ducks. Looking north, the main reedbed lies along the nearer eastern shore, giving the best chance of seeing a Bittern in flight, hearing a Bearded Tit or any of the other reedbed birds. Ruddy Ducks and various grebes seem to favour the more sheltered waters at this end of the lake. If the water is low, waders gather on the muddy shoreline either side of the point where the River Chew eventually emerges but the stumps of trees felled when the reservoir was flooded are numerous here and can often obscure resting waders for long periods. Not being used by bank fishermen, this area also attracts wildfowl disturbed from other parts of the lake. Chew Valley Ringing Station is situated in a wooden hut behind the house at the southern end of the bridge.

About ¾ mile (1.2 km) north towards Bishop Sutton a small lane runs left (opposite a gateway with ornate stone eagles) to a small car park. Permit-holders can walk along the back of the woodland to the south, then right through the trees to Sutton Wick Hide, often disturbed by fishermen, but good in the mornings for viewing the centre of the lake for deep-water diving species and feeding terns. On overcast days gulls gathering to roost can also be viewed satisfactorily. When water levels are low, the shore to the north often attracts dabbling ducks and a variety of waders.

To reach the western side of the lake it is necessary to drive via West Harptree and turn right at the church towards Chew Stoke. At the Blue Bowl Inn fork right down a no-through-road to a small car park at the bottom of the hill. Permit holders can enter the reservoir enclosure from the back of this car park to the Stratford Bay Hide along a wooden walkway. This provides alternative views of the southern part of the lake, and is particularly good if the water level is low and mud is exposed. Islands here attract resting birds, including Water Pipits as well as larger species, and at low water a shallow pool forms in front of the hide. In the early evening, the hide is a good spot for watching gulls flighting in from the south. A log book in the hide provides up-to-date information on sightings.

Permit-holders can walk north from the car park, over a stile, and eventually reach a small conifer plantation which shelters Moreton Hide. The hedges and fields en route sometimes hold migrant passerines such as Whinchats and Stonechats, as well as breeding Little Owl and warblers.

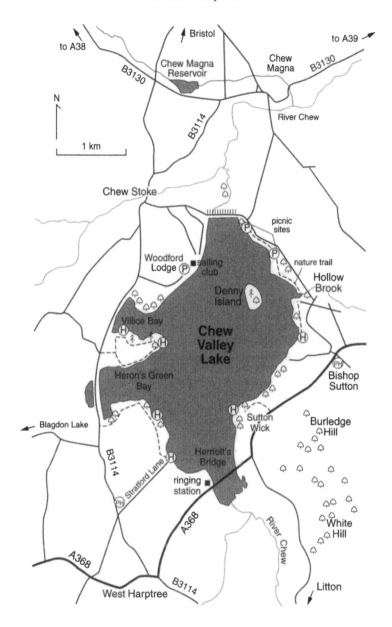

Moreton Hide is good for viewing waterfowl on the south central part of the lake, and for terns feeding offshore. The rocky shore when exposed at low water attracts a few waders.

Heron's Green Bay lies to the north again, and can be viewed from the road causeway (the private road at its southern end will bring permit holders to Moreton Hide from the north via a small car park). This large sheltered bay attracts diving species, especially the smaller grebes, Ruddy Ducks, Smew and other sawbills. The 'arm' to the south should be examined carefully as ducks often move well to the end, despite the proximity to the road. At low water levels, this is also an excellent spot for waders, especially when low enough to expose the old bridge in the middle of the bay. Gulls are rarely numerous, but terns sometimes rest or feed in the bay, or leave towards Blagdon to the west. On the opposite side of the road the formerly small pool has been opened up and hedgerows removed to create a larger expanse of water with shallow margins and an open aspect. Little Egrets, waders and dabbling ducks have already started to feed here, and birds like Spotted Crake and Jack Snipe can sometimes be seen. Continuing north, a lane to the right at the brow of the hill provides access (again only for permit-holders) to the 'Parkland' meadows, though out of the fishing season the gates may be locked and parking rather restricted. Paths lead to a hide overlooking Villice Bay on the north side of the grassland, or across it to another hide beyond the trees on Nunnery Point. Emergent vegetation around Villice Bay sometimes hides a spring Garganey, but Smew and the smaller grebes also appear occasionally, as well as a few waders when the water level drops. The Parkland itself holds a regular flock of Canada Geese, worth checking for exotics wild and tame, whilst Nunnery Point is a popular spot for an evening visit, as the main gull roost usually ends up off here. In the spring, there is a regular roost of Goldeneye, Goosanders and any rarer sawbills, the birds gathering just offshore at dusk. During the day, this is one of the best places from which to view feeding terns and Little Gulls: check the buoys for resting birds.

The next turning right beyond Villice Bay leads to Woodford Lodge, where there is a restaurant, toilets and car park, and from which permits can be purchased. The Lodge affords fine views over the central part of the lake, but there is no access to the shore itself.

The dam is best checked early in the morning for any waders, gulls or terns on the embankment before they are disturbed by traffic. Goldeneye and other diving ducks often feed close inshore, and divers sometimes favour this area, again mostly early and late. Another gull flightline enters here, but is rather difficult to view properly. The picnic site close to the dam is popular with the general public, and there are toilets, an information centre (from which birdwatching permits are also available) and snack bar here. It is linked by a path to a second picnic site a short way to the south (also accessible by car) which provides a good view of Denny Island. Ruddy Ducks often shelter here, joined by other species in rough weather from the west. Grey Herons and Cormorants gather in some numbers around the island. A muddy spit at the north end is exposed at low water and waders can be viewed distantly, although a telescope is essential. At very low water another island appears beyond the main one. Two waymarked public nature trails heading south start from this picnic site. First is the Grebe Trail, providing a circular walk on gravelled paths, suitable for wheelchairs, past a few pools and affording more views of Denny Island. At its far end a bridge crosses Hollow Brook (check for Kingfisher and Little Grebe in the channel) to the start of the Bittern Trail. This is often rather muddy and wet, but leads through lush undergrowth, willows and alders to the Bernard King Hide, which overlooks the east shore, often attractive to passage waders and usually holding good numbers of waterbirds. The trail continues past a raised viewpoint and through more damp woodland back to the starting point. This area is good for passerines, and rarer visitors like Lesser Spotted Woodpecker and Firecrest have been seen here.

Calendar

All year: Great Crested Grebe, Little Grebe, Cormorant, Grey Heron, Greylag, Canada and Barnacle Geese, Shelduck, Sparrowhawk, Buzzard, Little Owl, Kingfisher, Cetti's Warbler, Reed Bunting.

December–February: Possible Great Northern or other diver; rare grebe, Little Egret, Bittern, occasional Bewick's Swan. Wigeon, Gadwall, Teal, Pintail, Shoveler, Pochard, Tufted Duck, Goldeneye, Goosander, Ruddy Duck; probable Smew, Red-breasted Merganser; possible Scaup, Long-tailed Duck or rarity, e.g. Ring-necked Duck. Occasional Hen Harrier, Peregrine or Merlin. Water Rail, Lapwing, Jack Snipe, Snipe, sometimes Dunlin or other wader. Gull roost includes Mediterranean, Yellow-legged Gull, possible Ring-billed, Glaucous or Iceland Gull. Water Pipit. Stonechat, Chiffchaff, Firecrest and Bearded Tit all irregular. Siskin.

March–May: Bulk of winter ducks leave during March but Goldeneye peak end March–early April; rarities may linger or pass, e.g. Common Scoter. Garganey from mid-March. Hobby from late April. Chance of Osprey or Marsh Harrier late April–May. Thin wader passage, mostly Common Sandpiper (April), sometimes Ruff (March) or Sanderling (May). Mediterranean and Ring-billed Gulls to early April when roost disperses. Maybe Kittiwake April. Little Gull, Common, Arctic and Black Terns mid-April–May. Chiffchaff, Sand Martin from mid-March; Cuckoo, Reed and Sedge Warblers by late April. Light passage of passerines April including the odd Tree Pipit, Wood Warbler, Pied Flycatcher, a few White and Yellow Wagtails. Maybe overshooting rarity late April–May, e.g. Purple Heron.

June–July: Emergence of broods of grebes, ducks and Coots, often in large numbers. Moult flocks of Great Crested Grebe, Mute Swan, Canada Goose, Gadwall, Mallard, Tufted Duck, Pochard and Coot. Chance of Common Scoter (July). Ruddy Shelduck sometimes appears at this time, as do rare terns. Hobby irregular all summer. Returning waders from late June, especially Green and Common Sandpipers. Yellow-legged Gull from July.

August–November: Black-necked Grebe; Little Grebe peak before October dispersal. Little Egret influx in August. Occasional Grey Phalarope or seabird October. Sometimes Bewick's Swan from November. Garganey, Gadwall and Tufted Duck peak August; Shoveler peak August–November. Red-breasted Merganser from November when rarities sometimes appear. Possible Osprey August–September when Hobby regular. Water Rail from September, occasional Spotted Crake. Wader passage: from early August Ringed and Little Ringed Plover, Dunlin, Ruff, Wood Sandpiper, Black-tailed Godwit; then Little Stint, Curlew Sandpiper, Spotted Redshank through September–October when rarities more likely, e.g. Pectoral Sandpiper, Temminck's Stint, etc. Black, Common and Arctic Terns plus Little Gull July–October or other unusual tern. Gull roost builds steadily throughout. Chance of Mediterranean Gull in August or from November. Large numbers of common warblers pass August–mid-September, especially Sedge Warbler, maybe Aquatic. Bearded Tit may appear in October. Rock Pipit late September–October; Water Pipit from mid-October.

25 LITTON RESERVOIRS

Habitat and Species

Litton Reservoirs comprise two small pools (24½ acres, 10 ha) lying c.2 miles (3.2 km) up-river from Chew Valley Lake, and mainly used for trout-rearing. Because of their small size, only a few Mallard, Coot, Little Grebes and Tufted Duck are found in most winters, but, particularly early in the morning, fish-eating birds such as Goosander and Cormorants sometimes visit, and rarities such as Slavonian Grebe and Smew have also moved here temporarily from Chew. Kingfishers and Grey Wagtails are both regular visitors and Buzzard and Sparrowhawk can be seen over the nearby farmland and hillsides.

Access

A footpath between the villages of Coley and Litton runs next to the reservoirs, but birds are easily disturbed by passers-by.

26 COMPTON DANDO AREA

Habitat and Species

Just before reaching the Avon at Keynsham, the River Chew winds through some attractive rolling farmland dotted with a series of small copses and larger areas of conifer plantations. Southeast of the village of Compton Dando, large areas of land have been put into 'set-aside', and others are being farmed in an environmentally sensitive way. This, together with the varied landscape, has resulted in a richer mix of species than is often found in primarily agricultural areas these days. In one winter when small mammal populations were high, Short-eared, Long-eared and Barn Owls moved in to take advantage, the latter two species both having bred. The owls have mostly moved on, but the resident Buzzards, Sparrowhawks and Kestrels continue to thrive. Siskins and Redpolls can be found in the riverside alders in winter while Kingfisher, Dipper and Grey Wagtail all breed in small numbers along the Chew. Hunstrete Lake is heavily used by anglers but a pair each of both Great Crested and Little Grebes breed fairly regularly here. The conifers of the adjacent Lord's Wood shelter large numbers of Pheasants and there are a few Red-legged and Grey Partridges in some of the arable fields, all these species being reared for sporting purposes. To the southeast, the plateau south of Marksbury is a regular wintering site for Golden Plover and Lapwing, and the ornamental lakes of Newton Park, towards Bath, sometimes attract a few Teal and Tufted Ducks in winter. To the southwest, Folly Farm, near Bishop Sutton is an AWT reserve with wild-flower meadows and varied deciduous copses holding the usual mix of woodland birds.

Redpoll

Access

The general area lies between Keynsham and Chew Valley Lake, and is accessed along a network of minor lanes and well-marked public footpaths. Buses run regularly from Bristol to Wells along the A37, Pensford making a good starting point from this road. There is a small public car park at ST636655, near Compton Dando, which makes another good access point, with several waymarked paths starting from here. A detailed map is essential, the public footpaths being supplemented by permissive paths under Countryside Stewardship schemes.

27 BLAGDON LAKE OS Explorer 141 and 154

Habitat

Blagdon is a relatively long narrow lake overlooked by the northern escarpment of the Mendip Hills to the south and steeply sloping farmland to the north. There are several coniferous plantations along its shores, with mature gardens and mixed woodland around the dam at the western end, making this the most scenically attractive of the 'Mendip' reservoirs. The total area is c.430 acres (178 ha), roughly one third that of nearby Chew Valley Lake. Apart from the stonework of the dam the banks are entirely naturally vegetated, although emergent vegetation is mainly restricted to the eastern end, where the most extensive mud is exposed if and when water levels drop. The lake is well stocked with trout, but there are fewer coarse fish than at Chew; angling is popular but otherwise disturbance is low with no sailing activity. Current management activities include replanting of the surrounding woodland with native species by the AWT.

Species

There is no doubt that Blagdon is overshadowed by its famous neighbour, but nevertheless has an excellent selection of wintering wildfowl plus a good variety of passage species. Recently it has received rather more attention in the past, resulting in a series of rarities being found. As at Chew, this is a prime wintering site for Ruddy Ducks with up to 300 or so regularly seen in the bays and at the top end of the reservoir; contrary to a widely held belief, only a pair or two actually breed here. Controversially, both here and at Chew they have been the target of control measures designed to reduce numbers in the UK to protect the closely related White-headed Ducks of Spain and southern Europe. Other diving duck include very variable numbers of Pochard and Tufted Duck. For the former, there is a certain amount of interchange between Blagdon, Chew and even Cheddar, with weekend sailing activities at the latter sometimes causing birds to cross the Mendips to Blagdon. Peak numbers of Tufted Ducks occur in the autumn when there can be in excess of 500 here, though in winter there will usually be far fewer than this. Around 10–15 Goldeneye winter, but Goosander are erratic and are rarely into double figures here. Smew are virtually annual, although not predictable, with one to three red-heads considerably outnumbering the sought-after white males. A wide range of other diving ducks have included Ring-necked Duck (several times), Scaup, Long-tailed Duck and Red-breasted Merganser in small numbers over the years; recent rarities include, remarkably, two different Lesser Scaup in spring and autumn 2000. Among surface feeders, Teal are the most numerous species, although numbers vary depending on the water level. If levels are low there can be up to 1000 present, but they soon move away as waters rise. There can be up to 600 Mallard in autumn, and Wigeon numbers here (200–300) are now more significant than those at Chew. A few Pintail are regular, and both Gadwall and Shoveler winter in small numbers, with more (up to around 250) on autumn passage. As at Chew Bewick's Swans are now irregular visitors, mostly early in the winter. The grassland close to the lake attracts several hundred Canada Geese, accompanied by small numbers of feral Barnacle Geese, plus odd hybrids and escapes. Other wild geese and swans, apart from the resident Mute Swans, are unusual.

Ring-necked Duck

Both Little and Great Crested Grebes breed, though their success fluctuates widely with the water level. They occur in small numbers throughout the year, peaking in late summer prior to an autumn dispersal. Black-necked Grebes are tolerably frequent, though by no means annual, mostly on autumn passage. Slavonian Grebes are rarer, with Red-necked only in years of national influxes. Several Great Northern Divers have appeared in winter, with the two or three Black-throateds all in spring. Of other winter birds, small numbers of Common and Black-headed Gulls spend the day around the lake, numbers peaking in the afternoon before usually moving off to roost at Chew or the coast. Mediterranean Gulls have been seen with them several times, along with one or two Yellow-legged Gulls. A few Snipe winter along the margins, Redwings and Fieldfares use the nearby farmland for feeding, and there are small numbers of the commoner finches present.

High water levels usually restrict spring waders to the Common Sandpipers that join the resident Grey Wagtails along the dam. Feeding hirundines gather over the water, and the fringes of the reservoir have a good selection of the commoner breeding woodland species, and include one or two pairs of Sparrowhawks. Breeding waterbirds include around 10 pairs of Coot, plus a few broods of Mallard and Tufted Ducks.

Autumn wader passage is variable, but in recent years the water level has usually dropped enough to make watching here rather more rewarding than it has been at Chew! However, apart from Lapwing, numbers are relatively small, rarely into double figures on any one occasion. Dunlin, Ringed Plover, Green and Common Sandpipers and Greenshank are regular, with Little Stint and Curlew Sandpiper also to be expected in those years when their post-breeding population is high. 'Coastal' waders such as Sanderling, Knot and Curlew are irregular, perhaps discouraged by the enclosed nature of the shore. On the other hand there is a creditable list of rarer visitors of which recent highlights have been Avon's first Baird's Sandpiper, a couple of Temminck's Stints and a Red-necked Phalarope. Common, Arctic and Black Terns are regular in small numbers, normally less than ten at a time, with Little and Sandwich Terns occasionally noted, most species not staying long and often just using the valley as a route out to the coast from Chew. Hobbies hunting overhead are most likely to be seen in the autumn but Buzzards, which nest on the surrounding farmland, can be seen throughout the year over the nearby hillsides. Small numbers of a wide range of passerines pass through, including Crossbills, Redpolls and Siskins that sometimes remain in the lakeside woods. Stonechats fluctuate in numbers from year to year, but up to four can be found in the rougher patches around the lake in autumn and winter.

Timing

The lake is actively used by trout fishermen from mid-March to late November, and during the first few weeks of the season their numbers can make viewing unsatisfactory (also they arrive extremely early in the day and stay late to get their money's worth!); there are no 'refuge' areas until dropping water levels make the east end less productive from the angler's point of view. Low water is essential if waders are to be attracted, but otherwise factors are few. High winds in autumn may bring a seabird or two briefly, and also make ducks rather easier to view when they crowd into the bays for shelter. During winter afternoons small numbers of gulls gather at the western end to rest and preen before moving on to

Chew or the coast in the evening. Duck numbers tend to be highest on winter weekend afternoons when diving duck are displaced temporarily from Cheddar.

Access

The lake lies north of the A368 between the villages of Blagdon and Ubley. Access to the reservoir enclosure is strictly by permit only, obtainable from BW, the same permit allowing access to Chew and other local reservoirs, and is essential if the lake is to be viewed fully. However, a reasonable amount can be seen from the public roads. For the western end, take the turning signposted to Butcombe (Station Road) at one of the sharp bends in the middle of Blagdon village. This leads down past the old station to the stone dam, with good views of this end of the lake. The overflow channel at the far end usually holds Grey Wagtail and the adjacent woodland has the usual breeding species. A public footpath runs from here along the northwest shore of Butcombe Bay but this area is not particularly favoured by waterfowl. Returning to the south end of the dam, a minor road to the left gives several viewpoints over this normally sheltered area where a good variety of ducks often gather, and where Common Sandpipers can be seen on the stonework. Where the road bears away from the lake a gated private road gives access for permit holders to the southern side of the lake. Walk quietly behind the fringing trees to the black-and-white Blagdon Lodge area where the resting gulls may contain an unusual species if you are lucky. When water levels are low, the exposed shore here can be a productive area as far as waders

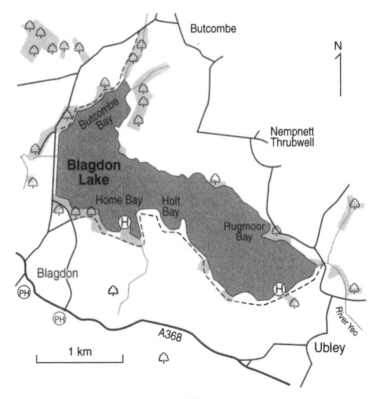

are concerned. The road continues past a couple of bays where waders and waterfowl can easily be missed unless you scan carefully. Kingfishers are quite often seen in this area, and the trees are worth checking for woodpeckers and passerines. There is a hide at the point, but it is rarely used these days. The road continues all the way along the southern side of the lake to the eastern entrance and another hide. Along the whole route, keep to the road itself, rather than wandering down to the actual shore, to minimise disturbance to the birds.

For direct access to the eastern end, return to the A368 and fork left into Ubley village, turning left again at the church and again at the T-junction in just under ½ mile (0.8 km) (turning right at this last junction leads directly to Chew Valley Lake). The reservoir entrance (gated here also) is at the point where the road crosses the River Yeo. There is only limited parking on the road here, although in the fishing season the gate may be open allowing permit holders to drive in and park within the reservoir boundary itself. The top-end hide lies to the right of the track c.½ mile (0.8 km) along, and is partially hidden by trees. This end of the lake is the most productive for waders if mud is exposed, and large numbers of duck also gather here. Back at the entrance gate, continue along the road to the left, and keep left at the next junction to another gateway overlooking Rugmoor Bay and the northern shore of the lake. Scanning from here with a telescope should, with patience, allow most birds at this end of the lake to be seen. Access to the rest of the reservoir enclosure is restricted to anglers only.

Calendar

All year: Great Crested Grebe, Cormorant, Grey Heron; Canada Goose, Barnacle Goose (feral), Mallard, Pochard, Tufted Duck, Sparrowhawk, Buzzard, Coot, Grey Wagtail, Goldcrest; Reed Bunting (rare in winter).

December–February: Occasional Great Northern Diver, maybe rare grebe; maybe Bewick's Swan (to end March); Wigeon, Gadwall, Teal, Pintail, Shoveler, Pochard, Tufted Duck, Goldeneye, Goosander, Ruddy Duck; maybe Scaup, Smew or rare duck. Snipe. Daytime gull roost may include rarity. Kingfisher (irregular), Water Pipit (scarce). Stonechat, winter thrushes, sometimes Siskin and Redpoll.

March–May: Little and Great Crested Grebe numbers increase. Winter wildfowl mostly leave during March. Passage of ducks (March–April) includes Tufted Duck, Goldeneye, chance of Garganey. Maybe Osprey April–May. Common Sandpiper April–May, other waders rare. Little Gull occasional March–April; trickle of Common, Arctic and Black Terns mid-April–May. Sand Martins pass from late March, other hirundines later.

June–July: Little and Great Crested Grebes usually breed. Small numbers of Pochard and Tufted Duck summer. Common passerines breeding, including Reed and Sedge Warblers. Hobby regular to late September. Large flocks of Swifts in bad weather. Autumn wader passage starts late July, and Little Egret most likely to occur at this time.

August–November: Little Grebes peak September. Chance of Black-necked Grebe. Maybe seabird after gales. Garganey peak August, Tufted Duck August–September, Gadwall and Shoveler October–November; Red-breasted Merganser possible November–December. Ruddy Ducks arrive from late August, other wildfowl mostly later. Wader passage August–October, timing and species similar to Chew Valley Lake. Lapwing numbers sometimes high October–November. Black, Common and Arctic Tern August–mid-October, plus occasional Little Gull. Trickle of passerines August–September include Yellow Wagtail, Whinchat, *Sylvia* and *Phylloscopus* warblers.

28 BARROW GURNEY RESERVOIRS

OS Explorer 154 or 155

Habitat

These three small reservoirs, which in area total 126 acres (51 ha), are raised and entirely stone-banked. They lie either side of the busy A38, a few miles southwest of Bristol, and function as storage tanks for water from other BW reservoirs, prior to treatment in the nearby purification beds. There is no emergent vegetation and mud is only exposed in drought years or when the reservoirs are drained for repair work. An old storage tank nearby contains some scrub and bush cover, and there is extensive woodland in the grounds of the nearby hospital, both of these areas being private.

Species

Although not in the same league as nearby Chew Valley and Blagdon Lakes, these reservoirs attract good numbers of diving duck and have a knack of turning up unusual visitors, particularly during adverse weather. Tufted Duck and Pochard numbers are generally between 50 and 100 but like other species are swelled in exceptional circumstances. Up to 20 Goldeneye are regular, but Goosanders have become rather erratic, possibly because of the reduction in numbers wintering at Chew. The site does not really suit surface-feeding ducks, although small numbers of Mallard, Teal, Wigeon and Shoveler can usually be found. Unsurprisingly, the more unusual waterbirds show a bias towards diving species. Among the grebes, Slavonian and Black-necked join the regular Great Crested and Little from time to time on passage or in winter but it usually needs cold weather to produce Red-necked. Long-tailed Ducks are seen intermittently, but when they do turn up tend to stay for long periods. The same holds for Smew, usually red-heads, although they, like other wildfowl, often commute to and from Chew Valley Lake and hence 'go missing' temporarily. Ring-necked Duck, Scaup, Red-breasted Merganser and Great Northern Diver have all appeared on more than one occasion, rarely staying for more than a few days, however. The open nature of the site makes it unattractive to the Ruddy Ducks that winter in large numbers at Chew and Blagdon, but if those waters freeze over, a large part of their populations will take up temporary residence here. The origin of the several Red-crested Pochards is a matter of speculation. In winter, the tanks form a staging post for gulls on their way to the Chew Valley roost, mostly Black-headed, Common, Herring and Lesser Black-backed, but Mediterranean, Ring-billed and Yellow-legged Gulls have all been seen, this last rather more frequently of late. Among small birds, Grey and Pied Wagtails are probably the most characteristic of the stonework, but Water Pipits also occur here from time to time.

In spring, hirundines skimming over the water, and Wheatears feeding along the grassy bank are the most obvious migrants but early-morning visitors can find small numbers of commoner warblers, chats and wagtails feeding nearby after their overnight flights. A few Common Terns and the occasional Black Tern or Little Gull may hawk for insects for a few hours, but then leave only a few pairs of Mallard, Coots and Great Crested Grebes as the major inhabitants for the summer, although Cormorants can also be seen throughout the year. In general, Common Sandpipers are the only autumn waders to find suitable feeding habitat along the banks, but if the water levels drop low enough to expose much mud, a wider variety of species can occur, Greenshank perhaps being the most regular. Common, Black and Arctic Terns pass through in small numbers, and ringing has produced evidence of a good trickle of commoner passerines in the nearby woodland and scrub. Autumn gales sometimes produce a surprise in the form of a storm-driven Grey Phalarope or seabird.

Timing
Not particularly critical at any time of year, Barrow Gurney being a place for a quick check on a frequent basis rather than a special visit. The main disturbance comes from fisherman (mid-March to late November) and to a lesser extent from sporadic sub-aqua diving in winter. Mostly the birds move out into the middle of the water or move to one of the other two tanks if disturbance occurs. Few waders will be present unless water levels are low. Freezing conditions elsewhere locally will bring an influx of water birds as these reservoirs take longer to ice over, but most birds leave again if they do actually freeze. Gale conditions sometimes bring storm-driven vagrants briefly.

Access
Access is by permit only, from BW. Leaving Bristol on the A38 towards Bridgwater, the reservoirs lie either side of the road by the B3130 turning to Clevedon. There is a car park on the right immediately before this turning. The largest (No. 3) tank lies north of the road, and the other two are just to the south, all accessible directly from the car park (take care when crossing the road). As each water is roughly circular, each reservoir can be scanned using a telescope from any point on their circumference, but it is often a good idea to walk all the way round each one (particularly Nos 2 & 3) to be sure that nothing is missed. The filtration beds, which attract gulls at times, can be scanned from the car park, and the edges of the nearby woods and hedges can be seen from the road or the reservoir enclosure.

Calendar
All year: Little and Great Crested Grebes, Cormorant, Mallard, Sparrowhawk, Buzzard, Kestrel, Coot, Grey Wagtail; common woodland passerines nearby.

December–February: Maybe diver or rare grebe. Cormorant, Grey Heron, Pochard, Tufted Duck, Goldeneye, Wigeon, Teal, Shoveler, Goosander;

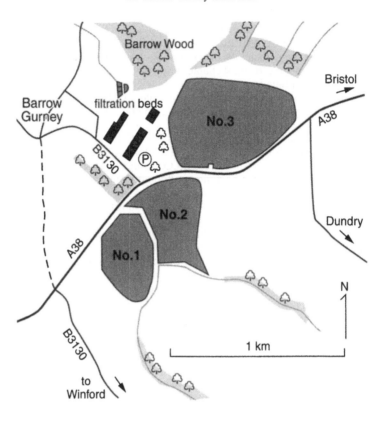

sometimes Long-tailed Duck, Smew, occasionally Scaup, Ruddy Duck. Green Sandpiper sometimes winters. Gulls may include rarities, e.g. Mediterranean, Ring-billed. Water Pipit.

March–May: Most wildfowl leave March–April. Passage of Common Sandpipers April–May, when also Black and Common Terns, Little Gull. Hirundines mid-April–May, Swifts later. Wheatear, White Wagtail pass April.

June–July: Quiet period; small numbers Great Crested Grebe, Mallard, Coot. Common Sandpiper from mid-July.

August–November: Chance of Black-necked or Slavonian Grebe. Winter wildfowl numbers build up from September, most arriving November. Passage of Common Sandpipers and small numbers of other waders, e.g. Greenshank, Dunlin, Green Sandpiper, mostly August–September. Chance of Grey Phalarope or rare wader September–October. Small numbers of Black Tern, Little Gull (mostly September). Trickle of passerine migrants August–September.

29 BROCKLEY & GOBLIN COMBES

Habitat and Species

These two steep-sided rocky combes cut into the limestone plateau c.9 miles (14.4 km) southwest of Bristol contain relicts of deciduous woodland, mostly oak, ash, beech, sycamore and yew, while on the higher ground, extensive conifer plantations cover what was formerly open heathland. There are more coniferous plantations to the southwest, making this one of the larger areas of woodland in a relatively treeless region. For this reason, it is a locally valuable place to look for the common woodland species, with Coal Tits and Goldcrests among the conifers, and woodpeckers, Marsh Tits, Nuthatches and Treecreepers in the mature deciduous trees. Both Buzzard and Sparrowhawk find conditions ideal, and can often be seen circling overhead. In some winters, flocks of Siskins and Redpolls move around the larch plantations, with singing birds heard in the spring. One or two Willow Tits used to occur among the conifers but there are no recent records, although it is possible that they are overlooked in such an extensive and underwatched area of cover. Passage Wood Warblers stop to sing for a few days in spring, but there have been few recent breeding records. Otherwise the usual summer warblers breed wherever the habitat is suitable. There is a heronry at Cleeve, containing nearly 50 nests. Currently, access to large parts of the conifer plantations is not encouraged, though there are some public footpaths through them. There are nature trails in both combes, however, and it may be that larger areas will become accessible in future.

Access

For Brockley Combe, take the turning to Bristol (Lulsgate) airport from the main A370 Bristol to Congresbury road. Near the top of the combe there is a triangular parking place on the right of the road, and a loop nature trail runs back along the upper southern side of the valley through a strip of deciduous woodland. Goblin Combe is reached by turning along the minor Cleeve Hill Road from the A370 south of Cleeve church; in a short distance there is a parking spot on the left, and a public footpath leads round to the start of the combe and on up through it to open country above Wrington. Cleeve heronry, among the trees on the slope northeast of Cleeve church, can be seen quite easily from the A370 directly below.

30 BACKWELL LAKE OS Explorer 154

Habitat and Species

Backwell Lake Nature Reserve is a small recreational lake on the outskirts of Nailsea, heavily used by the public but nevertheless holding a varied bird population. Before silt build-up altered the food supply the lake attracted up to 80 Gadwall in winter, but they are now seen only in ones and twos. On the other hand, Goosander have become quite regular winter visitors, up to a dozen at a time. Mallard, Tufted Duck and Pochard are the other mainstays among the wildfowl, with Ruddy Duck, Shoveler, Wigeon, Great Crested and Little Grebes seen occasionally. A pair of Mute Swans usually nests. More unusual visitors have included Common Sandpiper, Greenshank, Red-necked Phalarope, Scaup and Mediterranean Gull, so it is always worth a quick look for anyone passing.

Access

The lake (ST 478694) lies close to the minor road from Backwell to Nailsea, just north of the railway station, and can be viewed from its own car park. Smooth grassy paths run round the whole shore.

31 SAND POINT

Habitat

In some ways a smaller version of Brean Down to the south and also owned by the NT, the limestone promontory of Middle Hope, more often known by its western tip, Sand Point, lies just north of the holiday resort of Weston-super-Mare, where the coastline turns from southwest to nearly due south, and the estuary widens markedly towards the open sea. Cattle, sheep and rabbits combine to keep most of the higher open ground as fairly close-cropped grassland, but hawthorns, elder and brambles grow extensively on the southern slopes, and on the steeper parts of the northern side. The north-facing shoreline is mostly a narrow strip of weed-covered rocks, but to the south the point encloses the optimistically named Sand Bay, in fact mostly mudflats 1 mile (1.6 km) wide at low tide, with an interesting saltmarsh in the northern angle of the bay. The River Banwell emerges at the eastern end, where there is a small reserve managed by the AWT, and immediately inland are well-drained grazing meadows interspersed with ditches and hawthorn hedges.

Species

Most interest is centred on passage periods, both spring and autumn, and in those years when local birders have adopted it as 'their patch' some exciting birds have been found, not really surprising when its strategic position is taken into consideration. Wintering birds on the headland are relatively few, but Meadow Pipits and the resident pairs of Rock Pipits can usually be seen, and a careful search along the rocky shore may produce a Black Redstart. Up to six Purple Sandpipers have been seen at the point, one of the few places along the Severn Estuary where this elusive bird has occurred with any regularity in recent years. The mudflats to the south are not a major haunt of waders, but can hold up to 500 Dunlin, a 100 or so Curlew, plus a few Redshank and Oystercatchers. Shelducks are conspicuous out on the mudflats throughout the year, over 200 sometimes being counted in winter, but other wildfowl are mainly restricted to a few Mallard and the occasional Wigeon or Pintail down along the tideline. Snipe and a few Jack Snipe can be flushed from the saltmarsh, but the occasional migrant Short-eared Owl or Hen Harrier rarely lingers. In spring, Ringed Plovers appear briefly in flocks of up to 100 on their way north, with Grey Plover, Knot, Sanderling and Whimbrel the other wader species most likely to been seen at this time of year. On the headland itself, spring mornings often find the bushes full of Willow Warblers, Chiffchaffs and other small migrants, Grasshopper Warblers being among the more notable, while more open areas attract Ring Ousels and Tree Pipits. Pied Flycatcher, Redstart and even Tree Sparrow have been seen in spring, and rarities have included both Bee-eater and Golden Oriole. Offshore, counts of Common Terns moving up-river have topped the 100 mark in a few hours' watching on several occasions; no doubt Arctic Terns are also moving with them, though other species are unusual. Arctic Skuas are probably also regular. Of other seabirds, Kittiwake numbers in early summer have exceeded 100, likewise Manx Shearwaters at the same time. Gales at any time of year are likely to bring a variety of storm-driven birds offshore, including Gannets and

Common Tern

Great Skua, whilst petrels and vagrants like Sabine's Gull have appeared in autumn blows.

Breeding species are not remarkable, although Stonechats do seem to have returned at last, and the early autumn exodus of summer visitors has produced few surprises to date. At this time of year a walk to the point usually seems to produce a Wheatear or two, their white rumps flashing as they fly from one patch of grass to another, and the hawthorn scrub can be full of the commoner warblers. Visible migration is dominated by Swallows and House Martins at first, before the Chaffinches, Greenfinches, Meadow Pipits, Skylarks and Starlings pass through in October. As elsewhere along the estuary, these later migrants can be accompanied by a wide range of other species, Bramblings, Siskins and Redpolls among the more usual, while Woodlarks and Lapland Buntings have been picked out by those familiar with the flight calls. More intensive watching has proved that Firecrests probably occur most years, up to four at a time having been located among the more numerous Goldcrests and Coal Tits that feed in the dense scrub. Although less frequently seen than in the spring, the odd Ring Ousel can turn up in the autumn too. Peregrine, Merlin and Sparrowhawk all pass through, no doubt attracted by the passerine migrants. Offshore, sea-duck such as Common Scoter or Eider rarely linger very long, and other passing birds in the autumn have included Barnacle and Brent Geese, probably wild birds at this time of year. The mix of returning waders is much as in the spring, except that a few Common Sandpipers also occur. Once the main migration period is over, the relative quiet of winter sets in again, but finches may stay along the tideline until food there is exhausted, with Snow Buntings sometimes joining the more usual Linnets, Chaffinches and Reed Buntings. As elsewhere on the coast, there have been a few recent sightings of Dartford Warbler in the winter, and certainly there is plenty of cover for them to hide in.

Timing

High-tide visits are essential for waders, viewable as they congregate relatively undisturbed in the saltmarsh or start feeding again as the tide starts to drop. At low tide most birds are too distant for comfortable watching. Because Sand Bay is popular with visitors and consequently prone to disturbance, the shoreline is best covered early in the morning. The same applies to a lesser extent to Sand Point/Middle Hope where, moreover, both grounded and passing migrants are best seen during the first few hours of the day. Visible migration in autumn is usually most productive under overcast conditions with a headwind between west and south. Under calm clear conditions birds are often high up out of sight, or coastal fog may make viewing impossible. In spring, however, warm southerlies with morning mist have often produced the best falls of warblers and other migrants, and terns move through when the weather is relatively settled. Gales in autumn and winter are likely to bring seabirds offshore, although calm anticyclonic days in midsummer bring feeding flocks of shearwaters well up the estuary.

Access

The main access route is from the A370 Bristol to Weston-super-Mare road, just west of where it crosses the M5 (junction 21) and enters the outskirts of Weston. Bear left immediately after leaving the roundabout here, and follow signs to Sand Bay. Eventually the road emerges on the coast road, where there are several parking places, and the mudflats can be scanned from the promenade. For Sand Point, drive north along the coast road (or walk the tideline) to its far end where there is a large NT car park. An obvious path runs diagonally up to the triangulation point

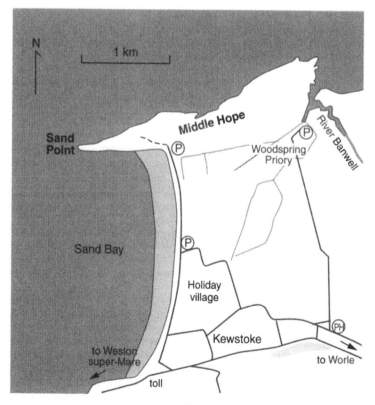

at 48 metres, traditionally a good spot for watching visible migration in autumn. The majority of birds fly west along the ridge before reorientating at the point, but some, particularly hirundines, tend to keep low on either side. A footpath leads along the ridge to the point itself, the best place for watching birds moving both up-river and down-river. The bushes on the south slope around the car park are one of best places for grounded migrants, but this habitat extends west to the point. An alternative route is to walk west along the foot of the southern slope (wellies may be needed), scanning the bushes on one side and the saltmarsh on the other, and then scrambling up onto a path which runs above the low cliffs to the point. At the east end of the car park some steps lead up to the fields of the central and eastern end of Middle Hope, where the bushy hollows on the northern side are worth checking for small birds though the shoreline on this side holds few waders.

This eastern end can also be accessed from the road leading to Woodspring Priory (although land around the priory itself is strictly private). Return towards the M5, but at the edge of Kewstoke a turning to the left by the Old Manor pub leads to Collum Lane and on towards the priory. Just before this, a (sometimes gated) track to the right leads to Hucker's Bow car park. From here follow the footpath left along the River Banwell bank to where the AWT manages a small reserve overlooking the estuary and Woodspring Bay. However, the grassland and bushes here are not usually so productive as those at the western end, and Woodspring Bay is best approached from the Clevedon direction.

Calendar

All year: Cormorant, Shelduck, Mallard; Eider (irregular and usually winter), Kestrel, Herring and Lesser Black-backed Gulls, Little Owl, Meadow Pipit, Rock Pipit, Stonechat.

December–February: Chance of Peregrine, Merlin. Water Rail, Snipe, Jack Snipe, Dunlin, Curlew, Redshank, Oystercatcher, occasional Grey Plover, Knot; Purple Sandpiper (elusive). Stonechat sometimes winters. Chance of Snow Bunting on beach.

March–May: Fulmar, Manx Shearwater, Kittiwake offshore, especially May. Common Scoter pass (mostly April). Waders late April–May include Ringed Plover, Sanderling, Whimbrel. Common and Arctic Terns, maybe Arctic Skua (late April–mid-May). Falls of spring migrants mid-April–May, including Tree Pipit, Whinchat, Wheatear, Grasshopper Warbler, common *Phylloscopus* and *Sylvia* warblers, Pied Flycatcher. Sometimes Ring Ousel (March–April) or rarity, e.g. Lapland Bunting, Golden Oriole have occurred in past.

June–July: Manx Shearwater regular, especially June. A few Fulmars and Kittiwakes. Breeding Rock Pipit.

August–November: Chance of rare seabird, e.g. petrel, Gannet, Great Skua, Sabine's Gull (especially September–October). Occasional passing wildfowl (October–November) including Brent Goose, Barnacle Goose, Pintail, Common Scoter. Passage raptors October–November include Peregrine, Merlin, Short-eared Owl. Return passage of waders August–September, wintering birds building up throughout. Trickle of common warblers and chats (August–September); visible migration peaks October, especially finches, pipits, larks, occasional Woodlark, rare bunting. Chance of Black Redstart or Firecrest October–November. Dartford Warbler may winter.

32 CLEVEDON/YEO ESTUARY os Explorer 153

Habitat

Four rivers emerge into the Severn along this 4 mile (6.4 km) stretch of low-lying coast, the Yeo being the largest, situated towards the southern end furthest from the Victorian resort of Clevedon, and their disruptive effect on access has left the area relatively undisturbed by roads and other development. The tide recedes for c.½ mile (0.8 km) at low tide, and the mud is backed in places by a strip of saltmarsh, much reduced recently. Coastal defence improvements have resulted in long stretches of unproductive concrete, and drainage of the meadowland behind has lost valuable breeding habitat for waders, but some rough shingly ground and damper areas still remain. Two reed-filled pools and a tidal inlet (Blake's Pools) have been created near the mouth of the Yeo by way of compensation, and are managed by the AWT. Near Clevedon, the sea-weed-covered Blackstone Rocks provide a refuge at high tide, and Wain's Hill, overlooking a small muddy harbour, has tree and bush cover for migrants in the vicinity of the church.

Species

Waders are the main group of interest here, wintering Dunlin averaging around 4000 in the past few years, though numbers have reached 10,000 in midwinter on several occasions. Up to 150 Redshank and 200 Curlew are also regular along this stretch of coast, and 20–30 Turnstones winter on the seaweed and rocks nearer Clevedon. The saltmarsh hides small numbers of Jack Snipe as well as Snipe, though both species can some-times be found feeding among the seaweed with the Turnstones. Grey Plover usually number less than 30, having declined again after a recent increase, and apart from a few Oystercatchers and Ringed Plover other waders are relatively unusual in winter, except when cold weather brings an influx of Lapwings and Golden Plover. Despite the loss of habitat, small birds feed along the seawall and in the remaining saltmarsh dur-ing the winter, Skylarks, Reed Buntings, Linnets, Greenfinches and Chaffinches dominating, but Bramblings join them in years of influx. There was a flurry of Twite records in the mid-1980s, but this species has currently reverted to its former rarity status. Among birds of prey, hovering Kestrels are a common sight over the fields, Merlins and Sparrowhawks skim along the seawall, while Peregrines have become regular visitors. Apart from the resident Shelduck the murky waters of the Severn attract few wildfowl to this part of the coast, Mallard, Wigeon and Teal in small numbers being the staple fare here, though Brent Geese can now be added to the list, up to ten appearing at the Yeo Estuary most winters. Scaup, Eider, Red-breasted Merganser, Common Scoter and Goldeneye are among a wide range of more unusual visitors that have all shown themselves to regular watchers along this stretch of shore in the past. Goosander also came into this category, but recently a few have taken up residence in winter at the Blackstone Rocks, feeding either here or on the nearby Blind Yeo river; it remains to be seen whether this will become a regular haunt for a bird otherwise associated with fresh water in this part of the world.

Among the waders passing through in the spring, Ringed Plover, Whimbrel and Bar-tailed Godwits are the most frequent, though 100 would be a good count for any of them. Apart from wader movements, spring passage is not particularly noteworthy, although Wheatears, Whinchats and White Wagtails are all regular, and Wain's Hill is always worth checking for a migrant Pied Flycatcher or Redstart. A pair or two of Lapwing sometimes manage to bring off young in the nearby fields, and the occasional Oystercatcher, of which up to a dozen are present all year, has been known to attempt to nest. The construction of Blake's Pools provided winter habitat for a handful of Pochard and Tufted Ducks for a time, but the encroaching reeds have driven away all but the Little Grebes, a pair or two of which sometimes breed. Cetti's Warblers are also resident here, joined in summer by part of the rather more widespread Reed Warbler population. Shelduck numbers increase on the mudflats during the summer as these inland-breeding birds bring their young to the safety of the shore almost as soon as they have hatched. Rock Pipits are a characteristic winter bird along the seawall, with one or two pairs usually to be found on Wain's Hill in the summer.

Although a few birds are present all year, late summer sees the annual influx of Little Egrets, the saltmarsh at the mouth of the River Yeo being a spot particularly favoured by these attractive birds. The double-figure barrier was recently broken, and only a severe winter seems likely to stop the increase for the time being. Their arrival coincides with the start of the return wader passage. Parties of Common Sandpipers along the shore surprise those who associate this species more with freshwater habitats, and Greenshank is another regular 'inland' species here. Little Stint and Curlew Sandpiper, Ruff and Knot are among the regular autumn migrants here, and rarities have included Pectoral Sandpiper more than once. Wain's Hill has received more attention in early autumn recently, and lucky observers have been rewarded with several Firecrests plus, to date, one each of Yellow-browed and Pallas's Warblers. Although numbers have reduced of late, significant numbers of finches and pipits move through in the early mornings, one advantage of this area being provided by the patches of saltmarsh, rough ground and the nearby farmland hedgerows which provide feeding opportunities for these migrants. Over the years good views have been had of Lapland and Snow Buntings, Richard's Pipit, Woodlark, Black Redstart and Great Grey Shrike amongst others. A Desert Wheatear in November 1997 is perhaps the star prize so far. Short-eared Owl and Hen Harrier sometimes linger for a time, but rarely winter. Autumn gales have historically brought few seabirds offshore, perhaps because this stretch is a little set back from the general line of the coast, but some intensive watching just up the coast at Ladye Bay, in the northern outskirts of Clevedon, has shown that a few auks, Gannets, Fulmars and skuas do occur offshore both in spring and autumn.

Rock Pipit

Timing

High-tide visits bring the best views of waders which gather on Blackstone Rocks, at the mouth of the River Kenn, and at the Yeo Estuary, sometimes roosting at these spots, or being forced into the fields if the tide is particularly high. Because the mudflats are relatively narrow, however, telescope users can usually manage reasonable views at other states of the tide apart from at very low water, although the birds are well dispersed, of course. Hunting birds of prey are often more active at high tide, when the waders are more concentrated. For visible migration in autumn the first three hours after dawn are the most productive, and winds from between south and west produce most birds. Cold weather in winter may bring unusual ducks and grebes to the sea if inland waters are frozen. The seawall is a popular walk with the general public, particularly near Clevedon, with afternoons seeing the most activity, and wildfowling and clay-pigeon shooting takes place towards the southern end.

Access

Clevedon lies on the coast due west of Bristol, and M5 junction 20 is the appropriate turnoff for those coming from further afield. In the town, follow signs for the seafront. Wain's Hill lies southwest of the main promenade area, Old Church Road being the cul-de-sac to take to reach the start of the seawall. There is usually room to park near the church, though sometimes restricted on Sunday mornings: a barrier marks the furthest point for cars. Just beyond this, a path up to the right leads onto Wain's Hill from which visible migrants in autumn can be watched from the top – birds pass either side as well as overhead, and usually in a southerly or southwesterly direction into the wind. The path along the seawall is obvious to the south, crossing the Blind Yeo (check for waterfowl) via a sluice, and then past a private golf course to Blackstone Rocks, which lie just offshore where the coast bends nearly due south. There is permissive access as far as the River Kenn, but it is private beyond this, but as far as small birds are concerned, the stretch of seawall and grassland between Blackstone Rocks and the River Kenn is generally the most productive.

A series of minor lanes south from Clevedon or west from Kingston Seymour lead to Channel View Farm, which is the point of access to the southern part of the bay. Roadside parking is extremely restricted, and a

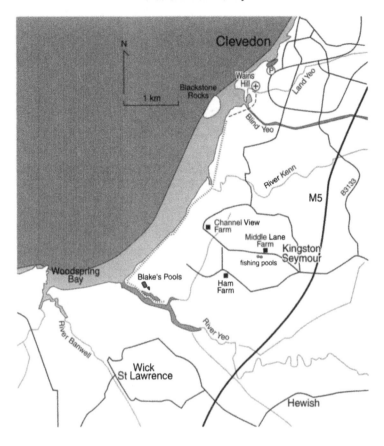

permit from the AWT is required for access to Blake's Pools and the Yeo Estuary area. A path leads to the seawall from Channel View Farm, and then south to the Yeo or north towards the Kenn, access usually being tolerated if a rarity has been found. Some recently constructed fishing lakes by the Perfect Bite café at Middle Lane Farm, nearer Kingston Seymour, hold a few ducks and common passerines, and may produce more birds with time.

Calendar

All year: Little Grebe, Cormorant, Grey Heron, Shelduck, Mallard, Sparrowhawk, Kestrel, Peregrine, Oystercatcher, Lapwing, Redshank, Turnstone, Herring Gull, Rock Pipit, Cetti's Warbler, Reed Bunting.

December–February: Little Egret. Chance of Great Crested Grebe, Goldeneye in cold weather. Brent Goose (scarce), Wigeon, Teal, Goosander, occasional Scaup or other duck. Merlin, Peregrine. Water Rail. Dunlin, Redshank, Curlew, Oystercatcher, Turnstone, Lapwing, Snipe, Jack Snipe, a few Grey Plover. Spotted Redshank has wintered. Black-headed Gull, occasional Mediterranean. Grey Wagtail, sometimes Black Redstart or Snow Bunting. Finch flocks (Linnet, Greenfinch, etc.) sometimes include Brambling. Winter thrushes in fields.

March–May: Passage waders, especially Ringed Plover (April–May), small numbers of Whimbrel and Bar-tailed Godwits (late April–May). Wintering waders leave March–early April. Wheatear, White and Yellow Wagtails pass late March–early May. Maybe Pied Flycatcher or other migrant on Wain's Hill.

June–July: Lapwing, Redshank, Oystercatcher sometimes attempt to breed. Shelduck bring young to shore. Small numbers of Curlew all summer. Rock Pipit (Wain's Hill) and Reed and Cetti's Warblers (Blake's Pool) breed. Green and Common Sandpipers from July. Little Egrets reappear from late July.

August–November: Little Egret. Occasional seabird in gales. Chance of Marsh Harrier early autumn, Merlin from mid-September, Hen Harrier or Short-eared Owl October–November. Passage waders include Common Sandpiper, Ringed Plover in August–September, small numbers of Knot, Sanderling, Little Stint, Curlew Sandpiper, Ruff, godwits, Greenshank peaking September–October before winter build-up starts. Visible migration of finches, pipits, larks, Starling through October into early November; rarities among them may stop on the shore, e.g. Snow and Lapland Buntings, Richard's Pipit, Woodlark, or on Wain's Hill (e.g. Firecrest). Black Redstart October–November, sometimes wintering.

33 GORDANO VALLEY & PORTBURY WHARF

OS Explorer 154

Habitat

Despite the proximity of large-scale industry, increasing housing development and the presence of the M5 motorway cutting its way along its southern side, the Gordano Valley continues to provide a complex web of varied habitats within a relatively small and scenically attractive area. The main valley floor stretches for c.4 miles (6.4 km) in a northeast/southwest direction and comprises a series of damp flower-rich fen meadows, interspersed with drainage ditches, woods dominated by alder and willow, and grazing meadows bordered by mature hedgerows. There are small reedbeds in a couple of areas, and even the old waste tips are grassing over now. The valley is sheltered on its north and south sides by two ridges, both of which have patches of open limestone grassland as well as much coniferous and deciduous woodland. More well-wooded rolling farmland lies to the southeast, around Failand.

At the entrance to the valley lies Royal Portbury Dock, with light industrial units and huge car parks for imported vehicles steadily covering the rough meadows, pools and shingle which previously surrounded the harbour itself. Outside the dock perimeter the some of the original meadows and tall thick hedges still remain at Portbury Wharf, there is a large freshwater lagoon and a strip of saltmarsh fronts the intertidal mud of the

River Severn. The AWT and EN manage several reserves in and around the Gordano Valley, including the areas with the richest flora, but the whole area is under threat of fragmentation by housing and industrial development.

Species

The main interest of the area to birdwatchers lies in the variety rather than the large numbers of individual species to be seen. With the increase in activity at the dock, its importance as a wader roosting site has declined. Dunlin, Curlew and Redshank are the most frequently seen species in winter, a few hundred of the first being the most numerous. Redshank tend to favour the banks of the River Avon, often some way upstream, to the open Severn shore preferred by the Curlew. Numbers of the latter peak in late winter prior to migration, and birds sometimes move into the fields at high tide. In recent years a handful of Purple Sandpipers have wintered on the rocky shore at Portishead, this currently being the most reliable spot in the area to see this unobtrusive wader. The scattered pools and ditches around Portbury Wharf have provided shelter for up to four Green Sandpipers in some winters. One or two Jack Snipe hide in the coastal *spartina*, with larger numbers of Common Snipe more widely scattered in damp areas. Parties of Mallard and Teal occur along the coast, with other species such as Wigeon, Shoveler, Pintail, Tufted Duck and Pochard tending to appear rather erratically, particularly in cold weather. Common Scoter have been seen several times passing offshore, and are the most likely of the seaduck to be recorded, although Eider and Long-tailed Duck have also been seen. Wild geese and swans rarely stop, even in cold weather, most birds merely flying straight over. The occasional Bittern has been seen in winter in the ditches and reeds, while Water Rails are regular visitors to both coast and valley, and have been suspected of breeding.

The damp fields and hedgerows of the whole area provide shelter for large numbers of winter thrushes, with Redwings usually predominating. Redpolls and Siskins are regular in the alder woods of the valley floor, while flocks of Chaffinches, Linnets and, in good years, a few Bramblings, feed on the rough ground near the coast, with Reed Buntings occurring in the *spartina*. Rock Pipits also like this latter habitat in winter, and a pair or two breed on the rocky sections of the coast. Water Pipits stop off from time to time in the freshwater habitat just back from the coast, being most likely on spring passage. Portbury Wharf, with its rough meadows and wet ditches, has long been a fairly reliable site for Short-eared Owls in winter, and a long-running re-introduction scheme has brought back a few pairs of Barn Owls as a breeding species to the area. In the past Long-eared Owls have come to roost in the thick hawthorns on several occasions, but rarely of late as the habitat has been whittled away by development. Peregrines can turn up almost anywhere in the valley in winter, and Merlins are also seen from time to time along the coast. Winter gales may bring a few Kittiwakes inshore, and Mediterranean Gulls have been seen on the coast on several occasions.

Early spring sees the emphasis change to the valley itself with Buzzards starting their soaring displays along the ridges. Recent studies have indicated a population of over 80 pairs in the Gordano/Failand area, more than doubling over the past decade, and it is not unusual to see ten or more birds in the air together. Sparrowhawks and Kestrels also find the mix of habitats ideal, Hobbies are frequent summer visitors, and

Buzzard

a few Ravens nest in some of the old quarries. Conversely breeding waders have declined, as everywhere in lowland Britain, though the calls of Lapwings and a few Redshank are still distinctive features of the valley meadows in spring, with one or two pairs of Snipe sometimes being noted. Green and Great Spotted Woodpeckers are common in the surrounding woods but any Lesser Spotteds tend to be just transient birds. The woodlands hold a good mixture of the commoner breeding passerines, while Sedge and Reed Warblers, Lesser Whitethroat and Reed Bunting are widely distributed on the lower ground. Shelducks in noisy groups are conspicuous against the lush grass in the spring, becoming very elusive once they are on eggs. Several pairs breed along the valley, with around 40 birds to be seen on the coast at most times of the year. Storm damage has removed all the heronries from the Gordano Valley, though feeding birds from nearby can often be seen stalking the ditches.

Despite disturbance, Ringed Plover have managed to raise young at the dock several times, and Oystercatchers also sometimes attempt to breed here. The spring wader passage is not remarkable, but includes Whimbrel, Common Sandpiper and Greenshank in small numbers. The valley seems to act as a channel for land migrants, and an active ringing group has trapped large numbers of common warblers, including good numbers of Grasshopper Warblers. The casual observer, however, is more likely to see birds like Wheatears, Whinchat and Redstarts along the hedges, or a Pied Flycatcher in the woodland near the coast. Among raptors, a Marsh Harrier or Hobby may pass through, and rarer visitors have included Red Kite and Honey Buzzard in recent years.

During the late summer the woods grow quiet and the valley hedgerows fill up with dispersing finches, tits and warblers. Small parties of Ringed Plovers are seen on the coastal mudflats, but now that the wader roost is difficult to observe, other wader migrants are recorded rather erratically, although in the past a good variety used to occur, albeit in small numbers. Common and Arctic Terns may stop briefly at the mouth of the Avon, and skuas are seen passing offshore from time to time. In gale conditions petrels, Manx Shearwaters and Gannets have been seen, but would otherwise be exceptional. Late autumn coasting movements by finches, particularly Chaffinches, Greenfinches and Goldfinches, occur regularly, and this period has seen the occasional appearance of Snow Buntings and Black Redstarts, the latter sometimes staying to winter either here or at nearby Avonmouth. Cold weather may bring an influx of Woodcock, which shooting records show to be probably regular in winter in the woodland.

Timing

Early morning is best for seeing the display flights of breeding waders, and most other valley and woodland species are more active then. Mid- to late morning in spring and again in the autumn is the best time for soaring Buzzards, which can become very elusive in midsummer when on eggs, and again in winter when they spend much time perched. Strong winds across the flat meadows keep most birds well out of sight. Pheasants are reared quite extensively in the valley, and autumn shoots can cause general disturbance. Because of the tidal range the best time to see waders is about two hours before high tide.

Access

The Gordano Valley lies between and inland from Portishead and Clevedon, and can be viewed generally from the B3124 that runs between the two towns and along its north side. The most productive fen-land areas are Weston and Walton Moors in the western half of the valley. For access to the AWT reserve on Weston Moor, take the B3124 from Portishead and turn left along a minor no-though-road (Cadbury Lane/Weston Drove) in the middle of Weston-in-Gordano. It is best to park before the first rhyne, and continue on foot: straight on takes you past some willows and reed-filled ditches to the main rhyne with views up and down the valley. For the reserve itself turn right before this point and then straight on past rough ground formed by past and current spoil-tipping activities to the gated entrance to the reserve. A board on the left shows the access paths round part of the reserve. The other fields should not be entered, but the whole area can easily be scanned from the main access track. About ½ mile (0.8 km) beyond Weston-in-Gordano an AWT plaque and a footpath sign indicate the start of a path, muddy in places, which crosses to the road on the other side of the valley, giving good views of the meadows and passing close to the main belt of alder wood-land. For quieter conditions, continue to Walton-in-Gordano, turn left along Moor Lane/Harley Lane across the EN reserve of Walton Moor to reach Clevedon Lane, which runs back along the south side of the valley. After c.1½ miles (2.4 km), a small gated car park on the left (opposite New Farm) marks the entrance to Clapton Moor reserve. An AWT board gives details of the short walk to a wheelchair-friendly hide overlooking more flower-rich meadows, flooded in winter. As elsewhere in the valley, do not forget to scan the ridges for soaring birds of prey, as well as keep-ing an eye on the valley floor.

Just west of the Moor Lane/Clevedon Lane junction a steep stony foot-path provides access to the woodland on Tickenham Hill. At the top, a track runs to the right through mixed beech and coniferous woodland, and there are a couple of points from which fine views of the valley are possible. Alternatively, a footbridge over the M5 leads to Cadbury Camp Lane which runs the whole length of the ridge in the opposite direction. A couple of other paths drop back down to the valley again further on. Alternatively, drive along Clevedon Lane to Clapton-in-Gordano and turn

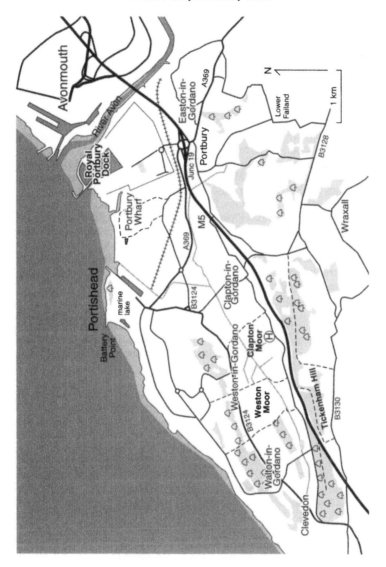

right over the motorway to a small parking spot at the fork in the road where Cadbury Camp Lane emerges. Vehicular access is strictly for residents only, but the road is a public bridleway. The mature gardens and adjoining woodlands hold the commoner breeding birds, and the open grassland of Cadbury Iron Age camp affords views of the southern side of the ridge.

For the Portbury Wharf/Royal Portbury Dock area, the starting point is the M5 junction 19 roundabout. From here take the A369 Portishead road, turning right after ½ mile (0.8 km) to Sheepway. At the far end of this village turn right along the narrow cul-de-sac of Wharf Lane, where there is limited parking at the end. Continue on foot to the shore past rough fields and thick hedges which are attractive to finches and buntings in autumn. Just before the coast, a steep bank on the left hides the CEGB pool, a freshwater lagoon with breeding Mute Swan, Coot, Moorhen and Little Grebe and which has attracted rarities such as Ring-necked Duck on occasion. The *spartina* marsh and the mudflats beyond can be scanned from the seawall, where the footpath runs to the right as far as a small sewage works and the dock perimeter fence. The creek here is often a favoured feeding spot for ducks and waders. The path continues, but it is fair to say that with the expansion of the docks this particular corner has lost much of its interest for the casual birdwatcher.

For more views of the estuary, follow the A369 to Portishead, and then signs to the seafront. The Marine Lake sometimes holds a few Pochard and Tufted Ducks in winter, and is worth a glance in passing for rarer visitors. The headland of Battery Point commands a good views both up and down-river, and Rock Pipits breed here most years. The half-dozen or so Purple Sandpipers that winter here favour the rocks beyond the navigation light, although at low tide it may be better to scan with a telescope from the promenade as the birds can be hidden by the slope. There are nature trails through the adjacent coastal woodland (Eastwood), worth checking at migration periods especially.

Calendar

All year: Grey Heron, Mute Swan, Shelduck, Sparrowhawk, Buzzard, Kestrel, Pheasant, Lapwing, Stock Dove; Barn Owl (irregular), Little Owl, Tawny Owl, woodpeckers including Lesser Spotted (but scarce), Rock Pipit, Skylark, Raven, Reed Bunting.

December–February: Cormorant, Teal, maybe Gadwall, Wigeon, Shoveler, Tufted Duck, Pochard on coast. Chance of other wildfowl in cold weather, e.g. Goldeneye. Merlin, Peregrine, sometimes Short-eared Owl. Water Rail, Dunlin, Redshank, Curlew, Purple Sandpiper, occasional Green Sandpiper; Snipe, Jack Snipe; Woodcock in woodland. Winter gull roost on coast (mostly Black-headed, Herring, Lesser Black-backed). Chance of Water Pipit, Black Redstart. Winter thrush flocks sometimes large. Parties of Chaffinches, Linnets, Reed Buntings on coast, Siskins and Redpolls on moors. Stonechats regular in winter, and may stay to breed.

March–May: Maybe rare migrant April–May. Sparrowhawk and Buzzard soaring displays most frequent. Chance of Hobby from May. Winter waders leave during March, passage of Ringed Plover, Whimbrel April–May. Redshank, Lapwing, Snipe displaying over moors, Oystercatcher and Ringed Plover sometimes nest on coast. Passage of Wheatear, Whinchat, White Wagtail April–May. Arrival of summer breeders from late April, e.g. Cuckoo, warblers.

June–July: Breeding species include Buzzard, waders as above, Reed and Sedge Warblers, Lesser Whitethroat, common woodland passerines, maybe Water Rail. Shelduck plus young on shore. Passage waders from late July.

August–November: Chance of seabird offshore in gales (September–October). Main wader passage, especially Ringed Plover in August, small numbers of Knot, Little Stint, Curlew Sandpiper, Ruff, Greenshank in September, when winter waders start build-up. Purple Sandpiper from

November. Passage thrushes, finches, pipits in October, occasional Snow Bunting October–November.

34 LEIGH WOODS & THE AVON GORGE   OS Explorer 154 or 155

Habitat

The steep limestone cliffs of the Avon Gorge form a spectacular natural western boundary to the city of Bristol, and are visually dominated by the Clifton Suspension Bridge. Immediately beyond the gorge is Leigh Woods, an important part of which comprises 156 acres (63 ha) of mixed deciduous woodland owned by the NT and managed by EN. This section has some fine mature beeches as well as oak, ash, sycamore and birch. Contiguous with this is a larger area of land owned by the Forestry Commission which was densely planted in the 1950s and 60s with conifers. As these mature, clearings are being opened up and replanted to give a much more varied mix of young trees and open spaces. One or two steep gullies with picturesque rocky outcrops run down to the tidal river, most notably at Nightingale Valley. Both sides of the gorge are popular with the general public, using a network of footpaths in the woodland itself and along the west bank of the Avon at the foot of the cliffs.

Species

Leigh Woods is a convenient area close to Bristol to see a good range of woodland species, with the added bonus of Peregrines on the cliffs for much of the year. In winter, the usual tits, Goldcrests, Treecreepers and Nuthatches are the most obvious inhabitants as feeding parties move through the trees, falling suddenly silent if a hunting Sparrowhawk should streak through among them. While berries last, Redwings and a few Fieldfares may join the resident Blackbirds and Song Thrushes within the woodland, all the thrushes also regularly feeding in the adjoining farmland, often alongside the numerous Pheasants. Woodcock are annual winter visitors, but their secretive habits mean that most views are chance ones of birds flushed from undergrowth. The build-up in song during the spring marks the start of the period of greatest interest as breeding birds move back into the area. Green and Great Spotted Woodpeckers are numerous, but Lesser Spotted no longer seem to nest here; in fact they have become very scarce in the Bristol area as a whole. Likewise, the Hawfinches which used to breed here regularly are merely an occasional winter visitor these days. Among summer visitors, Chiffchaffs, Willow Warblers, Blackcaps and Garden Warblers are all widespread, and one or two Wood Warblers can be heard singing most springs, sometimes remaining to breed, though no longer annually. Pied Flycatchers are also seen on passage but as yet have not used the nestboxes put up to attract them and other hole-nesting species. Otherwise, most of the common

Raven

woodland birds are present, and it is hoped that as the more varied vegetation structure develops some of the previous residents will return.

In midsummer attention turns to the Avon Gorge itself, where the Peregrines, if successful, will be feeding young, and therefore be relatively conspicuous. In 1990, the first young for many years were reared, and since then the nest site has been monitored by teams of local bird-watchers each season. Over the same period, a pair of Ravens has also returned to the cliffs, though by midsummer their young should be well on the wing. At least one pair of Kestrels breeds nearby, and there are myriads of Jackdaws to add variety. With round-the-clock surveillance, several rarer birds of prey have been noted passing the watchpoint, including Red Kite, Goshawk and Marsh Harrier, these birds possibly following the line of the river as they migrate through the area. Buzzards are quite commonly seen, as several pairs now nest within a few miles of the gorge. In the woodland, leaf cover and the cessation of song means that less is seen, but Crossbills sometimes move through in invasion years. Later, as the leaves fall, even many of the so-called residents move out into the nearby gardens, leaving a depleted winter population. A few Redshanks may be seen on the mud of the River Avon at any time throughout the year, and freezing conditions in winter may bring the odd Tufted Duck to join the small number of resident Mallard on the water. There are some large Pied Wagtail and Starling roosts around the Cumberland Basin road crossing just upstream from the Clifton Suspension Bridge, often attracting Sparrowhawks and even one of the Peregrines to attempt an evening kill.

Timing

Spring and summer is the most productive period for most species, although woodpeckers can often be seen more easily when the trees are bare. Song is at its maximum during the morning; the dawn chorus here is as good as in any woodland and birds are more easily seen before casual disturbance pushes them away from the most accessible areas.

Access

From central Bristol, the most direct route to Leigh Woods is from the Clifton area over the Clifton Suspension Bridge (toll for vehicles, free for pedestrians and cyclists). On the far side, turn immediately right into North Road, and in the dip near its far end it is possible to park by the roadside. An interpretation panel indicates the main access routes, including several colour-coded trails, the most productive deciduous woodland being approachable along a short gully and then across a grassy clearing. Alternatively, a path down Nightingale Valley to the right leads to the river bank, where the Avon walkway runs close to the shore from Bristol to Pill, a few miles down-river. To avoid the toll-bridge, cross the river at the main Cumberland Basin swing-bridge, and follow the A369 towards Portishead. This rises steeply along the west side of the woodland and passes the far end of North Road c.100 metres before the B3129 junction traffic lights. For the Forestry Commission area, continue west towards Portishead and turn right just beyond a stone archway, down a private road with a car park at its far end. The entrance is clearly signposted, and motorists are encouraged to use this access point. Tracks and paths lead west to the Paradise Bottom area and there are various waymarked paths to the east which link up with the nature reserve area and the cliffs. Several information boards along the way show the main paths.

The Avon Gorge cliffs can be scanned from the road that runs along the west side of Clifton Downs, which are immediately north of Bristol

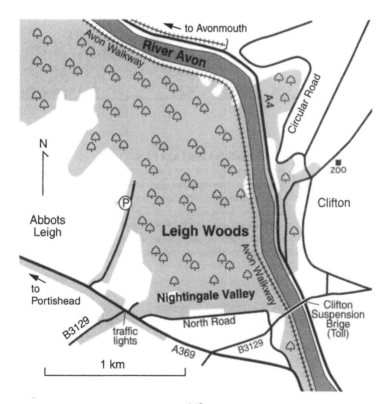

Zoo. This road (Circular Road) approaches close to the cliff edge in a couple of places. If the Peregrines are breeding, there is usually a group of watchers present to indicate the best viewpoint, the exact position of the nest varying from year to year.

Calendar

All year: Mallard, Sparrowhawk, Buzzard, Kestrel, Peregrine, Pheasant, Stock Dove, Tawny Owl, Green and Great Spotted Woodpeckers but Lesser Spotted now rare; Grey Wagtail, common woodland passerines including Nuthatch, Marsh Tit. Raven.

December–February: Redshank, Black-headed Gull, occasional Tufted or other duck by river. Woodcock. Woodland quiet, but birdsong builds up during February, when Ravens start nesting.

March–May: First Chiffchaffs late March; Cuckoo mid-April; most migrants late April–early May, including Wood Warbler, Garden Warbler, Blackcap, Whitethroat, etc. Pied Flycatcher on passage mid-April–May.

June–July: Peregrines feeding young. Breeding woodland birds as above, falling silent in July. Maybe passing Crossbills from July.

August–November: Summer migrants leave during August. Parties of tits, Goldcrest, Treecreeper active September–November. Sometimes influx of Woodcock in November.

35 CITY OF BRISTOL
OS Explorer 155

Habitat and species

Apart from Leigh Woods and the Peregrines of the Avon Gorge (see previous site), the City of Bristol has several sites worth visiting, particularly for locals, or for those with limited time to spare, ranging from waders by the River Avon, woodland birds in some of the parks and nearly 2000 pairs of Lesser Black-backed and Herring Gulls on the rooftops of the city centre. Several pairs of Sparrowhawks nest within the city limits, and Buzzard, Raven and Peregrine have all been seen over the city centre at various times.

Access

The River Avon downstream from the Avon Gorge holds small numbers of ducks, gulls and waders, conveniently viewable from the cycle path that runs from Ashton Gate (ST 721568) all the way along the left bank of the river to Pill (ST 526760). Waders such as Lapwing, Dunlin and Redshank tend to be found along the lower part of this route, but can occur anywhere. Sea Mills station (ST 550758) provides a good viewpoint from the Bristol side over what is often one of the more productive sections. Greenshanks often winter in this area, and Common Sandpipers also occur on passage. There have been several winter sightings of Mediterranean Gulls here, and a Long-tailed Skua took up residence for a few days one autumn.

Blaise Woods (ST 558787) is a public park in the Henbury area of north Bristol, with extensive woodland hosting breeding Green and Great Spotted Woodpeckers, Nuthatches, Treecreepers and Blackcaps, and has been the subject of some long-term monitoring.

The AWT has its headquarters by Brandon Hill (ST 578728), close to the city centre, and the adjacent park around the Cabot Tower makes a good viewpoint over the city and is used by warblers and other species as a migration stop-over.

Although on the surface an unpromising area in the Broomhill/ Frenchay district of northeast Bristol, the riverside walks of the Oldbury Court estate can be quite rewarding, particularly in winter when public pressure is not quite so great. Grey Wagtail, Dipper and Kingfisher can all be seen by the stream, and the park and woodland close by hold Nuthatch, Treecreeper, Great Spotted and, if you are lucky, sometimes Lesser Spotted Woodpecker. Siskins and Redpolls are regularly seen in the riverside trees. Access in the park is fairly general, but a walk upstream from Snuff Mills Park (car park at ST 623766) is usually the most productive.

Not far away, Eastville Park (ST 615755) holds a similar mix of wood-land species, with the lake attracting Mute Swans, Mallard, the occasional Cormorant and Common Sandpiper, and oddities such as Wood Duck and Mandarin. The most remarkable bird must be the Yellow-rumped Warbler seen here in November 1994, an extremely lost transatlantic vagrant.

On the southeast edge of Bristol, Stockwood Open Space (ST 625693) is a local nature reserve managed in partnership with the AWT. It com-prises 24 ha of former non-intensive farmland, some woodland and an in-filled rubbish tip, the whole area being surprisingly rich in wildlife. There are up to four pairs of Little Owls, Great Spotted Woodpeckers breed, and the summer visitors include Whitethroat, Blackcap, Garden Warbler, Chiffchaff and Willow Warbler. Grasshopper Warblers have been heard several times and have bred at least once. Sparrowhawks and Kestrels hunt the area throughout the year.

36 MARSHFIELD   OS Explorer 155 and 156

Habitat and Species

The open arable fields north of the village of Marshfield (northeast of Bath) still hold the most significant population of Corn Buntings near Bristol, although what the future holds for this declining species is hard to predict. Cereal crops dominate, though there are patches of set-aside, some reasonable hedges in places, and plenty of dry-stone walls. Other seed-eaters nesting here include good numbers of Yellowhammers and Linnets, and there are plenty of Skylarks. All these species can be found throughout the year, forming small flocks during the winter. Both Red-legged and Grey Partridges are reasonably common, their numbers, like those of the Pheasants, augmented by releases for shooting. During the summer they are joined by a few Quail, which can be heard calling from the cornfields, but rarely actually seen. Numbers vary from year to year, of course, but Marshfield is one of the more reliable sites for this elusive species in the region. Other species are not particularly noteworthy, but Lapwing and Golden Plover use the fields in winter, and Buzzards and Kestrels can be seen hunting across the open landscape throughout the year.

Access
The primary points of access are junction 18 on the M4 at Tormarton and the A420 which runs through Marshfield. A minor road between these two villages bisects the most productive area, which is best explored on foot along the network of lanes and footpaths east and west of this road, as far as West Littleton in one direction and West Kington in the other. The area is often best early in the morning or at dusk, as the Quail in particular tend to call more frequently at these times. Noise from the motorway can be intrusive.

37 CAM, MIDFORD & WELLOW BROOKS
OS Explorer 155

Habitat and Species
These small streams run through winding, steep-sided and picturesque valleys to join the River Avon near Monkton Combe, southeast of Bath. Although a variety of birds can be seen, their primary interest is for Dipper, Grey Wagtail and Kingfisher, which all breed in the area.

Access
The A361 Bath to Warminster road follows the valley of the River Avon immediately east of Bath. Access to the streams is possible at many points from a network of lanes and public footpaths around the village of Monkton Combe, and the Avon valley woodlands, some of which hold Nightingales in summer, are also accessible in several places. The ATW have reserves at Brown's Folly and Bathampton Meadows, near Bathford (contact AWT for access details).

Habitat

Severnside is the name generally used for the east shore of the River Severn between the mouth of the River Avon and the original Severn Bridge at Aust. The southern section is dominated by the industrial hinterland of Avonmouth, with its docks and chemical works, although there are some sewage lagoons and various small pools here. Chittening Warth has a strip of *spartina* and rough grassland, fronted by mud and then extensive shingle banks offshore exposed at low tide. The central section, between Severn Beach and New Passage, is protected by a concrete sea-wall overlooking stones and gravel but very little mud, and the second Severn crossing strides overhead here. North again, there are more mud-flats, but narrower and steeper here, although backed by some damp grassland at Aust and Northwick Warths. The fields behind the seawall hold some shallow marshy pools which have helped extend the range of species seen regularly on this stretch of coast.

Species

Passage and wintering birds are the main interest here, primarily waders but with a good scattering of other species using the river as a migration route. Numbers of wintering waders are dominated by around 4000 Dunlin out on the mudflats, accompanied by 200 or so Curlew. Lapwing numbers can sometimes be huge if driven to the coast by hard weather, but are normally highest on autumn passage. The gravel parts of the shore attract a regular flock of up to 200 Turnstones; in the past they were accompanied by a few Purple Sandpipers, but this species no longer winters here regularly, although odd birds still turn up on passage. There are small numbers of Snipe and Jack Snipe in the *spartina* and wet grassland, with up to 30 Ringed Plover and 150 Redshank scattered along

Redshank

the shore, but other waders at this time of year are few, although in some years Black-tailed Godwits have taken up residence. A few hundred Wigeon, Teal and Mallard winter along the shore, small numbers of the last being resident, but cold weather may bring brief influxes of far more, plus a scattering of other species including Goldeneye, Goosander, Ruddy Duck and Great Crested Grebe which are otherwise unusual. With the appearance of freshwater pools in various places behind the seawall, Coots, Tufted Ducks, Pochard and Little Grebes are now regularly recorded through much of the year, though still unusual on the river itself. Other diving and seaduck occur in small numbers on passage, Common Scoter being the only species to be expected annually. A few Shoveler and Pochard frequent the lagoons of Avonmouth Sewage Works, where Green Sandpipers have been known to winter. Parties of Bewick's Swans occasionally pass on their way to and from Slimbridge, and White-fronted Geese may appear briefly in cold weather. Small groups of Brent Geese, usually in single-figure numbers, are now seen regularly along the estuary, and turn up here as often as anywhere. Among predators, Peregrines and Merlins are annual winter visitors but any Hen Harriers and Short-eared Owls are usually just passing birds in autumn. There is a gull roost at Avonmouth, difficult to view, and rubbish tips in the area attract large numbers of Herring and Lesser Black-backed Gulls. Closer scrutiny of the gulls has produced several records of Yellow-legged Gulls from late summer to winter, while Mediterranean Gulls are now seen annually, primarily in the winter half of the year.

Spring brings a brief increase in the numbers of Ringed Plover and Turnstone as passage birds move through, and Sanderling, Bar-tailed Godwit and Whimbrel are regular in small numbers at the same time. Common and Arctic Terns, sometimes too far out to be identified specifically, pass up-river in small parties. Exceptionally, under the right weather conditions, thousands have been seen in just a day or two, sometimes accompanied by significant numbers of Little Gulls and Black Terns which otherwise usually occur in only ones and twos. Two or three Arctic Skuas also pass through, with the odd Pomarine Skua in late spring, all these birds presumably heading for an overland route. Kittiwakes sometimes appear in large numbers in the late winter or spring, usually after strong southwesterly gales: whether some of them are also heading overland on passage is uncertain. Passerine migrants such as Wheatears along the shore or a reeling Grasshopper Warbler in the scrub make a brief appearance and the area is rarely productive in the summer months, although parties of Manx Shearwaters and Fulmars sometimes make it this far up-river in early summer. As elsewhere, Little Egrets have recently started to appear at this time, often favouring the various pools and lagoons back from the coast, although they also feed on the shore. Wader numbers build up again in the autumn, Ringed Plover flocks regularly exceeding 300. Knot, Sanderling, Little Stint and Curlew Sandpiper are regular in small numbers, and there is a trickle of 'freshwater' waders such as Ruff, Common and Green Sandpipers. Finding unusual species on the open shore is difficult, but rarities such as Buff-breasted and White-rumped Sandpipers have been located (this last on several occasions), and the sewage works has held Lesser Yellowlegs and Pectoral Sandpiper in autumn. The return passage of terns and skuas is thin, the same species as in spring occurring in ones and twos, but with more chance of Pomarine and Long-tailed Skuas, though both are still infrequent.

Increased seawatching in the past few years has raised the numbers of seabirds recorded here at all seasons, with autumn gales producing pelagic vagrants such as Storm and Leach's Petrels and Sabine's Gulls on several occasions.

Visible migration of passerines along the shores of the Severn Estuary has been studied for many years, and the New Passage area has regularly produced good numbers, probably swelled by the addition of birds following the South Wales coast and crossing at this point. Strangely, the dominant direction of movement seems to be towards the northeast. Chaffinches and Starlings predominate, but Pied Wagtails, Greenfinches, Meadow Pipits, Skylarks and Linnets are also numerous. Among these is a scattering of a wide range of other species: Bramblings, Goldfinches, Redpolls, Siskins, Grey Wagtails and thrushes are regular, though it certainly helps to know the various flight calls to have any success in picking them out. Adding spice to life are the accompanying rarer passage birds such as the Lapland and Snow Buntings, and Richard's Pipit has occurred as a vagrant. Most of the finches and buntings continue through, but flocks of Chaffinches, Meadow Pipits and Bramblings sometimes remain into the winter if feeding conditions are good. Snow Buntings and the occasional Black Redstart may also linger, the latter more likely to be hidden among the docks and factories of Avonmouth.

Timing

High-tide visits are essential for waders, about an hour either side of high water being best: at low water most species are difficult to pick out on the vast mud and gravel banks. Lighting conditions are better in the morning, as the coast faces nearly due west. High water also gives the best chance of seeing water birds close to, and hard weather brings the biggest variety. The area is worth checking during southwest gales, particularly in autumn and winter, for a chance of storm-blown seabirds, and once again high-tide visits are always the most productive. Strong northeasterlies in spring often produce good numbers of skuas, terns and Little Gulls and headwinds from the same direction plus overcast skies produce the best conditions for visible passage in autumn: in clear calm conditions birds will pass high up over a broad front. The first three hours after dawn always produce the most birds, although a few trickle through later in the day. Coastal fog makes viewing very frustrating, although birds may still be passing not far overhead.

Access

The A403 running between Avonmouth and M4 junction 21 at the old Severn Bridge provides the main access route. Any turning marked Severn Beach (which is also accessible by rail from Bristol) will bring you eventually to the south end of the seawall that protects this section. Park nearby and scan from the seawall or walk south along the beach, checking the shore for waders and the saltmarsh for winter duck, passerines and raptors. Turnstones (and Purple Sandpipers when they were present) prefer the gravel beds off the Chittening shore to the rocks off Severn Beach itself. The seawall just south of the second Severn crossing is the best spot for sea-watching, as seabirds seem reluctant to pass beyond the second Severn crossing, and often linger offshore for a time before re-orientating back down-river. The path along the concrete seawall to the north passes under the new bridge to reach New Passage after c.1 mile (1.6 km) (this spot is also accessible by road, but parking is very limited). The promontory here is a good spot for scanning the mudflats at Northwick Warth, which also hold good numbers of waders. The way-marked Severn Way continues north along the seawall across a sluice, with grassland, sometimes flooded, on the left attracting Shelduck, waders and other wildfowl, particularly at high tide. Several of the rarer

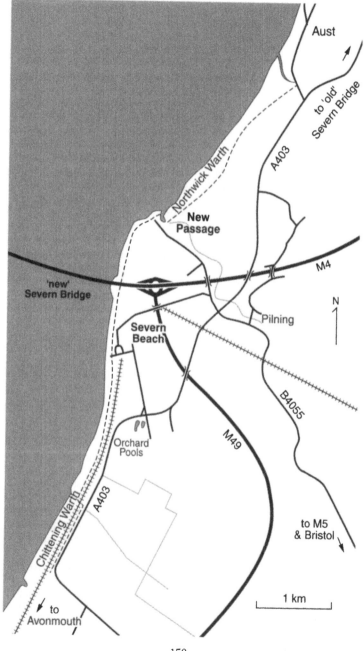

waders have been seen here. There is a rifle-range (active from April to October) on the right, and access is not permitted when the red flags are flying. At other times, the pools behind the seawall a little further on are worth checking for ducks, grebes and waders, while the hawthorn hedges may conceal interesting passerines. The path continues to join a minor road south of Aust.

There are various pools in the immediate hinterland, several not marked on OS maps, and not always clearly named. One group that has attracted Ring-necked Ducks several times, among other wildfowl, are those associated with Avonmouth Sewage Works. From Avonmouth go north along the A403, turning right at some traffic lights along Kings Weston Lane. After ¾ mile (1.2 km), just beyond Britannia Zinc Ltd, turn left towards the refuse transfer station/old incinerator. The lagoons can be partially viewed through the fence on the left, but for closer access a permit is needed from the AWT. Their reserve is now named Avonmouth Pools, while the outlying lagoon to the north, which also attracts wild-fowl, is known as Hoar Gout. Continuing north along the A403, the Honda Pools can be accessed along a path to the right immediately before the railway bridge beyond Cabot Park. They comprise several shallow reed-fringed lagoons immediately behind the Honda industrial units, and hold Mute Swans and Little Grebe throughout the year, with Reed and Sedge Warblers arriving in summer. Continuing north to Severn Beach, but turning right into a short cul-de-sac rather than to Severn Beach itself, brings you to Orchard Pools, two lagoons on the right, surrounded by rough ground, which often attract Little Egrets from the estuary as well as a few ducks and waders. One word of warning: the whole area is under constant industrial development, with the road layout, access and habitat changing rapidly, and during the week the roads can be full of heavy traffic.

Calendar

All year: Cormorant, Shelduck, Mallard, Buzzard, Reed Bunting.

December–February: Chance of passing White-fronted Goose, Bewick's Swan, Great Crested Grebe or unusual diving duck in cold weather. Maybe Brent Goose. Wigeon, Teal; other dabbling ducks scarce. Pochard and Tufted Duck regular (sewage works and Northwick Warth). Merlin, Peregrine, Oystercatcher, Dunlin, Curlew, Turnstone, Redshank, Ringed Plover, Snipe; sometimes Black-tailed Godwits; maybe Green Sandpiper (sewage farm) or Purple Sandpiper (rare). Sometimes unusual seabird, e.g. Little Auk, Great Skua, Kittiwake. Sometimes winter finches include Brambling. Maybe Black Redstart or Snow Bunting.

March–May: Little Grebe sometimes breeds (sewage farm). Sometimes Common Scoter in April. Occasional Marsh Harrier (May). Passage waders, e.g. Turnstone, Bar-tailed Godwit peak April, Ringed Plover, Sanderling peak May, Whimbrel late April–May. Main Common/Arctic Tern passage April–May, plus a few Little Gulls, Black Terns, Arctic Skua. Wheatear, Whinchat pass April–early May, when occasional falls of warblers.

June–July: Occasional groups of Manx Shearwater, Fulmar. Maybe Common Scoter in July (irregular all year). Return passage of waders starts July, especially Ringed Plover, Lapwing. Reed and Sedge Warblers at the pools just inland.

August–November. Chance of Manx Shearwater, petrel, skua or other seabird September–October. Little Egrets most often seen during this period. Maybe unusual wildfowl, e.g. Long-tailed Duck, Red-breasted Merganser, Scaup, Velvet Scoter towards end of period. Peregrine from August; passing raptors, e.g. Marsh or Hen Harrier, Short-eared Owl, October–November. Main wader passage August–October, including Knot, Sanderling (peak August), Ruff, Little Stint, Curlew Sandpiper (peak September); chance of rarity, e.g. American shorebird. Visible migration of passerines from mid-September (Grey Wagtail, hirundines) peaking through October into early November (finches, pipits, Skylark, Starling) with occasional rarity (Lapland and Snow Buntings). Black Redstart from late October.

39 LOWER WOODS & INGLESTONE COMMON   OS Explorer 167

Habitat

Lower Woods Nature Reserve encompasses a large part of the complex of woodland and heathland lying between the town of Wickwar and the Cotswold escarpment, having expanded from the original Wetmoor reserve managed by the GNT. Although ancient in origin, little resembling natural forest remains, but replanting and management has been varied, resulting in a patchwork of woodland types, varying from oak plantation in Wetmoor itself, through mixed oak and ash woodland to poplar and conifer plantations. Woodland blocks are intersected by broad open rides, which prove attractive to a wide range of butterflies, including white admiral, silver-washed fritillary and grizzled skipper. The heavy soil over much of the area, and the several small streams which cross it, mean that the ground remains waterlogged and sticky for long periods, discouraging access and clearance. The fringes of the woodland are dominated by thickets of hawthorn and blackthorn, particularly around Inglestone Common by which name the area is also often known. The surrounding farmland contains open cattle-grazed rough grassland on Inglestone and Hawkesbury Commons, as well as a few lush meadows in more inaccessible corners.

Species

Traditionally this has been the main site for listening to Nightingales in the Bristol area, with over 20 singing birds in some springs (though none at all in others!). Considering the extent and varied nature of the habitat, it is strange that the area has been rather neglected by observers at other times of year. Nevertheless, in the breeding season, most of the common passerines can be found, including Whitethroats, Lesser Whitethroats,

Blackcaps, Garden Warblers, Chiffchaffs and Willow Warblers in good numbers, plus the usual woodland residents. Grasshopper Warblers have been seen (or heard) on several occasions and much of the habitat looks ideal for this secretive species. Both Pied Flycatcher and Redstart have been heard singing in spring, and certainly the latter has bred several times in the past few years. The two common woodpeckers are widespread; Lesser Spotted has bred in the past, and although there are few recent records, they could well be being overlooked in such an extensive area. Sparrowhawks and Kestrels hunt the area regularly, and Buzzards can often been seen overhead, having moved in as a breeding bird from the nearby Cotswold escarpment, where numbers have been increasing for some time. The coniferous plantations sometimes attract passing Crossbills in eruption years, and the very occasional sighting of a Willow Tit indicates that they have not entirely deserted the woodland, formerly a regular breeding site, although they are becoming a hard bird to find in the Bristol area these days. In winter the woods are much quieter, but Woodcock find the damp ground ideal for feeding, and this is another species that is a potential breeder here.

Great Spotted Woodpecker

Timing

For Nightingales, warm evenings in late spring, or calm mornings after dawn provide the best conditions for hearing this magnificent songster, although birds sing intermittently throughout the day during the peak song period. For most other passerines, early morning visits are always the most productive throughout the year. Icy conditions in winter may force Woodcock more into the open. Heavy rain and strong winds make woodland birdwatching almost impossible.

Access

From the centre of Wickwar, take the B4060 north towards Wotton-under-Edge, but then fork almost immediately right down a narrow lane,

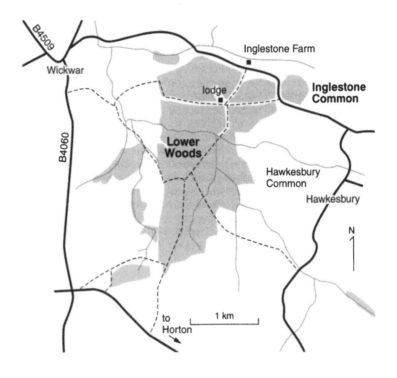

signposted to Inglestone Common; follow this for just over 1 mile (1.6 km) to where it crosses a cattle grid on to unfenced common land with scattered houses and farms. For the next mile (1.6 km) the road skirts the main block of woodland to the right and Nightingales can be heard in several of the dense thickets along this stretch. Opposite Inglestone Farm, where there is a postbox let into a wall, a track leads off to the right to Lower Woods Lodge, where there is space for cars to park, and where a map shows the main access routes. An unfenced gravelled track to the left leads on into the main woodland, through thickets which tradition-ally hold several pairs of Nightingales. It continues as a private road to Bucklebury Farm, but before then there is an obvious path branching right and down steeply to a bridge over a small stream. Grey Wagtail and, occasionally, Dipper can be seen here. The main ride through the centre of the woods starts from here, with many tracks branching off left and right for further exploration. In general one can walk along the rides throughout the woodland, but any access restrictions should be respected. Note also that waterproof footwear is often essential. The most productive areas are generally those in the northern half of the area, including north of the Lodge, where there is more broadleaved wood-land and dense scrub; the conifer plantations are mostly at the southern end, and there are some interesting meadows along the western edge. The bushy areas around Inglestone Common are worth checking for Lesser Whitethroat, and Skylarks can be heard singing overhead in the summer.

Calendar

All year: Sparrowhawk, Kestrel, Buzzard, Pheasant, Little Owl, Tawny Owl, woodpeckers may include Lesser Spotted; common woodland passerines including Goldcrest, Long-tailed Tit, Marsh Tit, Nuthatch, maybe Willow Tit.

December–February: Golden Plover sometimes on Hawkesbury Common. Woodcock. Song building up from February.

March–May: Chiffchaff from late March; Cuckoo, Willow Warbler, Nightingale from mid-April; Redstart and most warblers e.g. Whitethroat, Lesser Whitethroat, Garden Warbler, Blackcap late April–early May; Spotted Flycatcher mid-May. Maybe Grasshopper Warbler or Pied Flycatcher April–May.

June–July: Nightingale sings to early June, other passerines to early July. Maybe Crossbills passing late July.

August–November: Summer visitors leave during August. Woodcock from October. Woodland quiet from November–February.

40 TORTWORTH LAKE   OS Explorer 167

Habitat and Species

An attractive small woodland lake set in a steep-sided valley a few miles northeast of Thornbury. The outstanding species here is Mandarin, up to a dozen of which have been counted in autumn, and which probably breeds regularly, an offshoot of the population resident further north around Slimbridge. A few pairs of Little Grebes also nest, with post-breeding assemblies into double figures. Wildfowl include Mallard, Gadwall, Shoveler, Mute Swan and Canada Goose, with Tufted Duck being the most numerous, peaking at over 50. Kingfishers and Grey Wagtail occur by the waterside, while the surrounding woodland holds the usual common species, including Buzzard, Sparrowhawk and Kestrel.

Access

The lake lies in the private Tortworth Estate, and currently (2003) is closed to the public. It was previously accessible by taking the B4509 towards Wotton and Leyhill from M5 junction 14, and then turning right after c.200 metres, just beyond a layby on the right, onto a track into the estate. It may be that access to the path round the lake will be allowed again in the future, so this short account is retained for the moment.

41 OLDBURY-ON-SEVERN/ AUST

Habitat

Dominating the landscape on this stretch of the Severn Estuary between the 'old' Severn Bridge at Aust and the neck at Sharpness are the nuclear power stations of Oldbury and Berkeley, the former having introduced ornithologically significant additions to the landscape in the form of an empounded tidal reservoir just offshore, and some muddy settling pools (two now dry) next to the station itself. Also adjacent is a waymarked nature trail incorporating wildflower meadows, an old orchard, some young woodland and a few ponds. The shore itself is relatively featureless, the main channel running close to the near side to form steeply shelving mud banks backed by a narrow strip of wet grassland. At low tide, vast mud and sand flats are exposed out in the middle of the estuary and there are several outcrops of tide-scoured rocks north of Oldbury and at Aust. At Littleton, some disused brickpits are choked with *phragmites* and maintained as a nature reserve by the AWT, while at Aust there is a small sewage works close to the Severn Bridge. Otherwise, the immediate hinterland is mostly cattle-grazed fields with hedges, orchards and scattered trees.

Species

Wading birds, particularly at passage times, provide the main interest here, although, to be fair, it is not a particularly outstanding site. Dunlin, Curlew and Redshank are the usual species throughout the year, spread out over the mudflats at low water and concentrating on the upper shore or in the power station silt lagoons to roost. Dunlin may reach 1500 at peak times, and counts of roosting Curlews have been over 1000 birds on many occasions in autumn and winter. About 50 Turnstones winter on the rockier parts of the shore and a few Golden Plover may join the Lapwings which move from fields to mudflats depending on disturbance and feeding conditions. In the spring, Sanderling pass through in small numbers, with Ringed Plover, Whimbrel and a few Bar-tailed Godwits also occurring at this time.

Dunlin

Other species regularly found during the winter include up to a dozen Cormorants roosting around the tidal reservoir, and small numbers of Mallard, Wigeon and Teal along the shoreline. Other wildfowl are irregular passing birds, Pintail, Bewick's Swans and White-fronted Geese from the flocks up-river at Slimbridge being the most likely to be seen. Cold weather may force diving birds such as Tufted Duck, Goldeneye, Great Crested and Little Grebes on to the river, but these are unusual. Nevertheless, rarer wildfowl have included Long-tailed and Ring-necked Ducks, and there have been several sightings of Red-breasted Merganser. Kestrels are the commonest raptor, but Peregrines are nowadays seen throughout the year, sometimes perched on the power station buildings, and there is the chance of Merlin, Hen Harrier or Short-eared Owl on autumn passage. Buzzards nest a short distance inland, and can be seen circling over the nearby fields at all times of the year. Aust sewage works attracts a small number of wintering passerines, including several Chiffchaffs, and is a focal point for migrants at both seasons.

In spring, Wheatears and Whinchats appear in ones and twos along the seawall, but Swallows, together with smaller numbers of House and Sand Martins, move through in numbers of up to 500 birds per hour, following the bank closely on their way north. There is also a light passage of terns and the occasional Arctic Skua is recorded, both in spring and autumn. The summer is a quiet period, though there is a good population of Reed Warblers at Littleton brickpits, and Stock Doves and Little Owls nest in the hedgerow trees just inland. Throughout the autumn the silt lagoons at Oldbury attract migrant waders in small numbers, notably up to 300 Ringed Plovers but including 'freshwater' species such as Spotted Redshank, Greenshank and Common Sandpiper, as well as Curlew Sandpiper and Little Stint. Past rarities have included Broad-billed and Semipalmated Sandpipers. Autumn gales may bring seabirds offshore briefly, although the construction of the second Severn crossing has reduced the likelihood of many birds getting this far upstream. From autumn through to spring large numbers of gulls, mainly Common and Black-headed, roost on the open flats, and up to 40 non-breeding Great Black-backed Gulls are a regular feature through the summer months. From late summer the gulls are worth checking for Yellow-legged Gulls, which are regular migrants here, and Mediterranean Gulls also occur erratically right through to the spring. There is a trickle of autumn passerines such as Stonechat and Wheatear, and the power station sometimes attracts the odd Black Redstart.

Timing

High-tide visits are the most productive, particularly at Oldbury where roosting birds congregate on the main silt lagoon. At low tide most waders are spread thinly over the vast mudflats, although Turnstones feed throughout the day on rocks close to the east shore. Gale conditions may produce seabirds which are otherwise extremely rare here. From midday, gulls start to gather on the mudflats offshore, but distance makes identification difficult.

Access

For Oldbury Power Station, follow signs from the M5 (junctions 14 or 16) or A38 to Thornbury, then northwest towards Oldbury-on-Severn. You have to fork right before reaching the village but the power station is clearly signposted. There is a large car park and the visitor centre is open

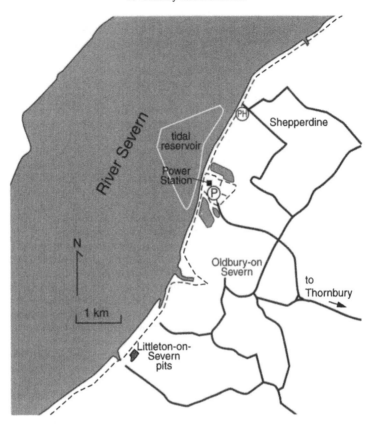

10 am–4 pm, Monday to Friday, from March to October). A leaflet describing the adjacent nature trail is available free. The trail has a series of information boards at strategic places, and is easy to follow. It runs right round the perimeter of the power station, taking in the dryland habitats as well as affording good views out over the estuary. Immediately to the north, partially viewable from the seawall, the two older silt lagoons sometimes flood in winter, and then can attract good numbers of duck, Snipe and Lapwings. The newest silt lagoon lies just south of the power station, and is the one most attractive to roosting waders. It is overlooked by a hide reached via a track starting just outside the main entrance gate, but visitors should report to the security office first for permission and directions to it.

For the shore to the north, return from the power station towards Oldbury, but bear left along narrow lanes to Shepperdine, eventually emerging at the seawall by the Windbound Centre, where there is a large car park – it would be tactful to patronise the café/bar if this is used. A public footpath runs in either direction along the seawall. The tidal reservoir lies immediately offshore, and parts of the settling pools can be seen from the seawall by the power station; the 2¼ mile (3.6 km) stretch north to Severn House Farm makes a reasonable walk for a scan of the estuary generally.

Littleton-on-Severn is signposted west from Thornbury. From the northern edge of the village take a no-through-road signposted to Whale Wharf, which leads in ¾ mile (1.2 km) to a car parking area behind the seawall. A path along the seawall to the north allows the brickpits to be scanned from a raised vantage point; the reedbeds themselves should not be entered. To the south, the Severn Way follows the seawall, and passes Aust sewage works a short distance before reaching the 'old' Severn Bridge.

Calendar

All year: Cormorant, Mallard, Buzzard, Peregrine, Kestrel, Red-legged and Grey Partridges, Stock Dove, Little Owl.

December–February: Passing White-fronted Goose, Bewick's Swan. Wigeon, Teal, maybe Pintail or diving duck. Dunlin, Redshank, Snipe, Jack Snipe, Curlew, Turnstone, sometimes Golden Plover. Gull roost, mostly Common, Black-headed, but maybe a rarity. Pied Wagtail roost at Oldbury; wintering Chiffchaffs at Aust sewage works.

March–May: Passage waders (April–May) include Oystercatcher, Ringed Plover, Sanderling, a few Whimbrel, Bar-tailed Godwit. Common/Arctic Terns, maybe Arctic Skua mid-April–May. Hirundine passage early May; Wheatear, White Wagtail (April).

June–July: Wader passage late July, e.g. Common Sandpiper, Ringed Plover. Yellow Wagtail moving from end July. Reed Warblers at Littleton brickpits.

August–November: Chance of seabird in gales. Maybe passing raptor, e.g. Merlin, October–November. Widest variety of waders August–September: Ringed Plover, Sanderling, Little Stint, Curlew Sandpiper; 'freshwater' waders include Spotted Redshank, Greenshank, Ruff, maybe a rarity. Stonechat, sometimes Black Redstart, on passage and may winter.

42 THE WEST BANK OF THE SEVERN

OS Outdoor Leisure 14

Habitat

Although lacking any obvious 'hot-spots' like the WWT at Slimbridge on the opposite side of the river, the west side of the Severn upstream from the 'old' Severn Bridge is not without interest, especially for those who like to see their birds far from the madding crowd. Aylburton Warth, which lies 6 miles (9.6 km) upstream from the bridge, is the central section of the first stretch of damp grassland along this side of the river, from Pillhouse Rocks in the south to Lydney New Grounds in the north, all fronted by broad expanses of mud and sand exposed at low tide. Just down-river the low, flat and seaweed-covered Guscar Rocks and a strip of shingle on the shore provide the main focus for the waders in this section of the estuary. The river narrows at Lydney harbour, before widening out again further upstream. At Awre, immediately opposite Slimbridge, vast mudflats are exposed at low tide, and can be viewed from footpaths along the grassy seawall which protects the grassland and old orchards immediately inland.

Species

Guscar Rocks are a traditional high-tide gathering spot for waders using this stretch of the river, particularly at passage times, although numbers in recent years have declined quite considerably. A few hundred Curlew and Dunlin are usually the most numerous species in winter, along with small numbers of Redshank and Lapwing. A handful of Snipe, Oystercatchers and Ringed Plovers also occur during the winter. The numbers of Lapwings feeding in the fields may increase many-fold if cold weather drives them to the coast, and they are sometimes joined by a few Golden Plover. Further upstream at Awre, a similar mix of species can be found spread out across the mudflats at low tide with, at least theoretically, any of the waders and wildfowl found at Slimbridge visible, if only distantly. In general, however, apart from Teal, Wigeon and Shelduck, and birds moving through and around the estuary, wildfowl are not a major feature of this side of the river. Prey is sufficiently abundant, nevertheless, to attract both Peregrine and Merlin, usually singly, the former being now a regular wintering bird along the whole estuary. The most spectacular sight, however, is provided by the vast gull roost in the Awre section of the river, where thousands of Black-headed, Common, Herring and Lesser Black-backed Gulls gather on the sands during the winter afternoons. Up to eight Mediterranean Gulls at a time have been located among the hordes, and no doubt others are overlooked. Yellow-legged Gulls also occur in small numbers, and Ring-billed Gulls have been seen virtually annually in recent years. There have been several records of Glaucous and Iceland Gulls, both of which are extremely rare elsewhere in the region, and storm conditions sometimes bring Kittiwakes to this part of the estuary in winter.

Spring passage sees an increase in the variety of waders, Ringed Plover being the commonest, while Sanderling, Grey Plover, Knot and Whimbrel are all regular in small numbers. Rarer species at Aylburton Warth in the past have included Dotterel and Broad-billed Sandpiper. Flocks of Meadow Pipits gather in the fields with one or two pairs remaining to breed, while White Wagtails and Wheatears are characteristic migrants along the seawall throughout. Summer is a relatively quiet period, although Oystercatcher, Lapwing and Yellow Wagtail sometimes attempt to nest in the Aylburton area. Autumn sees another build-up of waders, with again Ringed Plovers the most numerous migrant. Other species regular in small numbers are Knot, Curlew Sandpiper, Little Stint, Bar-tailed Godwit and Turnstone. Species more often associated with freshwater habitats, such as Greenshank, Ruff and Spotted Redshank, are only occasionally recorded, but small numbers of Common Sandpipers can sometimes be seen moving down-river.

Among passerine migrants, Whinchats and Wheatears are annual in and around the meadows, and parties Yellow Wagtails stop to feed for a few days. A trickle of other birds includes the odd Black Redstart later in the autumn, sometimes lingering around the old harbour at Lydney. Water Pipits are seen most winters in the Aylburton area, needing to be distinguished from the more widespread Rock Pipits. A few Tree Sparrows cling on to one of their last remaining outposts here while rough ground around the edges of the area attracts post-breeding flocks of Linnets and other finches. Ravens are seen in ones and twos at any time of year, but are most frequent in the winter.

Timing
At Guscar Rocks, high-tide visits will be the most productive, as later the waders disperse widely over the mudflats and become more difficult to watch. However, at Awre, most of the waders roost on the east side, and are easier to see, although still distant, as they move out and follow the receding tide. The gulls gather to roost throughout the afternoon and lighting conditions are ideal on this side of the river, with the setting sun at your back. The estuary is very exposed here so watching in wet and windy conditions can be difficult, although in autumn southwesterlies may bring the chance of storm-blown seabirds even this far up-river. Freezing conditions tend to concentrate birds to the coast, with large-scale weather movements of Lapwings and Skylarks into the area.

Access
Note that in several places parking is very restricted, and you may have to walk some way to reach the coast along rather rough paths. For Aylburton Warth, take the A48 from Chepstow north towards Lydney and after c.5 miles (8 km) turn right in Woolaston along the cul-de-sac of Station Road. Continue to a level crossing, where you can park by the roadside. Continue on foot across the railway and take the public footpath which follows the hedge to the seawall. Guscar Rocks lie just offshore to the right, and Aylburton Warth is up-river to the left. Both can be approached along the seawall, although there is no formal public access

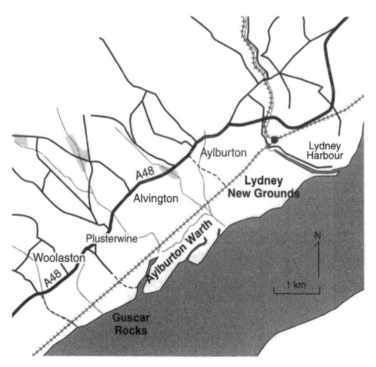

along the shore. Another public footpath emerges on the coast to the south of Guscar Rocks from the main road just before Woolaston, and both the rocks and the shore to the south can be scanned here at the mouth of Grange Pill. In gale conditions watches from the old ferry slip-way at the end of the B4228 at Beachley, almost under the 'old' Severn Bridge, have produced seabird sightings, but the coming of the second Severn crossing has reduced the numbers of birds reaching this point.

Lydney Harbour is at the far end of a minor road off the A48, sign-posted Lydney Industrial Estate; continue past the station (access by rail possible) to the end of the canal where a lottery-funded regeneration project is redeveloping this currently rather derelict area. The river and the grazing meadows to the south can be scanned from the seawall, and the buildings and bushes around the yacht club area are worth checking for migrants in spring and autumn.

A couple of minor lanes from the A48 between Blakeney and Newnham lead to the village of Awre (see also map with site 46, Slimbridge). Here, Woodend Lane, near the Red Hart Inn, leads to the seawall, though cars should be parked (considerately) back in the village, as there is no space anywhere in the lane itself. The Severn Way runs along the seawall to the north, and provides an excellent vantage point for scanning the river and mudflats, with the WWT immediately opposite. This is a good area for watching the gulls gathering to roost, but waders and migrants passing offshore are also visible.

Calendar

All year: Mallard, Kestrel, Redshank, Black-headed Gull, Skylark, Meadow Pipit, Raven; Tree Sparrow (scarce).

December–February: Shelduck, Wigeon, Teal; occasional diving or sea-duck offshore. Merlin, Peregrine, Dunlin, Curlew, Redshank, Snipe, Lapwing, Golden Plover, maybe Grey Plover, Ringed Plover. Snipe in damp fields. Chance of Kittiwake or other storm-driven seabird; gull roost peaks, with best chance of Glaucous, Iceland or other rare gull. Rock and Water Pipits, sometimes Stonechat.

March–May: Shelduck. Passage waders: Ringed Plover and Whimbrel peak April–May, Sanderling (mostly in May), Grey Plover, Knot, Bar-tailed Godwit. Wheatear from late March. Yellow and White Wagtails, Whinchats from April.

June–July: Breeding Meadow Pipit, Yellow Wagtail, Reed Warbler, occasional Shelduck, Oystercatcher or Lapwing. Wader passage (mostly adults) starts July, especially Ringed Plover, Common Sandpiper. Mediterranean Gulls start to appear from July.

August–November: Grey Heron. Ringed Plover peak August. Late August–mid-October: Knot, Curlew Sandpiper, Little Stint, Grey Plover, Bar-tailed Godwit, Turnstone, small numbers of 'freshwater' waders, e.g. Greenshank. Wintering waders build up from October. Gull numbers build up, with Mediterranean and Yellow-legged Gulls passing through (esp. August–September). Yellow Wagtail, Whinchat, Wheatear (August–September). Chance of Black Redstart (from October). Finch flocks include Linnet (especially August), later Chaffinch, Brambling. Most wintering birds present from early November.

43 FOREST OF DEAN & THE WYE VALLEY: GENERAL INTRODUCTION

This roughly triangular region between the rivers Severn and Wye north from their confluence at Chepstow to the A40/M50 is dominated by woodland, both deciduous and coniferous. Any of the woodlands will repay exploration and the whole length of the River Wye holds much of interest. However, for convenience three of the most productive areas with the easiest access have been picked out for more detailed treatment, each one holding its own specialities.

43a THE FOREST OF DEAN

Habitat

At some 25,000 acres (10,000 ha), the Forest of Dean is the largest area of continuous woodland in the region. It originally consisted mainly of sessile oak with ash, elm and hornbeam in the valley bottoms, but replanting under the auspices of the Forestry Commission, which manages the bulk of the woodland, has resulted in an overall mixture of half deciduous (mostly pendunculate oak plus beech, sweet chestnut, etc.), half coniferous, the latter comprising a wide variety of exotic and native species. Forestry operations mean that a mixture of habitats is continuously maintained, ranging from newly cleared open areas, through the thicket stages of the young plantations, to high forest in the mature woodland, and conservation management is now given a high priority. Coal mining has been a traditional land-use, but since the closing of the deep pits, mines are very small and unobtrusively scattered through the woods. Although the forest is ringed with villages, habitation within the woodland itself is sparse, leaving large areas undisturbed. There are several streams and forest ponds, the latter man-made. The public have access to large areas, with picnic sites and forest trails. The RSPB manage a reserve at Nagshead, notable as the site of a long-running nestbox scheme dating from 1942. Foxes and badgers occur widely, although not often seen, and there are small groups of fallow deer. In deciduous areas, butterfly species include white admiral, silver-washed fritillary and purple hairstreak.

Species

The Forest of Dean contains an extremely rich and varied woodland breeding population but in winter, large areas can be relatively quiet. In the bare trees species such as tits, Nuthatches and woodpeckers, including several pairs of Lesser Spotted, are perhaps more visible than in summer, but many so-called residents move out of the main woodland, to concentrate around the villages and gardens at the edges. Flocks of Chaffinches, Great Tits and fluctuating numbers of Bramblings gather to feed on beech mast in years when the crop has not failed. Redpolls and Siskins feed among the alders and birches by the streams, where the few pairs of Dippers are resident, and Woodcock may be flushed from cover almost anywhere. Single Great Grey Shrikes have occasionally wintered in some of the clearings, but the forest is not a traditional locality for this species. The larger woodland ponds attract small numbers of Tufted Ducks and Goosander in the winter, in addition to the Coots, Mallard and Little Grebes which are resident on some of them. The star waterbird is the Mandarin, which has a major stronghold here, with recent estimates of over 200 birds in the forest as a whole, though this secretive species is always hard to census accurately. Post-breeding gatherings have been as high as 150 individuals, and gatherings of 40 or more birds are not uncommon. A slightly wider, although still restricted, number of ducks can be seen on ponds in the more open fringing areas.

Among birds of prey, good numbers of Buzzards can be seen soaring over the woodland, particularly favouring the clearings and forest edges for hunting, and Sparrowhawks are similarly widespread. Both species are particularly visible during their display flights from early spring onwards, and it is at this time of year that the resident Goshawks are most easily viewed. Numbers have built up over the past decade or so to a level where it has been felt that an official viewpoint could be established, and this has quickly become one of the most reliable sites in Britain for viewing this magnificent raptor. Several birds are sometimes seen in the air at once at peak times in the spring, although for much of the year they remain well hidden, rarely venturing above tree-top level.

At the same time, the resident passerines start singing, providing the birdwatcher with a chance of learning or relearning their calls in stages. All the usual species to be expected in southern Britain are widespread but in addition there are concentrations of several species which are otherwise difficult to find elsewhere in the region. Amongst the earliest breeders are the Crossbills, with most occurring immediately after an irruption year, numbers steadily declining until the next influx arrives to replenish the population. Siskins tend to peak in the spring, with song heard quite commonly from the feeding flocks and one or two pairs remain to nest in the conifers. Redpolls are equally elusive breeders, with no records at all in some years. Another speciality is the Hawfinch. These are extremely secretive, but flocks of 40 birds have been seen feeding under hornbeams in winter. They often nest in loose aggregations with perhaps as many as 50 pairs present in the forest as a whole, though the most usual indication is only of a loud *tik* from a bird flying through the treetops and away. Outstanding among the summer migrants are the Pied Flycatchers, and although there are worrying signs that the population of this most attractive bird is declining, several dozen pairs can still be found. Likewise, Wood Warblers and Redstarts, although still characteristic birds of the deciduous woodland, are also less numerous than previously. Tree Pipits, Garden Warblers, Whitethroats and Willow Warblers all

Hawfinch

occur widely, particularly favouring the more open young plantations. Those at the denser thicket stage are the least attractive to most birds, but the small numbers of the localised Willow Tit seem to prefer them. Stonechats have recently returned as a breeding bird to one or two of the newly cleared and replanted forestry areas, with more moving in during the winter months. Conversely neither the Whinchats nor Grasshopper Warblers that used to favour the same type of habitat have stayed to nest in the past few years.

The more open clearings hold a few pairs of Nightjars, and observers waiting for these birds to start their evening songs will often be rewarded with the sight and strange high-pitched and grunting sounds of a roding Woodcock patrolling the treetops in the dusk. In recent years a fluctuating number of Firecrests have been proved to breed, scattered quite widely, but difficult to track down unless their song is known. The breeding birds are thought to be mainly summer visitors, although there are records from most months, with some song heard as early as February. Also, it is not clear whether the apparent variations in numbers are real, or just a reflection of observer effort. Hobbies are seen occasionally at any time during the summer, mainly over the more open areas, and wandering Peregrines drift over throughout the year, both species breeding not far away. Late summer and autumn sees a gradual diminution in activity, as song declines and summer visitors prepare to migrate, but Crossbills often reach their peak numbers at this time.

Timing

Not too critical for most species during the main breeding season, although windy days can be unproductive even in the shelter of the woodland. Goshawks tend to display most frequently from mid-morning to early afternoon and, like the other birds of prey, seem to prefer slightly breezy sunshine to tempt them into the skies. Songbirds are most active early in the day, particularly as the season progresses, while calm summer evenings produce the best chance of Nightjar and Woodcock. Nightjars do not normally begin to call until after 9.30 pm, or even later in midsummer; Woodcock start about half an hour earlier. On summer weekends, the picnic areas and roads can be crowded with visitors, but the majority do not venture very far from their cars.

Access

From the south, turnings off the main A48 Chepstow to Gloucester road at Lydney (B4234) and Blakeney (B4431/B4227) provide the main access, while the A4136 and B4226 cross the northern section between Coleford and Cinderford. Several minor roads and a multitude of Forestry Commission tracks traverse the whole forest; walking the latter to visit each of the various habitat types in turn should ensure finding the majority of species. There are plenty of picnic sites where cars can be left parked; in general you should not park on the roadside.

By far the best place for the widest selection of species is the RSPB-managed reserve at Nagshead, which contains the most extensive remaining area of mature oak woodland in the forest. Access is unrestricted, although parties of more than ten should contact the warden in advance. The reserve is signposted along a track to the north off the B4431 on the western outskirts of Parkend; follow this for c.½ mile (0.8 km) to a small car park at the edge of the reserve proper. Various trails are well marked, there are a couple of hides overlooking woodland pools, and an information centre is manned during the spring and summer. Around 50 pairs of Pied Flycatchers using the nestboxes are the star attraction – elsewhere in the forest they are much more thinly spread – but Wood Warblers and Redstarts also occur here, with Hawfinches, Woodcock, Nightjar and all three woodpeckers also present. Here, as elsewhere in the forest, listen out for Firecrests especially wherever holly and ivy are mixed in with other trees, whether deciduous or coniferous. The reserve extends well east of the B4234 and the Cannop Brook, and is part of the larger Cannop Valley Forest nature reserve: it is possible to continue on foot along waymarked trails to Cannop Ponds and beyond to add variety to the day's birding. The young plantations and clearings on the edges of the main oak woodland block are favoured by Tree Pipit. Remember to check any area of open water for Mandarins, although they are often difficult to see, especially when feeding on the forest floor.

The woodland around Parkend church, just off the road to Yorkley, is a fairly reliable site for Hawfinches in winter, and the clearings just to the east are worth checking. The bird-of-prey viewing area is at New Fancy View, on top of an old slag-heap. From Parkend, take the road northeast towards Blakeney, then left after c.1 mile (1.6 km) towards Speech House. The viewpoint and car park are signed to the right after a short distance. The nearby conifers are a regular haunt of Crossbills, famously joined by a Two-barred Crossbill in 1998, and this is as good a place as any to start exploring on foot through the conifers to the north. A Great Grey Shrike has wintered in the clearings here on at least one occasion.

The Speech House Hotel by the B4226 halfway between Cinderford and Coleford is a central spot from which to explore other parts of the forest, with several car parks nearby. A few Pied Flycatchers and Redstarts breed in this general area, and the mixed woodland and clearings in the large woodland block to the north of the road as far as the A4136 contain a good selection of the forest's birds, including Hawfinch and Nightjar. (Just following the sculpture trail from the nearby Beechenhurst picnic area/visitor centre can be rewarding both ornithologically as well as artistically!) About ¾ mile (1.2 km) east of the hotel, and also to the north of the B4226, the large shallow rush-fringed Woorgreen's Lake nature reserve (GWT) holds one or two pairs of breeding Mallard, Tufted Duck and Little Grebe, with the possibility of a Hobby hunting for dragonflies if you are lucky. Snipe and Jack Snipe occur here in winter, as do Goosander and Mandarin. Try the conifers and arboretum south and east of Speech House for Willow Tit, Siskin and Crossbills, although the latter range widely wherever there are mature conifers, and are attracted to any patch of standing water to drink. To the southwest, and clearly marked off the B4226 are Cannop Ponds, where wintering Siskins and Redpolls feed in the alders, and Dippers can be found along the stream. The woodland to the east has several productive clearings, with Lesser Spotted Woodpecker and Redstart to be found in the oaks southeast of the ponds.

In the eastern area of the forest, there are some fine stands of mature conifers north of Upper Soudley, with Little Grebe breeding on the ponds in the valley. The Dean Heritage Centre here is a good source of information, and Mandarins can often be seen on the adjacent pond. A short distance to the south there is some nice mixed oak, beech and conifer woodland around Blackpool Bridge and the Wench Ford picnic site, with Hawfinches sometimes to be found not far away.

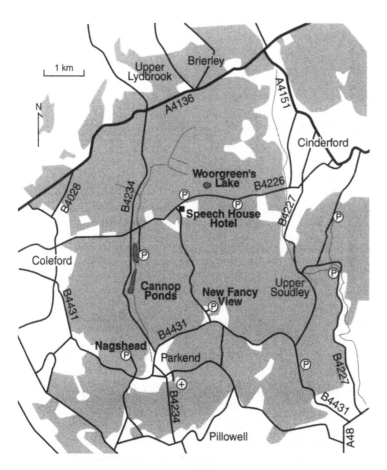

Much of the rest of the forest is dominated by conifers, the dense medium-age areas before thinning being the least productive. It is important to remember that forestry activities, particularly with fast-growing conifers, mean that conditions are continuously changing at any one spot, with clearings turning into woodland in one area, and vice versa in another. The many open areas of waste land, relics of earlier industrialisation, are always worthy of attention, particularly in winter, especially those areas where scattered trees, scrub and drainage channels are present. The areas listed above are meant only as an initial guide: an eye for the right habitat is the ultimate key to a successful exploration (don't be fooled by the decorative deciduous strip by the roads, hiding dense conifers beyond!)

Flaxley Pond lies on the edge of the forest, near Flaxley Abbey east of Cinderford. This relatively new farm pond attracts small numbers of winter duck, particularly Wigeon and Teal, and both Little Grebe and Tufted Duck usually breed. A whole string of other waterbirds have been seen here, including Pochard, Mandarin and Cormorant, with Common and Green Sandpiper on passage, so it's always worth a quick look. Going east from Flaxley church turn left after one-third of a mile (½ km), almost immediately crossing a small bridge. A footpath runs from here along the south side of the pond, although the water can also be viewed from the roadside a little further on. Do not trespass off the path, and take care not to block farm entrances (parking is very limited).

43b TIDENHAM CHASE   OS Outdoor Leisure 14

Habitat

This outlying part of the Forest of Dean is a plateau of former heathland bounded by the steeply wooded slopes of the River Wye near Tintern Abbey to the west while more gentle slopes to the east command fine views of the River Severn and the Vale of Berkeley beyond. Forestry Commission conifer plantations with a varied age structure cover a large part of the northern half of the area and include some large clearings. The southern part includes the largest remaining area of lowland heath in Gloucestershire at Poor's Allotment, and the RSPB and GWT are currently working to recreate similar habitat with heather, gorse and birches from the conifers at The Park, immediately to the west.

Species

The conifers hold good numbers of resident Coal Tits and Goldcrests, while Crossbills occur regularly, particularly after their periodic midsummer invasions. Willow Tits are still seen here, often preferring the denser young plantations avoided by other species; this is another bird for which, like the Crossbill, knowledge of the call is a definite advantage. Buzzards, Kestrels and Sparrowhawks soar over the slopes, taking full advantage of the updraughts. In spring and summer Siskins can be heard singing overhead, though definite breeding is difficult to prove. The young plantations and heathland remnants attract good numbers of Tree Pipits, Whitethroats, Yellowhammers and Linnets. The clearings sometimes hold one or two pairs of Nightjars, although this is a species which tends to fluctuate depending on the state and size of the clearings. Woodcock, another nocturnal species, can also be seen roding around the woodland rides at dusk. Migrant passerines such as Whinchat and Stonechat stop and feed in the autumn and the latter has bred at least once recently, both these birds being among the target species of the habitat restoration work currently in progress.

Timing
Not very critical, apart from for Nightjars and Woodcock which are best seen at dusk on calm evenings in spring and summer. Slightly breezy days in spring prompt birds of prey to soar over the slopes in display flights or preparatory to hunting, particularly in the mornings through to early afternoon.

Access
The B4228 north of Chepstow bisects the area and there is a car park by the road at Beacon Ash. The Poor's Allotment heathland is immediately opposite, with the east-facing slopes having unrestricted access along the paths. Tree Pipits are particularly common, and soaring Buzzards can be seen against the magnificent backdrop of the Severn Valley. A path to the west leads through The Park, along the edge of the habitat recreation project, with conifers currently remaining to the right. Several pairs of Tree Pipits have already moved in, with Whitethroat and Willow Warbler also prominent. The area became well known in 2002/2003 when a Little Bunting was found wintering along with a few Reed Buntings and Meadow Pipits, just to show that rare birds can be found almost anywhere! The path west past the triangulation point leads to Offa's Dyke

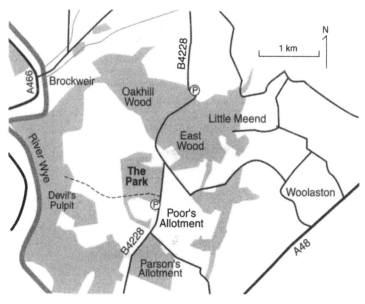

and the Devil's Pulpit viewpoint over Tintern Abbey, but the beech and conifer woodland here is not particularly rewarding although Wood Warbler and Lesser Spotted Woodpecker have been seen in the past. There is another parking place by the road at the far end of the northern sector of woodland (Oakhill Wood and East Wood). Forestry paths lead to west and east: currently the clearings, beeches and mature conifers to the east hold the most varied population.

43c THE WYE VALLEY & SYMONDS YAT

OS Outdoor Leisure 14

Habitat

This lowest stretch of the River Wye zig-zags between steep wooded slopes with fine limestone cliffs which rise to 90 metres in several places, before emerging into the River Severn near Chepstow. It is in part tidal, although the steepness of the banks means that only a narrow strip of mud is exposed at low tide. Much of the woodland is managed for forestry, with conifer plantations in places, but many parts have remained mixed and relatively untouched. The whole area is extremely scenically attractive, drawing large numbers of tourists to such spots as Tintern Abbey and Symonds Yat Rock, but there is a good network of footpaths including the Offa's Dyke path which runs along the upper eastern slope.

Species

The star species is the Peregrine, a pair of which have bred at Symonds Yat Rock since 1982; because of the relatively inaccessible nature of the nest-site itself (although it has been robbed) and the area's existing heavy use by the public, Symonds Yat has become a Peregrine equivalent of Loch Garten, with RSPB staff on hand and optical equipment permanently set up during the breeding season. Buzzards and Kestrels can frequently be seen in the same area, soaring in the updraughts anywhere

Peregrine Falcon

along the valley and both Sparrowhawk and Goshawk occur in the surrounding woodland, this also holding a good range of the commoner breeding birds, though not as wide a variety as in the nearby Forest of Dean. Grey Wagtails and a few Dippers are resident near the river itself, and winter parties of Siskins and Redpolls can be found in waterside alders. A few Sand Martins sometimes nest in the riverbank but by no means annually. Cormorants roost on the Gwent side near Lancaut while down nearer Chepstow a few Redshank and Shelduck appear along the river, and several pairs of Herring Gulls still breed on the cliffs between the old and new road crossings there.

Timing

The Peregrines are in residence the whole year round, but are most easily visible during the breeding season itself, particularly in June and July when young are being fed. Birds of prey tend to soar rather more on days with light winds and clear skies, but for most species timing is not particularly critical. Fine weather at weekends throughout the year brings large numbers of visitors which sometimes makes parking difficult at the more popular spots.

Access

From the south, Symonds Yat Rock is well signposted from Coleford along the B4432, and there is a large pay-and-display car park on the left when you arrive. There is parking for the disabled a little further on along the road, closer to the information centre and café.

Beyond the car park the road becomes very narrow as it drops down the hill to cross the river and join the B4229/A40 near Goodrich for access from the north. From the car parks a short walk via a footbridge brings access to the viewpoint on the neck of a huge horseshoe bend in the river. (Warning: in wet weather the rocks here can be very slippery.) The Peregrines nest on the cliff south of the river immediately upstream, and a telescope helps to get a good view of the birds when perched on the cliffs. During the breeding season the RSPB usually have telescopes ready-mounted for public use. Do not neglect to scan the hillside opposite for soaring birds of prey – Buzzards are numerous, and wandering Red Kites have been seen from here several times. To the south of the car park, forest trails lead through mixed woodland holding a range of the commoner breeding species including Wood Warbler. Further west, Redding's Inclosure and Highmeadow Woods are mostly coniferous, but mature enough and with clearings to make exploration worthwhile. There are several public car parks along the B4432 and A4136 with footpaths leading off into the woodland.

In the valley itself the busy A466 between Chepstow and Monmouth provides access to the riverbank in several places, with the footpaths along the east bank between Bigsweir and Brockweir and opposite Tintern (footbridge just north of the Abbey) making pleasant riverside walks. (See also entry under Tidenham Chase).

Calendar

All year. Little Grebe; Cormorant (River Wye), Grey Heron (River Wye); Mandarin, Tufted Duck, Goshawk, Sparrowhawk, Buzzard, Kestrel; Peregrine (breeds Symonds Yat), Coot, Woodcock, Tawny Owl, woodpeckers including Lesser Spotted, Grey Wagtail, Dipper, Stonechat, common woodland passerines including Nuthatch, Treecreeper, Goldcrest,

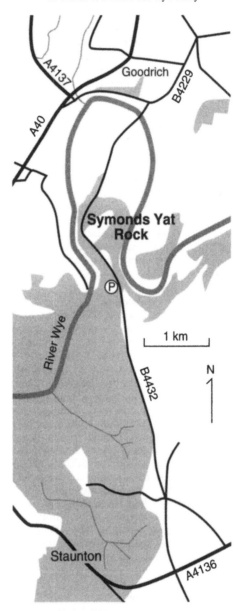

Marsh Tit, Long-tailed Tit, etc. Willow Tit; Redpoll, Siskin (both scarce in summer), Raven, Hawfinch (sometimes desert woods in winter), Yellowhammer.

December–February: Small numbers of duck e.g. Wigeon, Teal (Flaxley Pond), Gadwall, Goosander, maybe other diving duck. A few Snipe and Jack Snipe. Great Grey Shrike has wintered. Hawfinch flocks in places. Parties of Redpolls and Siskins; maybe Brambling with Chaffinches under beeches. Crossbills start breeding January. Herring Gulls return to Chepstow cliffs February.

March–May: Breeding residents active throughout. Summer visitors start arriving: Chiffchaff from mid-March; Cuckoo, Pied Flycatcher, Tree Pipit, Redstart, Willow Warbler from mid-April; Whinchat, Wood, Garden and Grasshopper Warblers from late April; Turtle Dove (rare), Spotted Flycatcher, Nightjar may not appear until mid-May or later. Chance of Hobby from May. Woodcock roding to early July. Firecrest singing March–June.

June–July: Peregrines active feeding young. Most passerines singing to early July, then falling silent; Pied Flycatcher and Wood Warbler especially difficult to find once song finishes but young Hawfinches sometimes conspicuous. Nightjar churring throughout. Maybe Crossbill irruption July.

August–November: Summer visitors mostly leave by end of August. Parties of tits, Nuthatches, sometimes with Lesser Spotted Woodpecker, active September–October. Quietest period November–January.

44 WALMORE COMMON   OS Outdoor Leisure 14

Habitat

Of the several low-lying areas of former meadowland either side of the River Severn down-river from Gloucester, Walmore Common, on the west bank, is nowadays the most rewarding from a birdwatching point of view. Surrounded by rolling farmland well endowed with orchards and hedgerow trees, the common itself (in fact mainly private farmland rather than a true 'common') is a large area of open damp grassland, intersected by drainage ditches, and prone to flooding in winter. Towards its western edge the ground is drier, with rather more in the way of hedges and trees, giving a varied landscape that is becoming increasingly rare in lowland agricultural areas.

Species

In winter, the numbers and variety of wildfowl present are dependent primarily on the degree to which the fields are flooded, but provided that they are reasonably damp, over 100 Bewick's Swans are often present, this being their main alternative to Slimbridge as a feeding site, with a regular interchange of birds throughout the winter. Whooper Swans are also occasionally recorded, although rarely are more than two or three birds present. Numbers of ducks fluctuate widely from season to season, depending also on the weather, but several hundred Wigeon still graze the fields under ideal conditions. Flooding will attract over 100 Pintail from across the river, with small numbers of Teal, Mallard, Gadwall and Shoveler also regular. Extensive flooding attracts Tufted Duck and Pochard, perhaps as many as 50 birds, and the occasional Goldeneye may also appear, but in general numbers of diving duck are low. Apart

Bewick's Swan

from wandering groups flying over, White-fronted Geese are unusual, the odd birds that do land rarely staying for more than a few days. Feral Canada and Greylag Geese are probably more likely to be encountered, while up to 50 Shelduck occur irregularly in the first few months of the year.

The damp fields are also attractive to waders. Lapwing throughout the year are the most obvious species, cold weather bringing flocks of several hundred, sometimes joined by twos and threes of Golden Plover. Parties of Dunlin sometimes move in from the estuary, with a small numbers of Redshank and Snipe also regular. A few Ruff may occur in winter or on passage, while ones and twos of Whimbrel are the most likely of the larger waders to appear on passage in the spring. Other wintering species include large numbers of thrushes, Fieldfare and Redwing predominating, while one or two Stonechats sometimes move down from higher ground.

At other times of year the area is less rewarding although a few pairs of Lapwing breed, and displaying Redshank in spring indicate that they may also attempt to nest in some years. Buzzard and Kestrel can be seen throughout the year, and Little and Tawny Owls are resident in the surrounding farmland, where the mixture of orchards, fields and hedgerow trees encourages a good breeding bird population, including most of the commoner warblers. In autumn, parties of migrating Yellow Wagtails stop off in the grassland, closely followed by larger numbers of Meadow Pipits and usually a few Whinchats. Common *Sylvia* and *Phylloscopus* warblers are much in evidence moving through the boundary hedgerows. The Severn Vale Ringing Group has been active here in the past and consequently the total list of species recorded is relatively high (over 150), but the more unusual migrants which have included Barred Warbler are unlikely to be seen by the casual visitor.

Timing

The degree of flooding is the main variable here with, in general, the more surface water the better. Cold snaps may bring an influx of Bewick's Swans and other wildfowl although most leave if the floods freeze. Wildfowl are often more active in late afternoon/evening, flighting in and out of the area. Shooting takes place from time to time, causing most of the wildfowl to leave temporarily. Fog is sometimes a problem.

Access

Walmore Common lies immediately west of the A48 c.6 miles (9.6 km) west-southwest of Gloucester, and is best viewed at Chaxhill, between Minsterworth and Westbury-on-Severn. The roadside verge provides a good viewpoint over the main eastern end which is the first to flood, but the road is busy and cars should be left parked off the road a little way east or west. Footpaths starting from near the school at Chaxhill lead to a gate overlooking the common. Any closer approach causes the birds to leave the area. The northern edge of the common can be explored by taking the first turning left towards Ley off the A48 just north of the Severn Bore Inn, and in ¼ mile (0.4 km) turning left again along Lower Ley Lane, passing several farms before it ceases to be drivable. A footpath continues straight ahead, with open fields viewable to the left, while the nearby hedges and bushes are worth checking for passerines. Between Chaxhill and Westbury, another lane leads north towards Grange Court; this western end of the common is, however, much drier and farmland birds rather than wildfowl are more likely to be seen.

The other low-lying areas in this part of the Severn Valley are less productive but Minsterworth Ham, c.4 miles (6.4 km) up-river, is sometimes worth a visit if flooding is extensive. Turn right down either of two small lanes off the A48 just north of Minsterworth, near the Apple Tree pub, and park where they peter out into farm tracks. The one straight ahead leads into a footpath which reaches the river bank after 1½ miles (2.4 km). Cormorants and a few duck occur by the river, including an occasional Red-breasted Merganser in winter and spring, and Grey Herons from the nearby Elmore heronry are sometimes present.

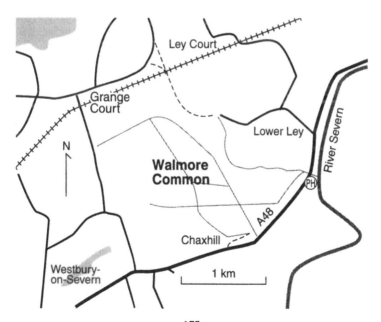

Calendar

All year: Grey Heron, Mute Swan, Sparrowhawk, Buzzard, Kestrel, Lapwing, Redshank, Stock Dove, Tawny and Little Owls, Green and Great Spotted Woodpeckers (Lesser Spotted sometimes seen); Skylark, Meadow Pipit, Pied Wagtail, common farmland passerines, Reed Bunting.

December–February: Cormorant (River Severn), Mute, Bewick's, maybe Whooper Swan. Occasional White-fronted, Canada and Greylag Geese. Shelduck, Wigeon, Gadwall, Teal, Mallard, Pintail, Shoveler; occasional Pochard, Tufted Duck or other diving species. Chance of Peregrine. Water Rail, Lapwing, Dunlin, Snipe, maybe Golden Plover, Ruff and Jack Snipe; gulls, especially Black-headed and Lesser Black-backed, sometimes numerous. Winter thrushes; sometimes Stonechat.

March–May: Bewick's Swans and most wildfowl leave February/early March; Shelduck may linger. Maybe Garganey mid-March–April. Occasional Ruff, Whimbrel (April). Lapwing and Redshank sometimes breed. Migrant hirundines from mid-April. Yellow Wagtails and Sedge Warblers from late April.

June–July: Breeding species include Sedge Warbler, Whitethroat, Lesser Whitethroat.

August–November: Cormorant (River Severn). Yellow Wagtails and common *Sylvia* and *Phylloscopus* warblers trickle through. Maybe a few Whinchats in September. Usually quiet until wildfowl and thrushes return from early November.

45 HIGHNAM WOODS

OS Outdoor Leisure 14 and Explorer 179

Habitat

Highnam Woods reserve, lying a few miles west of Gloucester, is one of the RSPB's more recent purchases. Oak and ash are the dominant trees, but there are sections of coppice-with-standards, both of hazel and of sweet chestnut, several more open areas of scrub and scattered birches, and one or two small ponds. The reserve itself covers 294 acres (119 ha), but is only part of a larger area of woodland once belonging to the Highnam Court estate, previous management being exemplified by a few remaining conifer and poplar plantations and a network of rides. The adjacent private woodland contains the bulk of what is reputed to be the earliest Victorian pinetum in Britain, and some fine specimens of exotic mature conifers can be seen scattered throughout the woods. In spring the ground under the trees is carpeted with bluebells, wood anemones and early purple orchids, with the rare upright spurge, one of the reserve's specialities, flowering a little later in the year. Woodland butterflies include silver-washed fritillary and white admiral.

Species

The key species here is Nightingale, around 20 pairs breeding in recent years, a remarkable number considering that Highnam lies at the very edge of its range. They are only part of a varied spring and summer avifauna, however, with Garden Warbler, Blackcap, Chiffchaff and Willow Warbler all to be heard at the same time in the main woodland, plus Whitethroats arriving to nest in the patches of scrub and undergrowth where there are fewer tall trees. Newcomers to birdsong identification may find it helpful to visit a little earlier in the year to sort out the songs of resident species such as Chaffinch, Great, Blue and Coal Tits, Nuthatch and Treecreeper, before the summer warblers come to add further confusion. Willow Tits are sometime seen here and, although their song is rarely heard, it is useful to learn their harsh calls to distinguish them from the more widespread Marsh Tits. With fewer leaves on the trees it is perhaps easier to locate the Green and Great Spotted Woodpeckers which excavate nestholes in the mature timber, and to attempt to track down the elusive Lesser Spotteds, a pair of which sometimes breeds. Sparrowhawks and Buzzards can quite commonly be seen soaring overhead, again particularly during their main display period in the first half of the year.

In winter, when the variety of species is inevitably less, the bird feeders in front of the main hide attract finches, tits, Pheasants and other residents, often giving stunning views at very close range. The rest of the reserve is not to be neglected, however, as Siskins and Redpolls come to the birch and willow scrub, Redwings and Fieldfares scour the woodland for berries, and there is always the chance of flushing a Woodcock from the side of one of the damp tracks.

Nightingale

177

Timing

For the first couple of weeks after their arrival, Nightingales will sing at times all through the day, but once they have settled in tend to be far more vocal in the evening and around dawn. For most woodland birds, morning visits tend to be more productive, and wet and windy conditions make most species difficult to locate. In winter particularly, the paths can be extremely muddy.

Access

From Gloucester, follow the A40 westwards towards Ross-on-Wye, as far as the junction with the A48. From this roundabout continue along the A40 for another 1 mile (1.6 km) to where, c.100 metres after a garage on the left-hand side of the road, the reserve entrance is located on the right. If the road is busy, which it often is, take care when turning across the traffic into the car park here. A surfaced path allows for wheelchair access to a hide a short way from the car park, overlooking a small pond and some open scrub. Bird feeders here attract birds throughout the year, and frogs can be heard croaking from the water in the spring. A waymarked trail, sometimes remaining wet and muddy throughout the year, leads off through the woodland, a main loop of c.1½ miles (2.4 km) in length; Nightingales can be heard (but are often notoriously difficult to see) from several places all along its length. Noise from the road can sometimes be intrusive in the southern part of the reserve.

The adjacent woodland is private, and although some footpaths do run through it, the reserve itself provides by far the best viewing conditions. About 5 miles (8 km) to the west, Newent Woods are mainly private coniferous plantations, with Tree Pipits breeding in the clearings, and Siskin, Redpoll and Crossbill are all seen from time to time. Public footpaths cross the adjacent May Hill, an open area of downland with gorse and a conspicuous clump of pines commanding fine views all round.

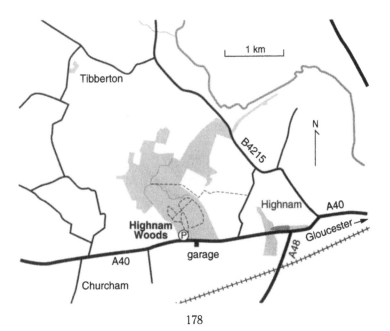

Wheatears and Whinchats sometimes stop off here on spring passage, and both Redstart and Stonechat have bred in the past. The National Birds of Prey Centre lies a short distance north of the woods, with captive and free-flying raptors on display, and holds wildlife art exhibitions from time to time.

Calendar

All year: Sparrowhawk, Buzzard, Pheasant, Tawny Owl, woodpeckers including Lesser Spotted; common woodland passerines including Goldcrest, Long-tailed Tit, Marsh Tit, Nuthatch; Willow Tit (erratic).

December–February: Chance of Woodcock. Fieldfare, Redwing, Siskin, Redpoll.

March–May: Chiffchaff from late March; Cuckoo, Willow Warbler, Nightingale from mid-April; Grasshopper Warbler, Whitethroat, Garden Warbler, Blackcap late April–early May. Spotted Flycatcher mid-May.

June–July: Nightingale sings to early June, other passerines to early July. Irrupting Crossbills sometimes move through from July onwards.

August–November: Summer visitors mostly leave during August. Parties of tits, Nuthatches and Goldcrests sometimes include a Lesser Spotted Woodpecker.

46 SLIMBRIDGE & THE NEW GROUNDS
OS Outdoor Leisure 14

Habitat

The New Grounds is the general name given to the extensive area of damp meadows and grazing marsh on the east bank of the River Severn between Purton and Frampton on Severn, and bounded to the east by the Gloucester and Sharpness Canal. At the centre lies the Slimbridge headquarters of the Wildfowl and Wetlands Trust, founded in 1946 by Sir Peter Scott, with its unrivalled collection of ducks, geese, swans and, more recently, flamingos. There are also two duck decoys, one of which is still operated, relics of the days when wildfowling was a major activity of the Berkeley Estate, who still own the area. The Trust's pools, bushes and trees provide shelter for wild as well as captive birds, and there are over a dozen hides overlooking the Dumbles grazing marsh and the river with its vast mud and sandbanks exposed at low tide. Shallow scrapes and pools have been created in the meadows adjoining the collection to increase the variety of species. There are small reedbeds near the shore at Frampton and Purton, and in places thick blackthorn and hawthorn hedgerows provide extensive cover for migrants.

Species

Wildfowl dominate the scene in winter, with European White-fronted Geese and Bewick's Swans being the most conspicuous. Although this is the most important wintering site for the first species, the incidence of milder winters in recent years has meant that many birds have stopped off in Germany and Holland rather than crossing to the UK, and have also tended to leave rather earlier. The peak numbers, rarely above 3000 these days, tend to occur early in the year, prior to the main departure in late February/early March. Bewick's Swans have stabilised at a current maximum of around 300 birds. Small numbers of the other British geese turn up regularly, including all the main rarities. Slimbridge remains the most reliable UK site for Lesser White-fronts, but they are by no means annual, and at least some recent records have related to neck-collared birds from the Scandinavian reintroduction programme for this threatened species. The Trust's free-flying geese rarely join the wild birds, but the usual caveat concerning the origin of any unusual wildfowl has to be borne in mind as strays from elsewhere sometimes get caught up on migration, and several hundred Greylag and Canada Geese breed ferally in and around the collection.

Numbers of Wigeon on the grassland reach around 3000, while up to 2000 Mallard and Teal also feed along the shore and in the various marshy pools. Several hundred Gadwall and Tufted Duck come in to join the captive birds in the Trust's grounds, often becoming almost equally tame, and the flock of around 200 Pintail also entering the enclosures is a particularly impressive sight. This last species has increased steadily over the years, as has the Pochard flock, over 1000 birds roosting here during the day and flighting out to feed elsewhere at night. Goosanders are now regular visitors to the estuary upstream in small numbers, with the occasional Red-breasted Merganser accompanying them, though both are rare at the Trust itself. Other diving ducks are relatively unusual, although as more pools are created there is a tendency for a wider range of species to be seen, including a series of recent records of Smew. Small parties of Common Scoter can appear at almost any time of year, but are most frequent in late summer. Inevitably, the collection attracts a range of vagrant ducks, with Green-winged Teal being virtually annual. Apart from wildfowl, winter birds present in large numbers include hundreds of Fieldfares and Redwings in the damp meadows, while numbers of Moorhens feeding opportunistically within the enclosures can be well in excess of 500 birds. They are often joined by Water Rails, over 30 having

White-fronted Goose

been counted, the grounds being an excellent place for seeing this normally elusive species at close range. Snipe and Jack Snipe also lurk in reedbeds and damp patches in various places in and around the Trust grounds. It is unusual for visitors not to see a Peregrine, with up to four wintering along this stretch of coast, and Merlins occur irregularly over the same period. Short-eared Owls occur most winters, usually passage birds, but they sometimes stay longer if the food supply is sufficient.

Wader numbers on the shore in winter are dominated by up to 4000 Dunlin and over 500 Curlew, while several thousand Lapwings are also present most winters, feeding on the grassland as well as on the mudflats, and numbers are even higher if cold conditions prevail further east and north. Up to 1000 Golden Plover occur most years, Redshank are present in small numbers, and up to a dozen Little Stints regularly accompany the Dunlin flocks. They are sometimes joined by a few Ruffs, particularly later in the season as passage birds move through. Vast flocks of gulls roost on the estuary in winter: Common and Black-headed can both top 10,000, with smaller numbers of Lesser Black-backed and Herring Gulls. More detailed study in recent years has shown that Mediterranean Gulls, up to eight at a time, are regular passage migrants in autumn and into the winter on the estuary, and odd birds can be seen within the grounds at times. Yellow-legged Gulls are also increasingly seen, especially in autumn, and there have been several sightings of Ring-billed Gulls at the roost.

Early spring sees the rapid departure of most of the wildfowl and many of the waders, but the strategic position at the head of the estuary ensures an interesting spring passage. Single Garganey are early arrivals, dropping into the Trust grounds for a few days before moving on. Wheatears are another early migrant, British birds first with the larger Greenland birds passing through later. Whinchats and Yellow Wagtails appear in the fields, with the occasional pair of the latter staying to breed. Out over the estuary, Common Terns pass through, sometimes up to 200 at a time, with smaller numbers of Arctic and Black Terns. Other tern species appear more erratically through the summer though peaking at passage times. Little Gulls, both adults and immatures, also pass up-river in small parties (usually up to five) in the spring, presumably continuing across country towards the Wash. Groups of a 100 or so Kittiwakes and the occasional skua offshore at this time also prompt speculation about the extent of seabird passage along the 'Cotswold Corridor'. Among waders, regular spring migrants include Ringed Plover, Grey Plover, Sanderling, Ruff, Whimbrel and Bar-tailed Godwit, daily counts of several of these being 50 or more, though birds tend to move on through very quickly at this time of year. Spring vagrants have included Temminck's Stint and Broad-billed Sandpiper, and Marsh Harriers are sometimes seen passing through both in the spring and the autumn.

Summer is relatively quiet, although a few Little Egrets are now a regular sight from late summer onwards, joining the Shelducks and their young on the sandbanks, and Hobbies come to chase the dragonflies over the reedbeds, particularly towards the end of the season. Common Terns have recently started breeding on the reserve, and can be seen at the South Lake throughout the summer. Mandarin and Gadwall breed in and around the collection, while Reed, Sedge and Cetti's Warblers are present in several of the reedbeds, including those at the Trust itself. From July onwards, moulting flocks of Lapwings can become quite large, heralding the best of the autumn wader passage. Flocks of over 100 returning Ringed Plover and Dunlin are joined by smaller numbers of Little Ringed Plovers, Little Stints, Curlew Sandpipers and Knot, while waders such as Black-tailed Godwit, Greenshank, Spotted Redshank, Ruff and Green and Wood Sandpipers are regular around the scrapes and freshwater pools higher up the shore. In recent years rarer waders have included Kentish Plover and Lesser Yellowlegs and there is little doubt that anything might turn up. There is a return passage of terns and Little Gulls, but with smaller numbers than in the spring. Passerines are often surprisingly numerous in the Trust grounds and nearby hedges, the hides allowing good views of such species as Lesser Whitethroat, Redstart and Willow Warbler, while parties of Yellow Wagtails occur in the nearby fields. Visible migration of Chaffinches, Skylarks and Meadow Pipits can be quite heavy here as elsewhere along the estuary, and Snow Buntings and Black Redstarts occasionally appear along the shore for a few days at a time. Rock Pipits join the resident Meadow Pipits for the winter, and sometimes a few Stonechats will stay. Severe gales may bring Gannets and Manx Shearwaters even this far up the estuary, and there have been records of Sabine's Gull, Leach's and Storm Petrel, and Grey Phalarope along the shore under such conditions.

Timing

For winter wildfowl, severe weather in Europe or elsewhere in Britain tends to bring larger numbers and the chance of vagrants. However, heavy snowfall around the Trust itself sometimes disperses the birds for a time if their feeding grounds are covered. Similarly, although high-tide visits are essential for those waders that spend most of their time down on the estuary flats, very high tides (particularly those in February) will flood the Dumbles for a time and likewise temporarily disperse both waders and geese. Bewick's Swans and many ducks flight back to the Trust enclosures in the evening to roost safely. Being low-lying, the area is sometimes affected by thick fog. Otherwise, factors are few although it is fair to point out that the Trust is very popular with visitors and those who like birdwatching in uncrowded conditions should try to come mid-week.

Access

The Trust itself is well signposted to the west off the A38 just south of Cambridge (M4 junction 13 is nearest). Continue for c.2 miles (3.2 km) through Slimbridge village and over the canal at Shepherd's Patch (the bridge is sometimes opened to let ships pass) to the end of the road where there is a large car park. The fields either side of the road west of the canal sometimes hold large numbers of geese, so are worth checking. The Trust is open from 9.30 am to 5 pm (6 pm in summer), free to members, otherwise a fee is payable, and is well supplied with hides overlooking the grassland. Geese usually feed on the Dumbles, where the Holden Tower and nearby hides towards the northern end give the best views, but may use other fields at times. At high tide waders are forced up on to this area to roost, but soon move back to the estuary where they are difficult to observe, even with a telescope. All the hides are worth checking carefully, particularly those overlooking the pools and scrapes where waders can easily be missed, and Kingfishers sometimes nest near the westernmost ones. Within the grounds themselves, the Rushy Pen, towards the northern end, attracts most of the wild ducks and swans that enter the enclosures, and South Lake, a large new lake on the southeast

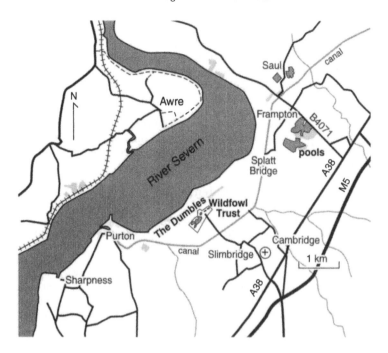

side of the grounds, is one of the best spots for seeing waders such as Black-tailed Godwits and Spotted Redshanks plus diving ducks such as Smew. Mediterranean and Ring-billed Gulls have also been seen here. Nevertheless the whole collection area is worth examining for wild birds, including the hedges for small birds at passage times, and the reedbeds for warblers in the summer. During the summer and early autumn, Landrover trips out to the seawall provide a good opportunity for closer views of the waders on the estuary and there is also a summer walkway out to Mid Point for the same reason. New facilities are being developed constantly so check the latest position on maps in the main building. There is good access for the disabled, and meals/drinks are available at the restaurant.

Access is not allowed to the fields around the Trust so geese are rarely viewable if dispersed from the immediate Trust area, though the canal path north and south from Shepherd's Patch is sometimes worth a try and the odd grebe or duck is sometimes found on the canal itself. At Splatt Bridge to the north, accessible by road via Frampton village green (see Frampton Pools entry), there is a small car park just before the canal bridge, and the river can be viewed distantly from the towpath. There is no public right of way along the seawall, and the area is leased for wild-fowling. Just to the north, a small reedbed and some damp fields are of interest, Jack Snipe, Short-eared Owls and passerine migrants sometimes being seen. A short distance to the south, a gate marks the start of the seawall in this direction. A series of shallow excavations here, in the '100 acre field', have created a mixture of pools and reedbeds which attract diving duck, Little Egrets, feeding Hobbies and breeding warblers among others. However, to avoid disturbance to both breeding and wintering birds this area can only be accessed on the Landrover trips organised by the Trust which include this area as well as the seawall.

South of the Trust, the shore can be reached at Purton along several narrow lanes (easiest to turn off the A38 just south of the railway bridge at Berkeley Road, and at Purton park just over the canal bridge). This is generally not a good spot for waders but under gale conditions, seabirds might be seen from the breakwater in front of the Berkeley Arms pub. This is also a good spot for viewing the gulls as they gather on the sandbanks offshore prior to roosting. Alternatively, walk along the canal path to the south where the narrowed river can be viewed on one side, while the reedbed and bushes around the disused (and inaccessible) Purton Timber Ponds across the canal hold breeding Reed, Sedge and Cetti's Warblers.

Calendar

All year: Cormorant, Grey Heron, Shelduck, Mandarin, Gadwall, Sparrowhawk, Buzzard, Kestrel, Peregrine, Moorhen, Lapwing, Redshank, Collared Dove, Barn and Little Owls, Kingfisher, Skylark, Meadow Pipit, Cetti's Warbler, Treecreeper, Chaffinch, Reed Bunting.

December–February: Bewick's Swan, occasional Whooper. Wild geese, especially White-fronted but any other species possible; peak numbers and variety January–February. Mandarin, Wigeon, Gadwall, Teal, Pintail, Shoveler, Pochard, Tufted Duck, sometimes Smew. Occasional Goosander or Red-breasted Merganser on river. Merlin, Peregrine, Water Rail, Curlew, Dunlin, Redshank, Snipe, Jack Snipe, Golden Plover, Little Stint. Sometimes Ruff, Black-tailed Godwit, Spotted Redshank. Gull roost may contain rarity, e.g. Mediterranean, Ring-billed, Yellow-legged Gull. Kittiwake flocks in bad weather. Short-eared Owl, Rock Pipit, winter thrushes, sometimes Stonechat. Huge Starling roost in some years.

March–May: White-fronted Geese and Bewick's Swans usually gone by first week of March (but sometimes by mid-February). Most winter ducks leave during March. Chance of Garganey from mid-March, Marsh Harrier in late April–May. Wader passage peaks April–May, especially Ringed Plover, Sanderling, Whimbrel, Bar-tailed Godwit; maybe Spotted Redshank, Greenshank; possibility of Temminck's Stint or other rarity. Rare gulls and Kittiwake may occur to April. Common, Arctic, Black Terns mid-April–May, possible Arctic Skua, Little Gull at same time. Whinchat, Wheatear, White and Yellow Wagtails pass during April–early May.

June–July: Breeding Redshank, Yellow Wagtail, Reed, Sedge and Cetti's Warblers; chance of feeding Hobby May–September, sometimes wandering Peregrine. Common Scoter most likely July–August. Wader passage starts July, especially Ringed and Little Ringed Plover, Whimbrel, Green and Common Sandpipers. Mediterranean and Yellow-legged Gulls from July. Occasional Sandwich or Little Tern. Little Egrets start to arrive, and Spoonbills sometimes occur during the summer.

August–November: Chance of Manx Shearwater, Gannet or other seabird in gales. Teal start returning from August; Bewick's Swan and White-fronted Geese usually from late October; most wildfowl increasing steadily through October–November. Raptors include Peregrine from August, Merlin from October, Hobby (August–September), Hen Harrier (October–November). Ringed Plover, Ruff, Spotted Redshank, Greenshank, Wood Sandpiper through August; Knot, Little Stint, Curlew

Sandpiper peak September when best chance of rare wader, e.g. Temminck's Stint, Pectoral Sandpiper. Wader passage mostly over by November. Gull numbers build steadily, with Mediterranean peaking August–September. Common *Sylvia* and *Phylloscopus* warblers through August, including Blackcap, Lesser Whitethroat, Willow Warbler, plus Yellow Wagtail, Redstart. Maybe Snow Bunting or Black Redstart among common larks, pipits and finches passing October–November.

47 FRAMPTON POOLS   OS Outdoor Leisure 14

Habitat

Frampton Pools comprise several disused gravel pits strategically placed close to the head of the Severn Estuary. There are two main pools, one deep, open and mostly steep-sided, and used by an active sailing club, while the other is less disturbed, containing several wooded islands and with quite extensive areas of emergent vegetation along its edges. Smaller, shallower pits nearby contain patches of rushes and are fringed by areas of dense bushes and tangled woodland. Close by is the attractive village of Frampton on Severn, with one of the longest village greens in England, its cottage gardens and the grounds of Frampton Court adding to the variety of the landscape. The amphibian and invertebrate fauna includes great crested newt and several species of dragonfly.

Species

Although numbers are rarely high, waterfowl in winter and a variety of waterside species on passage provide the main interest here, but there is usually something to see at any time of year. Cormorants are nearly always present, numbers swelled by birds from the estuary gathering in the trees to roost, over 60 having been seen together in winter. Up to 100 Tufted Ducks and rather fewer Pochard (though temporarily more if disturbed by ringing activities at the WWT) are present through the winter, numbers of the former peaking on spring passage, while a few may be present all year. Other diving duck are erratic, although up to five Goldeneye occur, and single red-head Smew appear reasonably frequently. Scaup, Goosander, Long-tailed Duck and Common Scoter have all been seen, although not very predictably. Among surface-feeders, small numbers of Mallard, Teal, Shoveler and Gadwall are regular, while Garganey are occasional on spring passage. Cold weather or storm conditions may produce one of the divers or rarer grebes, joining the 20 or so Great Crested Grebes that winter here. The same conditions may also bring the occasional Bittern.

The proximity of the WWT has inevitably meant that feral species of wildfowl occur. Around 50 or so each of Canada and Greylag Geese are usually present, along with a slightly smaller number of feral Barnacle Geese. All three species breed here, and also wander between here and Slimbridge. Mandarins are now well established in Gloucestershire, and

Great Crested Grebe

breed in the Frampton/Slimbridge area in good numbers. They are elusive when nesting, but gatherings can be as high as 50 birds in the autumn. Conversely, Ruddy Ducks have never really managed to maintain a permanent footing here, although ones and twos can be seen throughout the year. Water Rails are present in small numbers through the winter, and sometimes remain to breed, their presence usually indicated by sound rather than by sight.

Spring sees the arrival of hirundines and, later, Swifts over the water, and a variety of warblers singing among the willows and trees. Sedge Warblers are mostly passage birds but Reed Warblers remain to breed in the waterside vegetation, and Cetti's Warblers have been heard recently. The area continues to host two or three pairs of Nightingales, here approaching the edge of their range in Britain, but the Turtle Doves that used to nest have probably ceased to do so, though birds are still heard calling in spring in some years. Kingfishers usually breed and are regularly seen throughout the year. Common, Black and Arctic Terns pass through on both spring and autumn passage, together with Little Gulls and, less frequently, Sandwich and Little Terns, this being a noted site for this group of birds, which presumably are passing along the 'Cotswold Corridor' linking the Severn and the Wash. Other passage birds that may occur include raptors such as Osprey and Marsh Harrier while Hobbies can be seen from time to time all summer. The habitat is not, in general, suitable for attracting large numbers of waders, but if low water levels in late summer expose areas of mud and gravel a wide variety can occur, Common and Green Sandpipers, Spotted Redshank and Greenshank being the most frequently recorded. Early autumn sees large numbers of warblers and other migrants feeding actively in the trees and bushes around the pools, attracted by the rich food supply. Later most of these move away, to be replaced by parties of Siskins and a few Redpolls swinging among the alders, although small numbers of Chiffchaffs quite often attempt to overwinter if the weather is not too cold.

Timing

Not critical for most species, but singing Nightingales are best listened for early in the morning or again at dusk on reasonably calm days during their relatively short song period. Cold weather may bring an influx of wildfowl and other birds from further north and east, though if the pools freeze over most species move out until the thaw.

Access

Frampton is reached along the B4071, which leaves the A38 south of Gloucester (but north of Slimbridge), just south of the turning in the opposite direction to junction 13 of the M5 (see also map with previous site). Continue along this road (parking is not really feasible along this stretch) and turn left down the centre of Frampton village green to the far end where it narrows and where there is limited parking by the road. Alternatively there is a small car park by the Post Office at the north end of the green. The small pools on the village green sometimes attract a large Pied Wagtail roost from late summer into the winter or hirundine roosts in the autumn. The area is used by a variety of leisure interests as well as livestock, so access is controlled, but there is a good network of public paths from which everything can be seen.

A public footpath southeast from the south end of the green leads along a track to the sailing club, and on past the start of the large southern pool which can be scanned to the right. Sailing activities may disturb birds from here so it is best to visit this part first. The footpath runs diagonally left across a field to a gate which opens on to a track by some conifers and poplars. The northern pool can be seen through the trees straight ahead. The track then passes a small pool surrounded by taller trees, with a varied bushy area just beyond. Passerines, both resident and migrant, favour this section, and in particular several pairs of Nightingales can often be heard singing here. The landfill site further on attracts a certain number of scavenging gulls. Access further round the northern pool is not allowed but it can be viewed by returning along the track and continuing straight on via a clearly marked footpath along the edge of a meadow. This path eventually returns to the village green, but before reaching the first cottage, another path leads to the right along the western edge of the pool. Feral geese are often in the Frampton Court parkland here, and the pool and islands need careful scanning to ensure that everything is seen. Gulls and terns feed over both main pools, though preferring the more open southern one.

South from the village green, the first road on the left (Vicarage Lane) leads to a footpath by the southern side of the sailing club pool, for an alternative viewpoint. The next turning left, just before the church, leads past Denfurlong Farm to another small but very overgrown pool which attracts a few breeding warblers. To reach the estuary (see New Grounds, Slimbridge entry for more details) continue past the church to Splatt Bridge where there is a small car park just before the canal. Vagrant grebes and diving ducks sometimes occur on the canal so do not dismiss it without a glance.

Returning to the B4071 and then left over the canal to the village of Saul, there are two more small pools, rather derelict and heavily used by anglers, but sometimes worth a look. A footpath opposite Saul church leads to one while the other can be viewed from a pull-in under electricity cables just south of the village. Other lanes north and west bring access to the river again, here much narrower, scoured by the tides and less productive but incidentally one of the best spots to view the Severn Bore at the appropriate times of year.

Calendar

All year: Little Grebe (mostly winter, sometimes breeds), Great Crested Grebe, Cormorant (few in summer), Grey Heron, Mute Swan, feral geese including Greylag, Canada and Barnacle Geese; Mandarin, Tufted Duck; Ruddy Duck (scarce), Kestrel, Coot, Little Owl, Kingfisher; Nuthatch, Treecreeper, Reed Bunting.

December–February: Occasional rare grebe, diver or Bittern in adverse weather. Gadwall, Teal, Shoveler, Pintail, Tufted Duck, Pochard, Goldeneye; maybe Smew, Scaup, Long-tailed Duck, Goosander. Woodcock, Snipe, Water Rail. Pied Wagtails roosting; maybe Chiffchaff wintering; Siskin, Redpoll.

March–May: Chance of Garganey from mid-March. Maybe Marsh Harrier, Osprey or Hobby in late April–May. Common Sandpiper or other occasional wader on passage. Tern passage in April–May especially Common and Black plus Little Gull. Hirundines from April (Sand Martin from mid-March), Swift from late April. Yellow Wagtail from mid-April (has bred). Nightingale singing late April–early June. Common warblers arrive mid-April–mid-May.

June–July: Breeding wildfowl include Canada and Greylag Geese, Great Crested Grebe, sometimes Tufted and Ruddy Ducks. Water Rails may summer. Turtle Dove (rare). Common passerines breeding include Cuckoo, Blackcap, Garden Warbler, Whitethroat, Lesser Whitethroat, Goldfinch.

August–November: Cormorant numbers increase. Chance of passing Osprey or Hobby to end of September. Trickle of commoner waders August–September, e.g. Common and Green Sandpipers, Greenshank, Spotted Redshank, godwits. Common, Arctic and Black Terns, plus Little Gull to mid-October; maybe rare tern, e.g. White-winged Black (August–September). Common warblers peak August–early September; Pied Wagtail and hirundine roosts August–September in some years.

48 ASHLEWORTH HAM & COOMBE HILL CANAL   OS Explorer 179

Habitat

These two sites lie either side of the River Severn c.5½ miles (8.8 km) north of Gloucester, and are here treated together as their bird populations are fairly similar, both containing extensive areas of wet meadowland prone to winter flooding. At Ashleworth Ham, now being managed by the GWT, both the water levels and the mowing and grazing regimes are closely controlled to balance wildlife and farming interests; in summer, for instance, beds of meadow-rue, canary-grass and various sedges remaining uncut well on into the season. Tree cover is provided by pollarded willows fringing the many ditches that intersect the meadows while patches of woodland at Meerend Thicket and Sandhurst Hill overlook the area. On the east side of the river, the silted-up and overgrown Coombe Hill Canal is gradually being dredged out and cleared by the GWT. Again, willows line the ditches that often overflow into the nearby meadows in winter. Alders grow by the river itself, particularly around the Haw Bridge crossing.

Species

The alternative name of The Duckeries for the fields at Ashleworth Ham indicates that this area has long been known for wildfowl, and the retention of water into the spring has gradually increased its attraction for both breeding and passage waders. Surface-feeding ducks predominate in winter, and although numbers vary with conditions, up to 2000 Wigeon and 1000 Teal may be present. Mid-winter counts of Pintail have exceeded a hundred on several occasions, and it is a regular site for small numbers of Mallard, Shoveler and Gadwall. At peak flood periods numbers of Tufted Ducks and Pochard may reach 40 each, with twos and threes of Goldeneye joining them, and even at other times a few of any of these species may occur. More regular watching in recent years has produced sightings of several rarities from North America, including American Wigeon and Green-winged Teal, and other visitors have included Goosander, Mandarin, Ruddy Duck and Smew, usually on floodwater in the fields but sometimes on the river. With the WWT not so far away it is unsurprising that small parties of Bewick's Swans drop in from time to time, but Whooper Swans, in single figures mostly, have also started to appear here on a regular basis. It will be interesting to see if this new wintering trend continues. Apart from feral Canadas and Greylags, geese are only rare visitors, White-fronts on their way to or from Slimbridge occasionally being seen flying over. Up to five or six Shelducks may appear in late winter through to the spring and have bred. An increasing number of Cormorants are present along the river from autumn to spring, the riverside roosting/loafing sites at Wainlode Hill and Haw Bridge holding up to 40 birds each. Great Crested and Little Grebes on the other hand are fairly unusual visitors.

The wet cover attracts Water Rails every winter, and single Bitterns have been recorded, although actual sightings of both species are relatively infrequent owing to their skulking behaviour. Buzzards have steadily increased over the past few years, and are now probably the most conspicuous raptor, although Sparrowhawks and Kestrels can also be seen here all year round. In winter, Peregrines are regular visitors, and often scan for prey from high up on the electricity pylons that cross the area. Among small birds, Siskins and Redpolls can be found swinging acrobatically at the tops of the riverside alders.

Wintering numbers of Snipe can reach over 50 birds at Ashleworth, with smaller numbers at Coombe Hill, but there have been few recent signs of them staying to breed, unfortunately. However, the evocative calls of Curlew remain a regular spring sound, together with several 'yodelling' Redshank and 'peewitting' Lapwings. Despite all this spring activity, breeding success has been poor in recent years, and it is likely that water levels need to be managed over a wider area than just that of the current reserves if numbers are to increase in future. Other wader species drop in on spring passage, the most regular being Ruff and Whimbrel. Garganey are traditionally early migrants, and are reasonably regular

Grasshopper Warbler

here in spring; encouragingly, a pair in 2000 provided the first Gloucestershire breeding record for over half a century. The leading line effect of the Severn brings good numbers of other passing migrants through the area; among those that do stay for the summer are several pairs of Redstarts nesting in holes in the pollarded willows, Yellow Wagtails in the wet fields and Sedge, Reed and Grasshopper Warblers in the taller lush vegetation. A few Nightingales, getting close to the edge of their range here, can be heard singing from some of the nearby copses, and a dozen or so pairs of Sand Martins breed by the river near Haw Bridge.

Autumn migration starts with a trickle of Common Sandpipers following the Severn down-river from their high-ground breeding sites but, the scrape at Ashleworth excepted, the fields are usually too dry to attract many waders at this time of year. A few Greenshank and Green Sandpipers may appear, with the latter occasionally wintering in ones and twos. Passerine migrants such as Whinchat and Yellow Wagtail pass through in small numbers. The fields are attractive to wintering thrushes while cold weather may bring an influx of Woodcock to the damp thickets.

Timing

Displaying waders are always most active early in the morning, particularly if the weather is fine and calm, and during the summer other breeding birds are more likely to heard singing at this time, although Nightingales and Grasshopper Warblers have a resurgence of song at dusk. Wildfowl numbers, particularly those of diving ducks, will be swelled if heavy rainfall causes extensive flooding of the meadows, and the same conditions attract the highest numbers of waders. Cold conditions elsewhere in the country may bring an influx of birds, but because the water in the fields here is shallow it tends to freeze over easily, causing most wildfowl to leave, although many congregate on the nearby, unfrozen, river. General disturbance is much reduced once the shooting season ends in January.

Access

Ashleworth and Hasfield Hams. From Gloucester, drive north up the A417 and turn right at the Royal Exchange pub at Hartpury, skirting Ashleworth village and following minor roads signposted Hasfield and Tirley. About 1¼ miles (2 km) beyond Ashleworth the road passes under the second of two lines of electricity cables, with Ashleworth Ham immediately on the right beyond this. There is no access to the reserve itself, but the main area is easily viewable from the road, through various gaps in the hedgerow along the next mile (1.6 km). Two small GWT hides among the trees of Meerend Thicket on the bank on the left-hand side of the road provide a raised view over the area, and there is a roadside screen here also. A little further north, at the minor crossroads turning to Hasfield, the no-through-road to the east gives views over the northern, Hasfield Ham, area. The fields themselves should not be entered as, apart from their being private land, entry only puts up the birds which need this undisturbed refuge for feeding and breeding.

Access is also possible along the bank of the River Severn. Continue north to the B4213 junction and turn right to Haw Bridge over the river; a public footpath leads from the Haw Bridge Inn south along the river bank, eventually emerging at the Boat Inn at Ashleworth Quay. A few Sand Martins breed near Haw Bridge, and in freezing conditions this can be a profitable winter walk with many wildfowl on the river. The riverside alders are worth checking for Siskin and Redpoll, and a Kingfisher might be seen flashing past low over the water; the same species may be seen from the road across the river plain east of Haw Bridge. The B4213 continues east to join the A38 south of Tewkesbury for those approaching from that direction.

Coombe Hill Canal. About half way between Gloucester and Tewkesbury on the A38, a short no-through-road by the Swan Inn opposite the A4019 turning to Cheltenham leads down to the end of the now disused canal. There is limited parking here near some cottages, and a public footpath, sometimes very muddy, leads along the north bank of the canal. Information about the site is given on a GWT panel by the car park. The main floods occur in the fields to the north, though the fields to the south are also sometimes wet and thus attractive to birds. The whole area can be scanned from the towpath which eventually emerges after 2¼ miles (3.6 km) on a minor road from the B4213 near Haw Bridge to Norton village on the A38 to the south, this road providing alternative access, although parking by the narrow bridge over the far end of the canal is limited. There is another GWT panel at this end of the footpath. The main floods are by the eastern half of the canal walk, but lusher small meadows at the western end and the thick hedgerow by the canal provide cover for breeding birds such as Sedge Warbler and Reed Bunting.

Calendar

All year: Grey Heron, Mute Swan, Sparrowhawk, Buzzard, Kestrel, Little Owl, Reed Bunting.

December–February: Cormorant, chance of Bittern; sometimes Bewick's or Whooper Swans, Shelduck. Wigeon, Gadwall, Teal, Mallard, Pintail, Shoveler, Pochard, Tufted Duck, maybe Goldeneye or other diving duck. Chance of rarity, e.g. Green-winged Teal. Possible Peregrine. Water Rail,

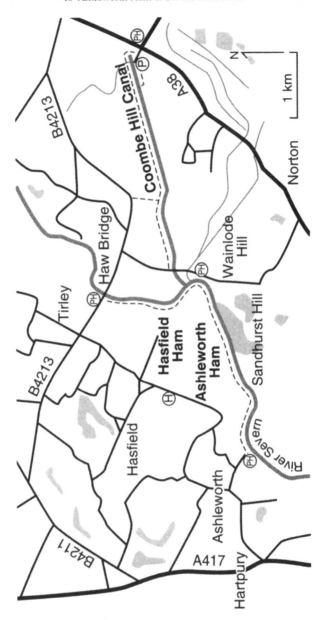

Coot, Snipe, maybe Jack Snipe, Redshank, Green Sandpiper. Winter thrushes; Siskin, Redpoll.

March–May: Maybe Shelduck; wintering wildfowl to end of March with passage birds (including rarities) through April; maybe Garganey mid-March–May. Trickle of waders in April, including Ruff, Whimbrel, Black-tailed Godwit, Greenshank. Displaying Lapwing, Curlew, Redshank. Summer breeding birds arrive from mid–late April: Cuckoo, Sand Martin, Yellow Wagtail, Redstart, Chiffchaff, Willow, Grasshopper, Sedge and Reed Warblers, maybe Nightingale. Peak song through May.

June–July: Breeding birds active, especially in June. Grasshopper Warbler sings through July. Common Sandpiper and occasionally other waders pass from July.

August–November: Cormorant; occasional Greenshank or other wader August–September; most summer migrants leave in August; Whinchat, Yellow Wagtail passing August–mid-September. Winter wildfowl from late October, when Woodcock may occur.

49 THE SEVERN & AVON VALLEYS OS Outdoor Leisure 14, Explorer 179 and 190

Habitat

From its junction with the Avon at Tewkesbury the River Severn winds through low-lying meadows devoted mainly to hay crops and cattle grazing. The lowest areas (notably the Avon valley, the Severn Ham at Tewkesbury and the meadows near Wainlode Hill) are completely flooded once or twice most winters. A footpath (the Severn Way) runs along the bank almost the whole way, and makes a convenient approach to an interesting if disjointed series of riverside habitats. At the extreme north of the area, above Tewkesbury, are old claypits at the Mythe, right by the Severn, some open with lilies and a few bulrushes, others choked with osiers and willows, and the nearby disused railway cutting is now managed as a nature reserve by the GWT. Up the Avon Valley lies Twyning Great Meadow, an ancient hay meadow still managed traditionally and of great botanical interest, despite being bisected by the M5 motorway. The Severn Ham near Tewkesbury is a broad island mostly devoted to hay, but edged with rough nettles and willow scrub. Between Tewkesbury and Gloucester, the river is lined by willows with alders and passes Ashleworth and Hasfield Hams (see previous entry); there are more former claypits at Apperley, Sandhurst (another GWT reserve) and Walham. Immediately west of Gloucester, Maisemore Ham, Over Ham and Port Ham together form the historic Alney Island, rather more built-up and cultivated than the ham at Tewkesbury. Sudmeadow, just to the south, is now partly occupied by Gloucester landfill site.

Species

In winter, flocks of up to 1000 Golden Plover and Lapwing may occur at Twyning, sometimes joined by a few Dunlin and Redshank. If floodwater is left lying in the fields, reasonable numbers of wildfowl can occur on the Avon meadows, including Bewick's Swans, Canada Geese and surface-feeding ducks such as Teal, Wigeon and Shoveler. Pochard, Tufted Duck and other diving ducks (including in cold weather Goldeneye and sometimes Smew) may be seen on the river, although usually in small

Reed Warbler

numbers. Moorhens, Mallard and Mute Swans are resident all along the river. Cormorants winter in increasing numbers (up to 50 in recent years), generally roosting at Wainlode Hill and Lower Lode and spreading along the Severn and Avon valleys to feed during the day. Snipe are found along most of the valley in suitable habitat, and the odd Green Sandpiper winters in the Gloucester area. Water Rails can be found at many of the pools in winter, and may breed. Gloucester landfill site attracts large numbers of gulls, mainly Black-headed and Lesser Black-backed, but intensive study has produced Iceland and Glaucous Gulls in several winters, and there are also records of Mediterranean, Ring-billed and Yellow-legged Gull from the same area.

During the spring, migrants moving along the line of the rivers stop off to feed and sing briefly, the waterside vegetation proving attractive to Willow Warblers and Chiffchaffs. Sedge and Reed Warblers breed wherever suitable vegetation occurs, particularly at Walham, Sandhurst, Severn Ham and the Mythe. Redstarts, breeding in pollarded willows, are something of a local speciality. The tangled scrub along the old Mythe railway attracts a few pairs of Nightingales in most years. Drainage has meant that breeding waders are few and far between, but the occasional pair of Curlew and Redshank appear here and there, notably at Twyning Great Meadow. There are breeding colonies of Lesser Black-backed and Herring Gulls on buildings in Gloucester, with over 2000 pairs of the former outnumbering the latter by over four to one. In midsummer and autumn the vegetation becomes lush and birds fall silent, but parties of Yellow Wagtails sometimes gather, and Common Sandpipers can be seen flying downstream from their breeding grounds, presumably in the Welsh hills.

Timing

Calm sunny weather is ideal for observing small birds in the tangled riverside vegetation and in summer brings out myriads of dragonflies. In autumn the area remains extremely dry until the first floods occur. At the height of any flooding, the water is usually too deep for wildfowl, and the most favourable conditions are found when the flooding is very light or has just receded. In very cold spells when other marshes and open water are frozen over, wildfowl take refuge on the river itself which almost invariably remains unfrozen. Casual disturbance peaks at weekends, and the riverbank and some of the pools are popular with anglers.

Access

For Tewkesbury Ham, it is usually possible to park in side streets across the A38 from the Abbey, and then walk to the old mill and weir, where a footbridge brings access to the island itself. Damper areas are at the southern and northern ends, and footpaths run all the way around the perimeter by the riverside, making a complete exploration fairly simple. There is a Cormorant roost at Lower Lode, just to the south.

Access to the Mythe area is from near the A38/A438 junction just north of the town, although parking is extremely limited. A signposted footpath along the east bank of the river starts at the junction itself, or can be reached via a short lane starting from the garden centre c.300 metres along the A38. The riverbank path passes all the more open pools, where Great Crested Grebes and Canada Geese are breeding species, and the old railway line at the foot of the escarpment runs close by areas of denser undergrowth where Nightingales and Reed Warblers can sometimes be heard singing.

Twyning Great Meadow is most easily viewed from across the river in the village of Bredon, reached along the B4080 north of Tewkesbury. In the village, follow signs to the church and riverbank. The newly created lakes at Bredon's Hardwick (Croft Farm Leisure and Water Park) can be seen from a public footpath along the west bank of the Avon from Tewkesbury to the Fleet Inn at Twyning, or from the B4080 south of Bredon, although a telescope is essential. These former gravel pits, on the Worcestershire side of the river, attract small numbers of diving ducks, but are also worth checking for migrant terns and waders, which have already included several rarities.

Sandhurst claypits can be reached via Twigworth (site, incidentally, of the interesting Nature in Art Museum and Gallery at Wallworth Hall) on the A38 north of Gloucester, turning left here and following signs to Sandhurst. In the village, turn left just beyond the church and continue to the end of the lane, although as parking is virtually impossible you may have to walk from the village centre. A muddy track and a public footpath across some meadows leads to the riverbank where the claypits lie to both the north and south. Access is not allowed to the pits themselves, which are managed by the GWT, but they can be viewed perfectly satisfactorily from the Severn Way riverside path which continues north to Wainlode Hill and south to Walham.

A footpath runs most of the way round Alney Island, but parking by the busy A40 is difficult both for this and for nearby Walham Pools and infilling and urban encroachment have reduced the interest of this area. The easiest point of access is along a track starting by the bridge at the south end of Maisemore village on the A417. The Gloucester landfill site at Sudmeadow can be viewed most easily from the Severn Way footpath where it follows the river bank from near the back of Gloucester Docks (Severn Road or Llanthony Road) to Hempsted.

Calendar

All year. Great Crested Grebe (the Mythe), Mute Swan, Canada Goose, Moorhen, Coot; Lesser Spotted Woodpecker (scarce); Willow Tit (Sandhurst), Reed Bunting.

December–February: Cormorant; Bewick's Swan (Avon Meadows and Twyning), Wigeon, Teal, Shoveler, Pochard, Tufted Duck, Water Rail, Lapwing; Golden Plover (Twyning), Snipe; Green Sandpiper (especially Sudmeadow), maybe Dunlin, Redshank. Gulls at landfill site may include rarity, e.g. Glaucous, Iceland Gull. Siskin, Redpoll.

March–May: Maybe breeding Curlew and Redshank (Twyning). First Chiffchaffs late March, Willow Warbler, Cuckoo, Yellow Wagtail, Nightingale, Redstart from mid-April, Sedge and Reed Warblers late April.

June–July: Breeding warblers, Yellow Wagtail. Common Sandpipers passing downstream from July.

August–November: Most summer visitors leave during August. Yellow Wagtail on passage (August–mid-September). Winter wildfowl from November.

50 THE CENTRAL COTSWOLD SCARP

OS Explorer 179

Habitat

This section of the steep indented Cotswold scarp holds a series of woodland and grassland sites, plus a couple of small reservoirs, where a good range of birds can be seen within close range of the two major centres of population of Cheltenham and Gloucester.

Starting in the north, Dowdeswell Reservoir is tucked into the steep-sided valley of the River Chelt just east of Cheltenham. In addition to the narrow strip of water, its north side is bordered by rhododendrons, conifers and the mixed woodland of Dowdeswell Wood, managed as a nature reserve by the GWT. Immediately south of Cheltenham, Leckhampton Hill is a plateau of rough grassland, gorse and scattered trees, with extensive worked-out limestone quarries on its western side. The quarries contain the famous pillar of rock known as the Devil's Chimney, as well as some fine cliffs. Plantations of conifers and deciduous trees grow below the cliffs, while scrub is encroaching on the steep grass slopes on the north side of the hill, posing a threat to the limestone flora. To the southwest, Crickley Hill has similar flower-rich grassland, only limited exposures of rock but some fine mature beech woodland. Southwest again, between Birdlip and Cooper's Hill, is an almost unbroken crescent of deciduous woodland comprising Witcombe, Buckholt and Brockworth Woods. The eastern section (Witcombe Woods), although having a large proportion of beeches, includes other species such as sycamore, oak, larch, birch and a few conifer plantations. The western section is dominated by beech but there are some bushy clearings, particularly at Cooper's Hill. Nestling at the foot of the slope are the three artificial lakes of Witcombe Reservoirs, their bare embankments separated by narrow causeways to form virtually a single unit of water covering 30 acres (12 ha). Almost due west, and partially enclosed by the city of Gloucester, the isolated and roughly conical Robinswood Hill holds a good mixture of open grassland, trees and bushes and rises to a height of 198 metres. It is designated a Country Park, with a golf course, ski-slope, etc., but parts are managed as a nature reserve.

Species

Setting aside the reservoirs, woodland and scrubland birds are the order of the day here. The Witcombe/Brockworth section plus Dowdeswell Wood hold the widest variety, with Tawny Owl, Great Spotted Woodpecker, Nuthatch, Treecreeper and the usual tits and finches all resident. Willow Tits breed at Dowdeswell Wood and are sometimes seen in the Witcombe area. Leckhampton Hill has the best selection of scrubland species, notably Yellowhammer, Linnet, Greenfinch and Meadow Pipit among resident species, while Jackdaws and Stock Doves breed in the quarries. Red-legged Partridge and Lapwing still breed on the nearby farmland, although the latter are declining fast. Kestrels are commonly seen all along the escarpment, using the updraughts to help them hang in the breeze, and Sparrowhawks are also widespread. Buzzards are steadily increasing in all the scarp woodlands, and in spring up to six together have been seen in territorial disputes over the Witcombe area. Likewise, Ravens are increasingly noted along the Cotswold escarpment, and there is certainly plenty of potential breeding habitat for them.

In summer the breeding population is swelled by the arrival of migrant species, the commoner warblers such as Blackcap, Garden Warbler, Willow Warbler and Chiffchaff being widespread in the woodland, while Whitethroats and Tree Pipits come to the more open bushy areas throughout. Wood Warblers can sometimes be heard singing in the Witcombe Woods, Crickley Hill and Leckhampton areas, especially where there are good stands of beech, but no longer seem to breed here. Redstarts are rather thinly scattered, being most often seen in the Witcombe to Sheepscombe area. Grasshopper Warblers have been recorded at several places, most notably Leckhampton Hill, but there are also records of this elusive species from Robinswood Hill and the Dowdeswell area.

Kestrel

The 'leading line' effect of the slope means that migration times can be quite rewarding. Wheatears and Ring Ousels are relatively frequent in spring on the tops of any of the more open areas, also occurring from time to time in autumn. Pied Flycatchers sometimes appear in the woodland, but have not yet bred. In late summer large numbers of Swifts, Swallows and House Martins hawk for insects along the escarpment lip at Leckhampton. Later in the autumn, visible migration of Skylarks, Meadow Pipits and finches takes place over the higher land, and grounded migrants include Stonechats and Whinchats.

In winter, fewer birds are to be seen, but there are usually a few Bramblings with the Chaffinches and Great Tits under the beeches, with numbers into the hundreds in good years. In the evenings, lines of gulls, mostly Black-headed and Common, stream along the escarpment on their way to roost on the Severn Estuary. However, at this time the reservoirs tend to command rather more interest. At Witcombe Reservoirs Pochard, Mallard, Tufted Ducks and Coot are the most numerous species, although inevitably overall numbers are never very high. Goosanders are increasingly noted here, with a dozen or so not unusual at times. Great Crested Grebes and Little Grebes winter in single-figure numbers, the former sometimes attempting to nest. Apart from a few feral Canada Geese, other wildfowl are unusual, but have included quite a range of species, for example Slavonian Grebe, Smew, Scaup and Long-tailed Duck, as often seems to happen with this type of small isolated reservoir. A few Common Sandpipers, Common and Black Terns appear on migration, usually singly, and again a variety of odd waders stop briefly, although suitable habitat is virtually absent. There have also been several records of Osprey, both in spring and autumn. The balance of species at Dowdeswell Reservoir is similar, although numbers are usually lower here, and both grebe species usually try to nest, though with variable success. Dippers from the nearby streams appear here from time to time, and may sometimes breed. Common Sandpipers are the only regular passage waders, but again the list of unusual birds is quite a long one, so it is always worth a quick check in passing.

Timing

Early morning is the best time for breeding passerines in the summer, and dawn for the best chance of grounded migrants or visible migration. Clear breezy days produce the most sightings of soaring birds of prey. Adverse weather may bring something unusual to Witcombe or Dowdeswell Reservoirs. Leckhampton, Crickley and Robinswood Hills are all heavily used by the public, particularly at the weekends, so an early start here is advisable.

Access

Dowdeswell Reservoir. This lies c.1 mile (1.6 km) beyond the outskirts of Cheltenham by the (very busy) main A40 road to Oxford (see also map with site 52, Cleeve Hill); the whole surface can be observed from the roadside footpath which runs the length of the southern side. For Dowdeswell Wood, a public footpath (part of the Cotswold Way) signposted Cleeve Hill starts a short distance below the dam, opposite the Waterside pub, the path crossing beneath the dam and then running along the west side of the wood. Waymarked trails within the wood start from the northern end of the dam. Also of interest for woodland birds, including Buzzards and Sparrowhawks, is the WT property of Lineover

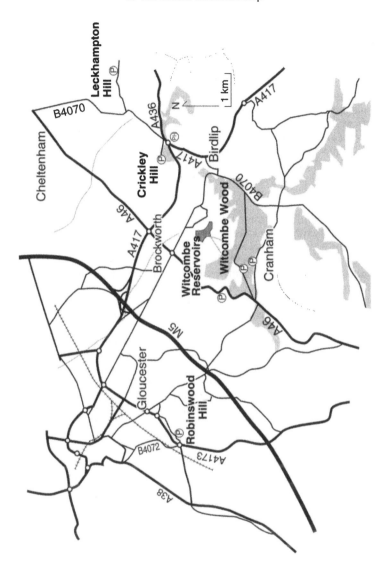

Wood, approached along a track to the south between the pub and the dam, and where there is limited parking.

Leckhampton Hill: The hill lies beyond the southern outskirts of Cheltenham, by the B4070. On the upward slope, turn left into Daisybank Road and park in one of two small car parks after c.200 metres on the right. For the energetic a rough track leads to the top past the Devil's Chimney. For a more leisurely approach continue along the B4070 and take the next road left to reach open farmland at the very top. After a short distance there is a large car park on the left with well-defined footpaths to the edge of the escarpment.

Crickley Hill Country Park: Continuing on along the B4070 brings you to the Country Park, which is signposted to the right just before the junction with the A436 near the Air Balloon Inn roundabout. This road leads to a large car park with information centre, toilets, etc. including facilities for the disabled. Guides to a variety of waymarked trails are available here.

Witcombe Woods: From the Air Balloon Inn roundabout, take the A417 Cirencester road for just under 1 mile (1.6 km) and then turn right to Birdlip. In the village, turn sharp right and then left on the B4070 towards Stroud. Just beyond the second bend a lodge on the right marks the entrance to Witcombe Woods, although cars cannot be parked here. A public footpath leads from here all the way to Brockworth Wood and Coopers Hill. Buckholt Wood NNR is just to the south, and there are various roadside parking spots and footpaths for further exploration of the whole area.

Witcombe Reservoirs: Instead of turning left in Birdlip, continue down a steep hill towards Brockworth, and then left into the village of Great Witcombe. A public footpath leads from just beyond the church across fields to the reservoirs, the public right of way continuing between the northern two and the southern one. Beyond Great Witcombe, a no-through-road to the left leads to Witcombe Farm and a car park reserved for anglers. However, birdwatchers are usually allowed to park here as long as permission is requested from the adjacent bailiff's office.

Robinswood Hill: This hill lies in the southern outskirts of Gloucester. At the junction of the A4173 Stroud road with the A38 southern ring road, a minor exit from the roundabout (Reservoir Road) leads, after a short distance, to the well-marked entrance to the Country Park where there is ample parking and an information centre. The GWT has its headquarters here, and is a useful source of information on the whole county. The other end of Reservoir Road emerges on the A38 at the next roundabout north, where a modern church spire provides a useful landmark. Churchdown Hill (sometimes called Chosen Hill) in the northeastern suburbs of Gloucester holds a similar range of species. Access is via footpaths from the church and nearby waterworks on the hill itself.

Calendar

All year: Great Crested Grebe, Grey Heron, Canada Goose, Coot (Witcombe and Dowdeswell Reservoirs), Sparrowhawk, Kestrel, Buzzard, Red-legged Partridge, Tawny Owl, Green and Great Spotted Woodpeckers; maybe Lesser Spotted (Witcombe Woods), Skylark. Maybe Dipper at Dowdeswell Reservoir. Willow Tit (Witcombe and Dowdeswell Woods), Nuthatch, Treecreeper, Linnet, Yellowhammer.

December–February: Little Grebe, Mallard, Pochard, Tufted Duck, Goosander, maybe Goldeneye or rarer duck (all Witcombe and Dowdeswell Reservoirs). Woodcock, Brambling, Siskin, Redpoll.

March–May: Common Sandpiper, chance of Common and Black Tern (April–May, Dowdeswell and Witcombe Reservoirs). Wheatear, maybe Ring Ousel, on high ground, mid-March–April. Arriving from mid-April–mid-May: Cuckoo, Tree Pipit; Redstart (Witcombe Woods, Crickley Hill), Whitethroat, Lesser Whitethroat; Grasshopper Warbler (Dowdeswell Woods, Leckhampton and Robinswood Hills), Garden Warbler, Blackcap, Willow Warbler, Chiffchaff; maybe Wood Warbler (Witcombe Woods).

June–July: Little Grebes may breed at Dowdeswell Reservoir. Woodland residents and summer visitors breeding. Maybe Common Sandpiper from July (Witcombe and Dowdeswell Reservoirs).

August–November. Maybe wader or tern (August–September, Witcombe Reservoirs). Ducks increase from September (Witcombe and Dowdeswell Reservoirs). Passage Stonechat, Wheatear, possible Ring Ousel, to end September. Visible migration of larks, pipits, finches in October. Brambling, Yellowhammer and finches in mixed roosts from October (Leckhampton Hill).

51 PITTVILLE PARK
OS Explorer 179

Habitat and species

This Cheltenham town park provides a convenient place to see a selection of commoner species, particularly if an early morning visit is made. There are two small lakes which attract small numbers of Mallard, Tufted Ducks and the occasional Pochard. There have also been several recent records of Goosander. Mute Swans, Coots and Moorhens are resident, Great Crested Grebes have attempted to nest and Little Grebe and Grey Heron visit from time to time. Common, Black-headed and Lesser Black-backed Gulls come to feed and bathe in winter, while Nuthatch, Coal Tit and Mistle Thrush are among breeding species. As often seems to happen in seemingly unpromising places, regular watchers have been rewarded by sightings of rarer visitors such as Osprey, Yellow Wagtail and Common Sandpiper.

Access

This town park lies in the northern part of Cheltenham, towards the race course, and is bisected by the A435 Evesham road. A tunnel connecting the two parts of the park means that a hazardous road crossing can be avoided.

52 CLEEVE HILL & COMMON
OS Explorer 179 and Outdoor Leisure 45

Habitat

Cleeve Common is a plateau approximately 2 miles (3.2 km) wide running northwest to southeast on the Cotswold scarp northeast of

Cheltenham. It contains the highest land in Gloucestershire with most of the area over 280 metres, and commands fine views to the west. The northwestern part is occupied by a golf course but most of the area is very open and windswept grassland with patches of scrubby gorse. It is good for orchids in early summer and there is a fair range of grassland butterflies to be seen. The steep slopes have some mixed woodland and scrub while to the east lie open rolling farmland and a number of dry wooded valleys, both with their own characteristic species.

Species

Breeding birds in spring and summer provide the main interest here, particularly in fine weather, with migration periods adding to the variety of species likely to be recorded. The sight of a Buzzard wheeling overhead is relatively commonplace these days as several pairs breed in the surrounding woodlands and hunting Kestrels can also often be seen. Ravens also are increasingly noted flying over, although exactly where they nest is something of a mystery. Both Grey and Red-legged Partridges occur on the adjoining farmland while a few Lapwings also still attempt to breed. In winter Golden Plover also occur here on an irregular basis. After an absence of several years it is good to be able to report the return of Stonechats as a breeding species, perhaps four pairs in the general area, several individuals remaining throughout the winter. Conversely, Corn Buntings continue to decline, although small numbers still remain on the high farmland to the east, with small flocks forming in the winter. Skylarks are abundant, their song being a characteristic sound of spring and summer. Meadow Pipits also occur throughout the year and are very numerous at times during the winter or on passage. In summer, the area is a good one in which to compare their songs, calls and plumages with those of Tree Pipits, the latter breeding on nearby West Down, although far outnumbered by the resident species. The presence of both species accounts for the fact that in spring the Cuckoo's call can be heard widely, the bird itself often to be seen searching for nests in which to lay its eggs. Grasshopper Warblers are still heard singing from the scrub on the edge of Cleeve Hill and Whitethroats, Willow Warblers and Linnets all nest in similar habitat rather more widely. A few pairs of Redstarts breed along

Ring Ouzel

the scarp edge around Corndean and Belas Knap Long Barrow but are not found on the Common itself. Arriving last of the summer visitors, the tiny Quail can sometimes be heard calling from the middle of one of the cereal fields; they are not numerous, perhaps three in a good year, and are notoriously difficult to actually see. Wheatears pass through in good numbers in both spring and autumn, and have occasionally bred in stone walls on the high farmland adjoining the common. Of the pure migrants, the most notable is the Ring Ousel, as Cleeve Hill in spring has become a reasonably reliable site for this species, usually in ones and twos although up to seven at a time have been reported, with the occasional bird also being seen in autumn. Dotterel have been reported in May on a few occasions, and a Buff-breasted Sandpiper on the golf course for a couple of days in September 2000 just goes to show that rarities can turn up almost anywhere that is watched regularly.

Timing
Early summer mornings are probably best for seeing breeding species such as Tree Pipit and Redstart. Quail often have a resurgence of calling in the late afternoon and evening. Being in such an exposed position the area can be very windy at times and watching birds then is almost impossible; in winter it can be very bleak and apparently almost birdless. The area is popular with the public and so an early start is advisable when looking for migrants.

Access
Cleeve Hill lies immediately northeast of Cheltenham, close by where the B4632 Stratford-on-Avon road rises onto the escarpment. Three approaches by car from Cheltenham are given below:

Route 1: At the brow of the hill on the B4632 1½ miles (2.4 km) beyond Southam turn right at a minor crossroads to the Municipal Golf Course on Cleeve Hill. This road leads past the clubhouse to a public car park on the left, in a disused quarry at the edge of the common.

Route 2: Leave Cheltenham east on the A40 past Dowdeswell Reservoir (see site 50) and c.1 mile (1.6 km) beyond this turn left into the village of Whittington. Here turn left again towards Ham and, after 1 mile (1.6 km), turn right where signposted Cleeve Hill Common; after nearly 3 miles (4.8 km) the road finishes by some radio masts on the south side of the common.

Route 3: Alternatively turn right in Whittington and then left after ¾ mile (1.2 km) towards Whitehall; after just over 2 miles (3.2 km) the road ends at West Down.
There are well-defined footpaths over the area from these three parking points with free access on the common and good footpaths and bridleways across the high farmland. The path from West Down to Wontley Farm and the Long Barrow at Belas Knap passes through the more varied eastern part.

Calendar
All year: Buzzard, Kestrel, Grey and Red-legged Partridges, Lapwing, Stock Dove, Skylark, Meadow Pipit, Stonechat, Raven, Linnet, Corn Bunting, Yellowhammer.

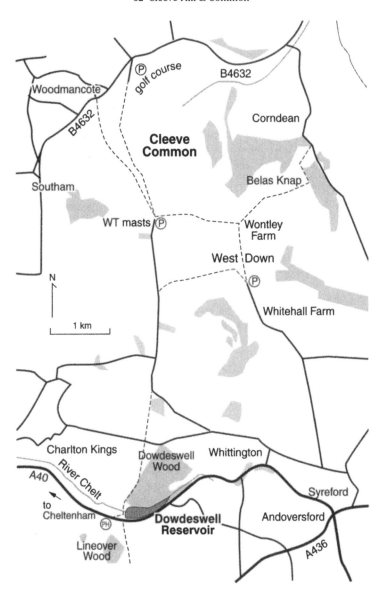

December–February: Quiet period. Sometimes Golden Plover. Stonechats may leave. Finch and bunting flocks in places.

March–May: Chance of Dotterel (but rare) in May. Wheatear; Ring Ousel (mostly April). Cuckoo, Tree Pipit, Redstart, Whitethroat, Grasshopper Warbler, Willow Warbler from late April.

June–July: Quail, Stonechat, Corn Bunting breed, occasionally Wheatear.

August–November: Wheatear, Whinchat, maybe Ring Ousel on passage September. Summer visitors mostly gone by end August.

53 GUITING WOOD

Habitat and species

This mixed deciduous wood with some conifer plantations covers nearly 500 acres (200 ha) and is situated in attractive undulating Cotswold farmland c.6 miles (9.6 km) east-northeast of Cheltenham. The usual commoner woodland species are likely to be seen, with a chance of Dipper along the River Windrush to the southeast. Buzzards can be seen soaring overhead at any time of year, and the surrounding arable fields hold both Grey and Red-legged Partridges, as well as plenty of Pheasants. The resident Skylarks and Yellowhammers of the farmland are joined in winter by wandering flocks of Fieldfares and Redwings.

Access

The nearest village is Guiting Power (SP 095248), the wood lying to the north of the minor road from there to Winchcombe. There is a small car park near the southern end, from where the Warden's Way runs through the wood, one of several public footpaths in the area. The lane along the eastern side (marked as unsuitable for motor vehicles) makes a pleasant walk, following a small stream which has been dammed in places to form small pools.

54 BOURTON PITS

Habitat

The village of Bourton-on-the-Water lies in the broad valley of the River Windrush where it is joined by the smaller Rivers Eye and Dikler and just to the southeast are several disused gravel pits. The northern group includes two fairly large lakes, both with bush-covered islands, plus several smaller pools. This area is heavily used for coarse fishing, including carp and pike. A little further south is a larger lake stocked with trout, close by the River Windrush. The banks of all the lakes are mostly open grass or rough weed-covered ground, with trees and hedges separating them from the surrounding farmland. Some poplars and deciduous copses adjoin the low-lying meadows just to the south.

Species

Whilst a good selection of garden and hedgerow birds can be seen in the vicinity of Bourton-on-the-Water, the gravel pits and their water birds are the chief reason for a birdwatching visit. Two or three pairs of Great Crested Grebes have raised young and up to about ten birds are to be seen at all seasons. Little Grebes are also usually present with a maximum of about 15 in autumn and winter. These too have bred successfully.

Single Cormorants can turn up at any time of year. Among surface-feeding ducks, Mallard are the most numerous in winter but do not usually exceed 100. Wigeon are erratic in their occurrence, although they have reached over 200. They tend to appear during spells of cold weather but disperse when it becomes milder as feeding is limited. Shoveler visit in very small numbers, usually less than five, mostly during the winter but also in spring and summer when passage birds may be involved, and a few Gadwall have also been noted. Among diving species, Tufted Ducks peak at around 150 in winter and a few pairs remain to breed. Pochard occur in slight lower numbers, again with a few birds sometimes lingering throughout the year. The odd Ruddy Duck can be seen at any time throughout the year, and they have nested at least once. Other wildfowl seem rather erratic, even birds like Goldeneye and Goosander being unusual, although more regular watching might increase the number of sightings. The most frequent 'vagrant' is the Red-crested Pochard which has occurred at various times of the year and has bred once, but the most likely origin for this species is the Cotswold Water Park where there is a thriving feral population. Mute Swans are resident, maximum numbers being around 20 in late summer/autumn and there are sometimes over 100 Canada Geese during the same period. A pair or two of both species breeds on a regular basis. Coots have reached over 300 in mid-winter and there are usually about 100 here throughout most of year. Water Rails are noted in winter but they are not easily seen. Black-headed Gulls, the most regular gull species here, sometimes stay to roost on the southern lake.

Spring brings a few Common Sandpipers passing through but, as there are no exposed margins of sand or mud, other waders are virtually non-existent. Rather more surprisingly, terns are also rarely reported on passage, but the occasional Common and Black Tern does occur. Sand Martins and other hirundines following the river valleys stop off to feed and Willow Warblers and Chiffchaffs also occur on migration in the waterside vegetation. Several pairs of Reed Buntings nest but suitable habitat is currently too limited to allow species such as Sedge and Reed Warblers to do so regularly. Willow Tits have been recorded here in the breeding season, in addition to the more numerous Marsh Tits, and there have been several sightings of Barn Owl. The vertical banks provide ideal nesting sites for at least one pair of Kingfishers and up to seven birds at

Kingfisher

one time have been noted. Grey Wagtails and Dippers are resident along the rivers nearby, although the latter at least is unlikely to be seen at the pits themselves. Hobbies hunt over the pits for insects and hirundines irregularly throughout the summer, and Buzzards can be seen soaring over the nearby hillsides, especially to the southeast. Flocks of Redpolls appear in the winter and Tree Sparrows, which still breed in the general area, are worth looking out for among parties of other seed-eating birds.

Timing

The main disturbance comes from anglers, who are on-site for most of the year. Otherwise not particularly critical although the village of Bourton itself is popular with tourists and can be very crowded in summer.

Access

Bourton-on-the-Water lies just east of the A429 Stow to Cirencester road. Drive the length of the village (towards Little Rissington) and, beyond the last of the houses, park in a layby on the left just before the bridge over the river. A short distance back towards the village a signposted footpath to the right crosses a paddock and runs through the northern group of pits. For the southern pits, return to the road and, almost opposite, another sign directs you south along a gravel track to the waterside. The footpath crosses the River Windrush, then passes through some riverside woodland, before returning to the pits at their southern end.

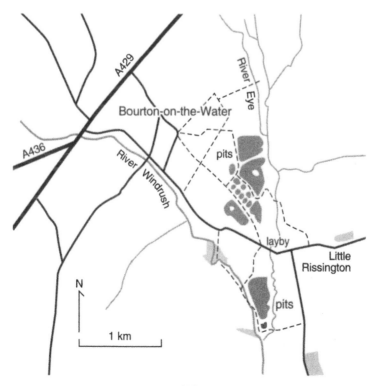

Calendar

All year: Great Crested and Little Grebes, Grey Heron, Mute Swan, Canada Goose, Mallard, Tufted Duck, Ruddy Duck, Buzzard, Coot, Kingfisher. Grey Wagtail, Dipper on nearby streams. Willow Tit, Tree Sparrow (both scarce), Reed Bunting.

December–February: Tufted Duck increase. Pochard, sometimes Wigeon, maybe Pintail, Shoveler or other more unusual wildfowl. Water Rail. Black-headed Gull roost. Redpoll.

March–May: Common Sandpiper (April–May), maybe other wader or Black Tern briefly. Hirundines from April.

June–July: Breeding waterfowl and common warblers. Chance of Hobby.

August–November: Pochard and other ducks increase from October.

55 CHEDWORTH & WITHINGTON WOODS   OS Outdoor Leisure 45

Habitat

These woods form a continuous belt of forest 3½ miles (5.6 km) long with an average width of c.½ mile (0.8 km), running mostly along a steep oolite slope on the south side of the River Coln. In the centre is an extensive area of deciduous woodland, mostly oak with hazel, while elsewhere are stands of pure hazel coppice, spruce and mature larches, and a variety of hardwoods. The River Coln itself is here merely a large stream, quite fast flowing, and winds through low-lying and rather bare grazing land with some alders in the western section. The river passes close to the eastern end of the woodland. Immediately south of the woods on the plateau near Chedworth village is a disused airfield where, although the runways are still partially in existence, the rest is composed of a flat, cultivated expanse. Otherwise the surrounding countryside is fairly open mixed grazing and arable farmland. A thriving population of fallow deer inhabits the woods and roe deer and muntjac are also present. The remains of a Roman villa (NT) in Chedworth Woods attract visitors to the site but not many of them walk the woodland paths. The large snails (*Helix pomatia*) that can be seen here were probably imported by the original inhabitants for food.

Species

This is primarily an area for woodland and farmland birds, not containing any great surprises, but as this is a relatively unexplored area of the county it is likely that some species are under-recorded. Sparrowhawk and Kestrel breed and Buzzards have also moved into the area. The Tawny is the commonest of the owls, but Little is also regular. Pheasants

Redstart

are extremely numerous and are extensively reared for shooting. Green and Great Spotted Woodpeckers occur and Nuthatch and Treecreeper are common residents. The usual range of other woodland birds can be expected, including Jays, plenty of Marsh Tits and a few Willow Tits. Goldcrests and Coal Tits are numerous in the coniferous areas and Bullfinches are to be found along the woodland edges. In some winters Bramblings arrive to join the Chaffinches searching the ground for beech mast and other seeds, while Siskins and Redpolls join the tit flocks searching the upper branches.

Of the warblers that arrive to breed in spring the Willow Warbler, Chiffchaff, Garden Warbler and Blackcap are numerous, but any Wood Warblers are usually just passage birds. Lesser Whitethroats occur in the areas of dense bushes, their presence usually only betrayed by their rattling song. A few Tree Pipits can be found in forestry clearings or along the woodland edge, and the same areas attract a few pairs of Redstarts. Woodcock has bred in the past, but seems to be only an elusive winter visitor these days.

The surrounding farmland holds Grey and Red-legged Partridges in reasonable numbers all year and in summer a few Quail are sometimes heard calling, particularly in the farmland to the south. Yellowhammers and Skylarks inhabit the nearby arable fields where Corn Buntings also bred in the past, although not frequently seen recently. Along the River Coln, Pied and Grey Wagtails and Moorhens are the most characteristic species. Suitable nest sites for Kingfishers are rather limited close by but single birds are seen intermittently. As far as Dippers are concerned, the River Churn to the west is rather better than the Coln as it has more in the way of the shallow rapids that this species prefers. A few pairs nest downstream, however, and dispersing birds move through from time to time. Little Grebes certainly visit in winter and single Grey Herons come to fish on an irregular basis at all times of the year. It is also always worth checking the river for Mandarins, which have been seen here on more than one occasion, although they are not yet an established species in the Cotswolds.

Timing

As in all woodland areas, calm, clear, warm mornings in spring and summer result in the greatest volume of birdsong, whilst windy weather at any time of the year makes watching difficult and the birds hard to locate.

Access

Chedworth and Withington Woods lie about half way between Cirencester and Cheltenham but away from the main roads. The main woodland is private but there are public footpaths both through it and along the edges, and much can be seen from the roads. Some main routes into the area are given below.

From the A429 Cirencester to Stow road turn west towards Yanworth near the Fossebridge Inn and follow signs to Chedworth Roman villa (c.3 miles/4.8 km). There is a small woodland car park at the entrance, with a footpath running back eastwards alongside the woodlands by the river. There are usually Redstarts to be seen here, and the woodland edge tends to be the more productive part. Alternatively, take the public footpath past the villa and up some steps to the disused railway line, which now forms a linear reserve managed by the GWT, providing some access to the centre of the wood, which is otherwise private. The footpath continues beyond the railway line to emerge near the disused airfield which can alternatively be reached either from the A429 via Chedworth village or along the White Way from the northern edge of Cirencester. In both cases follow signs to Chedworth then Withington. The rough ground around the airfield attracts finches, buntings, Skylarks and partridges, which are also scattered through the arable farmland to the south. From the airfield two roads cut north through the woodland. In addition a footpath starting from a telecommunications mast goes westwards along the southern edge of Withington Woods and through an area of bushes, open ground and conifer plantations of various ages, eventually coming out on the northern edge and joining a minor road to Withington village.

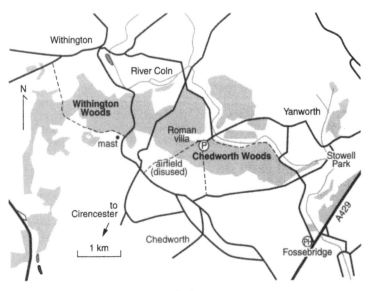

Calendar

All year: Mandarin (scarce), Mallard. Sparrowhawk, Kestrel, Buzzard; Grey and Red-legged Partridges, Pheasant, Tawny and Little Owls, Green and Great Spotted Woodpeckers; Skylark; Nuthatch, Treecreeper, Jay, Goldcrest; Dipper and Grey Wagtail on nearby streams; Bullfinch, Yellowhammer, maybe Corn Bunting.

December–February: Woodcock, Brambling, Siskin, Redpoll, possible Crossbill.

March–May: Cuckoo, Tree Pipit, commoner warblers, Wood Warbler (irregular), Redstart, all from mid–late April. Spotted Flycatcher in May.

June–July: Breeding residents and summer visitors. Possible Quail nearby.

August–November: Quiet period once summer birds gone in August.

56 CIRENCESTER PARK, OVERLEY, OAKLEY & HAILEY WOODS   OS Explorer 168 and 169

Habitat

Cirencester Park is an example of eighteenth century landscaping laid out by the first Earl Bathurst, whose family still own it, and the area has strong associations with the poet Alexander Pope. From the entrance gate on the western edge of the town, a spectacular straight avenue of tall, mature, broadleaved trees leads west for more than 1 mile (1.6 km) and broadens into an open grassy area surrounded by trees. Beyond this lies Oakley Wood, a large continuous tract of 2280 acres (923 ha) of mainly deciduous woodland – beech, oak, ash, sycamore and birch – but including some plantations of larches, pines and other conifers, the whole area being rather formally divided by long, wide, grassy rides. Overley Wood to the north and Hailey Wood to the southwest are outlying areas where woodland management is rather more obvious, although deciduous trees still predominate. Beech, oak, hazel coppice with standards, and conifer plantations are interspersed with open clearings. Fallow and roe deer, foxes, badgers and grey squirrels are all numerous. Several species of orchid, meadow saffron, columbine, and star of Bethlehem are specialities of a rich flora, and the woodland butterfly population includes several fritillaries.

Species

As one would expect in such an extensive area, a wide selection of woodland birds, both resident and migrant, are to be found. The presence of so many mature trees means that woodpeckers are fairly easy to find, even the elusive Lesser Spotted having been recorded on a few occasions. Nuthatch and Treecreeper, Coal, Marsh and Long-tailed Tits plus the usual Jays, Wrens, Robins, etc. are all common throughout the year. Records of Willow Tits seem to be more frequent in the winter but as breeding has been recorded they may well be more regular than appears on the surface. Buzzards are perhaps easiest to see soaring over the slopes of the nearby Frome valley, but they also occur in the main woodland block. Sparrowhawks find plenty of small prey to sustain them and Kestrels use holes in the larger trees as nest sites although hunting over more open country. Other hole-nesting species include good numbers of Stock Doves and Tawny Owls and a few Little Owls. Parties of Siskins and Redpolls can be expected in winter and Brambling flocks of up to 50 birds have been seen, joining the numerous resident Chaffinches under the beeches.

Sparrowhawk

Early spring is the best time to explore the woods, particularly before the leaves make pin-pointing singing birds even more difficult than it often is anyway! The Nightingales that used to occur in the dense hawthorn thickets between Overley and Oakley Woods seem to have deserted the area. In some years there are a pair or two of Redstarts but they are not recorded annually, although this is a bird easy to overlook, especially when not in song. However, Willow Warblers, Chiffchaffs, Blackcaps and Garden Warblers are numerous throughout the woods, Whitethroats can be found in some areas with plenty of undergrowth, and smaller numbers of Lesser Whitethroats nest where it is suitably bushy. Forestry activities have attracted a few Tree Pipits, which can be watched displaying and singing in flight from recently cleared areas, especially where scattered trees have been left standing. Spotted Flycatchers prefer the more mature parkland where they can chase insects over the open grass and return to a shady perch after each foray.

The only area of standing water is a small private lake in the gardens near the eastern entrance to the park. Visibility is restricted by vegetation in summer, but Little Grebe, Cormorant, Canada Goose, Shoveler, Pochard and Tufted Duck have all been recorded at various times, while Great Crested Grebe, Mute Swan, Mallard and Coot have all nested.

Timing

Mornings in spring and summer, especially if the weather is calm and sunny produce most activity. Casual disturbance can be fairly heavy on weekend afternoons at all times of the year.

Access

Cirencester Park lies immediately west of the town centre, and there is a small car park outside the park gates in Cecily Hill, with access during the day (8 am–5 pm). The A419 to Stroud skirts the southern side of both the park and then Oakley Wood to the west. Hailey Wood lies south of this road near the turnings to Coates and to Sapperton. Taking the latter, and then turning right towards Daglingworth takes you round the west and north sides of the estate, and an unfenced bushy stretch marks the start of Overley Wood to the left. The whole area is privately owned by Lord Bathurst but visitors are welcome on foot along the many paths and rides as long as they act responsibly and keep dogs under control. Entry is possible at many places, all of which are clearly marked by signs, though parking is limited by the roadsides. The areas furthest from the town are probably the most productive, and the nearby Frome valley from Miserden to Sapperton is also worth exploring using the network of footpaths.

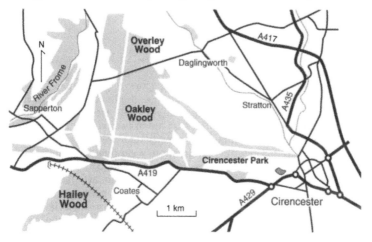

Calendar

All year: Buzzard, Sparrowhawk, Kestrel, Stock Dove, Tawny and Little Owls, Green and Great Spotted Woodpeckers (Lesser Spotted rare), Nuthatch, Treecreeper, Goldcrest, Jay; Coal, Marsh and Long-tailed Tits; Willow Tit (scarce), Bullfinch, Goldfinch.

December–February: Winter thrushes, a few Siskins and Redpolls, sometimes Brambling.

March–May: Most summer visitors arrive mid-April–mid-May: Cuckoo, Tree Pipit, Redstart, Blackcap, Garden Warbler, Whitethroat, Lesser Whitethroat, Willow Warbler, Chiffchaff; Spotted Flycatcher usually last.

June–July: Breeding species active. Song declines from late June.

August–November: Summer visitors leave by end August. Winter finches from October.

57 THE COTSWOLD SCARP SOUTH

OS Explorer 167 and 168

Habitat

In this area around the villages of Wotton-under-Edge and Dursley and north to Stroud, as elsewhere along the Cotswold escarpment, woodland dominated by beech and a variety of conifers grows extensively on the steep slopes, with mixed farmland below and arable fields on the plateau above. In addition, several long valleys with fast-flowing streams, private estates with secluded park lakes and rounded scrub-covered isolated hills add to the variety to the landscape in this little-explored area between Bristol and Gloucester.

Species

Although not outstanding, the area contains an interesting variety of breeding birds in pleasant surroundings. Buzzards have steadily increased and, together with Kestrels and Sparrowhawks, are to be seen soaring in the updraughts along the hill slopes, particularly in the spring. Tree Sparrows, however, once quite numerous here, are nowadays rarely reported, though a few may still occur. One or two pairs of Dippers are resident along the faster-running streams, particularly lower down near the mills and weirs. Grey Wagtails are more widespread in similar habitat. Mandarins occur in the woodland near some of the woodland lakes, but tend to be hard to locate, especially as their favoured habitat is often on private land. In summer, most of the commoner breeding woodland species can be expected, with Yellowhammers and a few Corn Buntings in the nearby fields. Tree Pipits bred in some of the newly replanted conifer plantations until recently but have been pushed out now that the trees have started to mature. Hopefully the birds will return in due course, and they breed elsewhere along the scarp to the north. The localised Willow Tit has also been recorded, as has the always hard to find Lesser Spotted Woodpecker. On spring passage, Ring Ousels and Wheatears stop off briefly on the more open hills and golf courses, while in autumn visible migration, dominated by Chaffinches, Meadow Pipits and Skylarks, can be quite heavy along the actual escarpment. In winter large flocks of Black-headed and Common Gulls pass back and forth between their Cotswold feeding areas and their Severn Estuary roosts.

Timing

For woodland species, early morning is by far the best time for the maximum output of song, and in midsummer, when song dies down, woodland birds can be difficult to find among the thick leaf cover. Breezy days in spring provide the best opportunities for seeing the Buzzards soaring. Visible migration in autumn usually occurs during the first three hours after dawn.

Access

This is a fragmented area, and large parts are private farmland or parkland, with narrow lanes and awkward parking. There are, however, plenty of signposted public footpaths, including the Cotswold Way winding along the escarpment, though an OS map is essential. The following areas provide a basis for further exploration.

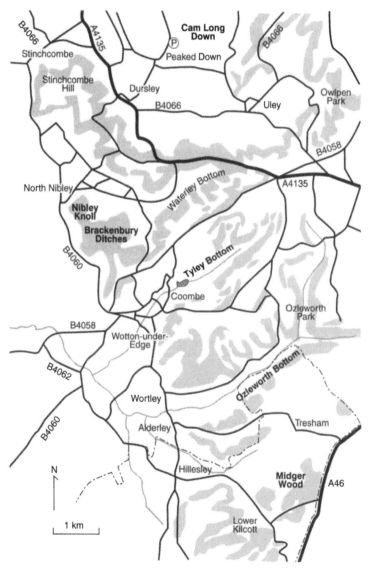

Immediately northeast of Wotton-under-Edge, a public footpath starting from Coombe pumping station runs up the centre of Tyley Bottom
valley, which has a mixture of farmland, rough grazing and woodland on
its steep slopes. South of Wotton, and then east from the village of Wortley,
a lane runs along Ozleworth Bottom, a similar but more extensive valley;
footpaths continue on by the streams while the road climbs out of the
side of the valley at Ozleworth Park. South again and east from Hillesley,
several small woods around Kilcott include Midger Wood which is managed by the GWT, notably for butterflies, dormice and orchids, but the
birdlife is also quite varied (park in layby 100 metres beyond the lower
entrance to the wood). North of Wotton, the conifer plantations on the
hill-fort area of Brackenbury Ditches/Westridge Wood are currently
rather dense, but Tree Pipits have bred here in the past when there were
suitable clearings. The nearby Nibley Knoll monument is one of several
vantage points for observing visible migration, particularly in the
autumn. Rather better from this point of view are the isolated hills of
Peaked Down (Cam Peak) and Cam Long Down, both north of Dursley,
where scrub also provides cover for resting or grounded migrants, Ring
Ousels being regular in spring. There is a small car park and information board at the western end of the hill. The ornamental lakes of
Woodchester Park (NT) have attracted both Dipper and Mandarin, and
the woodland (dominated by conifers) holds the usual common
species. There is a car park at the western end of the park, off the B4066
north of Uley, and there are several waymarked trails to follow through
this scenic valley.

Calendar

All year: Mandarin, Sparrowhawk, Buzzard, Kestrel, Grey and Red-legged
Partridges, Little Owl, Tawny Owl, Kingfisher, woodpeckers may include
Lesser Spotted. Skylark, Grey Wagtail; Dipper (scarce), Goldcrest, Coal Tit,
Marsh Tit; Willow Tit (scarce), Nuthatch, Treecreeper; Raven; Tree Sparrow
(scarce), Yellowhammer.

December–February: Black-headed and Common Gulls; Woodcock;
Fieldfare, Redwing, Brambling, Siskin, Redpoll.

March–May: Buzzards soaring. Common *Sylvia* and *Phylloscopus* warblers from mid–late April. Maybe Ring Ousel, Whinchat, Wheatear on passage, especially April.

June–July: Breeding residents and summer visitors.

August–November: Summer visitors leave during August, maybe
Whinchat or Redstart in September. Visible migration of Skylarks,
Meadow Pipits, thrushes, Chaffinches, Woodpigeons, etc. in October.

58 SILK WOOD & WESTONBIRT ARBORETUM

Habitat and species

Westonbirt Arboretum covers c.116 acres (47 ha) and contains around 18,000 trees of over 500 species, laid out in a series of broad, straight avenues, curving drives and paths. Being one of the finest collections in the world, it is extremely popular with visitors throughout the year. Immediately to the west, Silk Wood, 387 acres (157 ha), is a typical damp oakwood with scattered pendunculate oaks, ashes and wild cherry growing over a vigorous shrub layer. Part of the eastern side of the wood has been developed as an extension of the arboretum, displaying exotic conifers, hickories, walnuts, maples, etc., but much of the original hazel coppice with oak standards can still be seen. The GWT have a small reserve in part of the wood, but the whole area is managed sympathetically for wildlife, the overall aim being to increase the structural diversity of the wood. Flowers such as primroses and bluebells form a spectacular display in spring, and woodland butterflies include white admiral and silver-washed fritillary.

As far as birds are concerned, this is essentially a site in which to see the common woodland species in beautiful surroundings, both sections holding a good range although the greater variety is to be found in the less disturbed Silk Wood. All the usual species including Chaffinches, Robins, Blackbirds and Mistle Thrushes are common, being particularly easy to see on the lawns of the arboretum. The maintenance of plenty of mature timber means that Green and Great Spotted Woodpeckers are widespread, as are Nuthatches and Treecreepers, whilst Goldcrests and Coal Tits are typical birds of the conifers. Predators hunting in and around the area include Buzzards, Sparrowhawks and Kestrels. In summer the woodland residents are joined by Chiffchaffs, Willow Warblers, Blackcaps and Garden Warblers, with Spotted Flycatchers in the more open areas. To date there have been few surprises, but the controlled access has meant that it has not been watched intensively. The odd Pied Flycatcher has been heard singing in spring but so far they not been tempted to use one of the numerous nestboxes. The conifers attract Crossbills during their periodic irruptions, but they have not remained to breed.

Access

The entrance to the Arboretum is clearly marked, c.3½ miles (5.6 km) southwest of Tetbury on the A433. It is open every day of the year from 10 am to 5 pm with an admission fee payable. From the car park you may either walk a short distance to the entrance of the Arboretum or go down the slope in the opposite direction to Silk Wood. There are well-defined tracks and paths in both woodlands and trail guides are available in the visitor centre. Off the hard paths in the Arboretum waterproof footwear is advisable but much of the area has good facilities for the disabled. The Arboretum has plenty of facilities such as cafeteria, toilets, picnic area, shop, etc.

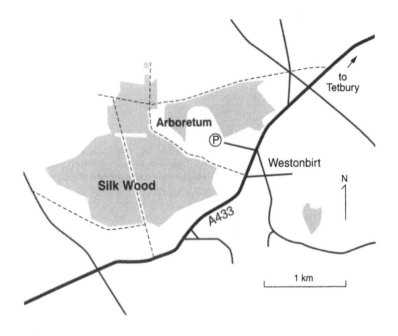

59 THE COTSWOLD
WATER PARK

OS Explorer 169 and 170

Habitat

The Cotswold Water Park is the largest area of sand and gravel extraction in southwest England, is still expanding, and is set to become one
of the largest man-made wetland complexes in Europe. It can be
divided into two main sections: the larger Cotswold Water Park (West)
has (in 2003) over 85 lakes or pits and straddles the meandering
Wiltshire/Gloucestershire border, while the Cotswold Water Park (East)
with over 30 lakes lies entirely in Gloucestershire c.7 miles (11.2 km)
away. It is convenient to consider both sections together as they form a
single ecological unit within one geological area, the Thames Basin. Here
the layer of Oxford Clay, on which the gravel beds lie, prevents drainage
of the water that floods a pit once it starts being worked. The general
water table is very near the surface, with the result that some surrounding fields may be temporarily under water. Two methods, wet and dry, are
employed to extract gravel and each results in a different habitat in the
short term. In the first, digging takes place under water to form a verti-
cally sided pit largely unattractive to birds until aquatic plant and animal
life become established. The dry method uses a pump to keep the pit relatively free from water during excavation, creating large areas of exposed
gravel, muddy or sandy areas, small pools, shallows, and long irregular
water edges which attract waders. These pits may have either steep or
sloping banks. Emergent vegetation of bulrush (reedmace), reeds and
willows (sallows) can become dense during the early life of a dry-dug

218

pit, but much of it disappears upon final flooding. The lakes vary in size and depth and are located in a typical English lowland valley landscape of small fields bordered by hedges and trees, with a few small woods and copses. There are several streams and, in places, water-filled ditches where vegetation can be quite dense. There are a number of flower-rich hay meadows, and the dragonfly population runs to 21 species, often in huge numbers. The whole area has been developed as a recreational centre, with activities such as sailing, angling, windsurfing, powerboat racing and jet-skiing subjecting waterbirds to varying degrees of disturbance. Fortunately they can, however, find refuge on the quieter lakes, some of which have been set aside as nature reserves.

Species

Those lakes in the Cotswold Water Park (West) located in Wiltshire give the county its most important wetland site and provide many of the wader and duck records. Over 200 bird species have been recorded, local birdwatchers finding the area increasingly interesting as new pits develop and young pits age. The peak period for waterfowl is of course the winter, the following approximate indications of the numbers involved in recent years being for the combined west and east sections of the Water Park. Coots have numbered between 5300 and 9100, Pochard 2000 to 2500, Tufted Ducks 1100 to 1600, Wigeon about 1500, Teal 250 to 650. Canada Geese numbers have increased steadily, sometimes reaching nearly 700 and maxima for both Mute Swans and Great Crested Grebes are about 300. Gadwall have increased in recent years to a winter maximum of about 350 and there can be up to 200 Goldeneye here. Adverse weather elsewhere has on occasions brought three species of diver plus Red-necked, Slavonian and Black-necked Grebes. Goosanders are regular winter visitors varying between about 20 to over 80, occasionally accompanied by single Red-breasted Mergansers, whilst Smew have been recorded in double figures in recent years. Bitterns are now recorded in most winters and other less common visitors have included Long-tailed Duck and Short-eared Owl. Wandering Peregrines can turn up at any time, though they are most likely to be seen in winter. The few Water Rails are not easily seen until cold weather freezes their normal haunts and forces them into the open by streams or reedbeds. They can be heard calling in most months of the year and probably breed. Very obvious are the numerous Cormorants which have steadily increased over recent years, with over 130 sometimes present. A pair nested in a tree in 1994 and successfully reared three young. Thousands of gulls roost near South Cerney: Black-headed are the most numerous but there is a considerable number of Lesser Black-backed Gulls, smaller numbers of Common and Herring Gulls, plus the occasional Great Black-backed. As elsewhere in southern Britain, Yellow-legged Gulls are increasing identified among the other species. Mediterranean Gulls are seen in most years, usually adults in February and juveniles in July and August. In some places small stands of alders attract wandering flocks of Siskins. In sustained cold weather most lakes completely freeze over and the majority of waterfowl are forced to go elsewhere, the small patches remaining open becoming a seething mass of birds.

Perhaps the most important factor in the ornithological character of the area is that it lies in the path of the flight routes of passage migrants and summer visitors. The early spring passage starts in earnest with small flocks of Pied and White Wagtails, Meadow Pipits, and, a little later, Yellow

Wagtails. A few Wheatears pause briefly on their way north and again in autumn when it is usually juvenile birds that are seen. Gradually the winter duck population declines and the common warblers arrive with the liquid notes of the Willow Warbler being a welcome sound in early spring. The bushy habitat favours species like Lesser Whitethroats, which may well outnumber Common Whitethroats here, Cuckoos come in search of nests for their parasitic offspring and in the denser vegetation a few Nightingales take up residence. Sedge Warblers become widespread and several pairs of Reed Warblers nest in the small scattered patches of *phragmites*.

In spring Common Terns appear in parties of up to about 30, while Black Terns, usually in ones and twos, and the occasional Arctic, move through quickly. On the more leisurely autumn passage, involving many juveniles, visits often last for several days. Waders trickle through steadily, over 30 species having been recorded in the area. Dunlin are regular visitors, sometimes in small flocks, and may be seen in every month of the year. They are often accompanied both in spring and autumn by a few Ringed Plovers. Small groups of Curlew arrive and some stay to breed in certain favoured fields. Post-breeding numbers can be quite significant and a small flock now remains throughout the winter. The presence of small groups of migrant Whimbrel is often only betrayed by their twittering calls. Winter flocks of Lapwings, sometimes 6000 strong, disperse in spring, a few pairs staying to nest on the open gravel or in nearby fields. By April the wintering Golden Plover flocks, sometimes comprising up to 3000 birds, have departed. Ruffs are regularly seen, occasionally in the fields with the few remaining Lapwings. Both Black-tailed and Bar-tailed Godwits may be encountered although the latter is scarce, but Turnstones, Oystercatchers and Greenshanks appear regularly, with Grey Plover and Sanderling not unexpected. Common Sandpipers feed around the edges of the quieter, mature pits as well as the dry-dug ones, while the more numerous Green Sandpipers favour the drier pits.

An abundance of insect life provides vital food for large flocks of Swifts and hirundines. Sand Martins are the first to arrive, some just passing through but many staying to nest in colonies of varying size in suitable steep-sided banks. Other hirundines soon follow and when cloud cover is low it is often possible to walk through dozens of wheeling and swooping Swifts, feeling the draught from their wings as they fly past at head height and hearing the soft clicks of their bills as they snap up an insect. Small parties of Shelducks, or the odd bird or two, regularly spend a short time at sandy or muddy places before moving on. They too have been recorded in every month and in recent years one or two have stayed to breed. In most years Garganey are to be found not far from fairly dense aquatic vegetation and breeding has been attempted. The Water Park is a noted site for Hobbies, with up to 20 sometimes to be seen, many of them non-breeding sub-adults. They have been joined on several occasions by Red-footed Falcons. Other unusual spring visitors have included Fulmar, Gannet, Night Heron, Purple Heron, Spoonbill, Avocet, Kentish Plover, Temminck's Stint, White-rumped and Pectoral Sandpipers.

During summer Little Ringed Plovers nest with varying success on exposed gravel. Ringed Plovers have also attempted to breed, raising young in 1999 at least. Corvid predation accounts for many losses and the presence of breeding plovers is entirely dependent on the continuing extraction of gravel as they are intolerant of encroaching vegetation.

Hobby

Another indication of how the changing character of the Water Park is attracting birds is the recent establishment of breeding pairs of Common Terns and Black-headed Gulls, encouraged by the installation of nesting rafts. On the quieter lakes Little Grebes breed and Great Crested Grebes are widespread with nest-building starting in January in some years. The more secluded areas with dense enough cover provide nest sites for Mallard and Tufted Ducks, Canada Geese are breeding in increasing numbers and there are several pairs of Greylag Geese. A feral population of Red-crested Pochards has considerably increased in number in recent years to about 80 birds. There are small heronries at Lakes 29 and 74. Other breeding species include Grey, Pied and Yellow Wagtails, Spotted Flycatchers and Kingfishers, this last species more easily seen in autumn when the young have dispersed.

Most of the waders seen in spring also occur in autumn, sometimes in larger numbers as is the case with Common and Green Sandpipers. Species that have been recorded include Wood Sandpiper, Knot, Spotted Redshank, Little Stint and Curlew Sandpiper, all mostly juveniles. Snipe arrive to winter followed by Jack Snipe in variable numbers. Birds seen on either spring or autumn passage have included Little Gull, Little Tern, Osprey, Sandwich Tern and small parties of Bewick's Swans. Little Egrets are now regularly recorded here, especially in autumn and winter.

Timing

The Cotswold Water Park is an area that is rewarding to both the casual and regular birdwatcher. Perhaps weekends are to be preferred, particularly for waders when the extraction of gravel on the dry pits ceases. It is surprising, though, how waders become less shy when on passage and tolerant of noise from machinery. Many of the mature pits are used for leisure purposes all year round, but tend to be less busy on weekdays, particularly in winter. A visit is always worthwhile after any spell of bad weather as unusual species may then turn up.

Access

The OS Explorer 169 (Cirencester and Swindon) shows most of the area in detail but map 170 is needed for some of the eastern section between Fairford and Lechlade. Unfortunately the OS maps do not as yet indicate the lake numbers, and also with such a rapidly changing area tend to become rapidly out-of-date. To overcome these problems the Park authorities publish an annual leisure guide, with maps showing the lake numbers, the current footpaths, hides, recommended observation points and parking places. This is available from the Cotswold Water Park Society, Keynes Country Park, Spratsgate Lane, Shorncote GL7 6DF (Tel: 01285 862777; website: http://www.waterpark.org). There is a good network of waymarked paths, often with good wheelchair access. Many of the lakes are easily viewed, but others are private, so any access restrictions should be respected. Some lakes can be seen from the roadside, but please note that the area is subject to heavy industrial traffic and care should always be exercised in both parking and watching.

The western section is much more developed for the visitor than is the eastern and includes several car parks and strategically placed toilet facilities. Access is best made from the A419 midway between Cirencester and Cricklade, at a point clearly signposted for the Water Park, along the Spine Road (B4696). After a short distance there is an information centre and car park on the left (currently under reconstruction). There are other parking areas to be found by travelling west along the Spine Road, all clearly signposted, and usually have maps showing the nearby rights of way. Towards the western end of the park, Keynes Country Park Visitor Centre is clearly signposted, and this is a good place to pick up the leisure guide and other literature, including the booklet *Wildlife in the Cotswold Water Park* which covers more than just the birds to be seen. The car parks here and at the nearby Neigh Bridge Country Park make good starting points for some productive walks. There is a hide overlooking Lake 34 (Coke's Pit), with Common Terns nesting on rafts here, while to the northeast, the Shorncote Lakes 84/85 and the

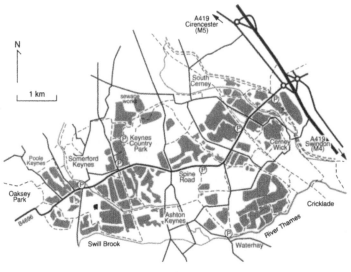

nearby sewage works are good for passage waders. A reedbed area, over-looked by more hides, is being developed here, and one target species, the Bittern, has already been seen here in winter. South of Neigh Bridge, a circular route runs past Lakes 46/48 (Swillbrook Lakes reserve) and 57, among others, an area particularly favoured by feeding Hobbies, and also good for warblers and Nightingales in the spring. It is also worth checking for Red-crested Pochard in this part of the Park, as they some-times breed on Lake 65. Southeast of Ashton Keynes, a path from the Waterhay car park winds past several more lakes, including the silted-up Lake 68c which attracts feeding and resting gulls and waders in good numbers, and which is viewable from a hide. Common Terns often feed over any of these lagoons, and nest on rafts on Lake 74. This last lake has also attracted Smew in winter, and Red-crested Pochard during their summer moulting period. In general the larger lakes in both these areas (e.g. 41, 57, 68, 74) are good for wildfowl in winter, although of course the whole Water Park is worth checking and birds can be very mobile. The roosting gulls also favour these larger lakes, with Lake 16 in the northern section also often holding good numbers.

The eastern section has been largely developed between Fairford and Lechlade with most of the gravel pits situated south of the A417. Starting from Fairford, going west for c.½ mile (0.8 km) along the A417, a minor road to the left leads towards Marston Maisey. At the first junction, take the left fork, signed for Fairford Tiles. A small layby on the right is con-venient for stopping to view the three lakes behind the hedge on the left. The first two, both silted up, are viewable from a stile a few metres further on, and the third is viewable from gaps in the hedge a bit further on again. The silted-up lakes are particularly attractive to gulls and waders. At the main crossroads in Fairford itself, take the Whelford road south, opposite the Marlborough Arms, and at the edge of the village turn right towards Hanson's gravel workings. A short way along on the right there is a small car park, with a footpath encircling the adjacent Lake 101. There are other lakes (129, 131) further on along this road, although lorry traf-fic to the active gravel works can be intrusive. From the A417 1 mile (1.6 km) east of Fairford another minor road leads south towards Whelford,

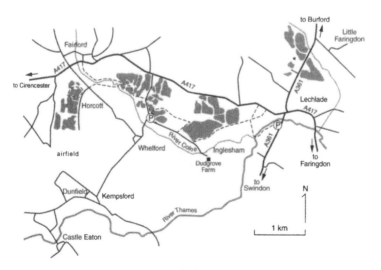

and shortly before the village a lane leads left towards Dudgrove Farm, eventually (beyond a slight bend) passing Lake 114 on the left, one of the larger and better pits for winter birds. A broad unsurfaced track to the left further on provides good views over this lake and Lake 116 beyond. Returning to the Whelford road and turning back towards the A417 brings you almost immediately to a gated entrance on the right to the small car park of Whelford Pools Nature Reserve (GWT), embracing three lakes (111, 111a, 111b) with two small hides overlooking them. These pools are often used as a refuge by wildfowl disturbed from other parts of the Water Park, especially at weekends. Further on again, at the bend by the Lakeside Inn, a footpath leads off left, providing a circuitous route to some more lakes, the most productive for wildfowl in winter being Lake 104. Eventually the path emerges on the A417 by the football ground at the eastern edge of Fairford.

There are also a few lakes on either side of the A361 just north of Lechlade where another small GWT nature reserve, the Edward Richardson Reserve, can be reached by turning left to the end of the cul-de-sac at the first roundabout beyond the northern edge of the town. One final point: when sending records to the county recorders it is extremely helpful if the lake numbers can be quoted, to ascertain which county is involved, if nothing else.

Calendar

All year: Great Crested and Little Grebes, Grey Heron, Canada Goose, Mute Swan, Mallard, Red-crested Pochard, Tufted Duck, Buzzard, Coot, Tawny Owl, Kingfisher, Green and Great Spotted Woodpeckers, Grey Wagtail, Reed Bunting.

December–February: Divers or rarer grebes may appear especially after bad weather. Cormorant, possible Shelduck; Teal, Gadwall, Wigeon, possible Pintail; Shoveler, Pochard, Ruddy Duck, Goldeneye, Goosander, Smew, possible White-fronted Goose or Bewick's Swan. Peregrine. Chance of rarer gull, such as Ring-billed, or Red-breasted Merganser. Water Rail, Golden Plover, Snipe, a few Jack Snipe; Green Sandpiper, roosting gulls in thousands; Siskin, Redpoll.

March–May: Most wildfowl leave during March. Shelduck may breed. Garganey and Little Gull; Common, Arctic and Black Terns (April–May). Outside chance of Marsh Harrier. Wader passage starts with Redshanks and Little Ringed Plovers at end March. Other waders include Ringed Plover, Grey Plover, Turnstone, Curlew, Whimbrel, Dunlin, Sanderling, Green and Common Sandpipers, Greenshank, Ruff, possible rarity. Arrival of common warblers, hirundines and Swifts from mid–late April.

June–July: Breeding species include Gadwall, Shelduck, Ruddy Duck, Sparrowhawk, Kestrel, Redshank, Little Ringed Plovers, Common Tern, Sand Martin, Nightingale, Sedge Warbler, Reed Warbler, Spotted Flycatcher, Pied and Yellow Wagtails. Hobby seen throughout the summer. Pochard numbers start to increase again. Autumn passage starts with Green and Common Sandpipers in late June. Mediterranean Gull late July to August.

August–November: Garganey in August. Continuing wader passage with Greenshank, Dunlin, Little Stint, Curlew Sandpiper, possible Wood

Sandpiper and other waders including perhaps a rarity (especially September). Black Tern and possible Sandwich Tern (August–September). Wintering ducks arrive in force from October.

60 WOODLANDS
WEST OF SWINDON   OS Explorer 168 and 169

Habitat

West of Swindon are the surviving remnants of the ancient Braydon Forest, several of which are accessible to the public and which contain a reasonably representative sample of woodland habitats. The first, Somerford Common, is an area of secondary mixed woodland 1 mile (1.6 km) long and ½ mile (0.8 km) wide containing relatively few mature trees, and where conifers previously engulfed the deciduous trees. Current Forest Enterprise policy is to remove the Norway spruce, generally thin out the woodland and to open up clearings and rides to enhance the wildlife potential, particularly for flora and butterflies. Some of the Corsican pine is being retained, to add variety.

Forest Enterprise and Wiltshire Wildlife Trust are working together at nearby Webb's Wood to encourage native broadleaves such as the small-leaved lime for which the wood is particularly important. Conservation work of thinning and scalloping forest rides has already benefited wildlife, particularly the plants and butterflies (at least 28 species noted). Ravensroost Wood, owned and managed by the WWT since 1987, is perhaps the most rewarding as far as birds are concerned, comprising many mature oaks with a shrub layer of coppiced hazel, and a diverse ground flora which indicates its ancient origins. Traditional coppicing has been reintroduced and wildlife includes roe deer, badgers and a good range of butterflies, including white admiral. Former claypits in the wood hold several species of amphibian as well as damselflies and dragonflies.

Finally, a mostly private wood contains what was once the largest body of fresh water in north Wiltshire, Braydon Pond. The establishment of the Cotswold Water Park has diminished its importance, this also having been affected by its use for raising trout and more recently for duck shooting. The pond, quite shallow and with a muddy fringe exposed when the level is low, is surrounded by mixed woodland with some fairly mature trees both coniferous and deciduous.

Species

Taking the four sites as a whole, all the usual common woodland species are well represented, but each one has its own specialities. At Somerford Common the current absence of mature trees means that breeding woodpeckers and Nuthatches are less frequently seen but finches, tits, and the usual smaller woodland species are plentiful; in summer they are joined by woodland and scrub-loving warblers such as Blackcap and Garden Warbler. Unfortunately, the Nightingales that used to occur here have suffered a drastic reduction in numbers, with no recent breeding records. Wherever there are conifers there are good numbers of Coal Tits and Goldcrests throughout the year and the spruce trees provide ideal nest sites for the Sparrowhawks which hunt the whole area. Ravensroost Wood, with its more mature trees, is particularly attractive as a breeding site for all three species of woodpeckers, Nuthatch, Treecreeper and Tawny Owl, although this last can be found in all the woodlands. Buzzards now regularly breed in the area and wandering Ravens are increasingly seen and heard almost anywhere. Of summer migrants, the Chiffchaff breeds in good numbers, and Willow Warblers and Blackcaps also occur. Both Willow and Marsh Tits are resident here so care should be taken with identification.

At Braydon Pond in winter, the resident Mallard may be joined by a few Wigeon, Goosander, Pochard and Tufted Duck, and Mandarins turn up fairly frequently. Grey Herons visit at all seasons and Cormorants from time to time. Siskin and Redpoll are both regular visitors to the fringing alders. In spring the pond is a good place to see early Swallows and House Martins, both of which nest nearby, and the usual migrant warblers, Blackcap, Garden Warbler, Chiffchaff and Willow Warbler, can be heard singing in spring and summer from the surrounding woodland. The pond attracts small numbers of Great Crested Grebes for most months of the year but usually only a single pair stays to nest, joining a few Coots and a pair of Mute Swans. Unusual birds appear from time to time, usually in winter or on passage. Among the more notable rarer visitors have been Red-throated Diver, Bewick's Swan, Osprey, Marsh Harrier and Black Tern.

More generally, the surrounding undulating farmland holds several resident Little Owls, while in summer a few pairs of Lapwings and Curlew sometimes attempt to nest in the damper fields, and Golden Plover may stop for a time in winter.

Timing
Calm bright weather in the mornings will give best results in the woodlands but a spell of hard weather in winter may bring an influx of Siskins, Redpolls or Bramblings.

Access
Somerford Common: From the roundabout north of Wootton Bassett take the B4042 towards Malmesbury and after 3½ miles (5.6 km) turn right at Brinkworth (Stopper's Hill) towards Minety. The road bends right as it enters the wood, and there is a small car park on the right-hand side another ½ mile (0.8 km) further on. Access is along the rides and public footpaths which emerge on the road in several places round the perimeter.

Webb's Wood and Echo Lodge Meadows: Continue to the northern edge of Somerford Common, and turn right at the staggered crossroads here. After another 1 mile (1.6 km) turn right at a T-junction, and after a sharp bend the entrance track for the wood can be found on the left-hand side, in the dip where the road crosses a small stream. There is a car park a short distance along this track, with a board indicating access to both the wood and the adjacent meadows, now managed for wild flowers by the WWT.

The Firs: Return to the T-junction mentioned above, and continue straight on for c.½ mile to where a notice board on the left marks the entrance to this privately owned wood. There is a circular trail through this area of relatively mature woodland, also now managed with wildlife very much in mind.

Ravensroost Wood: Take the road north from Somerford Common towards Minety and turn left at the first crossroads. After c.½ mile (0.8 km) there is a small car park behind a high bank at the corner of the wood, and again a board gives details of access along the various trails..

Braydon Pond: From Somerford Common take the road west towards Charlton and the second right towards Minety. Alternatively, c.1½ miles (2.4 km) west of Minety on the B4040 Cricklade to Malmesbury road, turn south towards Garsdon and Brinkworth. After a short distance the road enters the woodland, the pond, which can be observed from the roadside, being obvious on the left. Note, however, that currently (2003) this road is closed to vehicles (but not pedestrians) where it passes the lake, and the signposts have been removed. Note also that a public right of way crosses the wood from north to south.

Calendar

All year: Great Crested Grebe, Cormorant, Grey Heron, Mute Swan, Canada Goose, Mallard, Tufted Duck, Coot (Braydon Pond). Sparrowhawk, Buzzard, Kestrel, Lapwing, Little Owl, Tawny Owl, Green, Great and Lesser Spotted Woodpeckers; Jay, Willow Tit, Treecreeper; Nuthatch (Ravensroost Wood). Raven (scarce).

December–February: Occasional Wigeon, Pochard, Goosander, maybe Water Rail or Kingfisher (Braydon Pond). Golden Plover, Siskin, Redpoll, Brambling.

March–May: Curlew. Chance of Black or Common Tern (Braydon Pond). Summer visitors from mid-April: Cuckoo, hirundines, Blackcap, Garden Warbler, Whitethroat and other common warblers. Spotted Flycatcher not usually until May.

June–July: Breeding and resident species, gradually falling silent in July.

August–November: Quiet period. Maybe terns again on passage (August–September) at Braydon Pond or passage waders if the water level is low.

61 STANTON PARK   OS Explorer 169

Habitat

Stanton Fitzwarren Park is an ancient aristocratic estate dating from the 12th century and lies just north of Swindon. In 1995 Stanton House was sold and became a private hotel. Swindon Borough Council purchased the grounds (185 acres/74 ha) in 1996 to provide a new Country Park open to the public and began a long-term programme of restoration and woodland management. The park includes a grazed, traditional wild flower hay meadow with individual mature trees, a lake surrounded by an extensive reedbed, and some mainly deciduous woodland. Great Wood, south of the lake, is an ancient semi-natural woodland where tree cover has existed for more than four hundred years. Wetter soil conditions in the northern part encourage growth of alder, willow and grey poplar, while mature oak, ash and hazel dominate in the southern part.

Species

Stanton Park provides all year interest, resident woodland birds being the main attraction. These include Green and Great Spotted Woodpeckers which are common along with the much scarcer Lesser Spotted Woodpecker plus good numbers of Treecreepers, Goldcrests, Marsh Tits and Bullfinches. Among birds of prey, Buzzards, Sparrowhawks, Kestrels and Tawny Owls all breed in the park. In summer the woodland residents are joined by breeding Spotted Flycatchers, Chiffchaffs, Blackcaps and Garden Warblers. Hobbies are frequent visitors in late summer whilst Woodcock regularly occur in winter.

A variety of wildfowl visit the lake in winter in small numbers, such as Little Grebe, Teal and Shoveler. Great Crested Grebes and Mute Swans both breed, as have the feral Wood Ducks which are often present. Grey Heron and Kingfisher are regular visitors throughout the year with Water Rail and Reed Buntings coming to the reedbeds in winter. Reed Warblers can be heard singing around the lake in summer, whilst in winter Siskins and Goldfinches feed in the lakeside alders. In some winters, a few Bramblings can be found along with the commoner resident finches.

Timing

As the area is popular with the general public, morning visits are usually more productive and it is advisable to avoid weekends in summer if possible.

Access

This site is best approached from the A361 Swindon–Highworth road. Follow the sign towards Stanton Fitzwarren and after approximately 300 metres the entrance to the Park is on the left, leading to a large car park which is locked overnight. An information board shows the main access routes, and a surfaced path (suitable for wheelchairs) provides a circular route through parkland, woodland and around the lake.

Calendar

All year: Great Crested Grebe, Grey Heron, Wood Duck; Buzzard, Sparrowhawk, Kestrel; Coot, Tawny Owl, Kingfisher. Woodpeckers include Lesser Spotted (scarce); Long-tailed, Marsh and Coal Tits, Treecreeper, Goldcrest, Bullfinch.

December–February: wildfowl include Teal, Shoveler, Gadwall and Pintail. Water Rail, Woodcock, occasional Green Sandpiper. Grey Wagtail, Siskin, Reed Bunting.

March–May: Reed Warbler, Garden Warbler, Blackcap and Chiffchaff from mid- to late April, Spotted Flycatcher from mid-May.

June–July: Resident and breeding species.

August–November: Quietest time; roving tit flocks; chance of Hobby to end of September.

62 COATE WATER OS Explorer 169

Habitat

Coate Water, although still surrounded by open countryside, lies close to the southeastern edge of Swindon, just to the north of the M4 motorway. Its name is familiar to many people through the writings of the naturalist Richard Jefferies (1848–1887) who lived in a farmhouse nearby. Although from several directions the lake appears natural, it was in fact constructed to supply the locks of the Wiltshire and Berkshire Canal, passing from private ownership to that of Swindon Corporation in 1914 to become part of a park and leisure area. The original lake, a single elongated shape, was formed by damming a shallow valley. Now an SSSI, it is mostly open water but with beds of *phragmites* and aquatic marginal vegetation in places and willow scrub and some swampy woodland, mainly deciduous, at the southern tip. In 1974 a nature reserve extension was added in the form of a second lake to the southeast, separated from the original one by a narrow causeway. Islands and peninsulas were incorporated to provide feeding areas and cover for waterbirds, two observation hides have been constructed by the Borough Council and a tern raft has recently been installed. The surrounds of the new lake have been planted with various trees and shrubs and its banks are quite marshy in places.

Species

Although a variety of birds can be seen at all times of the year, the main attraction of Coate is the chance of seeing something unusual at times of migration in spring and autumn and usually a good selection of wildfowl in winter. Mallard can number over 100 while Shoveler and Wigeon are both regular visitors, though numbers vary and usually do not exceed 40. Counts of Teal often exceed 100 and have reached 250. Gadwall occur regularly in small numbers and have bred. The elegant Pintail turns up in most years, though usually only singly. Among the diving duck a few Pochard and Tufted Duck are annual winter visitors, the latter occasionally staying to breed. Goldeneye and Goosander are much scarcer, although up to 70 of the latter have been recorded, and Smew have rarely been seen here. Ruddy Ducks, on the other hand, are regular visitors and have bred. A selection of other wildfowl has occurred at various times in very small numbers, including Greylag Goose, Shelduck, Mandarin, Red-crested Pochard, Scaup and Common Scoter. In addition there has been the usual range of undoubted escapes from collections (e.g. Snow Goose). The rarer grebes sometimes occur and all three species of diver have appeared a few times in winter. Cormorants are very regular, sometimes reaching over 20 and can be expected at any time of year. Water Rails are annual in winter and were proved to breed in 1982 when one chick was raised. More than 50 Coots remain throughout the year. Numbers of wintering Snipe have dropped in recent years and now rarely exceed double figures, and the tiny Jack Snipe, often missed because of its superb camouflage and skulking behaviour, is an even more irregular visitor in ones and twos. Among the gulls the Black-headed and Common are the usual species in winter, with Herring Gulls regular in small numbers; Lesser Black-backed Gulls are recorded throughout the year. The dainty Little Gull has been seen several times both in spring and autumn.

Among the resident species, Great Crested Grebes have bred on the lake since 1913 and nowadays about five pairs attempt to nest with varying success each year. In winter around 30 birds may be present. Although not recorded as a feral breeding bird in Wiltshire until 1968, a single pair of Canada Geese reared young at Coate in 1976 and since then several pairs have bred annually. Autumn numbers now build up to over 250. Over 20 pairs of Grey Herons nest by the new lake.

During the migration periods, the lake is worth checking on a daily basis as birds tend to move through quickly. One or two Garganey sometimes occur, mostly just on spring passage. Common Terns, usually singly, are annual in spring and early summer, and a single pair has already remained to breed on the raft. Arctic Terns are more occasional spring visitors, but Black Terns regularly pass through on both passages. Sandwich and Little Terns have been recorded very occasionally. Migrant waders are uncommon with Common Sandpipers being the most regular but several other species appear from time to time. Greenshanks turn up in most years as single birds in spring or late summer and the smaller Green Sandpiper is not unusual from July into the winter. Both Dunlin and Redshank are irregular visitors in small numbers. Scarcer species in recent years have included Oystercatcher, Little Ringed Plover, Black-tailed Godwit and Whimbrel. In addition to these waders there have been single occurrences of Night Heron, Purple Heron, Spoonbill and Great White Egret with several records of Little Egret.

Turning away from waterbirds, resident species which usually breed in the area are Sparrowhawk, Kestrel, Kingfisher, all three woodpeckers, Grey Wagtail, Nuthatch, Treecreeper and Reed Bunting. Among summer visitors Sedge Warblers and Reed Warblers nest among the reeds and willows but Yellow Wagtails are now only seen on spring and autumn passage. Chiffchaffs, Willow Warblers and Blackcaps are the commonest warblers away from the waterside with smaller numbers of Lesser Whitethroats, Common Whitethroats and Garden Warblers also nesting. In October 1980 the first Cetti's Warbler in Wiltshire was recorded at Coate and singing males have been recorded subsequently. At any time during the summer, particularly in the evenings, a Hobby is a frequent sight hunting House Martins or other prey.

Timing

With the growth of Swindon, Coate Water is no longer in a really rural situation and on fine summer weekends or during holiday periods hundreds of people visit the lake and its surroundings, so early in the morning will be a more productive time and if possible weekdays are preferable to weekends. In winter timing is not so important but the early part of the day is usually the best.

Access

From M4 junction 15 take the A419 north for c.1 mile (1.6 km) and at the large roundabout here turn off left onto the A4259 towards Coate and Swindon. The entrance to Coate Water Country Park is on the left at the next roundabout after nearly another 1 mile (1.6 km) with a car park at the dam at the north end of the lake. A daily, or annual, permit for entry into the nature reserve on the new lake, which has two hides, can be obtained from the Ranger's Office near the dam or the Activity Centre a

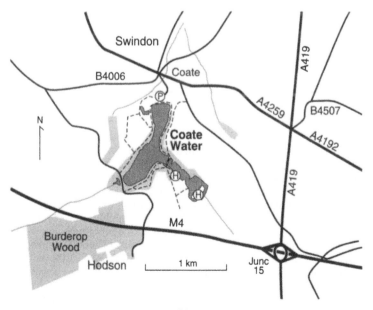

short distance along the west shore. A footpath runs all the way round the lake, emerging for a short distance by a minor road at the southern end, and there is wheelchair access to much of the area.

Calendar

All year: Great Crested Grebe, Grey Heron, Canada Goose, Ruddy Duck, Buzzard, Sparrowhawk, Kestrel, Coot, Lesser Black-backed Gull, Little Owl, Kingfisher, Green, Great Spotted and Lesser Spotted Woodpeckers, Grey Wagtail, Nuthatch, Treecreeper, Goldcrest, Bullfinch, Reed Bunting.

December–February: Possible diver or rarer grebe. Gadwall, Teal, Mallard, Shoveler, Pochard, Tufted Duck; possible Wigeon, Pintail, Goldeneye or Goosander. Water Rail, Snipe, gulls; maybe Siskin or Redpoll.

March–May: Possible Garganey. Other ducks include Gadwall and Shoveler seen in April on passage. Common Sandpiper and other occasional migrant waders (April–May); possible Common, Arctic or Black Tern at same time; also Yellow Wagtail. Arrival of summer visitors from mid–late April: Cuckoo, Sedge Warbler, Reed Warbler, Lesser Whitethroat, Whitethroat, Garden Warbler, Blackcap, Chiffchaff, Willow Warbler, Spotted Flycatcher. Possible Redstart, Wood Warbler and Pied Flycatcher passing through.

June–July: Breeding residents and summer visitors. Common Sandpiper and Green Sandpiper from July. Hobby irregular all summer.

August–November: Occasional Greenshank, Green and Common Sandpipers and terns August–September. Yellow Wagtails pass August–early September. Most winter ducks from October, but some, e.g. Shoveler, earlier.

63 MARLBOROUGH & FYFIELD DOWNS

OS Explorer 157

Habitat and species

The Marlborough Downs are the most northerly part of the great chalk area which covers almost two-thirds of Wiltshire and are separated from Salisbury Plain to the south by the Vale of Pewsey. The most level or gently sloping land of these uplands is intensively cultivated, growing a variety of arable crops or heavily grazed. Racehorse training is another major land use. Fyfield Down, between Avebury and Marlborough, is a NNR containing some fine examples of sarsen stones (silicified sandstone boulders). There are a few small copses and windbreak trees but the development of scrub is limited by grazing. This is not an area with an abundance of birds, but it does have some species not always easy to find elsewhere. Throughout the year Buzzards circling overhead are a typical sight almost anywhere, and Ravens are noted more and more frequently. Wintering Hen Harriers are not seen as often as in the past but other raptors such as Merlin and Peregrine still can be seen hunting over the wide-open downland at this time. Golden Plover sometimes flock on the ploughed fields in winter. Among small birds, Tree Sparrows, Yellowhammers and Corn Buntings still breed quite widely in good numbers, joined in summer by a few Yellow Wagtails. Quail also sometimes occur in summer and Dotterel have been recorded on spring passage. Other migrants in small numbers in both spring and autumn include Wheatear, Redstart and Ring Ouzel.

Access

From the A345 at the northern edge of Marlborough a minor road, signposted Broad Hinton, bisects the downs, eventually dropping steeply at Hackpen Hill, where there is a car park/viewpoint, to reach the A361 just before Broad Hinton itself. From the car park, the Ridgeway path provides access both to the north towards Barbury Castle and to the south to Fyfield Down, both routes following the escarpment. Another pleasant access route is on foot from Avebury, taking a well-marked track to the east to cross the Ridgeway on Overton Down and continuing to the copses and sarsen stones of Fyfield Down. There are plenty of other public footpaths across the whole area.

64 THE KENNET VALLEY EAST OF MARLBOROUGH OS Explorer 157

Habitat

The River Kennet, a tributary of the Thames, rises from the downs near Avebury and is a typical chalk stream, its clear waters being renowned for trout. East of Marlborough it winds through a wide valley between rolling farmland with copses and more extensive areas of woodland. The river itself is fringed by a series of damp fields and water meadows for much of its course and there are alder and willow thickets in several places, particularly at Axford and Chilton Foliat. At Ramsbury Manor, parkland on the north bank has been enhanced by a large lake formed by damming the river and another 'broadwater' has similarly been formed at Chilton Foliat, on the county boundary. Here woodland containing both conifers and deciduous trees grows on both banks. The riverside and the water meadows contain an interesting flora including ragged robin and marsh orchids.

Species

The mixture of habitats in a small and attractive area means that there is always something of interest to see whatever the time of year. The river is something of a stronghold of the Little Grebe, over 30 having been counted in the winter and several pairs nest. Mallard and Tufted Duck are always present with Gadwall in smaller numbers, all species breeding, and they are joined in winter by Wigeon and Pochard, particularly on the two lakes. Teal, and less commonly Shoveler, can be found more widely along the valley in winter. A word of warning concerns Ramsbury Lake where there is a varied collection of ornamental waterfowl – do not be surprised to see an exotic species swimming past! In fact Black Swans seem to breed regularly in this general area, with family parties often noted in the summer. The Canada Geese are arguably wild; certainly breeding pairs are well scattered along the river, and late summer concentrations have reached over 200. Cormorants have been increasing in numbers and can be seen all the year round, often perching in mature trees at Chilton Foliat and Axford. Up to twenty may be present.

The damp habitat combined with the 'leading-line' effect of the river valley means that in spring most years a trickle of migrants will pass through, including Common Sandpiper, Sand Martin and perhaps Whinchat. Reed Buntings can be heard wherever there is damp cover and both Pied and Grey Wagtails nest near the river. Spring is a good time to look for soaring Buzzards, now a common species in this area. Woodcock breed in the surrounding woodland.

Once the summer visitors are in, Sedge Warblers and a few Grasshopper Warblers can be located by listening for singing males while a few Reed Warblers can be found in the patches of *phragmites*. A recent arrival among resident species is the Cetti's Warbler – up to nine have been heard singing. Other common woodland and hedgerow warblers, including Garden Warblers and Blackcaps, are quite frequently found, and a few Nightingales can be heard wherever the woodland is sufficiently dense. Cuckoos are regular in spring and summer and are probably parasites of the Sedge and Reed Warblers. A good number of Spotted Flycatchers also breed in the valley. During the summer there is always quite a good chance of seeing a Hobby passing over and in irruption years Crossbills have been attracted to the riverside to drink. Kingfishers also breed, but perhaps late summer is the best time to see them as young birds disperse away from their parents' territories.

Siskin

In autumn increasing numbers of Green Sandpipers pass through and odd birds usually stay for the winter. Other species arriving at this time include the ever-elusive Water Rail, and parties of Siskins, Redpolls and Goldfinches attracted by the riverside alders. As the river is unlikely to freeze even in very severe weather, Grey Herons find good feeding conditions throughout the year. Ospreys are seen more regularly now on passage than in the past and Bitterns have sometimes occurred in winter. Little Egrets have appeared in recent years at Axford whilst Red Kites are also becoming noted more frequently, presumably wanderers from the reintroduced population in the Chilterns. Small numbers of Bramblings are seen in most winters, often under beeches near Ramsbury Lake.

Timing

Roding Woodcock should be listened for on warm, still evenings, from about an hour before it gets dark, and both Nightingales and Grasshopper Warblers have a resurgence of song at the same time. Very cold weather may bring a wider variety of birds to the riverside or force the more skulking ones into the open.

Access

From the church at the east end of Marlborough High Street, a minor road runs along the north side of the Kennet Valley via Mildenhall, Axford and Ramsbury to join the B4192 west of Chilton Foliat (see also map with next site). In places the river can be viewed from the roadside and various lanes cross over and provide access to the south side where footpaths follow the course of the river although not always close to it, access to the actual banks mostly being reserved for anglers. Exploration is best carried out using an Ordnance Survey map, but some better places are Axford, where there are alders, willows and *phragmites*, Ramsbury Manor Lake (viewable from the public footpath over the footbridge at its eastern end), and the stretch between Knighton and Chilton Foliat where the water meadows are particularly extensive. At Chilton Foliat itself there is a lay-by just west of the church; park here and cross through the willow and alder woodland of Stew Close, across the river and back east to the main roadbridge, from which the Broadwater downstream can be viewed. A public footpath through Littlecote Park to Ramsbury and back to Chilton Foliat via Knighton is one of several circular walks that could be devised.

Calendar

All year: Little Grebe, Grey Heron, Cormorant, Mute Swan, Canada Goose, Gadwall, Mallard, Tufted Duck, Buzzard, Sparrowhawk, Kestrel, Red-legged and Grey Partridges, Moorhen, Coot, Little Owl, Tawny Owl, Kingfisher, Green and Great Spotted Woodpeckers, Cetti's Warbler, Marsh Tit, Nuthatch, Treecreeper, Grey Wagtail, Reed Bunting.

December–February: Teal, Wigeon, Shoveler, Pochard, occasional Goldeneye and Goosander. Water Rail; Green Sandpiper and Snipe may winter; Siskin, Redpoll.

March–May: Woodcock. Maybe Common Sandpiper. From mid–late April Cuckoo, Sand Martin pass through; Nightingale, Reed, Sedge and other common warblers arrive to breed. Perhaps Grasshopper Warbler. Tufted Duck broods May–August.

June–July: Breeding species. Canada Geese flock. Chance of Hobby and perhaps wandering Crossbills from late June.

August–November: Green Sandpiper (wintering birds from November). Water Rail from September, most ducks from late October.

65 SAVERNAKE FOREST & HENS WOOD OS Explorer 157

Habitat

Savernake is an area of ancient woodland and was a Royal Forest under William the Conqueror. It is currently managed by the Forestry Commission whose policy of selective ride widening and thinning has greatly enhanced the area for wild flowers, butterflies and birds. The main area, which is roughly triangular in shape and covers approximately 2300 acres (930 ha), lies immediately southeast of Marlborough and is bounded by main roads on the northern and southwestern sides. A notable feature is the Grand Avenue, a perfectly straight metalled road which runs for 3 miles (4.8 km) through the middle of the Forest, northwest to southeast. Part way along is the junction of eight other avenues which radiate to the main points of the compass. Many smaller tracks and paths criss-cross the whole forest. Broadleaved trees predominate in the main block and include several fine beech avenues planted under the direction of the ubiquitous Capability Brown in the eighteenth century. More recent plantings of oak have also been successful. In addition to the main woodland there are several areas of sparse scrub along shallow valleys as well as thickets of hawthorn and other bushes. A coniferous arboretum and some areas of newly-planted and mature conifers, such as Scots and Corsican pine, European and Japanese larch, Douglas fir and Norway spruce, add to the variety of habitat. Open areas include the two Forestry Commission nurseries by the track from Cadley to Eight Walks and a few arable clearings. Fallow and roe deer and the numerous grey squirrels require control measures to restrict damage to tree regeneration and growth. Recently muntjac have arrived and are breeding very rapidly. Many species of butterfly are to be seen, including white admiral and purple emperor.

Hens Wood is an extension of the Savernake block covering approximately 370 acres (150 ha) on its northeast corner, and is also managed by the Forestry Commission. It has a preponderance of coniferous plantations of various ages but also some areas of broadleaves.

Species

In winter the plentiful supply of beech mast provides one of the favourite foods of the Bramblings which visit the forest in variable numbers each winter and are often to be found with the Chaffinch flocks. Also in winter bands of tits roving the forest – Blue, Great, Marsh, Coal and Long-tailed – are joined by Goldcrests and Treecreepers, and with the trees bare there is perhaps a better chance of seeing a Lesser Spotted Woodpecker. Nuthatches and the other two species of woodpecker are far more widespread. The presence of mature timber is particularly attractive to hole-nesting species, and in damp places with rotting stumps a few Willow Tits are able to excavate their nesting holes, this species also being found among the conifers often avoided by other birds. Among other residents, Jays are common and many pairs of Tawny Owls breed. In winter, Siskins and Redpolls both occur regularly, particularly in the larches of Hens Wood, and Goldfinch flocks here are a feature in spring. The conifers are a favoured haunt of Crossbills, flocks of over 150 having been noted. Elsewhere in the forest, Hawfinches occur as a winter visitor in small numbers.

Nuthatch

Spring and summer sees the woods full of a variety of warblers. The Garden Warbler prefers areas of hawthorn and other tall scrub in which to nest but others can be found elsewhere in the forest in early spring, some being passage birds pausing for a short time before going further north. Blackcaps and Willow Warblers are both widespread summer breeders, while Chiffchaffs are generally commonest where there are taller trees. Wood Warblers used to breed in small numbers but now only occur occasionally as spring migrants. A few pairs of Redstarts also bred until very recently but likewise have become increasingly scarce of late. A few Nightingales can be heard singing where the habitat is suitable. Several pairs of Woodcock breed in the forest and can been seen during their 'roding' display flights; in winter sightings are more dependent on disturbing one at its daytime roost. Nightjars are also recorded on a more irregular basis. The open glades and forestry clearings usually hold several pairs of Tree Pipits and Yellowhammers while Spotted Flycatchers are often found where the trees are less dense. Unhappily, the Turtle Dove, which used to be a common nester in the forest, is no longer so. However, singing Firecrests have been seen several times in Hens Wood in summer, but whether they breed or not is difficult to prove.

Species associated with the woodland edge and surrounding farmland include Barn Owls, sometimes to be seen hunting among the trees in the evening. The Sparrowhawk and Kestrel both nest in the forest, both hunting more widely, and Buzzards are now a common sight. In summer Hobbies can sometimes be encountered flying over and these days Red Kites are no longer as unexpected as in the past, although always an exciting find.

Timing

As for most woodland areas, early mornings in spring and summer are the best time, particularly before the leaves become too dense. Woodcock and Nightjar should be listened for around open clearings from about an hour before it gets dark. Casual disturbance is not usually too bad away from the roads but weekend afternoons see the highest numbers of people out for a walk.

Access

From Marlborough the A4 Hungerford road runs along the north side of the forest and two pillars mark the Forest Hill entrance 1½ miles (2.4 km) east of the A346/A4 junction. The Grand Avenue leads from here straight through the middle of the woodland to join a minor road from Stibb Green on the A346 north of Burbage to the A4 west of Froxfield. Just under halfway along, at Eight Walks, another driveable road leads back to the A346 at Great Lodge Farm. These roads provide the main access routes. There is a large car park and picnic site at the northwest end by the A346 c.1 mile (1.6 km) south of the A4 junction in Marlborough and there are other small parking places by the roadside. Although there are few rights of way, the Marquess of Ailesbury and Forest Enterprise kindly permit the public to have access on foot over the many roads, rides and footpaths. Fenced-off areas should not be entered unless there is a footpath, and vehicles should not be left where they may block forestry access.

For Hens Wood, take the A4 east from Marlborough for c.3½ miles (5.6 km). Just past the turning to Bedwyn station, there is a lay-by on the left, and a short distance beyond this a track leads north into the wood.

Calendar

All year: Sparrowhawk, Buzzard, Kestrel, Red-legged Partridge, Woodcock, Barn and Tawny Owls; woodpeckers include Lesser Spotted; Goldcrest (particularly Hens Wood); Long-tailed, Marsh and Willow Tits (the latter particularly Hens Wood); Nuthatch, Treecreeper, Jay, Goldfinch; Crossbill (Hens Wood); Bullfinch, Yellowhammer.

December–February: Finch flocks may include Siskin, Redpoll, Brambling; Hawfinch (scarce) in Savernake.

March–May: Woodcocks roding. From mid-April: Cuckoo, Tree Pipit, Redstart (scarce), Blackcap, Chiffchaff, Willow Warbler. Wood Warbler (scarce), Whitethroat, Lesser Whitethroat, Garden Warbler. Turtle Dove (scarce) and Spotted Flycatcher from late April–mid-May. Firecrest (Hens Wood).

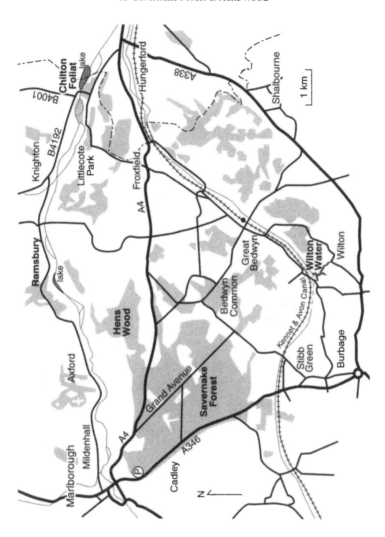

June–July: Breeding residents active, including Nightjars. Young Tawny Owls sometimes easy to find and chance of Barn Owl in late afternoon. Maybe Hobby.

August–November: Relatively quiet period once summer birds leave in August. Winter visitors from October.

66 WILTON WATER & THE KENNET & AVON CANAL OS Explorer 157

Habitat and species

Wilton Water is a small reservoir that feeds water to the Kennet & Avon Canal at one of its highest points, southeast of Marlborough. It is a good site for breeding Little Grebe, Canada Goose, Mallard and Tufted Duck, recently joined by Gadwall. Other nesting species include Kingfisher, Mute Swan, and both Sedge and Reed Warblers. Since 1996 a heronry has become established in the nearby trees and bushes, with six nests in 2002. More occasional visitors are Great Crested Grebe, Cormorant, Goosander and Shoveler whilst Teal, Wigeon and Pochard may occur in winter in very small numbers. Common Sandpipers and Common Terns are seen annually on passage, and records of migrant Ospreys have shown a welcome recent increase. A Barn Owl can often be watched hunting over the area at dusk and in summer Hobbies are regularly seen overhead.

Access

Wilton Water lies between the village of Wilton (SU268616) and the canal, with a public footpath along its eastern edge. The canal itself makes a pleasant route through a predominantly farming landscape all the way from here to the point where it joins the Avon near Bath, with a towpath which can be walked or cycled the whole of its length. The section from Pewsey to Devizes is perhaps the most productive, as it has been widened into a small lake at Wilcot and also contains several stretches where reedmace and *phragmites* provide breeding habitat for Reed and Sedge Warblers, Reed Buntings and other waterside birds. Grey Wagtails and Kingfishers can be seen almost anywhere along the route. Moorhens, Mute Swans and a few Coots also occur along most of the canal, which is accessible at the many bridges along its length. Since renovation of the canal has been carried out, the pounds at the Devizes flight of locks have provided ponds where Coots, Tufted Ducks and other waterfowl are attracted to breed or visit in winter.

67 COLLINGBOURNE & COLDRIDGE WOODS OS Explorer 131

Habitat and species

This large area of Forest Enterprise woodland covers approximately 1730 acres (700 ha) and lies just north of Ludgershall. Some of the wood is dense and dark with few birds, though it provides a refuge for both fallow and roe deer. Forest Enterprise is continuing a programme of thinning and natural regeneration, and together with the introduction of other indigenous species of trees, this is improving the biodiversity of the woods to the benefit of birds and other wildlife. Scalloping of selected rides reduces the density of the wood and encourages a more varied fauna and flora. Birds to be seen include Sparrowhawk, Buzzard, Green and Great Spotted Woodpeckers, Nuthatch, Treecreeper and other common woodland species with, in summer, Blackcap and Chiffchaff.

Access

From the A342 at the eastern edge of Ludgershall, turn left into Biddesden Lane, then left again into Crawlboys Lane. Where this bears sharp left back to Ludgershall, an unsurfaced track straight ahead leads to the southern entrance to the woods, with space for a few cars (SU 267518). Various tracks and paths allow the whole area to be fully explored.

68 JONES'S MILL   OS Explorer 157

Habitat and species

This Wiltshire Wildlife Trust nature reserve lies close to the Kennet & Avon Canal near Pewsey. The reserve covers 81.5 acres (33 ha) in total of which 27 acres (11 ha) is fen and carr. Here the infant River Avon flows through what were formerly water meadows, but which have now been invaded by sedges, rushes and wild flowers. Other parts are dominated by alder and willow, forming a mosaic of wetland habitats managed mainly for their plant and insect life. However, it is a very attractive place, supporting a good variety of bird species. There is a fairly large pond which holds Little Grebes and Tufted Ducks, while Kingfishers and Grey Herons come to fish in the clear waters of the river. In spring and summer, there are the usual common warblers, plus the possibility of Sedge Warbler, while Cuckoo, Reed Bunting, and Willow and Long-tailed Tits also breed. Sparrowhawk, Kestrel, Green and Great Spotted Woodpeckers, Bullfinch and Treecreeper are all resident. A few Snipe winter here although they no longer breed at the site.

Access

There is a large car park by the Waterfront café and shop at Pewsey Wharf, where the A365 Marlborough road crosses the Kennet and Avon Canal. A fifteen-minute walk along the towpath eastwards brings you to a footbridge over the canal and by climbing up onto this you will see the reserve entrance immediately on the right. A board indicates the various permissive paths that allow for a full exploration. The reserve is open to members of the public, as long as the habitat is not damaged. Other minor lanes and paths approach the reserve from the B3087 Burbage road, but parking is extremely limited. Note also that there are regular train services to Pewsey station.

Habitat and species

Lying southwest of Marlborough, these woods of over 1000 acres (400 ha) were formerly part of Savernake Forest and consisted of traditionally managed oak with hazel. Between 1931 and 1950, having been mostly felled, the area was replanted by the Forestry Commission with beech and some conifers. Forest Enterprise has a management plan aimed at creating a forest nature reserve here, gradually removing conifers, thinning the beeches and introducing other native species of trees. Naturally regenerated oaks are being selected and retained, and rides widened to allow in more light, and the resulting display of bluebells in the spring is particularly fine. As the trees have matured all three species of woodpecker have been seen, especially Great Spotted, and Nuthatches and Treecreepers are resident. Three or four pairs of Tawny Owls breed in the wood and winter brings Bramblings to join the Chaffinches, small flocks of Siskins and a few Redpolls. Recently, Hawfinches have occurred on the fringes of the central open area known as Hursley Bottom.

Access

Leave Marlborough west on the A4 but, before reaching Fyfield, take a minor road to the left, signed Clatford, then Pewsey. In 1½ miles (1.2 km) the entrance to the woods is clearly marked on the right. A gravelled track leads to a car park with picnic tables. Alternatively, continue to Fyfield itself and turn left to Lockeridge. Here, just beyond the school, turn left along a lane marked 'unsuitable for heavy vehicles'. Then at the junction take the road opposite with a 'no-through-road' sign. This enters the wood at a sharp right-hand bend where there is another car park. Note that in spite of the conservation work that has been done, and the network of forest paths and tracks, it is easy to get lost in the extensive and dense woodland here.

70 BOWOOD & SPYE PARKS   OS Explorer 156

Habitat and species

These two aristocratic parkland and woodland estates lie next to each other in undulating countryside between Melksham and Calne. The majority of the trees are deciduous with a fair proportion of oaks, and there is a good scattering of exotics in the parkland. Both resident and migrant woodland birds are well represented, including all three woodpeckers, Nuthatch, Spotted Flycatchers and maybe the odd Redstart. Buzzard, Sparrowhawk and Kestrel all breed locally. More unusual species seen recently include Red Kite, Pied Flycatcher and Firecrest, while there have been several sightings of Crossbills. Bowood contains a lake ½ mile (0.8 km) long, with two arms at the southern end, and this attracts breeding Canada Geese and Great Crested Grebes, plus visiting Kingfishers and a variety of waterbirds. Rarer visitors have included Kittiwake and Bewick's Swan. There is also a small heronry nearby, containing about 15 nests.

Access

A fee is charged for admission to Bowood House and gardens but a public footpath crosses the park. The main entrance, marked with white gates, is just off the A4 at Derry Hill/Studley, near the church. Footpath signs indicate the way to the arms of the lake at its southern end. The path then splits to lead southwest to the hamlet of Sandy Lane on the A342 or northeast along a track which emerges just south of Calne on the A3102. Spye Park, which lies to the southwest, is private but is skirted by lanes and footpaths.

71 CORSHAM LAKE   OS Explorer 156

Habitat

Corsham Lake is a decorative feature of the park belonging to Corsham Court and lies some distance to the east of the house. The grounds were landscaped by Capability Brown who provided for the 13 acre (5.26 ha) lake which was constructed by Humphry Repton. It lies in the southeast quarter of the roughly rectangular parkland which is typical open pasture with scattered mature hardwood trees. A narrow belt of deciduous woodland with a few pines shelters the bulk of the park, running north from the house, then east to the northeast corner and south along the eastern boundary of the park. A block of mixed deciduous woodland is to be found at the eastern end of the lake where a stream runs out towards the River Avon c.2½ miles (4 km) to the east. The lake itself is mainly open water, the formerly large reedbed on the north side having become small and fragmented since the lake was emptied and dredged in 2000/2001. A small island near the west end had many of its trees felled when the lake was emptied but a few mature trees remain, including poplar and oak. The south shore has some low marginal vegetation and open banks where cattle come to drink. Until recently the lake was relatively undisturbed but it is now used for water sports and for angling, especially during the summer months. During June, July and August camping clubs are allowed to use the field by the lake and this causes considerable disturbance to the birdlife.

Species

In winter the main birds of interest are wildfowl and grebes. Apart from the ever-present Mallard and Coot, Tufted Ducks and Pochard are the most numerous wildfowl although numbers have declined in recent years. Tufted rarely reach double figures and Pochard seldom exceed 40 in number. Both species have bred in the past but, because of disturbance, both ducks and Coots find it difficult to raise their young successfully. However, both Great Crested and Little Grebes have managed to breed successfully in recent years. Up to 20 or so Goosander are regular winter visitors, the birds sometime to be seen flighting into the lake at dusk after feeding on the nearby river systems during the day. Small numbers of Wigeon, Teal, Shoveler, Gadwall and Goldeneye appear from time to time, rarely staying long. An extensive list of rarer visitors includes Red-necked Grebe, Shelduck, Pintail, Ferruginous Duck, Scaup, Red-crested Pochard, Ring-necked Duck and Common Scoter. Ruddy Ducks have bred on the lake several times in recent years as well as occurring at other times. Usually obvious are the Canada Geese, a species which has rapidly expanded in number and range in Wiltshire in recent years. A single pair first bred here in 1982 and now flocks of well over 100 visit the lake and surrounding fields.

Turning to the residents, a pair of Grey Wagtails has nested on more than one occasion and birds can often be seen around the lake. Reed Buntings occur throughout the year but are most noticeable in winter when they come to the reedbeds to roost but in smaller numbers than in the past. The nearby parkland provides feeding and nest sites for large numbers of Rooks and Jackdaws, while Stock Doves, Mistle Thrushes and Nuthatches are reasonably frequent. Lesser Spotted Woodpeckers have bred on several occasions, this being as good a site as any for trying to track down this elusive bird.

Spring sees the arrival of Sedge and Reed Warblers with about four and six pairs respectively usually breeding. Perhaps surprisingly, Common and Black Terns sometimes stop off here for a while on migration and the odd Arctic Tern has sometimes been identified among them. The occasional Cormorant fishes in the lake at this time and both Green and Common Sandpipers are regular passage migrants. In summer the main interest centres on the breeding warblers and waterbirds while from August the return passage south of terns and sandpipers occurs and sometimes at this time the unexpected visitor such as a Bearded Tit, Black-necked Grebe or Ringed Plover turns up. You never know what it may be next.

Timing

As the park is visited by quite a number of people, particularly in late spring and summer, early morning is probably the best time for seeing the more unusual birds or the Grey Herons that come to the lakeside to feed. A period of cold weather or violent gales will often result in the appearance of an unusual visitor.

Access

There are several car parks in Corsham, which is also accessible by buses that run between Chippenham and Bath. Corsham Court is well signposted, and two public footpaths starting from here cross the adjacent park. One path runs east to Westrop village while the other cuts northeast across the parkland to the Mynte crossroads on the A4. Alternative access is along South Avenue from the B3353. Although much of the park grounds are private, the southern part, up to the lake shore, is accessible on a permissive basis under a Countryside Stewardship Scheme, and so the lake is now more easily scanned than it was in the past.

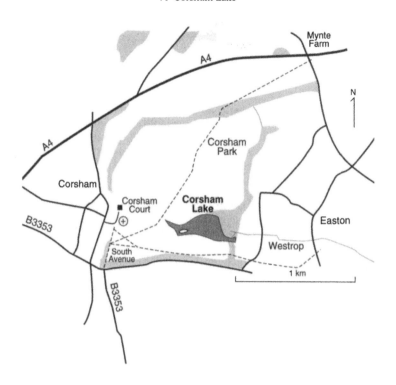

Calendar

All year: Great Crested Grebe, Little Grebe, Grey Heron, Canada Goose, Mallard, Buzzard, Coot, Moorhen, Stock Dove, woodpeckers including Lesser Spotted; Grey Wagtail, Nuthatch, Reed Bunting.

December–February: Little Grebe, maybe rarer grebe; occasional Cormorant; possible Shelduck or other uncommon duck. Wigeon, Gadwall, Teal, Pintail, Shoveler, Pochard, Tufted Duck, Goldeneye and Goosander all possible. Black-headed Gull flocks. Water Rail, Siskin.

March–May: Ducks include Goosander to April. Great Crested and Little Grebes sometimes breed. Common Sandpiper, maybe Common or Black Tern on passage April–May. Sedge and Reed Warblers from late April.

June–July: Breeding species, with young waterfowl noticeable.

August–November: Thin passage of Common and Black Terns, Common and Green Sandpipers in August–September. Winter ducks from October.

Habitat

The By Brook is a picturesque stream running from the edge of the southern end of the Cotswolds as far as the Bristol Avon, which it joins near Bath. The part under consideration here runs south through a fairly narrow if flat-bottomed valley with interlocking spurs of land on either side, well covered with deciduous and mixed woodland on the valley sides, before turning west through more open countryside with scattered trees. The land along the brook is composed of a variety of flat grazing meadows and cultivated fields throughout its length and the banks have willows, alders and intermittent small scrubby bushes providing some cover for birds. Over the centuries the brook water has been harnessed at intervals for milling, the resulting weirs having produced stretches of deeper, slower-moving water alternating with fast shallower sections, the latter being naturally most frequent further upstream. There is access by public footpaths to nearly the whole valley either along the edge of the brook or along the valley sides but fishing rights are reserved in several places. Large numbers of visitors come to admire the Cotswold stone buildings, particularly at Castle Combe.

Species

Many common woodland species can be found along the valley including Nuthatch, Treecreeper, Green, Great and Lesser Spotted Woodpeckers, although this last is rarely seen. In winter Siskins often come to the brookside alders. Perhaps the main attractions are the Dippers, as many as a dozen pairs in all, which occur wherever there is fast-flowing water, and the Kingfishers which burrow their nesting holes into vertical riverside banks in several places along the whole length of the brook. Other commonly occurring waterside birds include Mute Swan, Mallard and Moorhen, Pied and Grey Wagtails, a few Reed Buntings and the occa-

Dipper

sional Little Grebe. Grey Herons can be seen at any time of year, but are particularly widespread in winter. At this time Snipe can be flushed from marshy and damp areas and variable numbers of Bramblings are attracted to beech mast in the woodland. Buzzards are resident, being most frequently seen in the upper, more wooded, sections, with Sparrowhawks and Kestrels the other main predators. The Willow Tit, local in Wiltshire, can be found here, together with the commoner Marsh Tit. In spring there is a passage of migrant passerines along the valley including Redstarts, which have been recorded breeding in the past, and the occasional Pied Flycatcher. A variety of warblers also occurs with, in summer, the commonest species being Willow Warbler and Chiffchaff. Plenty of Swifts, Swallows and House Martins hunt for insects along the valley and nest in the farms and villages.

Timing

Factors are relatively few but resident birds, including Dippers and Kingfishers, are probably more easily seen before the leaves are fully out. Buzzards are more visible on slightly breezy days in the early part of the year when displaying. As far as general disturbance is concerned Castle Combe village is a very popular tourist attraction and is therefore congested in the holiday periods and at weekends. However, an early start will avoid parking problems and few visitors to the village walk very far away from it.

Access

This is an area best explored on foot, especially as parking places are few and far between. Along the whole valley the footpaths are generally well signposted but can be very muddy at times.

The nearest main roads are the B4039 near Castle Combe, the A420 at Ford, and the A4 at Box, all of which cross the valley. Starting at the northern end, there are several public car parks close to Castle Combe and a footpath from the village signposted to Long Dean leads south along the east side of the river. It follows the hillside away from the brook, which is shallow and faster flowing here, though with stretches of deeper water winding through flat grassland. The valley sides are steep and fairly well wooded with some open unimproved meadow with gorse and hawthorn scrub around Rack Hill. Conifer plantations and mixed woods can be found nearby. Long Dean is also accessible by road but parking here is virtually impossible. In the opposite direction, other footpaths start at the north end of Castle Combe and lead upstream across a golf course to Nettleton Mill where there are belts of deciduous woodland alongside the tributary Broadmead Brook.

The next stretch as far as Slaughterford can also be viewed from footpaths but then only from the roadside until Weavern Farm is reached. This section is well wooded, with beech hanger and hazel coppice on the valley sides, and provides the best chance of seeing a Buzzard. Park just off the A4 in a wide cul-de-sac by the entrance to RAF Rudloe Manor, opposite the entrance to Rudloe Hall Hotel. From here walk c.½ mile (0.8 km) along the adjoining lane then track leading through private mixed woodland to Weavern Farm. Cross the brook here to another public footpath on the west side downstream to Drewett's Mill. For a short way at Widdenham (about halfway) the path follows a lane leading in from Colerne, this providing alternative access. At Drewett's Mill roadside parking is virtually impossible and vehicular access from the A4 is not

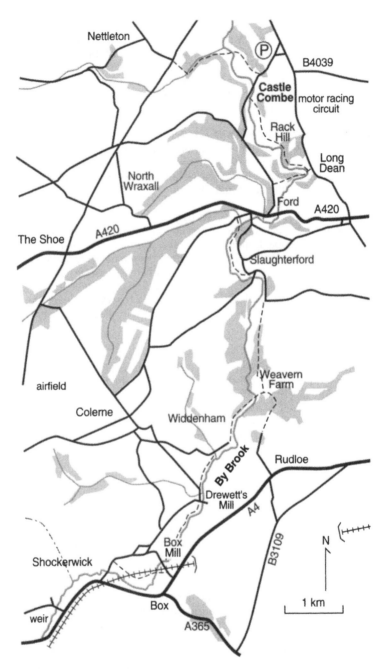

allowed but the path continues as far as Box Mill. The brook on this stretch is mostly slow-flowing and meandering, with weirs at Widdenham and Weavern providing faster, shallower water. Flat meadowland, damp in places, lies either side of the banks which are fairly bare with a few patches of willow, hawthorn and bramble. The valley sides are mostly open, cultivated farmland with scattered mature trees.

Box lies at the junction of the A4 Bath to Chippenham road and the A365. Parking is probably best at Box Mill which is reached along Mill Lane 400 metres east of the A4/A365 junction. The path upstream starts from the entrance to Box Mill, on the east bank but soon crosses a wooden bridge to the west side. The path downstream starts next to the railway bridge. This stretch to Shockerwick weir (accessible by road off the A4) has rather more in the way of willows and alders by the river and vertical banks provide nest-sites for Kingfishers. Dippers can be seen at Shockerwick and Box.

Calendar

All year: Grey Heron, Mute Swan, Mallard, Sparrowhawk, Buzzard, Kestrel, Moorhen, Red-legged and Grey Partridges, Little, Tawny and Barn Owls, Green and Great Spotted Woodpeckers, maybe Lesser Spotted; Grey Wagtail, Dipper, Willow Tit, Treecreeper, Nuthatch, Jay, Yellowhammer, Reed Bunting.

December–February: Little Grebe. Snipe in places; winter thrushes, Siskin; Redpoll (scarce), Brambling.

March–May: Summer visitors arrive mid-April–mid-May: Cuckoo, Tree Pipit, possible Redstart; Lesser Whitethroat, Garden Warbler, Blackcap, Spotted Flycatcher. Sometimes Pied Flycatcher on passage during same period.

June–July: Resident and breeding species, gradually becoming less vocal.

August–November: Swallows and House Martins around the villages to September, but other summer birds slip away in August. Quietest period of the year.

73 SOUTHWICK COUNTRY PARK

OS Explorer 156

Habitat and species

Southwick Country Park lies immediately southwest of Trowbridge and consists of over 100 acres (40½ ha) of undulating grassland with extensive old hedgerows, some fine old oak and ash trees and several newly planted copses. Despite being very heavily used by dog walkers, to the detriment of ground nesters such as Skylark and not having any outstanding features, the Park can be quite rewarding for many common species, especially the quieter areas away from the car park and main paths. The area is owned and managed by West Wiltshire District Council and a regime of minimal herbicide use has increased the range of flowering plants, and numbers of several bird species, including Song Thrush, also seem to have grown in recent years. Residents include the two larger woodpeckers, Little Owl and Bullfinch. Winter produces flocks of Goldfinches, Linnets and Meadow Pipits and the occasional Stonechat and Reed Bunting. Spring and summer bring Spotted Flycatcher, Common and Lesser Whitethroat, and other warblers. Kestrel, Sparrowhawk and Buzzard are regular throughout the year and Hobby is sometimes seen during the summer.

Access

The Park lies close to the A361 Frome road southwest of Trowbridge, shortly before Southwick village (see also map with next site). On leaving Trowbridge, after c.½ mile (0.8 km) at the bottom of the hill, the clearly signed entrance and car park can be found on the right-hand side of the road. Here, a map of the site gives full details of the various footpaths, and there is good access for wheelchairs.

74 WOODLANDS NEAR TROWBRIDGE & WESTBURY

OS Explorer 143

Habitat

The woodlands described under this general heading are remnants of the ancient woodland, originally dominated by oaks, which once covered most of the Oxford Clay outcrop around Trowbridge. Clanger and Picket Woods form a continuous block covering 166 acres (67 ha) and, under the ownership of the Woodland Trust, are currently undergoing restoration to broadleaved woodland with the creation of paths, rides and small clearings. Green Lane Wood (39 ha) is an ancient woodland of oak, field maple, hazel and ash, and is now managed as a nature reserve by the Wiltshire Wildlife Trust with coppicing being reinstated. Brokerswood, c.2 miles (3.2 km) northwest of Westbury, is a privately owned woodland park of 80 acres (32 ha), interlaced with nature trails and incorporating a small lake, museum, shop, tea room and adventure playground. The wood is almost entirely deciduous, with hazel coppice managed commercially on the traditional seven-year cycle for pea and bean sticks, etc., but there are plenty of mature trees of a wide range of species including wild service trees, an indicator, along with the woodland flowers such as wood anemone, of the wood's age. All the woods are noted for their butterflies, which include white admiral.

Species

All these sites hold a good population of typical woodland birds, although the range of species in Green Lane Wood is slightly less wide than in the others. Among residents, Sparrowhawks, Kestrels and

Buzzards can regularly be seen hunting over or around the woodland and Tawny Owls can be heard hooting at night, particularly in the early part of the year. Green and Great Spotted Woodpeckers are well established residents, but Lesser Spotted are unusual, though sometimes seen in Brokerswood. Typical woodland birds such as Treecreeper, Robin, Chaffinch, Jay, Goldcrest and the five common species of tit can all be located relatively easily, and nestboxes erected in Clanger Wood are helping to establish high populations of hole-nesting birds.

With the coming of summer, Willow Warblers, Chiffchaffs, Blackcaps and Garden Warblers can be found in all the woods. Nightingales were once numerous, particularly in Brokerswood, Clanger and Picket Woods but at the time of writing have become either absent or extremely scarce. A few Whitethroats are sometimes at the edges of the woods but are more likely to be seen in nearby hedges.

In autumn roving parties of tits include good numbers of Long-tailed and there is often an influx of Bullfinches, but other winter finches are unusual. Ringing has shown there to be a good passage of migrant passerines through Clanger Wood in autumn, and the careful observer might see at least part of this. Apart from a few Mallard, Coot and, in winter, the odd Teal, Brokerswood lake holds only Canada Geese and a motley collection of domestic and hybrid wildfowl.

Timing

As ever with woodland birds, early morning in calm weather provides ideal conditions for finding singing birds, but a visit during the last couple of hours before dusk is the best for listening to singing Nightingales when they are present. At Brokerswood it is probably better to avoid weekends and holiday periods if possible.

Access

Clanger Wood: This lies immediately east of the A350 halfway between Trowbridge and Westbury. If approaching from the former, the entrance track is on the left c.¾ mile (1.2 km) beyond the Yarnbrook crossroads/roundabout (Longs Arms); from Westbury it is on the right shortly after you pass a church on the brow of the hill at Heywood. A small car park (easy to miss) is set back from the road, next to the gated entrance which should not be blocked. A wide track starting from here traverses the whole of Clanger Wood and other paths lead off to other parts of the woodland. The Woodland Trust welcomes responsible public access to its properties, but visitors should bear in mind that it is a nature reserve and act accordingly.

Green Lane Wood: From the Yarnbrook crossroads/roundabout, take the A350 towards Melksham. The entrance to the wood is on the left after c.2 miles (3.2 km), where there is a small car park (also easy to miss). Although the wood is a Wiltshire Wildlife Trust reserve it is open to the public, but dogs should be kept on a lead.

Brokerswood: All the approaches to Brokerswood are along narrow winding lanes. From Trowbridge, turn left off the A361 Frome road at the church in Southwick. The woodland park is clearly signposted here and again at the sharp bend ½ mile (0.8 km) further on where you turn right. Following this road for 2 miles (3.2 km) brings you to the entrance to the wood on the right. The road straight ahead is also well signposted and,

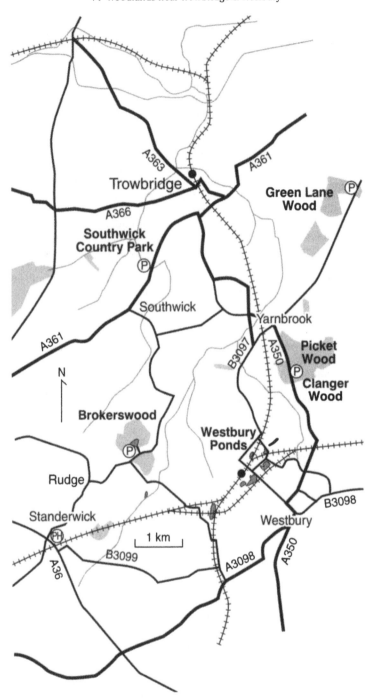

after passing the village of Rudge, emerges by the Bell pub on the A36 Bath to Warminster road at Standerwick, an alternative access route. The park is open all year from 10.00 am to 5.00 pm, with a charge for admission, and has good disabled access.

Calendar

All year: Grey Heron, Mallard, Tufted Duck and Coot (Brokerswood). Sparrowhawk, Buzzard, Kestrel, Tawny Owl, Green and Great Spotted Woodpeckers. Nuthatch, Treecreeper, Jay.

December–February: Chance of Woodcock.

March–May: Song from residents building up. Summer visitors arrive from mid-April–mid-May: Cuckoo, Nightingale (now scarce), Blackcap, Garden Warbler, Willow Warbler, Chiffchaff; perhaps Whitethroat and Lesser Whitethroat.

June–July: Nightingales stop singing early June, most other species by early July.

August–November: Young birds and passage migrants about in August, then relatively quiet period through autumn and winter.

75 WESTBURY PONDS   OS Explorer 143

Habitat and species

These two lakes, each c.7½ acres (3 ha) in area, plus one smaller pool nearby, are the remains of old ironstone pits close to the northwest outskirts of Westbury. The southern Station Lake contains an island but is used by a dingy-sailing club in the summer, while Frogmore Pond to the north has rather more in the way of willows, sedges and reedmace to provide cover, though trees and bushes surround both lakes. Although subject to disturbance by anglers, wildfowl are regular visitors and in the past have included unusual species such as Bittern, Scaup, Smew and Red-breasted Merganser. One or two pairs of Great Crested Grebes breed annually and several Canada Geese are usually present, numbers sometimes reaching over 100. Various gulls also drop in for a drink and a bathe. Frogmore Pond has seen an increase in angling and other activities in recent years and this has resulted in fewer wildfowl and other species visiting the pond.

Access

The ponds are at ST 864520, on the northwest edge of Westbury, close to the railway station, and both can be viewed from the roads that run alongside them (see also map with previous site).

Habitat and species

Smallbrook Meadows is a nature reserve covering 34½ acres (14 ha) on the southern edge of Warminster, and is managed by Wiltshire Wildlife Trust. A stream, the Were, flows from Warminster Park at the northwest end, through what were once water meadows, to join the River Wylye which forms the southern boundary of the reserve. Over the years the drainage ditches have silted up and today Smallbrook Meadows is a mixture of marshy grassland and fen interspersed with scrub and white willows. Around the edge of the area are hawthorns, hazel, blackthorn and some mature oak and ash trees. A pond dug in 1989 has matured into a fine habitat for freshwater plant and animal life, including water voles and grass snakes. Warminster Park boating lake, although not part of the reserve, joins it at the western end. Tufted Ducks are usually to be seen here and Grey Herons visit when it is quieter. Kingfishers hunt along the Were as well as visiting the pond and lake. The pond also attracts Snipe in winter whilst in summer Coot and Little Grebe nest by it. Water Rails regularly occur in the marshy areas. The reserve has a good number of common resident woodland birds such as Nuthatch, Treecreeper and Long-tailed Tit. These are augmented in summer by migrants including Sedge Warbler, Blackcap, Garden Warbler, Willow Warbler and Chiffchaff. Sparrowhawk and Kestrel hunt through the area and Buzzards fly over from nearby woodlands. In summer Swifts and hirundines appear in some numbers hunting the abundant insects. Common Sandpipers pass through on passage and in autumn flocks of Goldfinches and Linnets are attracted to the seed heads of various plants. Dippers and Grey Wagtails can sometimes be seen along the River Wylye.

Access

To reach the reserve, walk through Warminster Park from Weymouth Street, near the centre of town, passing the boating lake on the way. Alternatively, turn right off the A36 into either Smallbrook Road or Chain Lane, a little way to the east of the town centre, and after a sharp double bend you will come to a car park by the eastern end of the reserve, where there is rather more in the way of woodland. A board indicates the route through the reserve, the paths having been designed with wheelchair access in mind.

77 SHEARWATER LAKE & WOODS & SOUTHLEIGH WOOD

OS Explorer 143

Habitat

Shearwater (or Shear Water) Lake is an artificial woodland lake of 35 acres (14 ha) constructed in the late eighteenth century by the Duke of Bridgwater by damming a valley running east/west fed by two streams. A small pool (Crockerton Pond) lies below the dam at the eastern end. Rhododendrons grow over the water's edge along most of the shore except near the dam, but have been thinned out in places. Along the north shore and at the eastern end is a narrow belt of beeches, oaks and other broadleaved trees planted over 100 years ago and another, including many alders, borders the western edge. The bulk of the surrounding estate is more recent coniferous plantation but there are plenty of groups of mature conifers including Douglas fir, sequoia, western red cedar, larch and Norway and Sitka spruces. Some clearings with scattered birches add variety. The whole area is visited by the public but the main pressure, particularly in summer, is around the lake where the presence of anglers, walkers and an active sailing club can be intrusive. However, relatively few visitors walk the woodland paths away from the lake and the tarmac road. In autumn a great variety of fungi can be found but botanical interest is somewhat limited. Roe deer may be encountered in the quieter parts, and fallow deer are known to occur. The lake itself is up to 12 metres deep and holds a plentiful stock of fish, in particular bream, roach and perch.

Southleigh Wood is also part of the Longleat Estate and lies to the east just across the River Wylye valley. Apart from a belt of broadleaved and mixed woodland on the western slope overlooking the river, the bulk of the woodland is coniferous plantation.

Species

Shearwater is most notable for its woodland birds and whilst some of the denser plantings are almost devoid of birdlife at all seasons, there is usually something of interest to see. The lake itself does not attract large numbers of waterbirds or a great variety of species. Winter flocks of Mallard may reach over 300 but are usually considerably smaller and a number of feral and hybrid birds mingle with the genuinely wild ones. The Tufted Duck is resident and a regular nester at the lake. In winter a small number are usually present although there has been a decline in recent years. Also recorded in small numbers in winter are Pochard, Teal and Wigeon, and Goosander have appeared rather more frequently of late. Mandarin, Gadwall and Shoveler are occasional visitors and the odd diver or rarer grebe has occurred very infrequently. Great Crested Grebes can be found throughout the year and several pairs breed, unlike the Little Grebe which usually is only seen in winter. However the latter are sometimes present in other seasons at Aucombe Pond in the woods northwest of the lake. Grey Herons make fleeting visits, favouring the nearby marshy field just to the southwest. Coots are nearly always present, but are not very numerous, probably due to a shortage of aquatic vegetation. Kingfishers turn up, usually singly, between autumn and spring but there are no suitable nest-sites at the lake. Both Grey and Pied Wagtails breed and can often be seen on the lakeside or at Crockerton Pond, numbers of the latter being augmented by winter visitors and birds on passage. An Osprey once stayed for nearly ten weeks, and single migrant individuals have stopped briefly on other occasions.

Turning to the woodland birds, Sparrowhawk, Buzzard and Kestrel are the resident raptors and several pairs of Tawny Owls nest in both the deciduous and coniferous woodland. In summer a Hobby may pass over from time to time, but it is decidedly scarce. The Woodcock breeds in the area, its numbers augmented in winter by birds from elsewhere. All three woodpeckers are present, although the Lesser Spotted is by far the least common and difficult to locate. Nuthatches, however, are usually to be found fairly easily by listening for their characteristic calls – among the oaks near the lake is a good place. Treecreepers are also fairly common but are not always easy to find without hearing their calls. In winter they often join wandering flocks of other small birds. Six species of tit breed, five of them quite numerously but the Willow Tit is rather uncommon.

Probably the most interesting species in the area is the Crossbill, which has been proved to breed here. Flocks sometimes numbering up to 100 have been located regularly in recent years but they are wary birds and often feed silently in the tops of tall conifers, a quiet crunching being the only indication of their presence. Siskins sometimes form large flocks in the spring and it is worth keeping a lookout for mixed parties with Redpolls in winter wherever alders and birches grow, the west end of the lake being one of the better places. Redpolls have bred on at least one occasion.

Crossbill

Because of the abundance of conifers, Goldcrests are extremely numerous at all times of the year unless decimated by cold weather. Firecrests have been found among them on several occasions and reports have been received of this species regularly nesting in the Center Parcs village. This species seems to fluctuate in numbers quite considerably from year to year, but it is always worth examining Goldcrests carefully as Firecrests are easily overlooked unless they are singing. In summer, the resident Robins, Chaffinches and other songsters are joined by warblers – Garden Warbler, Blackcap, Chiffchaff and Willow Warbler the most usual. Wood Warblers are sometimes heard singing in the spring and may well breed here. Tree Pipits occur in several places where there are clearings, either open areas in the deciduous woodland or in young conifer plantations.

Southleigh Wood does not have quite such a wide range of birds as Shearwater, though the commoner ones are all to be found, particularly those associated with conifers. When there were suitable clearings, Nightjars bred but currently they are not to be found here.

Timing

As Shearwater is a popular recreation area, early morning is the best time at any season of the year, and weekdays are preferable to weekends. However, away from the lake itself, the woods are relatively undisturbed. The woodland rides and clearings are worth watching at dusk for roding Woodcock in the summer.

Access

Shearwater can be approached by car from the A350 Warminster to Shaftesbury road. Follow this for c.1 mile (1.6 km) from its junction with the A36 Warminster bypass, and turn right at Crockerton where the lake is signposted. Turn again at the Bath Arms and after c.½ mile (0.8 km) the lake is obvious on the right-hand side with a small car park (fee payable) opposite the entrance. The road over the dam leads to other car parks on the north side of the lake. The building of the Center Parcs Holiday Village in the western half of the woods has resulted in a large area being surrounded by a high fence and no longer accessible to walkers. Adjacent woodland to the west can be approached from the A362 Warminster to Frome road. Follow this for c.½ mile (0.8 km) from its junction with the A36 Warminster bypass and turn left at the Picket Post roundabout towards Horningsham. A further 1½ miles (2.4 km) brings you to a car

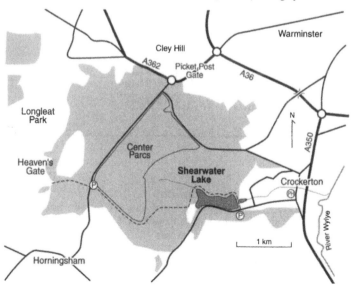

park on the left. Footpaths from here lead to the viewpoint of Heaven's Gate or back to Shearwater Lake. The woods around Shearwater are open free of charge to the public by generous permission of the owner, the Marquess of Bath, but visitors must comply with any requests given by authorised estate staff.

For Southleigh Wood, return to the A350's junction with the A36 Warminster bypass. After only a short distance towards Shaftesbury, the first turning on the left leads over the River Wylye and up a steep hill. After c.1 mile (1.6 km) a public footpath to the right crosses through the wood, eventually leading to Longbridge Deverill. Other tracks from this path allow further exploration.

Calendar

All year. Great Crested Grebe; Grey Heron (irregular); Mallard, Tufted Duck, Sparrowhawk, Buzzard, Kestrel, Coot, Woodcock, Tawny Owl; woodpeckers including scarce Lesser Spotted; Grey and Pied Wagtails, Goldcrest, perhaps Firecrest; Willow Tit (scarce), Treecreeper, Nuthatch, Jay, Crossbill, Bullfinch.

December–February. Pochard, Teal, perhaps Little Grebe, Gadwall or Goosander. Possible Kingfisher. Maybe Brambling, usually Siskin and Redpoll.

March–May. Siskin flocks in March. Cuckoo, Tree Pipit, Blackcap, Garden Warbler, Wood Warbler, Willow Warbler, Chiffchaff arrive from mid–late April; Spotted Flycatcher not usually until May.

June–July. Resident and breeding species active, but less song from end June. Chance of Hobby or even an Osprey any time from May to September. Crossbills often more widespread from end June.

August–November. Summer visitors gone by end August. Winter finches and ducks from October.

78 WOODLANDS OF THE SOMERSET/WILTSHIRE BORDER

OS Explorer 142

Habitat

The west-facing escarpment along the Somerset–Wiltshire border from the estate of Longleat Park south to Penselwood is clothed in an almost continuous belt of woodland c.8 miles (12.8 km) long. Great Bradley Wood at the northern end, and some areas at the southern end, are mostly broadleaf, with oak, beech and birch dominant. The majority of the rest is coniferous plantation, largely larch, spruce and Douglas fir, though with a scattering of deciduous trees, and some felled clearings. Nature conservation and habitat diversity now play a major role in forestry management here, and waymarked rails as well as the extensive network of tracks facilitate access. Fallow and roe deer are common and fox, badger and stoat are among the mammals to be found.

At the southern end, lakes have been formed by damming the valley at the head of the River Stour. The largest, the Garden Lake, at the NT estate of Stourhead, is surrounded by an 18th century 'pleasure ground' of exotic trees and shrubs and has two islands. A little to the south is the smaller New Lake, often called Gasper Lake, both waters containing plenty of fish such as roach, perch and bream.

Species

These woodlands, relatively remote from other popular birding sites, are watched only sporadically, but have been proved to hold several specialities rare, or overlooked, elsewhere in Somerset and Wiltshire. Visits early in the year are sometimes very worthwhile, as Crossbills can been found moving through the conifers almost anywhere, their chipping calls being the best way to locate them. They have certainly bred in the recent past, though numbers need to be 'topped up' by influxes from elsewhere to maintain the population. Buzzards and Sparrowhawks soar overhead in display flights on sunny days in late winter through into spring, both species breeding in good numbers here, with Kestrel and Tawny Owl the other two main avian predators. Ravens have expanded into this part of Wiltshire, with at least one pair nesting in the area. All the common tit species nest, Coal Tits being particularly evident among the conifers, though the few Willow Tits tend to be restricted to damp woodland, such as at Lower Woods at the northern end. The areas of deciduous woodland at both ends of the escarpment are also the best places to search for Lesser Spotted Woodpeckers, though like the other two species, which breed rather more widely, wandering birds may turn up almost anywhere in winter. Otherwise all the usual woodland residents occur, game rearing accounting for large numbers of Pheasants.

Chance sightings of Woodcock can be made during the winter, but they also occur, at least in some years, in summer, when they can be seen at dusk during their 'roding' display flights. In the past as many as ten pairs have been located, the majority in the northern half of the woods where there are more deciduous trees. Again, although not reported annually, Nightjars have been heard churring at dusk near recently cleared areas in the central section of the woodland, this being a species which tends to fluctuate in numbers along with the presence or absence of open ground among the trees. Other specialities of the summer are a few Wood Warblers, particularly where there are beech trees, and a scattering of Tree Pipits in newly planted clearings. Whitethroats and sometimes Grasshopper Warblers can be heard singing from the younger plantations, particularly where brambles and scrub have not been cleared. Blackcaps, Garden Warblers, Chiffchaffs and Willow Warblers are widespread where the conifers are not too dominant. Conversely, Norway spruce and Douglas fir, two species shunned by most birds apart from Goldcrests, are the places to look for its close relative, the Firecrest, or rather to listen for its distinctive song. Over ten singing males have been located in some years, though none in others! It is likely that natural fluctuations in numbers as well as in observer effort account for the changes from year to year.

Firecrest

Other species which may or may not breed every year include Redstart, Siskin and Redpoll, ones and twos of which have been heard singing in the spring and summer, but which have proved difficult to pin down for sure. It is certainly an area in which discoveries are still be made. The latter two species are, of course, characteristic winter birds of the conifers.

The lakes near Stourhead add variety to a day's birdwatching in the area. Mallard, Tufted Ducks and Coots all breed, and Great Crested Grebes manage to find nest-sites by the islands at Stourhead. Grey Herons visit at less disturbed times of day, and Common Sandpipers have been noted on passage, as has the occasional Osprey. In winter, small numbers of other duck occur, particularly Pochard, Goldeneye and Goosander.

Timing

Early morning is always the best time to visit woodland sites, as most species will be active and calling then. In addition, the gardens at Stourhead are very popular with visitors, especially in the afternoons, so it is worth visiting the lakes there early rather than later. For Nightjars and Woodcock in summer you will also need to be there in the half-light, when birds start their evening display flights. Weather conditions on the escarpment tend to be a bit worse than on lower ground nearby, which is often worth bearing in mind before setting out.

Access

The nearest large towns are Frome and Warminster to the north, and Wincanton to the south. Minor roads run through parts of the woodland, though parking places are limited. There is a good network of footpaths, and an Explorer 1:25,000 OS map is essential for a full exploration. Circular walks are possible in some places: a few starting points for the main areas are given below. Remember, however, that conifer plantations change rapidly – in general areas with mature trees and/or clearings are the most productive.

Gare Hill area: From Frome, take the B3092 south for c.3 miles (4.8 km), then turn right towards Witham Priory. Turn left after c.1¼ miles (2 km) at the railway bridge, then on for another 1¾ miles (2.8 km) to a sharp bend

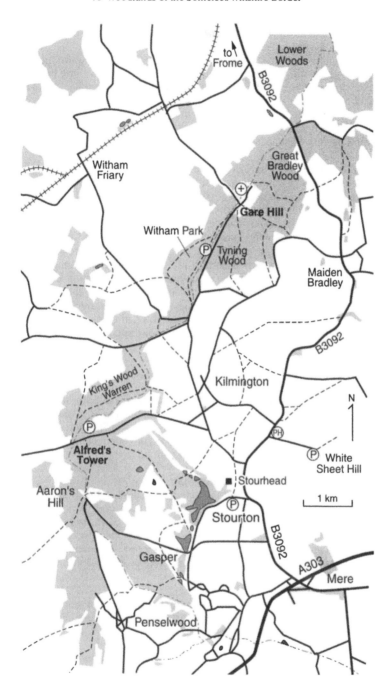

at the top of the hill where Gare Hill church (now used as a house) is a prominent landmark.The narrow lane to the left past the church leads to a public footpath through the northern part of Great Bradley Wood, where there is a good mixture of deciduous trees as well as plenty of conifers. Alternatively fork right at the start of the wood and take a circular route, always turning right, eventually emerging back on the road near the church.

For Tyning/Penstones Wood, turn left here, then left again down a footpath towards Yarnfield. For Witham Park Wood, continue a little further along the road to a track on the right, signposted Deer Wood Picnic Area, which is a short distance down on the right. There are a couple of waymarked walks starting from here. Both these woods have more in the way of conifers, but the latter has proved reliable for Crossbills, Grasshopper Warblers and Nightjars in the past.

Alfred's Tower area: From Gare Hill continue south for c.3 miles (4.8 km) and turn right in Kilmington, where Alfred's Tower is signposted. After 1½ miles (2.4 km) there is a car park on the right, the starting point for several more walks. Information boards nearby give a certain number of possible routes, including down to Stourhead. King's Wood Warren lies to the north, and its conifers have also held Nightjars in the past. To the south, the area around Aaron's Hill has a fair number of broadleaved trees, open fields, brambly clearings and damp meadows, though you have to walk some way to cover all the habitats. Wood Warblers and Tree Pipits are rather more numerous at this end of the escarpment. Firecrest has been heard from the car park, though it should be listened for almost anywhere along the escarpment. For a fee, you can climb to the top of Alfred's Tower itself for fine views over the whole area, and the chance of soaring raptors.

Stourhead and New (Gasper) Lakes: The NT property at Stourhead is well signposted off the B3092, c.1½ miles (2.4 km) north of where it joins the A303 near Mere. There are well defined paths close to both lakes, and there are suggested walks through the surrounding farmland as well. The chalk downland at White Sheet Hill to the northeast of Stourton (turn off B3092 at Red Lion Inn) adds a little variety to a day spent in the area, and is noted for its orchids and butterflies in particular.

Calendar

All year: Great Crested Grebe, Grey Heron, Mallard, Tufted Duck, Mute Swan, Canada Goose, Moorhen, Coot (Stourton and New Lakes). Sparrowhawk, Buzzard, Kestrel, Pheasant, Tawny Owl, woodpeckers (Lesser Spotted scarce), Pied and Grey Wagtails, common woodland residents including Nuthatch, Treecreeper, Goldcrest, Long-tailed, Marsh, Coal, Blue and Great Tits; Willow Tit scarce. Jay, Raven, Crossbill, Bullfinch, Goldfinch.

December–February: Cormorant, Pochard, Goldeneye, sometimes rarer waterbird on the lakes. Wintering Woodcock, Fieldfare, Redwing. Crossbill, Siskin, Redpoll, sometimes Brambling.

March–May: Passage migrants. Possible Common Sandpiper at lakes (April). Roding Woodcock. Summer visitors from mid–late April: Turtle Dove (scarce), Nightjar, Cuckoo, Tree Pipit, Redstart (scarce), Whitethroat, Blackcap, Garden Warbler, Wood Warbler, Chiffchaff, Willow Warbler. Firecrest singing from April to June.

June–July: Breeding residents and summer visitors. Most song ceases by end of June.

August–November. Summer visitors mostly leave in August and September. Perhaps Common Sandpiper at lakes. Winter wildfowl from October.

79 SALISBURY PLAIN ARMY RANGES

OS Explorer 130 and 143

Habitat

Salisbury Plain is a plateau of chalk dissected by dry valleys and has provided the Army with training grounds since Napoleonic times, the main area stretching from Warminster in the west to the Avon Valley in the east, a distance of 16 miles (26 km). The chief characteristic of the ranges is grassland, not the close-cropped turf associated with rabbit or sheep grazing, but wild, wiry long grasses, reminiscent of savanna. A number of copses of broadleaved trees with some pines are scattered over the downs and there are also some more recently planted conifer plantations. Quite large tracts of the area have considerable amounts of gorse or hawthorn scrub. On the northern boundary rows of hawthorns have been planted to provide another army training environment. The whole area is criss-crossed by tank tracks and in some places there are low-lying depressions subject to flooding and dew ponds which support frogs and crested newts. These also attract a few birds which would otherwise not be seen on the waterless plain, for example, migrating Greenshanks. There are many deserted farms and one village, Imber, which lies in a dry valley in the heart of the chalk downs and is now almost entirely composed of dummy houses and shops constructed by the Ministry of Defence for training purposes. Imber nestles amongst a number of deciduous trees of varying ages, as well as hawthorn bushes and other shrubs which provide cover for small birds. Salisbury Plain is now designated a Special Protection Area for birds, especially for wintering raptors. It is nationally important for breeding populations of Stone Curlew, Hobby, Quail, Barn Owl, Skylark, Whinchat, Stonechat, Grasshopper Warbler and Corn Bunting, and also supports a varied population of butterflies and other insects, foxes, badgers, stoats, weasels, roe deer, rabbits, brown hares, and thousands of small mammals.

Species

Winter is probably the most rewarding season for the birdwatcher when there is a good chance of seeing Hen Harriers, Short-eared Owls, a Merlin or a Peregrine. However, be prepared for disappointment. This is a vast area and quite often you can go for miles and see nothing more than a few Meadow Pipits or Skylarks. Luck plays a big part in your success. Hen Harriers can often be surprisingly difficult to spot, especially if they are flying low, and it is quite easy to drive past one quartering a gully and not notice it. Buzzards are a regularly encountered resident and the odd Rough-legged Buzzard sometimes penetrates this far west. Kestrels are

Hen Harrier

usually frequent and the Sparrowhawk too is not uncommon, often hunting in the open. The installation of strategically placed nestboxes has increased the breeding population of Barn Owls to nearly 100 pairs, and they can sometimes be seen quartering the ground in daylight. In some winters small roosts of Long-eared Owls form in the copses and clumps of bushes and very occasionally a pair or two will stay to breed. Another winter speciality of the area is the Great Grey Shrike, virtually annual in recent years, although this wide-ranging species can be very hard to pin down. This and the birds of prey are the star attractions in winter but other species do occur. Golden Plover are regular, often flying with the Lapwings, which are mostly to be found on the perimeter of the ranges and Snipe come regularly to flooded tracks and wet ground. Both Red-legged and Grey Partridges are resident but the latter is not as numerous as in the past. Woodpigeons are very common with roosts sometimes building up to as many as 2000. Stock Doves have taken up residence in some of the derelict buildings, tanks and other vehicles which are scattered over the ranges while both Green and Great Spotted Woodpeckers breed where there are suitable trees. A few Stonechats stay for the winter, with single birds or pairs to be seen flitting along the roadside; hard weather forces them away and numbers are always higher in summer when the migratory part of the population returns to nest. Flocks of Fieldfares and Redwings come to feed on the hawthorn berries and Chaffinches and Bramblings are attracted to the lines and clumps of beeches where they feed on the fallen mast. Yellowhammers and Corn Buntings nest in places and both form flocks in winter, though the latter species has become scarcer in recent years. Reed Buntings pass through in spring and autumn and some regularly breed where the vegetation is sufficiently tall and dense, the presence of water not seemingly essential.

The spring brings passing Wheatears and the possibility of a Ring Ouzel (again in autumn). The Wheatear used to breed quite commonly 50 years ago, but available nest-sites were reduced by ploughing of downland during the Second World War and again when the lower rabbit population in the 1950s led to fewer holes and longer grass. The odd pair may still breed occasionally. In summer the grasslands of the open plain swarm with Skylarks and there are plenty of Meadow Pipits. The presence of the latter accounts for the fact that Cuckoos are usually very noticeable in spring and early summer as they fly around searching for victims to parasitise. The long grass and scattered bushes are ideal for a wide range of warblers including Grasshopper Warbler, Lesser Whitethroat, Whitethroat, Garden Warbler and Willow Warbler. Good numbers of Tree Pipits and Whinchats breed each year in several areas. Nightingales are a summer visitor in the more thickly covered areas, and Blackcaps and a few Chiffchaffs can be found in places. The occasional pair of Redstarts breed. Among the more special birds of summer Quail can sometimes be located by their strange call. They usually remain unseen and in any case vary considerably in numbers from year to year. Particularly on the more eastern parts, small numbers of Stone Curlews still find suitable breeding and feeding habitat, and are slowly increasing in numbers under strict protection, this crepuscular wader having suffered over much of Britain from recent changes in agricultural practice. Perhaps the most exciting bird at this time is the beautiful migratory falcon, the Hobby, several pairs of which nest around the scattered copses. There is little to compare with the sight of one pursuing one of the numerous Swifts and hirundines that sometimes gather to feed on the swarms of flying insects over the ranges under the right climatic conditions.

In late summer Whinchats, Redstarts, warblers and other passerine migrants gather prior to migration and there is always the chance of a wandering Montagu's or even Marsh Harrier. Seed-eating birds such as Goldfinches and Linnets find plenty of food in autumn and into the winter on the numerous thistles and other plants. Passage rarities which have turned up on the Plain over the past few years have included Purple Heron, Black Kite, Red-footed Falcon, Dotterel, Hoopoe, the Siberian race of the Stonechat, Hawfinch and Ortolan Bunting.

Timing

For the general public the opportunities to penetrate the area are limited because of army training. On the few days that access is allowed an early start is advisable before there is too much traffic. Most people do not stop on the narrow roads but quite a large number of visitors concentrate in Imber village, so a morning visit here is best, the earlier the better. A bright, calm day at any time of year is more likely to produce good results than a windy or wet one but remember that in winter the number of species is very small. In winter Short-eared Owls are most likely to be seen during the afternoons. Hen Harriers can be seen at any time of day but gather at dusk to roost, though the exact sites vary from year to year. Stone Curlews may be spotted standing sentinel on open ground at any time of day, but are often more active and vocal at dusk.

Access

When the ranges are not in use and the red flags are not flying, public rights of way on the ranges are generally open to the public. A regularly updated recorded message (Tel: 01980–674763) should be checked before setting out, however.

Imber Ranges are generally open to the public on national holidays but notices are always placed in the local newspaper giving the precise dates. Visitors are not permitted to walk or drive off the roads, but a car can be a useful form of hide in this bare environment and most species can in fact be seen from the roads. The three roads of the western area converge on Imber itself. When the ranges are open to the public, the following are the points of entry by car.

From Bratton village: On the B3098 Westbury to Market Lavington road take the small lane, Stradbrook, at the eastern end of the village. The road climbs through a gap in the escarpment with many hawthorns which in winter often attract large numbers of wintering thrushes, finches and other birds. At the top check the Reeves Farm area for finch and bunting flocks. After passing the vedette post it is worth stopping at concrete lay-bys to see what turns up. Go on to Ladywell Barn (no barn here now) where the road meets the east–west road across the ranges passing through Imber village.

From Warminster: Take the road (Imber Road) to the army's School of Infantry but carry on past this and up the valley to the vedette post. Huge expanses of land stretch into the distance and a scan with the telescope is needed to pick up birds at any distance.

From Heytesbury: The ranges are signposted north from the A36 village bypass road. The vedette post is ½ mile (0.8 km) beyond East Hill Farm. Towards Imber the road passes several copses of mixed woodland worth checking for perched birds of prey.

On the eastern side: The entry is from St Joan à Gore (no cross!) 1 mile (1.6 km) south of West Lavington on the A360 Devizes to Amesbury road. The vedette post is 1 mile (1.6 km) to the southwest. This road, leading to Imber village, passes a line of beeches on the highest ground which often attract feeding Bramblings and Chaffinches.

When the Imber Ranges are closed the road between Chitterne via Tilshead to St Joan à Gore's Cross may give you an opportunity of sighting many of the birds mentioned in this account. The tracks and roads on the north side of the ranges and the footpaths on the southern side between Chitterne and Heytesbury are also worth exploring on foot using an Ordnance Survey map.

West Down and Larkhill Ranges: The same general conditions apply as for Imber, but there are rather more in the way of public footpaths in this part of the ranges. When the ranges are not in use and the red flags are not flying, all public rights of way on the ranges outside the Impact Area (the perimeter of which is marked by signs at 100 metre intervals, and with no admittance at any time) are open to the public. Two rough roads, the Centre Range Road from Redhorn Hill to the Bustard Hotel and the route from Market Lavington vedette to West Down and Orcheston are also open at these times. However, on no account should anyone leave either road. Hen Harriers can often be seen, late on winter afternoons, from the Centre Range Road, prior to roosting, though the exact roost sites tend to change from year to year. Short-eared and Barn Owls also hunt over this part of the Plain on a regular basis.

The Ridgeway route, now open to the public, runs along the northern edge of these ranges from St Joan à Gore's Cross on the A360 to West Chisenbury on the A345, with good views over the ranges in places.

In the east, the road from Netheravon (on the A345 Upavon to Durrington/Amesbury road) to Everleigh on the A342 is open to the public at all times and Short-eared Owls and Hen Harriers may be observed from it in winter.

There are also several approaches to the edge of the ranges along minor roads leading from the A345 on the east side and from Shrewton on the south.

Calendar

All year: Sparrowhawk, Buzzard, Kestrel; Peregrine (scarce). Red-legged and Grey Partridges, Stock Dove, Barn, Little, Long-eared (rarely breeds) and Tawny Owls, Green and Great Spotted Woodpeckers, Skylark, Meadow Pipit, Stonechat, Raven (scarce), Yellowhammer, Corn Bunting.

December–February: Hen Harrier, Merlin. Golden Plover, Lapwing, Snipe, Woodcock. Short-eared Owl. Stonechat. Fieldfare and Redwing flocks sometimes large. Possible Great Grey Shrike; Brambling, Goldfinch, Linnet.

March–May: Hen Harrier to mid-April; Merlin to end March; Hobby from late April. Maybe a passing Marsh Harrier or Red Kite. Quail from late May. Lapwing breeding; Stone Curlew from end March. More Stonechats from March. Wheatear and maybe Ring Ouzel pass from early April. Most summer visitors arrive from late April: Cuckoo, Tree Pipit, Whinchat, Grasshopper Warbler, Lesser Whitethroat, Whitethroat, Garden Warbler, Blackcap, Willow Warbler.

June–July: Breeding residents and summer visitors include a few Redstarts and Reed Buntings. Large numbers of feeding Swifts and hirundines under some conditions.

August–November: Hen Harrier, Merlin from September; Hobby to end September. Maybe passing Montagu's or Marsh Harrier or Curlew. Dispersing or migrant chats, flycatchers and warblers sometimes numerous in August–early September. Wheatear, Whinchat, maybe Ring Ouzel in September. Finch flocks sometimes include Brambling from October.

80 LANGFORD LAKES   OS Explorer 130

Habitat

Langford Lakes lie in the Wylye valley close to the village of Steeple Langford, c.5½ miles (8.8 km) northwest of Wilton. Here, three former gravel pits are being developed into a nature reserve particularly for wetland birds. The gravel pits were excavated in the 1970s and then became a fishery until acquired in 2001 by the Wiltshire Wildlife Trust. The 12 ha of open water is surrounded by aquatic vegetation and some areas of wet woodland and the Trust has already carried out extensive earth-moving operations to create islands for nesting birds. Other enhancements are aimed at increasing the extent of the marginal vegetation and making the shoreline shelve more gently to improve the exposed mud and gravel habitat in late summer and autumn. Also part of the reserve, but with very restricted access, is ½ mile of the River Wylye. This is of international importance as a chalk stream containing wild brown trout and grayling. Otters are known to visit this stretch as well as the lakes and there is a population of water voles.

Species

To date, 146 species of birds have been recorded at this site of which 50 breed regularly on or near the lakes, or have bred in the past. Breeding waterfowl include Great Crested Grebe, Coot, Moorhen, Mallard and Tufted Duck and the damp meadows nearby often hold over 200 Mute Swans. A pair or two of Pochard usually breed and it is hoped that they will be joined by Gadwall in the near future. There is also potential for Lapwing, Little Ringed Plover and Common Tern to nest here. Kingfisher and Grey Wagtail are breeding residents in the area and the small reedbed holds a few Reed Warblers, this species being likely to increase as the reed fringes become more extensive. In winter, the numbers of the resident wildfowl increase: typical maxima are 100 Pochard, 100 Tufted Ducks, 70 Gadwall, 150 Mallard and 200 Coots. Smaller numbers of Wigeon, Shoveler and Teal occur and there are occasional visits by other species such as Pintail, Goldeneye and Bewick's Swan. Water Rails are seen or heard through the winter and occasionally a Bittern turns up.

Regular passage migrants, especially in autumn, include Common Sandpiper, Green Sandpiper, Black Tern and Osprey, and the list can only get longer, especially as the habitat improves.

Gadwall

Timing

Adverse weather conditions might produce more in the way of winter wildfowl or passage migrants, but otherwise factors are few.

Access

The village of Steeple Langford lies just south of the A36 between Wilton and the east end of the Warminster by-pass, and is served by a regular bus service (see map with next site). In the centre of the village turn south into Duck Street, signposted for Hanging Langford; after a short distance the road crosses the River Wylye, with the entrance to the reserve clearly marked on the left. There are already four hides, as well as a car park, in place, and other facilities for visitors are under construction. Note that advance notice is required for coaches, that no dogs are allowed on the reserve, and that the gates are closed at 4 pm (5.30 pm in summer). All the hides are accessible to wheelchairs. Although not part of the reserve, the private White Bird Lake (Salisbury & District Angling Club) on the north side of the River Wylye also attracts wildfowl and is viewable from the public footpath at its western end.

Calendar

All year: Little and Great Crested Grebes, Cormorant, Grey Heron, Canada Goose, Tufted Duck, Pochard, Ruddy Duck, Buzzard, Sparrowhawk, Kestrel, Kingfisher, Great Spotted Woodpecker, Grey Wagtail, Long-tailed Tit.

December–February: Little Egret, Bittern, Gadwall, Teal, Shoveler, Wigeon, Water Rail. Occasional visitors include rarer grebes, Pintail, Smew, Bittern and Bewick's Swan.

March–May: Sand Martin, Sedge Warbler, Reed Warbler, and other warblers. Maybe Osprey on passage.

June–July: Breeding species and commoner warblers.

August–November: Little Egret, maybe Osprey. Hobby, Common Tern, Black Tern, Common Sandpiper, Green Sandpiper, Redshank and possibly other waders.

81 GREAT RIDGE & GROVELY WOODS
OS Explorer 130 and 143

Habitat

Great Ridge and Grovely Woods are remnants of a prehistoric belt of oak forest on the range of chalk downs between Salisbury west-northwest to the Deverills south of Warminster. Both are elongated and irregularly shaped areas each c.3 or 4 miles (4.8 or 6.4 km) in length and 1½ miles (2.4 km) in width at the broadest point. The course of a Roman road following an earlier Iron Age track through the centre of both can still be traced today. Great Ridge Wood contains a wide variety of woodland types including oak standards with hazel, birch and hawthorn scrub, rhododendron thickets, stands of mature beech, oak with bramble and other low ground cover as well as some dense conifer plantations. Parts of the nearby downland are relatively untouched, especially to the north, with a good calcareous flora including several orchid species, and dry valleys running out from the woodland have a mixture of hawthorn scrub and brambles which, together with the patches of gorse on the more open areas, add to the variety of the habitat. Heather grows in a few places where the soil is more acidic. Grovely Wood is similar, but contains rather more in the way of coniferous plantations, particularly in the western part managed by the Forestry Commission. The wood has become extremely dense and gloomy in many parts but the Commission plans to carry out a thinning programme in the near future. A complex of overgrown roads and areas of very thin topsoil over the chalk suppress the cover at the western end (Middle Hill). Further east there is plenty of overgrown hazel coppice as well as similar mixed woodland to that found in Great Ridge Wood. There is one large clearing devoted to arable crops while the privately-owned eastern end has mature beech trees with rather sparse undergrowth. The surrounding downs are used for both arable and grazing and there has been a marked return to sheep rearing more recently. The area supports plenty of badgers, foxes, brown hares, roe deer and a small number of fallow deer. Woodland butterflies are well represented, white admirals, speckled woods and several fritillaries all being quite numerous and there are a few purple emperors. Glow-worms are still present and can be seen in June. These woods are not explored by many birdwatchers and all records are welcomed by the Wiltshire Recorder.

Species

The area holds a good selection of woodland birds and a morning's walk through the centre will usually yield Green and Great Spotted Woodpeckers, Goldcrests, five species of tit, Treecreeper, Nuthatch, Linnet, Bullfinch and a fair number of other common woodland species. The Lesser Spotted Woodpecker has bred in these woods but is now extremely scarce. Willow Tits are present but not common. At least seven species of raptor have been recorded in or around the woods. Both Sparrowhawk and Kestrel are common residents and Buzzards are quite often to be seen, particularly when they are performing their soaring display flights in spring. Hen Harrier, Peregrine and Merlin, probably wanderers from Salisbury Plain, sometimes appear in winter, the harriers sometimes passing right over the wooded areas as well as quartering the

Woodcock

open downland nearby. The seventh species, the Hobby, can be seen hunting during the summer. The small numbers of resident Woodcock are swelled in winter by visitors from elsewhere, although sightings at this time are likely to be chance ones of singles flushed from the undergrowth. Both Red-legged and Grey Partridges and, in summer, sometimes Quail are to be found on the fields surrounding the wood. Woodpigeons abound with Stock Doves more thinly scattered. The Tawny appears to be the only resident owl species; although Barn Owls are occasionally seen in the Middle Hills area, they are only transient birds. In winter lack of foliage means that resident birds are often more easily seen although large areas of the woods are apparently vacated. However, at this time of year Siskins and Bramblings may be found, the latter attracted in particular to the beeches at the eastern end and flocks of Fieldfares and Redwings as well as parties of Mistle Thrushes roam through the woods in search of berries.

Spring brings a few Lapwings to display over the surrounding fields and Stonechats reappear where suitable open scrub and grass can be found. Wheatears are regular on migration both in the spring and again in the autumn. A little later comes the main influx of summer migrants from the south. Warblers are well represented by Whitethroat, Lesser Whitethroat and Garden Warbler in glades and wood edges where there is shrub and ground cover. Blackcaps and Willow Warblers are found where there are taller trees with bushes or other undergrowth below while Chiffchaffs are particularly numerous where larger mature hardwood trees grow. Wood Warblers formerly bred in Great Ridge Wood but have not done so in recent years. Likewise, Redstarts have become very scarce with only a single pair or none at all being noted of late. Nightingales breed in both woods where there is dense enough cover, this being a high altitude for this species in Britain but their numbers have also dwindled recently. A few Turtle Doves can usually be located by their purring song and for the period while they are calling Cuckoos are very much in evidence. Three or four pairs of Nightjars have continued to be recorded in the plantations of Grovely Wood in recent years, and used to be seen in Great Ridge Wood until the conifers became too tall and dense. Their future status will depend on the existence of suitable clearings, the same holding for the Grasshopper Warblers using the same habitat.

Timing

In winter, calm clear days give the best chance of finding the thinly scattered woodland birds and for scanning the surrounding fields for hunting raptors or ground-feeding birds. As ever, early mornings produce the best birdsong in summer, and mammals are also more likely to be observed before they retire into cover for the day. A visit around dusk is essential for Nightjars and roding Woodcock, and Nightingales are usually more vocal at this time.

Access

Both woods lie on the high ground south of the River Wylye valley, and the busy A36 on its north side provides the main route to the area, with a minor road on the opposite side of the river from near Warminster to Wilton providing a pleasanter if slower alternative.

To reach Great Ridge Wood turn off the A36 at Codford and cross the river towards Sherrington, turning left immediately after crossing the rail-

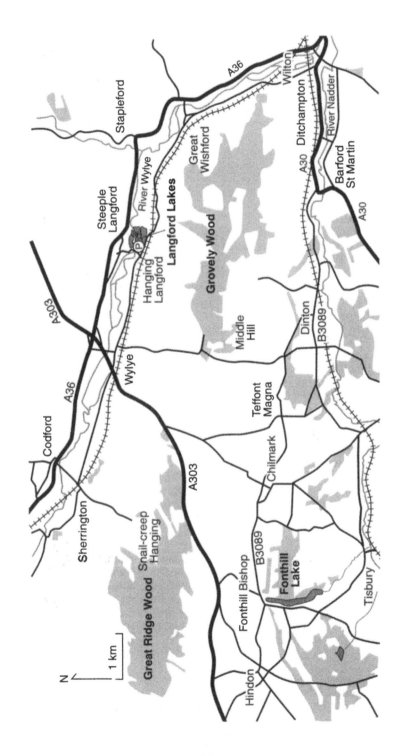

way bridge, and continue 1.25 miles (2 km) to where the road veers left through a gate marked private. It is possible to park by the roadside here and walk on into the woodland along a chalky track known as Snail-creep Hanging. This soon joins the straight Roman track which runs the length of the wood. Although Great Ridge Wood is part of a large private estate there are plenty of public footpaths which are quite adequate for watching the birdlife. Several paths lead north to Tytherington, Corton, Boyton and Sherrington on the minor road along the Wylye valley and the more energetic could use these to devise circular routes taking in the surrounding downland as well as the woods to see the widest range of species.

For Grovely Wood take the road from the east edge of Wylye south over the railway to Dinton (on the B3089 west of Wilton) and at the summit of the downs, where there is a sharp double bend, turn left onto the narrow metalled lane which runs east along the edge of the wood. After ⅔ mile (1.1 km), past a barn, the road is gated. Park here and continue on foot into the Forestry Commission section along the central track which goes the length of the wood. This is a public right of way but other paths, especially in the eastern section, are private. However, public paths lead down to the minor valley road to the north at Hanging Langford and Great Wishford, while the central track eventually drops down to join this road in the outskirts of Wilton, just north of the railway bridge at Ditchampton. As at Great Ridge Wood, circular walks taking in the more open ground will give a more varied range of species, particularly if both woods are included in a longer exploration using the footpaths linking the two.

Calendar

All year: Sparrowhawk, Buzzard, Kestrel, Red-legged and Grey Partridges, Woodcock, Stock Dove, Tawny Owl, woodpeckers; Goldcrest; Willow Tit (scarce), Long-tailed, Marsh and Coal Tits; Nuthatch, Treecreeper, Jay, Linnet, Bullfinch, Goldfinch, Yellowhammer.

December–February: Occasional Hen Harrier, Peregrine or Merlin; Golden Plover flocks on nearby fields. Fieldfare, Redwing, Siskin, Brambling. Reed Buntings on downland with other buntings.

March–May: Chance of Hobby from early May. Woodcock roding. Passage Wheatear April–early May. Cuckoo, Tree Pipit, Nightingale (scarce), Blackcap, Willow Warbler, Chiffchaff from mid–late April; also Redstart (Great Ridge). Turtle Dove, Whitethroat, Lesser Whitethroat, Garden Warbler, Spotted Flycatcher mostly early May. Nightjar (Grovely) from late May.

June–July: Breeding residents and summer visitors.

August–November: Summer visitors mostly leave in August but dispersing birds and passage Wheatears, Stonechats and parties of Meadow Pipits present through September–early October. Flocks of Lapwings and Golden Plover nearby from early October, when other winter visitors start arriving.

Habitat

Fonthill Lake is a narrow artificial water formed by damming a tributary of the River Nadder and was created to enhance the grounds of Fonthill Abbey, the Gothic residence built in the eighteenth century for William Beckford. He had a million trees planted here in one year and today there are still extensive areas of mixed woodland in the vicinity. At the lake's northern end is a large pool separated from the main lake by a small road bridge. Some years ago the marginal trees and bushes were removed from this stretch of water making it much more open than previously. South of this point the west shore is damp with alders and other trees and shrubs which give way to larger trees on steeper banks and more open shores further south. On the east side there is open grassland with yellow iris, reedmace and other marginal vegetation at the water's edge, with, further south, mature deciduous woodland coming right down to the edge of the lake. The stream cascades over stonework at the southern end and flows from the lake into damp meadowland to join the River Nadder at Tisbury.

Species

The larger lakes are always of interest to the birdwatcher because there is always a chance of the unexpected arrival. This is true of Fonthill where over the years such species as Grey Phalarope, Black-necked Grebe and Great Northern Diver have been seen. The more normal population of the lake in winter consists of moderate numbers of Mallard and Tufted Ducks, up to 200 or so, and around 40 Pochard, although parties of Shoveler are seen from time to time in very variable numbers. Other species which have stayed for short periods in winter include Teal, Wigeon, Pintail, Shelduck, Long-tailed Duck, Goosander and Goldeneye.

Coot numbers build up in winter to between one and two hundred, a few pairs breeding in the summer. Great Crested and Little Grebes can be seen at almost any time with numbers rising in winter. At least two pairs of the former and up to five pairs of the latter breed here each year. Mallard and Tufted Duck have both reared young and the odd pair of Pochards sometimes nest. Mandarins have recently started to establish themselves in parts of Wiltshire, and Fonthill Lake is one place that holds a small breeding population, with a flock of 15 or more usually to be seen on the lake in winter. Ruddy Ducks, another naturalised introduction, have also taken up residence, with over 20 sometimes present and breeding taking place most years. Both Grey Herons and Kingfishers come to fish and the Grey Wagtails which nest along nearby streams are also often seen by the lake. The waterside alders and birches attract winter flocks of Siskins and Redpolls, sometimes accompanied by Goldfinches and tits.

Spring brings a few passing Common Sandpipers, but the only other wader likely to be seen is the Lapwing which breeds in declining numbers on the surrounding chalk downland. The area has a good selection of woodland species, including Willow Warblers, Chiffchaffs, Robins, Chaffinches, Spotted Flycatchers, Nuthatches and Treecreepers, all of which are numerous. Great Spotted Woodpeckers are common residents,

Mandarin

and a pair or two of Green Woodpeckers inhabit the parkland. Dippers used to be seen frequently on the stream but have only occurred very rarely in recent years. On the other hand, a Little Egret was first seen here in 1993 and since the expansion of this species' range, it has occasionally visited the lakeside since then.

In summer you may get a glimpse of a hunting Hobby and if you are lucky a better view of one pursuing insects or hirundines up in the sky. Kestrels, Sparrowhawks and Buzzards are to be seen frequently, all three species breeding in the area and wandering Ravens are sometimes seen or heard passing over. Ospreys have been seen on more than one occasion, this spectacular bird turning up on passage in Wiltshire quite often in recent years, though very erratically at any one particular spot. The occasional Black Tern is sometimes seen in autumn, when again a few Common Sandpipers can appear briefly.

Timing
Not generally critical but during severe winter conditions, or after a period of gales, rarer visitors may turn up.

Access
Fonthill Bishop lies on the B3089 Mere to Wilton road (see also map with previous site). A minor road to Tisbury runs south from here along the west side of the lake, passing under an impressive arch, a relic of Beckford's days. The lake and surroundings can be viewed from the road. Where the road curves away from the lake, a public footpath runs from a lay-by along the southern part of the west shore and takes you to the dam. The east shore is private and not accessible. The large area of park and woodland to the west of the lake is not open to the public but woodland species can be seen from the surrounding lanes and public footpaths.

Calendar
All year. Great Crested and Little Grebes, Grey Heron. Mandarin, Mallard, Tufted Duck, Kestrel, Sparrowhawk, Buzzard, Coot, Moorhen, Tawny Owl, common woodland passerines, Pied and Grey Wagtails, Green and Great Spotted Woodpeckers, Nuthatch, Treecreeper, Raven.

December–February: Pochard, other ducks irregular. Water Rail (scarce), Kingfisher, Siskin, Redpoll, Brambling; finch and tit flocks.

March–May: Maybe Common Sandpiper April–May. Chance of Hobby from late April. Summer residents arrive late April: Blackcap, Willow Warbler, Chiffchaff. Spotted Flycatcher from early–mid-May.

June–July: Breeding species. July rather quiet. Post-breeding gatherings of Lapwings and Pied Wagtails nearby.

August–November: Cormorant. Possible Black Tern in September. Sometimes Common Sandpiper in August. Migrant warblers and Spotted Flycatcher.

83 THE AVON SOUTH OF SALISBURY

OS Explorer 130

Habitat

The Salisbury Avon with its very shallow gradient is, like other chalk rivers in this part of England, noted for the clarity of its water. South of the city it is joined by the Nadder and the Bourne while a little further south the Ebble flows in near Longford Castle. As the river broadens on its way south to the county boundary it runs through a series of rough, tussocky and damp water meadows which may be divided into three sections: Britford water meadows, the Longford Castle Estate and Charlton water meadows.

In the past the Britford meadows were traversed by a series of parallel water courses running through sluice gates out of and back into the main river. A trout farm has now been established and, in consequence, many of these have been reduced to minor channels or have even dried out completely except in near-flood conditions. Clumps and lines of mainly deciduous trees occur at intervals. Immediately downstream is the Longford Castle Estate, comprising a mixed habitat of cereal and dairy farmland with parkland. The houses of the estate workers are enclosed by well-established trees and stand close to the castle which is itself alongside the river. Beyond this, and stretching as far as the village of Downton, on the county border, are the Charlton water meadows with rather fewer, but deeper water-channels which contain water throughout the year. The main river is also deeper and slower flowing here and stretches of reeds (*phragmites*) line the banks. Near the weir and footbridge and east of the main river is some good deciduous woodland.

In addition to the river's importance as a wetland site, the woods and copses on the valley sides provide habitat for woodland species and migrant passerines. Other more open areas away from the river flood plain are mostly farmland with some downland and scrub.

Species

In winter the water meadows and the ever-flowing river are particularly attractive to birds in cold weather. On the deep stretch at Charlton, diving duck such as Pochard and Tufted Duck occur in small numbers every winter along with Gadwall, Pintail and the odd Goldeneye. The colder the winter weather, the more wildfowl appear. The adjacent water meadows attract flocks of Wigeon and Teal, the former not usually numbering more than 400 and the latter usually less than 100. Mallard reach 300–400 in the autumn or winter with smaller numbers all year. Up to 100 Canada Geese move freely throughout the area in winter although most often seen at Longford. In the breeding season, widely dispersed pairs become harder to find. Other wildfowl are less numerous, Shoveler and Bewick's Swans staying for a few days, the latter probably wanderers from the regular winter haunt at Ibsley (north of Ringwood in Hampshire). In nearby Salisbury, Peregrines sometimes roost on the cathedral spire and can be seen during the day hunting in the valley, mostly in winter. Water Rails are regular at this time but usually manage to keep out of sight. Green Sandpipers winter in most years but also occur at almost any season. Groups of Snipe often exceed 50 during cold weather which also brings Lapwing, Redshank, Dunlin and occasionally Ruff, with the chance of a rarer wader. Formerly numerous, Cormorants now occur only sporadically throughout the year; shooting to protect fish stocks is suspected as causing the decline. Varying numbers of Fieldfares, Redwings and Meadow Pipits can be seen in the fields and one or two Stonechats usually turn up near the river. In wooded places Bramblings and Redpolls appear rather erratically according to weather conditions and food supply.

Grey Herons can be seen all year and in the wood at the northwest corner of the Longford Castle Estate, near Manor Farm, there is a well-established colony of 30–50 pairs, viewable from the main road. Up to 150 birds may occur along the river in autumn and winter. Following the first Wiltshire record of Little Egret at Britford in January 1992 there has been an unprecedented expansion of the range of this species and

Little Egret

egrets have now been recorded in all five river valleys around Salisbury. They now appear frequently in the meadows between Britford and Salisbury, usually in ones and twos but sometimes up to 50 can be found. Peak numbers occur between January and April but some are present all year and breeding in the heronry is likely to occur in the not too distant future, as they are often seen in the trees there. The river provides habitat for Little Grebes, Coots, Moorhens and Kingfishers and it should be possible to see this last species on almost any visit to Britford or Longford although they are less frequently seen at Charlton. Great Crested Grebes now occur here throughout the year, up to ten pairs breeding regularly between Downton and Salisbury. Grey Wagtails haunt the sluice gates and Dippers have been recorded occasionally. In summer both Sedge and Reed Warblers nest along the river, joining the resident Reed Buntings, and Grasshopper Warblers can be heard giving their reeling song from thicker cover. Cetti's Warblers have established themselves here in small numbers, with around ten singing birds sometimes to be heard, and breeding has been proved on several occasions.

The more open farmland of the valley sides has most of the species to be expected in this kind of habitat, including Kestrel, Little Owl and Buzzard. This last species has increased greatly in recent years and may be seen on almost any visit. Other birds to be found here are Grey and Red-legged Partridges, Skylark and Yellowhammer, while the woods and copses hold a good selection of common passerines. Great Spotted and Green Woodpeckers, Nuthatches and Treecreepers are resident. In spring the woodland birds are joined by Spotted Flycatchers, Willow Warblers, Chiffchaffs, Blackcaps and other common migrants.

At migration times, besides movements of wildfowl and waders, a considerable number of hirundines and Swifts pass along the valley. Other passage species have included Hobby, Merlin, Hen Harrier, various pipits, warblers and finches. Ospreys on passage are now regularly noted in spring and autumn in small numbers, birds sometimes remaining for up to five days, usually at Britford or above Downton. Common and Black Terns have been noted on passage and probably occur regularly. Although it is hard to predict what might be seen on any one visit, there is nearly always something of interest at this time.

Timing

Cold weather in winter will drive more birds to the riverside, and wildfowl onto the river itself if there are hard frosts. Skulking birds such as Water Rails are easier to see under such conditions. An early morning visit in spring and early summer is best for singing warblers and any migrants that may have appeared overnight on their way through the valley.

Access

Britford water meadows: About 1 mile (1.6 km) south of Salisbury on the A338, turn left along a lane signposted to Lower Britford and continue past the turning to the church as far as the small village green. A public bridleway follows the gravel track which goes east from one corner, then south, and shortly after the bend a public footpath to the left leads to an extensive area of rough grazing interspersed with channels of water. The path continues past the trout farm to the river. You can walk downstream along the riverbank for c.300 metres but then you have to retrace your steps. Back at the gravel track, you can in addition

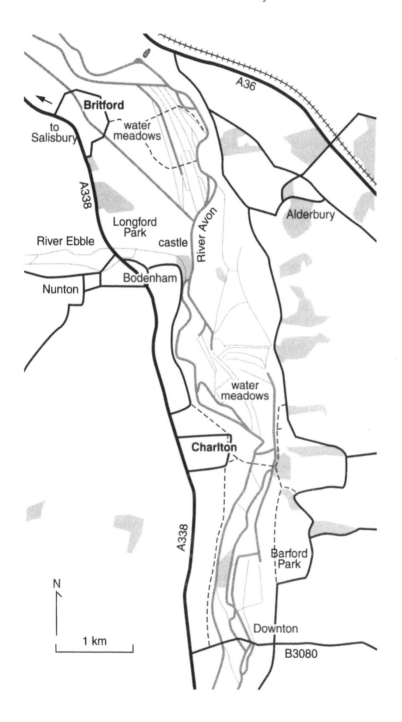

continue south past Lower Farm and across the meadows to the river, but again you have to return to Britford by the same route as there is no other public access.

Longford Castle Estate: A little further south on the A338, just after the start of the dual carriageway, turn left towards Bodenham and after c.200 metres turn left again. The entrance to the estate is immediately on the left. Access to the estate is by permission in writing from the Estate Manager but much of the area can be viewed from the road which continues south through Bodenham.

Charlton water meadows: Either continue on the minor road from Longford Park through Bodenham, or alternatively south along the A338 to turn left along the next unsignposted lane (just beyond the turning to Matrimony Farm). There is an obvious pull-in near the sharp bend by the river, and good views of the meadows can be had from this area. A public footpath runs southeast from the bend to Charlton village. Here you can continue past the church and in a short way turn left along another waymarked path to the meadows. The path leads through the meadows and across a weir and sluices to the far side of the river. After a short climb, a track and then a waymarked narrow path left runs through the woodland fairly close to the river, passing a bridge where more views of the meadows can be obtained. You have to retrace your steps as the meadows themselves are private; note that the route may be rather overgrown and obscured in summer.

The northern section of the minor road from Downton to Alderbury on the east side of the valley allows distant views of the meadows, as well as running through arable farmland with scattered woodland.

Calendar

All year: Little and Great Crested Grebes, Grey Heron, Little Egret, Mute Swan, Canada Goose, Mallard, Tufted Duck, Sparrowhawk, Buzzard, Kestrel, Grey and Red-legged Partridges, Little Owl, Kingfisher, Green and Great Spotted Woodpeckers, maybe Lesser Spotted; Coot, Green Sandpiper, Grey and Pied Wagtails; a few Blackcaps and Chiffchaffs usually overwinter. Cetti's Warbler, Goldcrest, Treecreeper, Nuthatch, Jay, Reed Bunting.

December–February: Cormorant, occasional Bewick's Swan; Gadwall, Teal, Wigeon, Shoveler, Pochard, possible Pintail. Chance of Peregrine. Water Rail, Lapwing, Snipe, Redshank, sometimes Ruff. Occasional Stonechat; winter thrushes, Brambling (sporadic).

March–May: Grey Herons active at heronry. Common Sandpiper, possible Greenshank or Ruff (April–May). Lesser Black-backed and Herring Gulls. Possible Common and Black Terns on passage (mid-April–May). Cuckoo, hirundines and Swifts, commoner warblers arrive mid-April–mid-May.

June–July: Residents and summer visitors include breeding Reed, Sedge and Cetti's Warblers.

August–November: Cormorant. Duck numbers build up from late September. Snipe, Redshank, possible Greenshank or other less common wader on passage (especially August–September). Water Rail. Possible

Osprey, Common or Black Terns in September. Trickle of passerine migrants August–October.

84 WOODLANDS EAST OF SALISBURY

OS Explorer 131

Habitat

These woodlands are the remains of the great Clarendon Forest which was established in the Middle Ages, two main sections of which are still in existence. One, comprising large areas of coniferous woodland with smaller groups of deciduous trees, is contained within the Clarendon Estate and is not very accessible. The other is grouped into three main blocks: Bentley Wood and Blackmoor Copse, Hound Wood, and the outlying Ashley's Copse. The whole area is surrounded by rolling chalk farmland, with Hampshire Clay on the lower areas.

Bentley Wood is a former Forestry Commission site of c.1700 acres (688 ha) but the Trustees who have owned it since 1983 have developed the wood as a nature reserve and forest park whilst also retaining its commercial forestry. The conifers have been thinned to the benefit of the oaks and other hardwoods, and rides have been widened. At the northern end and at the southwest corner there are cleared areas which are regenerating or being replanted with native broadleaves. Several ponds have been created, providing habitat for frogs, newts and dragonflies. The adjoining Blackmoor Copse (36 ha) is very different in that it is almost totally broadleaved, divided by rides, with oaks, birches and hazel dominant. It is managed by the Wiltshire Wildlife Trust who have introduced hazel coppicing into the northern part to improve the habitat for rare butterflies and dormice. The lower southern section of the wood is much damper with plenty of sedges, rushes and water mint. Hound Wood lies a short distance to the northwest of Blackmoor Copse. At its northern end it has some fine old beeches, while on the eastern side there is more damp oak woodland with one or two clearings. The remainder of the wood is predominantly conifers of different ages with a good growth of bramble thicket.

These three woods are an extremely important haunt for butterflies, with over 40 species listed, including white admiral, purple emperor and several species of fritillary. Fallow and roe deer are widespread, and muntjac, badgers and foxes also occur.

Species

All the usual common resident woodland species are to found here, including Sparrowhawk, Buzzard and Tawny Owl in good numbers. Kestrels hunt over the area, and the occasional Barn Owl is sometimes seen. All three species of woodpecker breed, Lesser Spotted as ever being the most difficult to locate. Passerines include Nuthatch, Treecreeper, Marsh, Willow, Coal and Long-tailed Tits, Jay and Bullfinch. Woodcock occur frequently in winter, whilst at this time of year flocks of finches such as Siskins, Greenfinches and Crossbills are encountered.

With the coming of spring, migrant warblers arrive to set up territory, including Whitethroats, Blackcaps and Garden Warblers. Wood Warblers may stop to sing for a few days, but have not been proved to breed and the Turtle Dove just maintains a foothold. Tree Pipits are to be found near the rides and woodland edges. Woodcock nest in some of the clearings and can often be heard roding at dusk but the Nightjars that used to breed in Bentley Wood seem to have disappeared.

Lesser Whitethroats breed not far away, though not in the woods themselves. Other species of the general area include Hobby, which might be seen flying over at any time during the summer. The autumn brings a light passage of Redstarts and Whinchats to the higher ground along the northern edges, with perhaps a Stonechat or two at the same time. Flocks of Fieldfares and Redwings also appear along the wood edges a little later.

Timing

Mornings in spring and early summer will produce a good list of residents and summer visitors but for Nightjar and Woodcock a visit at dusk is essential. This will be best on a calm, warm evening. Nightjars, now extremely scarce if present at all, usually do not start to call until at least 9.30 pm in midsummer, Woodcock being active a little earlier. Soaring Buzzards and Sparrowhawks are most evident on sunny but slightly breezy days, especially in spring.

Access

Route 1: From Salisbury take the A30 Andover and Winchester road and 2½ miles (4 km) from the A338 junction bear right to reach West Winterslow. From here carry straight on towards East Grimstead for another 2 miles (3.2 km) to reach the western edge of Bentley Wood. A track on the left leads into the woods, with space for a few cars near the gated entrance. A further ½ mile (0.8 km) will bring you to a crossroads and another point of entry to Bentley Wood, and also to Blackmoor Copse on the right. The paths through the latter are indicated on a board close to the entrance. Hound Wood can be reached by turning right here to the village of Farley and taking the path north near the church across the fields.

Route 2: From Salisbury take the A36 Southampton road and after c.3½ miles (5.6 km) at Whaddon turn left towards the Grimsteads, and then follow signs to East Grimstead. Here turn left and, beyond the village green, right towards Winterslow. Just over ½ mile (0.8 km) will bring you to the entrances to Bentley Wood and Blackmoor Copse, and the turning to Farley mentioned above.

Route 3: From West Dean, south of Bentley Wood, turn left off the road to West Tytherly. After c.500 metres a rough track to the left leads to small car park from which the eastern part of the wood can be explored.

Access to both Bentley Wood and Blackmoor Copse is allowed along the many footpaths, although dogs should be kept under strict control. Hound Wood is a private wood, but several public footpaths run across it and skirt the southern edge.

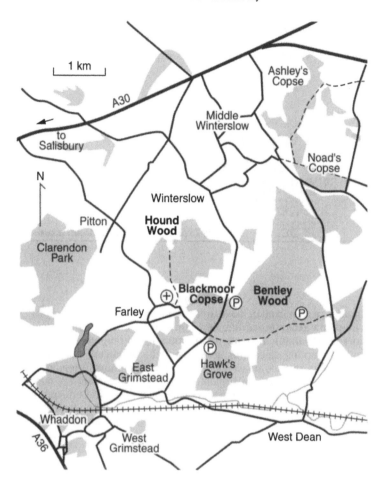

Calendar

All year: Buzzard, Sparrowhawk, Kestrel; Barn Owl (scarce), Tawny Owl, Green and Great Spotted Woodpeckers (Lesser Spotted scarce), Nuthatch, Treecreeper, Marsh and Willow Tits, Goldcrest, Jay, Bullfinch. Crossbill in variable numbers.

December–February: Wintering Woodcock, winter thrushes, Siskin, sometimes Brambling.

March–May: Chance of Hobby from May; Woodcock roding. From mid–late April: Cuckoo, Tree Pipit, possible Nightingale; Whitethroat, Garden Warbler, Blackcap, Chiffchaff, Willow Warbler, maybe passage Redstart or Wood Warbler (rare). Goldfinch, Siskin. Turtle Dove and Nightjar (if present) arrive in May.

June–July: Breeding residents and summer visitors. Other species quieter in July.

August–November. Possible Hobby to end September. Passage warblers August–September with perhaps a few Redstarts, Whinchats and Stonechats. Winter thrushes from October. Goldfinch, Siskin, Redpoll.

85 FRANCHISES WOOD, CLOVEN HILL PLANTATION & LOOSEHANGER COPSE
OS Explorer 131 and Outdoor Leisure 22

Habitat

This area of woodland in the extreme southeast of Wiltshire is essentially a northerly extension of the New Forest, lying on a northeast facing slope, higher and undulating in the southern half but more level in the northern. Among deciduous trees, oak is the dominant species, interspersed with smaller areas of birch and sweet chestnut. There are also some quite extensive conifer plantations, varying from stands of mature trees to newly established ones in clear-felled areas. The undergrowth and shrub layer varies considerably from one part of the woodland to another. There are pastures in the centre which create a rich woodland edge, and other parts are low-lying and very damp. Both fallow and roe deer are found and in summer butterflies and dragonflies are numerous in the glades and walks.

Species

As might be expected, the bird population here is very similar to that in the nearby New Forest woodland, and is best during the breeding season. In winter the interest is not quite so great but, given reasonable weather, it can provide a few extra specialities. Hawfinches are relatively numerous in the New Forest, where they can be seen throughout the year, but in winter they wander more widely and are quite often to be seen across the border in these Wiltshire woodlands. At this time of year these elusive finches are best seen in bare tree tops, where their dumpy short-tailed appearance and ticking calls aid identification even on a brief view. In recent years they have been seen much more frequently in spring and summer and it may well be that a few pairs breed in these woods. Crossbills are recorded fairly regularly and can be seen in any month, although their numbers fluctuate from year to year. Again they are best located by their calls. Siskins and Redpolls are recorded from time to time, the former being seen in small numbers in most months and the latter mostly in winter. Siskins at least have been proved to breed. As one would expect, all the usual woodland residents can be found. All three species of woodpecker breed here and Treecreeper and Nuthatch are relatively easy to locate in several places. Jays can often be heard

Wood Warbler

squawking and there are plenty of Robins, Wrens, Chaffinches and six species of tit, though populations in the main woodland are very much reduced in the winter. Coal Tits and Goldcrests are numerous at all times in the coniferous areas. Among predators Sparrowhawks, Buzzards and Kestrels are all frequently seen overhead. One rather irregular speciality of the more open areas is the Woodlark, but these birds are extremely scarce and are best sought across the county border in the New Forest.

In spring the woods come alive with the arrival of several summer visitors of which the two star attractions are the Wood Warbler and the Redstart. These two birds are relatively scarce breeding birds in Wiltshire and whilst both species have declined here in recent years, the Wood Warbler is still relatively frequent in areas of mature oak and birch. Redstarts have declined more noticeably but are still recorded in most years, especially in open glades and on the edge of clear-felled plantation areas. Far rarer, and certainly not recorded annually, is the Firecrest, a species which breeds patchily in the New Forest, and which has been seen here in summer also. It is essential to learn the song, an accelerating series of high-pitched notes, to stand a realistic chance of locating this tiny bird amongst the leaves. The resident birds are now also joined by Blackcaps, Garden Warblers, Willow Warblers and Chiffchaffs. Turtle Doves give out their purring notes and the Tree Pipits ascend from their perches on the higher boughs, singing as they fall back again. Several pairs of Woodcock breed in the area and Nightjars can be found relatively commonly in the young conifer plantations throughout. The New Forest is something of a stronghold of the Hobby so it is not surprising that sightings of this attractive falcon are reasonably frequent during the summer. They prefer to feed in the open so are unlikely to be seen in the denser woodland but can often be seen in the open areas created by the electricity pylon runs. In recent years there has been a number of sightings of Peregrine in the area, most of these being of birds perching on the pylon line running through the woods.

Timing

In winter, when leaves have fallen, it is easier to see those species that are present but it is often possible to walk a long way with hardly a bird in sight. At all times of year most birds keep under cover in poor weather so fine conditions without strong winds are the most productive. Look for soaring Buzzards on fine spring mornings and go at dawn for the chorus of passerines and roding Woodcock. Dusk is necessary for observing Nightjar or Woodcock again, though the former may not start churring until after 9.30 pm in midsummer.

Access

The easiest starting point is Hope Cottage at the junction of the B3080 Downton/Cadnam road and the B3078 from Fordingbridge, where there is a car park at Telegraph Hill just east of the junction. From just to the right of the cottage a well-defined track leads into the woodland. After a short distance the public path branches off left down a slope and, c.200 metres beyond a line of electricity cables, reaches a minor road from Hamptworth to Nomansland where access is also possible. Turn left here along a lane and take the footpath (often very wet and muddy) straight ahead at the point where it re-enters the woods. After c.1 mile (1.6 km) through varied woodland a track joins from the right and shortly after this you turn left past an isolated house to reach Loosehanger Copse. A narrow footpath skirts the edge of the copse and eventually joins a more well-defined track. Turn left here and keep straight on for c.1 mile (1.6 km) to the line of electricity cables. Keep straight on both here and where the path splits three ways, and again where the track veers off to the left. The footpath skirts Franchises Lodge to emerge, via the latter's access track, on the B3080 c.100 metres west of the starting point. This circuit is c.5 miles (8 km) in length and takes about two or three hours to walk. Other access to these private woodlands is relatively limited and

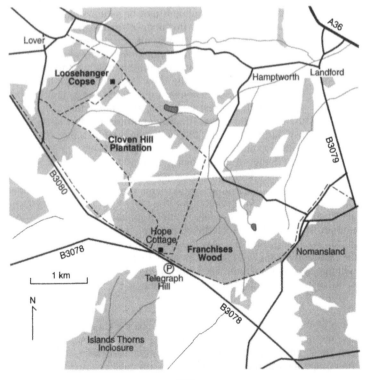

286

adjoining land in the New Forest would probably be more productive for further exploration.

Calendar

All year: Buzzard, Sparrowhawk, Kestrel; Woodcock; Green, Great Spotted and Lesser Spotted Woodpeckers, Goldcrest, Nuthatch, Treecreeper, possible Siskin or Woodlark.

December–February: Winter thrushes. Siskin, Redpoll. Possible Brambling with other finches. Possible Hawfinch. Crossbill in small numbers.

March–May: Woodcock active. Occasional Hobby from May to September. Cuckoo, Tree Pipit, Redstart, Blackcap, Garden Warbler, Wood Warbler, Willow Warbler, Chiffchaff arrive mid–late April. Turtle Dove and Spotted Flycatcher from early May; Nightjar from late May. Chance of Firecrest.

June–July: Residents and summer visitors breeding. Nightjars active throughout.

August–November: Summer visitors leave during August, then fairly quiet period until winter birds arrive in October. Hawfinches start their autumn and winter movements.

LIST OF ORGANISATIONS, WITH ABBREVIATIONS USED IN THE TEXT

The following list gives some useful contacts and sources of further information. Any records of unusual species should be sent to Recorder for the county concerned.

Avon Ornithological Group, Harvey Rose (Recorder), 12 Birbeck Road, Stoke Bishop, Bristol BS9 1BD. Publishes annual *Avon Bird Report*. [AOG]

Avon Wildlife Trust (aka The Wildlife Trust, Bristol, Bath and Avon), 32 Jacobs Wells Road, Bristol BS8 1DR. Web site: http://www.avonwildlifetrust. org.uk. [AWT]

Bristol Ornithological Club, Mrs J. Copeland (Membership Secretary), 19 St George's Hill, Easton-in-Gordano, Bristol BS20 0PS. Publishes monthly newsletter, *Bird News*, and a journal, *Bristol Ornithology*. Web site: http://www.boc-bristol.org.uk. [BOC]

Bristol Water plc, Recreations Department, Woodford Lodge, Chew Stoke BS40 8XH. Web site: http://www.bristolwater.co.uk [BW]

Dursley Birdwatching and Preservation Society, Maurice Bullen, 20 South Street, Uley, Dursley, Glos GL11 5SP. Publishes monthly *Bulletin*. [DBWPS]

Exmoor Natural History Society, Ms Caroline Giddens, 12 King George Road, Minehead, Somerset TA24 5JD. Publishes annual *Exmoor Naturalist*. [ENHS]

Gloucester Ornithological Coordinating Committee, Richard Baatsen (Recorder), 1 Prestwick Terrace, Bristol Road, Whitminster, Gloucester GL2 7PA. Publishes annual *Gloucestershire Bird Report*. [GOCC]

Gloucester Wildlife Trust (formerly Gloucestershire Trust for Nature Conservation), Dulverton Building, Robinswood Hill Country Park, Reservoir Road, Gloucester GL10 3EU. Web site: http://www.gloucester-shirewildlifetrust.co.uk. [GWT]

Kenneth Allsop Memorial Trust (Steep Holm). Mrs Joan Rendell (Tel: 01934 632307). Publishes annual *Steepholm Magazine*. [KAMT]

English Nature (formerly Nature Conservancy Council), Northminster House, Peterborough PE1 1VA. Regional Offices: South-west, Roughmoor, Bishop's Hull, Taunton, Somerset TA1 5AA. West Midlands, Attingham Park, Shrewsbury, Shrops SY4 4TW. South, Foxhold House, Thornford Road, Crookham Common, Newbury, Berks RG15 8EL. Website: http://www.english-nature.org.uk. [EN]

North Cotswold Ornithological Society, Tim Hutton, 15 Green Close, Childswickham, Broadway, Worcs WR12 7JJ. Publishes annual *North Cotswold Bird Report*. [NCOS]

National Trust, 36 Queen Anne's Gate, London SW1H 9AS. Website: http://www.nationaltrust.org.uk. [NT]

Oldbury Power Station, Thornbury, Bristol BS12 1RQ. [OPS]

RSPB, The Lodge, Sandy, Beds SG19 2DL. Regional Offices: Central England, 46 The Green, South Bar, Banbury, Oxon OX16 9AB. South-west, Keble House, Southernhay Gardens, Exeter EX1 1NT. Website:http://www.rspb.org.uk. [RSPB]

Somerset Ornithological Society, Brian Gibbs (Recorder), 23 Lyngford Road, Taunton, Somerset TA2 7EE. Publishes annual *Somerset Birds*. Web site://www.somornithosoc.freeserve.co.uk. [SOS]

Somerset Wildlife Trust (formerly Somerset Trust for Nature Conservation), Fyne Court, Broomfield, Bridgwater, Somerset TA5 2EQ. Website: http://www.wildlifetrust.org.uk/somerset. [SWT]

South West Water plc, 3–5 Barnfield Road, Exeter. Web site: http://www.southwestwater.co.uk [SWW]

Wiltshire Ornithological Society, Rob Turner (Recorder), 14 Ethendun, Bratton, Westbury, Wilts BA13 4RX. Publishes annual report, *Hobby*. [WOS]

Wiltshire Wildlife Trust (formerly Wiltshire Trust for Nature Conservation), 19 High Street, Devizes, Wilts SN10 1AT. Web site: http://www.wiltshirewildlife.org. [WWT]

The Woodland Trust, Autumn Park, Dysart Road, Grantham, Lincs NG31 6LL. Web site: http://www.woodland-trust.org.uk. [WT]

Wildfowl and Wetlands Trust, Slimbridge, Gloucester GL2 7BT. Web site: http://www.wwt.org.uk. [WWT]

Wessex Water plc, Wessex House, Passage Street, Bristol BS2 0JQ. Web site: http://www.wessexwater.co.uk. [WW]

The Birdwatcher's Yearbook, available annually from Buckingham Press, 55 Thorpe Park Road, Peterborough, Cambs PE3 6LJ, provides an up-to-date list of addresses and telephone numbers of most of these and many other organisations relevant to birdwatching.

The Fatbirder website (http://www.fatbirder.com) is a useful portal, with links to many other sites of local, national and international interest.

Information about rare birds in the area can be accessed on the premium rate phone lines Birding South West (09068 884500) and the Regional Birdlines: South West (07626 923923) and Midlands (09068 700247).

CODE OF CONDUCT
FOR BIRDWATCHERS

Today's birdwatchers are a powerful force for nature conservation. The number of those of us interested in birds rises continually and it is vital that we take seriously our responsibility to avoid any harm to birds. We must also present a responsible image to non-birdwatchers who may be affected by our activities and particularly those on whose sympathy and support the future of birds may rest.

There are 10 points to bear in mind:
1. The welfare of birds must come first.
2. Habitat must be protected.
3. Keep disturbance to birds and their habitat to a minimum.
4. When you find a rare bird think carefully about whom you should tell.
5. Do not harass rare migrants.
6. Abide by the bird protection laws at all times.
7. Respect the rights of landowners.
8. Respect the rights of other people in the countryside.
9. Make your records available to the local bird recorder.
10. Behave abroad as you would when birdwatching at home.

Welfare of birds must come first
Whether your particular interest is photography, ringing, sound recording, scientific study or just birdwatching, remember that the welfare of the bird must always come first.

Habitat protection
Its habitat is vital to a bird and therefore we must ensure that our activities do not cause damage.

Keep disturbance to a minimum
Birds' tolerance of disturbance varies between species and seasons. Therefore, it is safer to keep all disturbance to a minimum. No birds should be disturbed from the nest in case opportunities for predators to take eggs or young are increased. In very cold weather disturbance to birds may cause them to use vital energy at a time when food is difficult to find. Wildfowlers already impose bans during cold weather: birdwatchers should exercise similar discretion.

Rare breeding birds
If you discover a rare bird breeding and feel that protection is necessary, inform the appropriate RSPB Regional Office, or the Species Protection Department at the Lodge. Otherwise it is best in almost all circumstances to keep the record strictly secret in order to avoid disturbance by other birdwatchers and attacks by egg-collectors. Never visit known sites of rare breeding birds unless they are adequately protected. Even your presence may give away the site to others and cause so many other visitors that the birds may fail to breed successfully.

Disturbance at or near the nest of species listed on the First Schedule of the Wildlife and Countryside Act 1981 is a criminal offence.

Copies of Wild Birds and the Law are obtainable from the RSPB, The Lodge, Sandy, Beds. SG19 2DL (send two 2nd class stamps).

Rare migrants

Rare migrants or vagrants must not be harassed. If you discover one, consider the circumstances carefully before telling anyone. Will an influx of birdwatchers disturb the bird or others in the area? Will the habitat be damaged? Will problems be caused with the landowner?

The Law

The bird protection laws (now embodied in the Wildlife and Countryside Act 1981) are the result of hard campaigning by previous generations of birdwatchers. As birdwatchers we must abide by them at all times and not allow them to fall into disrepute.

Respect the rights of landowners

The wishes of landowners and occupiers of land must be respected. Do not enter land without permission. Comply with permit schemes. If you are leading a group, do give advance notice of the visit, even if a formal permit scheme is not in operation. Always obey the Country Code.

Respect the rights of other people

Have proper consideration for other birdwatchers. Try not to disrupt their activities or scare the birds they are watching. There are many other people who also use the countryside. Do not interfere with their activities and, if it seems that what they are doing is causing unnecessary disturbance to birds, do try to take a balanced view. Flushing gulls when walking a dog on a beach may do little harm, while the same dog might be a serious disturbance at a tern colony. When pointing this out to a non-birdwatcher be courteous, but firm. The non-birdwatchers' goodwill towards birds must not be destroyed by the attitudes of birdwatchers.

Keeping records

Much of today's knowledge about birds is the result of meticulous record keeping by our predecessors. Make sure you help to add to tomorrow's knowledge by sending records to your county bird recorder.

Birdwatching abroad

Behave abroad as you would at home. This code should be firmly adhered to when abroad (whatever the local laws). Well behaved birdwatchers can be important ambassadors for bird protection.

This code has been drafted after consultation between The British Ornithologists' Union, British Trust for Ornithology, the Royal Society for the Protection of Birds, the Scottish Ornithologists' Club, the Wildfowl Trust and the Editors of *British Birds*.

Further copies may be obtained from The Royal Society for the Protection of Birds, The Lodge, Sandy, Beds SG19 2DL.

INDEX OF SPECIES

Species index listed by site number

INDEX OF SITES

Site index listed by page number

Lightning Source UK Ltd.
Milton Keynes UK
UKOW06f1006090415

249356UK00013B/238/P